EMPIRICAL RESEARCH IN LOGOTHERAPY AND MEANING-ORIENTED PSYCHOTHERAPY

An Annotated Bibliography

EMPIRICAL RESEARCH IN LOGOTHERAPY AND MEANING-ORIENTED PSYCHOTHERAPY

An Annotated Bibliography

Alexander Batthyany and David Guttmann
In collaboration with PsycINFO, a department of
the American Psychological Association (APA)

Zeig, Tucker & Theisen, Inc.
Phoenix, Arizona

Published by
ZEIG, TUCKER & THEISEN, INC.
3614 North 24th Street
Phoenix, Arizona 85016

Manufactured in the United States of America
10 9 8 7 6 5 4 3 2 1

CONTENTS

FOREWORD

Unfortunately, I never actually met Viktor Frankl. But early in my career I read his work, and it turned my life around, giving me the sense of professional purpose I was seeking. In my early years of teaching, research, and practice, my orientation had shifted from the psychoanalytic emphasis of my graduate training and internship to a humanistic approach, through my encounter with Carl Rogers' Counseling Center at the University of Chicago. Although this humanistic approach struck a resonant cord with me, it somehow was not enough. What I needed, and then found, was Frankl's approach, with its emphasis on discovering the meaning and purpose of your life through the day-to-day, moment-to-moment decisions you make. I was also struck by the importance of existential courage in this process, if meaning and purpose are to continue to unfold. Through courage, you can choose the future, in the decision-making process, rather than holding on to the past and avoiding change and development. And, Frankl's logotherapy seemed effectively designed to help clients reach this goal.

Before long, I was highlighting existential psychology and logotherapy in my teaching of personality to undergraduate and graduate students. They responded enthusiastically, convincing me even further of the value of, and need for, this approach. I also emphasized logotherapy techniques in my psychotherapy practice, and saw clearly the dramatic difference in made in the lives of my clients. Their dedication to courageously pursuing meaning in their lives justified my strenuous efforts. And in my research and writing, I concentrated more and more on existential psychology. For example, my contributions concerning hardiness structure it as the courage and motivation not only to survive, but also to thrive under the stress of everyday decision making and the imposition of additionally stressful circumstances in these turbulent times. In all this, I have been fortunate to have helped to form and participate in a small, but intense, international support group of psychiatrists and psychologists who are dedicated to studying and enhancing the personal search for life's meaning.

I am delighted with this book, which is appearing on the 100th anniversary of Frankl's birth. It is much needed at this point in the development of psychology and psychotherapy. The basic concepts of existential psychology and psychotherapy are covered in the first part of the book. The emphasis is on the fundamental importance of discovering the meaning of your life by the decisions you make day after day. If you choose the future in these decisions, your life is vibrant and involving, despite the uncertainty associated with changing. If, instead, you choose the past, your life becomes more stultifying and meaningless as the years go by. Clearly, we all are responsible for how our lives go. And a major aim of existential psychotherapy is to provide the client with this insight, and instill the courage whereby he or she can face choosing the future, rather than shrinking into the past.

The second part of the book details specific techniques of existential psychotherapy. Among those that were most important for Frankl were paradoxical intention and dereflection, both of which have had an impact on contemporary practice. In paradoxical intention, the client learns to gain control over symptoms by trying to exaggerate them. And in dereflection, the client is helped to tolerate overwhelming emotions by putting them in perspective. The aim of all of these psychotherapeutic techniques is to give the person control through the decision-making process.

The final part of the book emphasizes current trends in logotherapeutic development and research. It is fascinating, and suggests the value of further effort in the future. The annotated bibliography is valuable in bringing together the work on existential psychology and psychotherapy that has been going on throughout the world.

This is an especially good time for this book to appear. Psychology in the United States is being increasingly influenced by a positive outlook on living. But the emphasis is too exclusively on happiness. Lest this focus be too superficial, it is important to emphasize the courage that is needed to meet the inherently stressful nature of life and to do the hard work of turning it to advantage. This other positive psychology owes much of its sophistication to Viktor Frankl and the other existentialists.

Salvatore R. Maddi, Ph.D.
University of California, Irvine

DEDICATION

We dedicate this book to the two people who, more than anyone else, stand for logothera-py and its message to the world: Viktor E. Frankl and his wife Elly (Eleonore) Frankl. The Frankls' apartment in Mariannengasse 1 in Vienna was the place where the authors met for the first time, and it was also the place where we shared many memorable afternoons.

Now that this book has been completed, we happily use the opportunity to express our deep gratitude in writing – to Dr. Eleonore Frankl and the family of Viktor E. Frankl, (especially Dr. Gabriele Vesely-Frankl and Professor Franz Vesely), for their friendship, trust, and their fine and important work in keeping Viktor Frankl's legacy alive. We will never be able to repay the gift of logotherapy that Viktor Frankl gave us and the world, and the sup-port his wife and family showers on us; nonetheless, we try. In the meantime, our unceas-ing gratitude goes out to you.

ACKNOWLEDGMENTS AND SPECIAL THANKS

This book would not exist had it not been for the labor of others, specifically, that of the researchers who conducted the more than 600 studies presented in the main section of this bibliography. Our sincere thanks go to them. Moreover, we would like especially to thank those researchers who sent us their studies, most of which are included in this book.

Collecting scientific papers from over such a long timespan (almost 30 years) can be a difficult task; however, wherever we went, we were met with a cooperation and support that we had never expected. For the staff of the Vienna University's Psychology Library, no request was too obscure, no source too old, no partial information too incomplete, and no list of requests and questions too long not to be met with an encouraging smile (and, in most cases, a positive reply).

There is one person to whom we owe the very existence of this book: Marion Harrell of the American Psychological Association's PsycINFO department. No simple acknowledgment can repay her generous assistance, and so we decided to elaborate on her role in our introduction. In addition to the practical help she provided, her friendliness and personal support were extraordinary.

Thanks also to our good friend Patti Havenga-Coetzer of the Viktor Frankl Foundation of South Africa, who kindly publicized our call for papers and helped us to unearth a whole lot of studies of which we otherwise probably wouldn't have become aware. Furthermore, Patti encouraged us with her lovely letters to continue with our project. We especially thank her for her help and what perhaps was the first instance of logotherapy per email.

The gratitude continues. We wish to express our sincere thanks to Marie Elisabeth Henckel von Donnersmarck for her invaluable technical help in converting the entries of this bibliography into an easily accessible and usable text file, and for her kind support whenever help was needed (which was quite often).

Then there is our friend and colleague Marysia Miller-Aichholz, on whose carefully thought-through advice we could always rely. Surprisingly enough, she never lost patience, but always was eager to help. She would deserve her own entry in the section on value- and meaning-based pro-social behavior.

Special thanks go to our friend Christopher Wentworth-Stanley for proofreading this book. He didn't just read the manuscript — he sifted through it, line by line, word by word. We also owe our thanks to Emanuela Ivanova for incorporating the first editor's handwritten remarks and numbers on the original printout of this bibliography; no doubt deciphering the numbers and notes was a major task in itself.

And finally, we are especially grateful to Jeff Zeig, our publisher, whose enthusiasm when we first presented him with the idea of this book never waned. His advice helped us tremendously, and we would like to thank him for his untiring support throughout the entire time this book was being written.

INTRODUCTION

The 100th birthday of logotherapy's originator, Professor Viktor Emil Frankl (1905-1997), is an appropriate occasion on which to review the research produced in the past three decades in logotherapy and related disciplines: How comprehensive is it? How can it best be used and accessed by concerned parties? Which areas need further strengthening and more research? These were some of the questions we posed as the authors of this book. Our aim was to gain a systematic and easy-to-use knowledge base related to research in logotherapy and to make this information available to researchers, practitioners, and students in the helping professions, academic psychology and related disciplines.

Twenty-six years ago, in the first issue of the *International Forum for Logotherapy,* published in 1978/1979, Frankl expressed his hope that this new journal would present articles based on experimental and empirical validation of his concepts. He said:

> Logotherapy is concerned with the search for meaning not only as a matter of health, and in no way as a matter of morality, but rather as one of the most intrinsic human phenomena. You cannot turn the wheel back and you won't get a hearing unless you try to satisfy the preferences of present-time Western thinking, which means the scientific orientation or, to put it in more concrete terms, our test and statistics mindedness [...]. That's why I welcome all sober and solid empirical research in logotherapy, however dry its outcome may sound. (Fabry, 1978/79: 5-6)

When this statement was made, logotherapeutic research had already reached a state in which some of its major concepts and methods had gained validation in research using psychometric tests and sophisticated statistical procedures. Nevertheless, the need for further testing and the refinement of research techniques and tools to assess the therapeutic value of logotherapeutic intervention was, and still is, evident.

RESEARCH IN LOGOTHERAPY: HISTORICAL BACKGROUND

Research in logotherapy can be divided roughly into three consecutive, and somewhat overlapping, periods: In the first period, which lasted from the appearance of Frankl's two central books in English, *The Doctor and the Soul* (published in 1955), and *Man's Search for Meaning* (published in 1959), researchers from clinical, social, and experimental orientations in psychology and psychiatry were eager to show that Frankl's concepts and theory of logotherapy could be verified by scientific investigation. This was also the period in which research efforts centered largely on studying the therapeutic effects of paradoxical intention with various clients suffering from sleep and speech disorders, and from a host of phobias, obsessions, and compulsions.

1

The second period in logotherapeutic research can be characterized as centering on the development of new tools and instruments with which logotherapeutic concepts, such as meaning in life and existential vacuum, could be objectively measured. This period lasted approximately from the appearance of the "Purpose in Life" test (Crumbaugh & Maholick, 1964) until the mid-1980s. And the third period in logotherapeutic research, from that time on, can be seen as concentrating on logotherapy's impact on clients' mental health in many fields of practice.

Historically speaking, research in logotherapy began in earnest with the development of specifically logotherapeutic measuring tools in the 1960s. By that time, Frankl's major efforts in developing logotherapy into a well-constructed theory of human motivation were sufficiently refined in his books, articles, and presentations around the world, and yet they still needed scientific validation. Until the new instruments appeared on the scene, and made inroads in the research and psychotherapeutic practice establishments, logotherapy was sometimes accused of being too subjective, too anecdotal, and too impressionistic. As Damon, Menon, and Brock put it in their short historical overview:

> The notion that ethereal constructs such as "meaning" and "purpose" could make a difference – that they could motivate someone to do something, or even shape a person's basic choices about how to live – seemed impossibly soft-headed and sentimental to mainstream psychologists of that time.
>
> If the behaviorist and psychoanalytic schools (the two best-known bodies of psychological work at midcentury) agreed on anything at all, it was that meaning, purpose, and other such belief systems were the products of more fundamental drives; that they were dependant on the drives for their shape, substance, and very existence; and that meaning and purpose were no more than marginal factors in behavioral development. (Damon, Menon & Brock, 2003)

Perhaps partly in reaction to such reservations by the predominant schools of psychological thought, and also because Frankl, as a neurologist, was deeply interested in empirical research and validation, Frankl and the first generation of logotherapists were eager to show the world that logotherapy has more to offer than just a theoretical-philosophical basis, namely, that its major tenets about a will-to-meaning, the motivation to find meaning in life, and the existential vacuum can be empirically researched and validated. Frankl himself was particularly concerned that logotherapy might remain an abstract concept. As he told the editor of the newly established *International Forum*:

> Why should we lose, unnecessarily and undeservedly, whole segments of the academic community, precluding them a priori from understanding how much logotherapy "speaks to the needs of the hour"? Why should we give up, right from the beginning, getting a hearing from the modern researchers by considering ourselves above tests and statistics? We have no reason not to admit our need to find our discoveries supported by strictly empirical research. (Fabry, 1978-1979:5)

At the time this statement was made, logotherapeutic research was concentrating mainly on dissertations in psychiatry, psychology, philosophy, and related disciplines. The research done was aimed at verifying the therapeutic value of logotherapeutic concepts and the clinical efficiency of several methods and techniques of logotherapeutic intervention, such as paradoxical intention, dereflection, and modification of attitudes. Today, the situation is entirely different, as the more than 600 studies presented in this book attest to (excluding an even larger number of dissertations and master theses, books, book chapters, and conference presentations not surveyed here). We may say, with all due respect and modesty, that Frankl would have been very pleased to find that the research in logotherapy has far surpassed his dream.

THE RATIONALE FOR THIS BOOK
This annotated bibliography of scientific and empirical studies in logotherapy published in professional journals in many disciplines, aside from, and in addition to, logotherapy, is the first book on this subject.

The book provides the necessary information on what has been achieved so far in making Frankl's dream about logotherapy-oriented research come true: what has been tested, assessed, and found useful or in need of further refinement of the many logotherapeutic test instruments, tools, and techniques currently available to interested parties; which concepts are most in use and which need additional clarification; and where the major gaps in logotherapeutic empirical knowledge are at present.

The reason for compiling a separate book on research studies on logotherapy is not difficult to state: Aside from Frankl's express wish to see his logotherapy supported by empirical research, researchers, clinicians, practitioners, and students, as well as educators, the clergy, and others, need access to easily available and up-to-date information about what is known and what is missing on this subject. In addition to the above, this book can also serve training purposes in research and statistics at professional schools of social work and in faculties and departments of psychology, medicine, education, theology, and the like.

We believe that this book can fill an important function in expanding and supporting logotherapy's knowledge base, and that our work will make a needed contribution, not only to Frankl's theory, but also to psychotherapy in general. Last but not least, we hope that our endeavour will inspire other researchers and scholars to conduct further studies, and to carry on and expand the scientific tradition of logotherapy.

METHODOLOGY AND INCLUSION CRITERIA
All entries in this research bibliography were selected and assessed on the basis of their relevance for the intended users. Each entry was evaluated using two criteria:

1. The particular study refers to logotherapy and/or existential analysis and is relevant to
logotherapeutic knowledge, theory, and practice.

2. The particular study presents empirical research using logotherapeutic concepts, tools, and instruments, and was reported in a professional journal published between 1975 and 2004.

The methodology employed in securing available data about research in logotherapy included all the abstracts of studies selected from professional journals that were available through the database of the American Psychological Association (APA), PsycINFO®. PsycINFO is an electronic bibliographic database that provides abstracts and citations from scholarly literature in the fields of the behavioral sciences and mental health. The database includes material of interest to psychologists and professionals in related fields, such as psychiatry, neuroscience, education, social science, management, business, and social work. PsycINFO offered more than 1,900 titles and psychological literature from the 1800s to the present, with almost two million records and nearly 10 million references in journal articles, books, and book chapters as of March 2004.

This comprehensive database was the main source for the entries in this book. The first editor started a broad search, using all the keywords related to logotherapy and Frankl's thoughts and ideas. The search was then refined step by step and studies were scanned for their methodology, relevance, and quality. Only empirical research studies were included (that is, no single-case studies or theoretical papers were accepted). Relevance to logotherapy and meaning-oriented psychotherapy was, of course, the most important criterion. Yet it soon became evident that a number of researchers measured and correlated the impact of logotherapeutic concepts within the context of other data, often stressing the latter over the former. In other words, in some instances, the logotherapeutic concepts investigated in the entries are only mentioned relatively briefly in the abstracts, and in such cases, it is advisable to take a closer look at the test constructs and data investigated and discussed in these studies. If logotherapeutic concepts were mentioned relatively briefly, the first editor checked the original article to see whether the logotherapeutic data were a prominent enough part of the study to merit inclusion in this research bibliography. Only then was the study included.

In other cases, methodology and quality were an issue, too. This was true especially for descriptive studies, which, although not empirical in the stricter sense, were included in this bibliography if they measured concepts and ideas not otherwise accessible to more conventional research methods (for example, individual sources of personal meaning in coping). In the same vein, there were a few borderline cases in which either the number of subjects was too small for an elaborate statistical analysis or the investigated conditions and constructs were too diverse for the study to qualify as a classical empirical research paper. If this was so, the decision as to whether or not to include the entry was made on a case-by-case basis.

The second source of entries was provided by the authors themselves and a few friendly persons who were kind enough to distribute our call for papers and studies around the world. Nevertheless, the studies received as a result of the call make up a considerably smaller section of the entries than those found through PsycINFO (less than 3% as compared with the 97% of PsycINFO).

Meeting enthusiastic kindred spirits is not something that one would necessarily expect in the world of bibliographies, research data banks, humming computers, and silent libraries. For us, it was a journey into a world of its own. And within this world we met exceptional people. One such was Marion Harrell of PsycINFO. Thanks to her help and generosity, we were allowed to reprint the full abstracts in this book for a merely symbolic fee. Ms. Harrell was a kind, friendly, unfailing, and important help: her and PsycINFO's roles in making this book possible cannot be praised highly enough. It is a delight to be able to thank Marion Harrell and all those involved in APA's PsycINFO for their support in making this book possible.

Despite the first editor's attempts to collect all studies fitting the inclusion criteria, given the sheer number of studies found, some research papers that should have been included probably have been omitted, either because they were not available on PsycINFO, or because the first editor failed to notice them. A sincere apology is due to the authors whose studies were overlooked. Their authors are encouraged to inform the first editor of such studies so that these can be included in subsequent editions of this bibliography (for more information, see below).

THE STRUCTURE OF THIS BIBLIOGRAPHY

All entries are numbered consecutively for easy access. The material is organized in such a way as to provide the relevant information by using either the chapter or part of the chapter that covers the topic, or the cross-references and numbers of the entries.

Many of the studies presented investigated more than one concept, disorder, or technique, and hence it was necessary to structure these studies accordingly. Each entry contains the main finding, plus other findings of relevance. We decided to focus on the main finding, or most severe condition, and present the secondary findings, or the (relatively) less severe conditions, in a shortened form. For example, a study on suicide and substance abuse would be presented like follows: In the section on "suicide," the full study would be quoted; whereas under the heading "Substance Abuse," only the bibliographical reference would be given, together with the number of the full citation.

Furthermore, a relatively small number of studies explicitly refer to certain age groups; others either do not mention the age range of the subjects, or neglect potential age differences. Although it is true that the importance of certain existential themes varies across the life span, the same is true for any other external influence on subjects; hence, rather than presenting such findings in age-related sections of their own, the entries in each chapter and section are sorted alphabetically.

In some cases, especially in the sections on basic research findings and on suicide, the respective studies were primarily conducted to test the reliability and validity of certain new psychometric instruments measuring logotherapeutic concepts. Depending on the content of the studies themselves, in the majority of cases, such findings are presented not in the chapter on logotherapeutic tests and research instruments, but under the chapter referring to the conditions that were investigated from a logotherapeutical viewpoint — in this case, on meaning and its general role in psychology and therapy. We decided to follow this path for several reasons: First, for the purposes of this bibliography, research findings rather than research methods were of prime interest. Second, some of these studies used translations of tests already known to be of high validity. And third, we felt that the main findings of these studies were too important or clinically too relevant for them to be merely presented as validity and reliability studies of new research instruments in logotherapy and meaning-oriented psychotherapy.

This bibliography covers all the relevant information on logotherapy-related research available. The references are arranged in three parts, each with subheadings and sections. The three main parts of this bibliography are dedicated respectively to Theory, Application, and Evaluation. Each contains several chapters, and each chapter is divided into several sections. The major findings in each of the relevant parts of this book constitute the heart of this work.

Structure of Part I

The first part of the book summarizes studies on Frankl's motivational theory (the will to meaning).

Chapter 1, titled "Meaning in Life (General)," presents studies related to the concept of meaning in psychology, with special emphasis on logotherapy and existential analysis. Logotherapy differentiates three "kinds" of meaning: the meaning of life, ultimate meaning, and the meaning of the moment. Research findings alluding to these are elaborated on in more detail in this chapter. Our review of the research landscape shows that, in recent years, psychologists have become increasingly aware of the psychohygienic and therapeutic value of the awareness of meaning in life, both in itself and as a way of coping and protection. The studies in Part 1, Chapter 1, offer a broad overview of what is known about meaning fulfilment, the expressed search for meaning and the sources, categories, and depths of meaning of diverse populations. These entries present studies on these concepts within a wide variety of demographic criteria. Studies are structured in the following sections.

1. Meaning: General findings
2. Sources of Meaning
3. Value-Orientation and Pro-Social Behavior
4. Family and Relationships
5. Meaning and Spiritual Quest

Chapter 2 explores the different sources of meaning. Whereas meaning fulfilment and the search for meaning are personal and individual paths, and, according to logotherapy's predictions, cannot be generalized, a number of researchers have been able to show that sources and categories, and also the depth of meaning, can be measured. These research findings are yet another example of the increasing sophistication of measurement instruments of concepts, which, at first sight, would not have seemed to lend themselves to psychometric research.

Sections 3 and 4 explore the more social aspects of meaning: Section 3 deals with pro-social behavior, its association with value and meaning and their often-complex interrelationship, whereas Section 4 presents research findings on meaning in family and relationships.

Although most of these sections' titles are self-explanatory, a number of entries (Section 5) describe research on ultimate meaning and its psychological aspects. This section needs some clarification and elaboration: While, as a school of therapy, logotherapy has to, and does, remain neutral on the question of religiosity and ultimate meaning, Frankl acknowledges religiosity and spirituality as genuine manifestations of the noetic dimension of humans, and hence as something irreducible to lower drives, homeostatic functions, defence mechanisms, and the like. Nonetheless, Frankl urged practitioners not to impose values and sources of meaning on the patient, and this is, of course, especially important in the context of religion and spirituality. Yet Frankl also recognized the psychohygienic potential of an authentic and healthy spirituality, and, provided that a person "stands on firm ground of religious belief", stated that "there can be no objection to making use of the therapeutic effect of his religious convictions and thereby drawing upon his spiritual resources" (Frankl, 2004:122). Since religion, as a basic belief in ultimate or super-meaning, is – albeit in a highly restricted sense — a potential topic in therapy, a smaller number of studies pertaining to this issue and its relationship to meaning in general are also presented in Section 5. Whereas there exists a vast amount of studies on the psychology of religion and spirituality's relationship to mental health (and disorder), only a small percentage of these were included in this bibliography — namely, those that explicitly were judged to be of relevance to its general theme. Given the relatively high number of such studies as compared with their somewhat restricted relevance in the context of logotherapy, inclusion criteria were considerably stricter than for most other studies.

Chapter 2, "Meaning in Suffering: The Homo Patiens," presents studies that allude to the problem of meaning and unavoidable suffering. In this context, meaning is not a primary source of well-being, but is a potent way of coping with what otherwise would be barely bearable for the patient or his or her relatives:

> We must never forget that we may also find meaning in life even when confronted with a hopeless situation, when facing a fate that cannot be changed. For what then matters is to bear witness to the uniquely potential at its best, which is to transform a personal tragedy into a triumph, to turn one's predicament into a human achievement. [...]
> It is one of the basic tenets of logotherapy that man's main concern is not to gain pleasure or to avoid pain but rather to see meaning in his life. That is why man is even ready to suffer, on the condition, to be sure, that his suffering has a meaning. (Frankl, 2004:116)

However, in order to avoid misunderstandings, Frankl repeatedly stressed the point that suffering is not necessary in order to find meaning; rather, he held the position that meaning can be found even in suffering and that life is meaningful despite the tragic triad of suffering, guilt, and death. Yet certainly, if the suffering is avoidable — for example, as with a treatable disease, the priority (and, in fact, the most meaningful thing to do) is to look for an alleviation of the suffering rather than to search for meaning in a suffering condition that can, in principle, be changed (Frankl, 2004:117).

In this chapter, then, research findings are presented that deal with the search for meaning in the context of chronic, sometimes terminal, diseases (Section 1), or death (Section 3) and bereavement (Section 4), or traumata and other conditions that can be summarized under the more general heading of unavoidable (that is, unalterable) suffering (Section 5). A new addition to the classical logotherapeutic list in this context is the perspective not only of the person in need of care, but also of the caregiver (Section 2). Current trends in healthcare studies devote increasing attention to the burden that relatives and friends, and, more generally, caregivers in hospitals and hospices of the severely (or terminally) ill have to carry in their service. While not necessarily unavoidable suffering in the stricter sense of the word, the perspective of the caregiver is included in this chapter since it is closely related both to unavoidable suffering and to a person's ability to rise above himself or herself and to transform tragedy into triumph.

The general outline of the sections in Chapter 2 is as follows:

1. Chronic Diseases and Disabilities
2. The Caregiver's Perspective
3. Death and Mortality
4. Bereavement
5. Coping: Miscellaneous Conditions and Findings

Structure of Part II

Part II of this book deals with one, albeit major, theme: logotherapeutic intervention and therapy. Problems affecting people's well-being are presented in here. This part gives an overview of empirical research whose subject areas include conditions that Frankl termed the results of living in an "existential vacuum." These are, among others, aggression and antisocial behaviour, addictions, depression, and suicide. Frankl repeatedly emphasized that lives devoid of clear purpose and marked by boredom and emptiness lead to conditions that border on psychopathology, and when left unattended, may result in serious harm to the well-being of the individual. Logotherapy's predictions about the relationship between (or, in some cases, direct mediation of) awareness of meaning and a number of psychopathological conditions were described by Frankl as follows, in a paragraph, that, because of its conciseness, deserves full quotation.

> The existential vacuum, according to Frankl:
> [...] is causing, and certainly bringing to psychiatrists, more problems to solve than distress. And these problems are growing increasingly crucial, for progressive automation will probably lead to an enormous increase in the leisure hours available to the average worker. Let us consider, for instance, "Sunday neurosis", that kind of depression which afflicts people who become aware of the lack of content in their lives [...]. Not a few cases of suicide can be traced back to the existential vacuum. Such widespread phenomena as depression, aggression and addiction are not understandable unless we recognize the existential vacuum underlying them. This is also true of the crises of pensioners and aging people. (Frankl, 2004:112)

The conditions discussed in Part II, however, are not necessarily, nor in all cases, directly and only caused by the existential vacuum; rather, a number of them are likely to be multicausal. Yet even if the psychopathological condition is not by itself caused by the existential vacuum, it unquestionably is aggravated by living in a meaningless void. For example, addiction and aggression are more likely to blossom in certain social environments, or might, to some degree, be dispositionally preformed. On the other hand, a strong awareness of meaning and purpose can serve as a protective factor, even if certain triggers and causes generally might predispose certain populations to specific mental problems or disorders. Still, according to logotherapy, humans are free to take a stand on such conditions, and an awareness of meaning and purpose – and responsibility – strengthens one's coping resources and healthy nucleus, and so can serve as a potent protective factor in neurosis prophylaxis. Also, even in cases where someone has already been involved in one of the problem behaviors or disorders referred to in this section, logotherapy can serve as an important and effective recovery tool – for, according to logotherapy, a person "is capable of changing the world for the better if possible, and of changing himself for the better if necessary" (Frankl, 2004:133). Thus, recovery, even on an existential level, is possible once the patient has found a purpose for whose sake it is now worthwhile to rediscover life and health where disorder and despair used to reign.

In addition to disorders and conditions that are, to some degree, co-caused by repeated wrong choices (as in addictions), other mental disorders are not self-afflicted, but are aggravated by the lack of awareness of meaning and purpose:

> In such patients, what we have to deal with is not a noogenic neurosis. However, we will never succeed in having the patient overcome his condition if we have not supplemented the psychotherapeutic treatment with logotherapy.
>
> For by filling the existential vacuum, the patient will be prevented from suffering further relapses. Therefore, logotherapy is indicated not only in noogenic cases [...], but also in psychogenic cases, and sometimes even the somatogenic (pseudo-) neuroses. (Frankl, 2004:113)

Having said this much, it has to be kept in mind that each person's journey toward healing and recovery is highly individual. According to the understanding of logotherapy, each and every person is unique and irreplaceable; and furthermore, each individual's meaningful tasks – that which life asks from him or her – changes not only from subject to subject, but also from situation to situation. Hence, meaning cannot to be prescribed according to a fixed schedule and program, but has to be found by the individual himself or herself, with or without the help of a therapist. Taking these individual paths into account, the entries in Section 1 summarize main findings according to broad categories rather than highly specialized keywords and diagnoses. Section 1 thus presents entries that address the role of meaning awareness in a large array of diverging psychological disturbances and disorders. Only in the following sections (2-5), are specific conditions discussed. These are, in addition to Section 1 (Psychopathology [general]):

2. Depression and Despair
3. Suicide
4. Substance Abuse and Addictions
5. Antisocial Behavior/Delinquency/Violence

In the section on suicide, a number of studies that refer to the "Reasons for Living Inventory" (RFL) are presented. While this research instrument measures a number of constructs that are not directly related to logotherapy (e.g., fear of social disapproval and fear of suicide), the test has a number of subscales that directly refer to logotherapeutic concepts (e.g., responsibility to family and child-related concerns). These meaning- and values-oriented subscales are prominent features of the RFL, which is why we decided to include RFL studies in the section on suicide.

The entries of Chapter 2 specifically address the two main techniques of logotherapy, paradoxical intention (Section 1) and dereflection (Section 2) and the particular model and psychological mechanisms underlying the effectiveness of these techniques. The findings presented in each section can be divided into two kinds of empirical data, dealing either with the respective technique and its clinical efficiency or its underlying mechanism.

1. OCD and Anxiety Disorders (Paradoxical Intention)
2. Hyper- and Dereflection

Readers will note a certain assymmetry in the entries of these subsections, though. Whereas relatively few studies which the mechanism underlying paradoxical intention as compared with the number of studies showing its therapeutic efficiency, there is a relatively larger number that refer to the detrimental effects of excessive self-focus as compared with those that address the clinical efficiency of dereflection. Such studies are to be found mainly in the preceding sections of Part II, Chapter 1. Dereflection cannot be achieved by merely explaining to the client that he or she ought to ignore that which has often already become part of a vicious circle of symptom -> attention -> magnification of symptom -> increased attention. From the viewpoint of logotherapy, not thinking about a certain topic hardly is meaningful in itself; rather, the basic idea of dereflection is to direct one's attention and efforts toward a meaningful task that deserves, needs, and is worthy of it. Thus, there is an obvious overlap between renewed meaning awareness and dereflection. As Lukas says with regard to hyperreflection's role in sexual and sleeping disorders:

> A man who drops into bed at night thinking about what he has accomplished that day will soon fall asleep. A woman who in the union with her partner thinks of his pleasure instead of her own, will find sexual gratification. When patients concentrate not on themselves but on their work or their partner, the body functions automatically. (Lukas, 1984:90)

Consequently, most studies that address the therapeutic potential of a renewed or improved awareness of purpose and meaning directly or indirectly make use of dereflection. The same is true for other logotherapeutic techniques that were developed by Frankl and his students mainly as aids for the patient's discovery of meaning. According to logotherapy, the path to meaning differs from person to person, and from hour to hour – and, in therapy, from one therapeutic dyad to the other; thus, relatively few studies make explicit reference to the individual processes that lead patients to a new sense of responsibility and purpose. We view such confines of empirical research on the techniques of dereflection and finding meaning as indications of the richness and individuality of human lives – and thus as confirming one of the tenets of logotherapy (the individuality and irreplacability of each and every person) – rather than as a shortcoming of current research methods in logotherapy.

> For a long time – for half a century, in fact – psychiatry tried to interpret the human mind merely as a mechanism, and consequently the therapy of mental disease merely in terms of technique. [...] A doctor, however, who would still interpret his own role mainly as that of a technician would confess that he sees in his patient nothing more than a machine, instead of seeing the human being behind the machine! (Frankl, 2004:135)

Structure of Part III

Efforts at assessing Frankl's intuitive concepts surfaced early when his best-seller *Man's*

Search for Meaning made a lasting impact on those who read it. This was not an easy ride for researchers in logotherapy, as much in Frankl's theory was not straightforward, within the reach of scientific measurement and validation. For example, the concept of the "freedom of the will" is outside of any experimental paradigm since it is defined by the very absence of determining causes that are the basis of standard research procedures. On the other hand, other concepts related to the spiritual dimension in Frankl's logotherapy, such as the "defiant power of the human spirit," can be, if only indirectly, measured. A circumstantial connection also can be made between "freedom of the will" and the latter indicating that no circumstance whatsoever can be sufficiently overpowering as to totally eliminate a person's last freedom – the freedom to take a stand toward otherwise trying circumstances.

Also, the search for meaning is not a subject that lends itself to easy categorization and measurement. The same applies to "unavoidable suffering" or to Frankl's concept of "self-transcendence." Nevertheless logotherapists should not be content with descriptions of "successful logotherapeutic interventions" in clients' lives without empirical proof. Anecdotal accounts about logotherapy's influence on behavior, impressive as they may be, are not sufficient in themselves to convince researchers in the mental health professions of logotherapy's value for psychotherapy.

Attempts to develop tools and instruments for the scientific and empirical evaluation of some major concepts in logotherapy and their impact on patient and client well-being have been continuing since the 1960s. In the last chapter of the bibliography, studies of the internal validity, reliability and statistical relevance of a number of tests – some well known, others less so – are presented. As already explained above, we decided to list some of those studies that researched the reliability, factor structures, and validity of certain tests under the respective conditions which were correlated with the measured meaning construct. Hence, for some studies, only references are given in this chapter (the reference number will point readers to the full citation with abstract in the respective sections), whereas others are presented with abstracts. The chapter on research instruments in logotherapy concludes this bibliography on empirical research in logotherapy and existential analysis, its concepts, methods, and models.

Crumbaugh, J.C. (1977). The Seeking of Noetic Goals Test (SONG): A complementary scale to the Purpose-in-Life Test (PIL). *Journal of Clinical Psychology*, 33, 900-907.

Crumbaugh, J.C., & Henrion, R. (1988). PIL Test: Administration, interpretation, uses, theory and critique. *The International Forum for Logotherapy / Journal of Search for Meaning*, 11, 76-88.

Crumbaugh, J.C., & Maholick, L.T. (1964). An experimental study in existentialism: The psychometric approach to Frankl's concept of noogenic neurosis. *Journal of Clinical Psychology*, 20, 200-207.

Damon, W., Menon, J., & Bronk, K.C. (2003) The development of purpose during adolescence. *Applied Developmental Science*, Vol. 7, No. 3, 119–128

Fabry, J.B. (1978-1979). Aspects and prospects of logotherapy: A dialogue with Viktor Frankl. *The International Forum for Logotherapy Journal of Search for Meaning*, 2, 8-11.

Frankl, V.E. (1955). *The Doctor and the Soul.* New York: Knopf

Frankl, V.E. (1959). *Man's Search for Meaning / From Death-Camp to Existentialism. A Psychiatrist's Path to a New Therapy.* Boston: Beacon Press

Frankl, V.E. (1962). *Man's Search for Meaning; An Introduction to Logotherapy; a revised and enlarged edition of From death camp to existentialism* (Preface by Gordon W. Allport). New York: Touchstone.

Frankl, V.E. (1963). *Man's Search for Meaning: An Introduction to Logotherapy.* New York: Washington Square Press.

Frankl, V.E. (1981). The future of logotherapy. *International Forum for Logotherapy Journal of Search for Meaning,* 4, 71-78.

Frankl, V.E. (1986). *The Doctor and the Soul: From psychotherapy to logotherapy.* New York: Vintage Books.

Giorgi, B. (1982). The Belfast Test: A new psychometric approach to logotherapy. *The International Forum for Logotherapy Journal of Search for Meaning.* 5, 31-37.

Guttmann, D. (1996). *Logotherapy for the Helping Professional. Meaningful Social Work.* New York: Springer Publishing Company.

Hutzell, R.R. & Peterson, T. J. (1985). An MMPI Existential Vacuum Scale. *The International Forum for Logotherapy Journal of Search for Meaning,* 8, 97-100.

Lukas, E. (1986). *Meaningful Living; A logotherapeutic guide to health.* Foreword by V. E. Frankl. New York: Grove Press/Institute of Logotherapy Press.

Starck, P. L. (1983). Patients' perceptions of the meaning of suffering. *The International Forum for Logotherapy Journal of Search for Meaning,* 6, 110-116.

THE LOGOTHERAPY RESEARCH PLATFORM

The Logotherapy Research Platform is an international and interdisciplinary Web-based meeting point for professional and student researchers in academic and applied settings. It was established on the occasion of the publication of this bibliography and is hosted by the Viktor Frankl Institute, Vienna. The Research Platform's address is: www.viktorfrankl.org/research.

Its primary purpose is to promote empirical research related to Viktor Frankl's logotherapy and existential analysis. It will serve as a meeting point where the international logotherapy research community can receive feedback and encouragement and develop ideas and joint research projects. To that end, it will host or provide links to descriptions of ongoing or completed research projects, individual manuscripts, or abstracts to promote information sharing and communication among researchers. A resource section with links will give access to logotherapeutic research instruments, and books and journals of interest.

The platform will provide an Internet forum (bulletin board service) for both young and senior researchers to share ideas and experiences relevant to logotherapeutic research. A further aim is to establish an academic support and mentoring program for post-graduate and early- career researchers. Participation is free; the platform is open to everyone who is interested in current topics and future trends in logotherapy research.

HOW TO USE THIS BIBLIOGRAPHY

- The entries in this bibliography are grouped by subject.
- The bibliography is divided into three parts: Part I presents findings on the scope, depth, and sources of meaning both in everyday life and in the context of diverse life situations and conditions. Part II presents findings relevant to logotherapy in psychopathology. In Part III, studies are listed that address the reliability, validity, and structure of logotherapeutic test instruments, or deal, in one way or another, with meta-research in logotherapy.
- Parts I and II are divided into two chapters; each chapter is divided into several sections that specifically address concrete concepts and conditions. Part III consists of only one main chapter.
- Within each section, entries are listed alphabetically according to the name of the first author.
- All entries are numbered consecutively. In those instances where articles refer to more than one condition, the entry is listed in the section on the more severe condition (or more basic finding) with full quotation (i.e., with abstracts). A shortened reference is listed in the section on the less severe condition (or less basic finding) and the number referring to the main entry.
- Some abstracts make only relatively brief references to the logotherapeutic concepts the researchers investigated. Such studies were included only if the logotherapeutic aspects of the study justified the inclusion in this bibliography; hence, it is worthwhile to take a closer look at the abstract or the study itself.

PART I

MEANING: BASIC FINDINGS AND CONCEPTS

Meaning in Life (General)

[001]
Adams, Troy B.; Bezner, Janet; Drabbs, Mary E.; Zambarano, Robert J.; Steinhardt, Mary A.

Conceptualization and measurement of the spiritual and psychological dimensions of wellness in a college population.
To explore the relationship between measures of spiritual and psychological wellness and perceived wellness in a college student population, the authors administered a series of survey instruments to 112 undergraduate students (aged 16-58 yrs) under quiet classroom conditions. They used the Life Attitude Profile to measure spiritual wellness, the Life Orientation Test and the Sense of Coherence Scale to measure psychological wellness, and the Perceived Wellness Survey to measure overall wellness. Path analysis performed with a proposed theoretical model revealed that the effect of life purpose on perceived wellness was mediated by optimism and sense of coherence, which had independent effects on perceived wellness beyond that of life purpose. The findings suggest that an optimistic outlook and sense of coherence must be present for life purpose to enhance a sense of overall well-being.
Journal of American College Health. 2000 Jan Vol 48(4) 165-173

[002]
Akande, Adebowale; Odewale, Funmilayo

The relationship between adolescent satisfaction and goal directedness.
Estimated correlations of satisfaction with goal-directedness for 59 Nigerian college adolescents using different questionnaires. The Spearman rank-difference coefficient was used to assess the extent to which the future could be predicted from these measures. The sample comprised 28 boys and 26 girls, of whom 34 were Southerners and 47 were oriented toward graduate study. It was hypothesized that Ss' perceived satisfactions as measured on the Adolescent Satisfaction Questionnaire would be correlated with the goal-directedness measured on the Purpose in Life Test. Data significantly supported this hypothesis. Data for Southern boys and graduate study oriented Ss supported the hypothesis.
International Journal of Adolescence & Youth. 1994 Vol 4(3-4) 245-252

[003]
Balcar, Karel

Standardization of the Logo-Test questionnaire with a sample of Czech university students.
(Standardizace dotazniku Logo-test na vzorku studujicich ceskych vysokych skol.)
Studied the usefulness of the Logo-Test questionnaire (E.Lukas)—an existential frustration measure developed for research, counseling, and clinical use—with Czech university students. Human Ss: 353 normal male and female Czech adults (aged 18-29 yrs) (undergraduate and graduate students). The norms and psychometric properties of the Czech version of the questionnaire were established. Multivariate analysis and factor analysis were performed.
Ceskoslovenska Psychologie. 1995 Vol 39(5) 400-405

Meaning: General Findings

[004]
Balcar, Karel

Meaningfulness of life and personality.
(Zivotni smysluplnost a osobnost.)
Eventual relationships between the Logo-test (an existential frustration measure by E. Lukas) and psychological scales of the Cloninger's TPQ, Eysenck's EPQ and IVE, Amthauer's IST, Leary et al.'s ICL (all in their Czech versions) have been examined in a sample of 131 Czech university medical students. Statistically significant correlations have been found predominantly with the more experience-determined traits than with those considered to be more genetically determined. This finding is interpreted as supporting the logotherapeutic conception of specific kind of independence as well as interaction between the "meaning-in-life" quality and personality dimensions.
Ceskoslovenska Psychologie. 1995 Vol 39(6) 496-502

[005]
Balcar, Karel

Meaning in life, well-being, and health.
(Zivotni smysluplnost, dusevni pohoda a zdravi.)
Expected relationship among experienced life meaningfulness, experienced well-being, and self-rated objective health has been subject to statistical evaluation using the Logo-test (a life meaningfulness questionnaire by E. Lukas), Dep36 (a subjective emotional reactivity questionnaire by J. Kozeny), and Health rating (objective health self-evaluation scale by the author) in a sample of 353 undergraduate and graduate level Czech university students. Through correlational analysis of the data, the hypotheses, deduced from the theoretical frame of V. Frankl's existential analysis, of an unequivocal functional relationship between experienced meaningfulness and well-being and of two mutually contrary functional relationships between experienced meaningfulness and objective health are supported.
Ceskoslovenska Psychologie. 1995 Vol 39(5) 420-424

[006]
Cathcart, N. L., & Schulenberg, S. E.

Meaning, gratitude, and psychological health: A psychometric investigation of Logotherapy.
In this study, the relationship between meaning, gratitude, and psychological well-being was examined using the Life Attitude Profile-Revised (LAP-R), the Gratitude Questionnaire (GQ-6), and the Personality Assessment Screener (PAS). Meaning and gratitude, and meaning and well-being, are statistically related to one another such that greater meaning is associated with greater gratitude and greater psychological well-being. The relationship between gratitude and psychological well-being is small, but statistically significant such that greater

gratitude is associated with greater psychological well-being. These data are consistent with the Logotherapy paradigm.

Manuscript submitted for publication at the time of inclusion in bibliography (2004).

[007]
Chang, Rosanna H.; Dodder, Richard A.

The modified Purpose in Life Scale: A cross-national validity study.
Although the original 20-item Purpose in Life Test (PIL) has been subjected to various reliability and validity tests, its use has been limited largely to American culture. In this paper 10 items were selected from the original scale, and both directionality and response categories were modified. This 10-Item Modified PIL was then validated through item analyses using 2 cross-national samples of elderly people. One sample consisted of 177 retirees from the school system in Payne County, Oklahoma (average age 73 yrs), and the other consisted of 202 retired teachers in Taipei, Taiwan (average age 67 yrs). It is concluded that the 10-Item Modified PIL can be reduced to the 7-Item Modified PIL as an alternative measure for comparing the psychological well-being of the elderly cross nationally.
International Journal of Aging & Human Development. 1983-1984 Vol 18(3) 207-217

[008]
Coffield, K. E.

Student apathy: A comparative study.
Administered the Purpose in Life (PIL) Test to 175 male and 280 female undergraduates. Data is compared to that of J. C. Crumbaugh's findings. It is concluded that the level of apathy being shown by student groups is equal to that which was manifested earlier. However, the present data indicate that females are finding more meaning than their male counterparts as their PIL scores indicate more meaningful behaviors. The changing status of females and the increased number of options open to them are addressed.
Teaching of Psychology. 1981 Feb Vol 8(1) 26-28

[009]
Coffield, K. E.; Buckalew, L. W.

University student apathy: Sex, race, and academic class variables.
Examined student apathy among 112 female and 88 male Black undergraduates using the Purpose in Life Test. Comparisons of data with those of a heterogeneous university sample by K. E. Coffield showed that both groups had similar apathy levels. In applying sex-race dichotomies, however, Black males showed significantly less apathy than Black females or heterogeneous university males. Black juniors and incoming heterogeneous freshmen displayed greater apathy behaviors than did other academic classes. Potential explanations are offered for the differential behavior noted.
Psychological Record. 1985 Fal Vol 35(4) 459-463

[010]
Coffield, K. E.; Buckalew, L. W.

Student apathy: An analysis of relevant variables.
Investigated potential gender and academic level influences on apathy levels as measured by

the Purpose In Life Test. Findings, based on 137 female and 93 male university students and 65 female and 42 male high school respondents, suggest a diminution of previously reported gender differences. Educational level was not reflected as a significant variable, although data suggested that the freshman year is potentially critical in making a commitment to education. No appreciable difference between high school and university students was found. Supplementary data point toward the potential importance of the college major as it relates to student apathy.

College Student Journal. 1986 Sum Vol 20(2) 211-214

[cf. 597]
Coward, Doris D.

Self-transcendence and correlates in a healthy population.
*Nursing Research. 1996 Mar-Apr;45(2):116-21 ***

[011]
Crumbaugh, James C.; Henrion, Rosemary

The PIL Test: Administration, interpretation, uses theory and critique.
Reviews the literature concerning the Purpose in Life Test (PILT), an attitude scale constructed with the logotherapeutic orientation and designed to detect existential vacuum. Three areas of critical inquiry are explored: whether the PILT is so heavily contaminated with the tendency to give socially desirable responses that its usefulness is impaired, whether it is cross-culturally valid, and whether it really measures meaning and purpose in life. The PILT reflects relationship to both material and noetic success. The PILT and the Logotest may be used to determine the effectiveness of therapeutic treatments or the status of various populations and their need for such treatments.

International Forum for Logotherapy. 1988 Fal-Win Vol 11(2) 76-88

[012]
Debats, Dominique L.

The Life Regard Index: Reliability and validity.
Principal component factor analyses performed on the responses of 122 undergraduates gave two factors, Fulfillment and Framework, confirming the theoretical structure. Alpha estimates of internal consistency of the factor scales ranged from satisfactory to good. Analysis supports the predicted moderate negative correlations with anxiety, hostility, and depression and a positive correlation with elation. Discriminant validity was good: the index discriminated persons who are happy and satisfied with their lives from unhappy and dissatisfied ones. A clear philosophy of life, education, and psychological counseling correlated significantly with the degree of meaning in life.

Psychological Reports. 1990 Aug Vol 67(1) 27-34

[013]
Debats, Dominique Louis; Drost, Joost; Hansen, Prartho

Experiences of meaning in life: A combined qualitative and quantitative approach.
Investigates the relation of aspects of meaning in life with indices of psychological well-

being by means of a combined qualitative and quantitative design. Content analysis of 122 college students' (aged 18-46 yrs) answers to open questions about personal experiences with meaning in life showed findings that are in line with phenomena that are reported in the literature. Meaningfulness was strongly associated with contact with self, others and the world, whereas meaninglessness was associated with a state of alienation from self, others and the world. The Life Regard Index (LRI) was associated with the interpersonal dimension of well-being. The exchange of both positive and negative feelings was associated with positive life regard. As predicted, effective coping with stressful life events in the past was associated with a current sense of meaningfulness as measured with the LRI.

British Journal of Psychology. 1995 Aug Vol 86(3) 359-375

[014]
Debats, Dominique L.; Van der Lubbe, Petra M.; Wezeman, Fimmy R.

On the psychometric properties of the Life Regard Index (LRI): A measure of meaningful life: An evaluation in three independent samples based on the Dutch version.
Evaluated the reliability and validity of the LRI, a 28-item scale designed to assess the degree of experienced meaningfulness of one's life. The theoretical LRI structure, which distinguishes 2 dimensions (Framework and Fulfillment) was supported by data from distressed student (n = 116), normal student (n = 169), and general population (n = 176) samples. Other measures included the Rokeach Value Survey, SCL-90—Revised, and a happiness index. Findings show that the LRI scales have high internal consistency and good test-retest reliability. The LRI strongly discriminated between distressed and nondistressed Ss. Associations with happiness, psychological well-being, and primary relationships were established, thus confirming the LRI's construct validity.

Personality & Individual Differences. 1993 Feb Vol 14(2) 337-345

[015]
Delle Fratte, Alessandra; Steca, Patrizia; Capanna, Cristina

Well-being and quality of life in adolescence: An empirical contribution.
(Benessere e qualita della vita in adolescenza: un contributo empirico.)
The aim of the present study is to explore the psychological dimensions identified in 1989 by the theoretical model of Carol Ryff (Autonomy, Self-acceptance, Positive relations with others, Purpose in life, Personal growth, and Environmental mastery) in a group of Italian adolescents. In particular, their relationships with the Big Five personality factors and various self-efficacy beliefs involved in the emotional and interpersonal domains were investigated. 296 boys and 306 girls ranging in age from 14 to 19 years participated in the study. Analyses of variance were performed to trace gender differences. Correlational and regression analyses were performed to explore the relationships among the different constructs. Significant gender differences were seen in the various dimensions of psychological well-being, as well as in personality traits and self-efficacy beliefs. Numerous positive relationships among the various constructs were shown. In addition, the concurrent value of personality traits and self-efficacy beliefs compared to the psychological well-being of the participants was shown. The study confirms the importance of personality traits for individual psychological well-being of adolescents and emphasizes the role of self efficacy beliefs in psychological well being.

Bollettino di Psicologia Applicata. 2003 Jan-Apr Vol 239(1) 35-47

[016]
Do Valle Freitas, Christa Hildegard

Experimental investigation of the `collective neurosis' symptomatology.
(Ein Versuch, die Symptome der kollektiven Neurosen nach Viktor Frankl testpsycholo-
gisch zu erfassen.)
This is a study of the collective neurotical symptoms according to Viktor E. Frankl through
an empirical research using a questionnaire. In addition to the issues originally formulated
by Frankl, additional questions were added probing those behaviour patterns which, as
observed by several autors, are characteristic of the collective neurotical symptoms. The survey of the data obtained confirmed the following hypotheses: (a) the symptoms are present
in the population tested, (b) less than 5% of the population tested is free of symptoms, (c)
over 50% of the population tested show two or more symptoms.
*The International Journal of Logotherapy and Existential Analysis / The Journal of the Viktor
Frankl Institute. 1996: Vol 4, Nr 1 (Spring 1996)**

[017]
Denne, Julene M.; Thompson, Norman L.

The experience of transition to meaning and purpose in life.
Investigated the establishment of meaning and purpose (M&P) in life as generated from
self-reported descriptions of the transition (T) from meaninglessness and purposelessness to
M&P. 19 "mature age" university students were recruited for taped interviews in which the
T to an experience of M&P was described. Five invariant constituent elements were identified in the structure of the T: (1) acceptance and enactment of personal responsibility, (2)
integration of resisted aspects of experience, (3) congruence between personally meaningful
concepts and experience, (4) decisional turning points, and (5) greater balance of self in relation to the world. While nonessential to the underlying structure, idiosyncratic content was
experienced as essential by the individual, thus indicating the need for an existential-phe-
nomenological therapeutic mode.
Journal of Phenomenological Psychology. 1991 Fal Vol 22(2) 109-133

[018]
Doerries, Lee E.; Ridley, Dennis R.

Time sensitivity and purpose in life: Contrasting theoretical perspectives of Myers-Briggs
and Viktor Frankl.
This study investigated the relationship between the sensitivity and purpose in life. Time
sensitivity was operationally defined by scores on the Judging-Perceiving dimension of the
Myers-Briggs Type Indicator and by whether Ss reported habitual watch-wearing. Scores
indicating the Judging orientation and watch-wearing defined individuals who were most
responsive to the dimension of time. Purpose in life was operationally defined by scores on
the J. C. Crumbaugh and Maholick Purpose in Life Test. A multiple linear regression analysis showed no difference in scores on the Purpose in Life Test between Judgers and
Perceivers, apparently supporting the Myers-Briggs perspective that having a specific tem-
perament does not convey any special advantage in added value or meaning to one's life.
Watch-wearing best predicted scores on the Purpose in Life Test. The results are discussed
in terms of competing theoretical perspectives.
Psychological Reports. 1998 Aug Vol 83(1) 67-71

[cf. 103]
Ejaz, Farida K.; Schur, Dorothy; Noelker, Linda S.

The effect of activity involvement and social relationships on boredom among nursing home residents.
Activities, Adaptation & Aging. 1997 Vol 21(4) 53-66

[019]
Ebersole, Peter; DePaola, Steve

Meaning in life depth in the active married elderly.
Investigated 2 dimensions of depth of meaning in life as expressed by 32 elderly persons and 2 groups of younger adults. The Purpose In Life Test (PIL) was used to measure self-satisfaction with personal depth of meaning in life, and a meaning essay document (MED) consisting of statements about Ss' strongest meaning in life was rated for depth by outside judges. The elderly Ss scored significantly higher on the PIL than the younger adults reported in the PIL manual. However, elderly Ss' MEDs were rated significantly lower in depth than a previous sample of younger adults (P. Ebersole and K. L. DeVogler). It is suggested that elderly Ss were better able to appreciate life but were less able to communicate their depth of appreciation to others.
Journal of Psychology. 1989 Mar Vol 123(2) 171-178

[cf. 601]
Ebersole, Peter; Quiring, Gogi

Social desirability in the Purpose-in-Life Test.
Journal of Psychology. 1989 May Vol 123(3) 305-307

[020]
Estes, Kent; Welter, Paul

The university department as a base for promoting the study and practice of logotherapy.
26 adults who had completed one or more logotherapy (LT) training courses at a university completed a 7-item, open-ended questionnaire. Ss were asked to indicate (1) the concepts in LT that motivated them to seek the training and (2) the differences that LT training had made in their lives and work. Responses support V. Frankl's belief that LT is "teachable and learnable" and also support the university department as a workable setting for the teaching and learning venture.
International Forum for Logotherapy. 1994 Spr Vol 17(1) 27-31

[021]
Halama, Peter

Dimensions of life meaning as factors of coping.
Examined the relationship of meaning in life and the preference of coping strategies in 166 17-19 yr olds. Three meaning dimensions were measured: (1) intensity, a level at which the individual perceives that his her life has meaning and purpose; (2) the breadth, a number of sources, which the individual derives meaning from (a number of different values in one's life); and (3) depth, a level of self-transcendence of meaning in life. A picture frustration

test, adapted for recognizing coping strategies, was completed. Results show positive relationship of meaningfulness and constructive strategies as well as positive relationship of
meaninglessness and the preference of aggressive strategies. Depth of life meaning was
found as the strongest predictor of coping strategies. Ss with more self-transcendent values
tended to use constructive strategies and Ss with self-focusing values used more aggressive
strategies.

Studia Psychologica. 2000 Vol 42(4) 339-350

[022]
Halama, Peter

Meaning and hope – two factors of positive psychological functioning in late adulthood
The collaborative role of life meaning and hope in positive human functioning is investi-
gated.The research sample consisted of 94 persons in late adulthood (50-79). Reker's
Personal Meaning Index (PMI) was used measuring life meaningfulness and Snyder's Hope
Scale for measuring the level of hope. As indicators of mental functioning use was made of
Rosenberg's Self-Esteem Scale (SES), Spielberger's State-Trait Personality Inventory (STPI),
which measures one positive characteristic (curiosity) and three negative characteristics
(depressiveness, aggressiveness, and anxiousness). The model with a suggested statistical
causal influence of positive life regard to positive and negative functioning was tested by
LISREL analysis. This analysis showed a strong positive causal influence of positive life
regard on positive functioning and a negative causal influence on negative functioning. The
discussion deals with the possible contribution of internal locus of control to positive life
regard index, as ensued from the result.

Studia Psychologica. Vol 45:2. 103-110

[023]
Harlow, Lisa L.; Newcomb, Michael D.; Bentler, P. M.

Purpose in Life Test assessment using latent variable methods.
Conducted a psychometric assessment of a revised version of the Purpose in Life Test
(PIL—R) with 722 Ss (mean age 21.93 yrs). Factor analyses revealed a large general factor
plus 4 primary factors comprising Lack of Purpose in Life, Positive Sense of Purpose,
Motivation for Meaning, and Existential Confusion. Validity models showed that the PIL—
R was positively related to a construct of happiness and was negatively related to suicidali-
ty and meaninglessness; reliability was acceptable. It is suggested that the revised version can
be presented compactly and may be less confusing to Ss than the original PIL.

British Journal of Clinical Psychology. 1987 Sep Vol 26(3) 235-236

[024]
Harris, Alex H. S.; Standard, Samuel

Psychometric properties of the Life Regard Index-Revised: A validation study of a measure
of personal meaning.
A validation study of the English version of the 28-item Life Regard Index-Revised was
undertaken with a sample of 91 participants (74.5% female, aged 20-80 yrs) from the general population. The Index appeared to have adequate evidence supporting its concurrent
and discriminant validity when compared with measures of hopelessness, spiritual well-
being, and other measures of personal meaning. A significant positive association was found

between the index and the Marlowe-Crowne Social Desirability Scale. The Index was also significantly associated with sex (women scoring higher) and marital status (divorced people scoring lower). Revisions of the English version may address the restriction of range problem by employing a 5-point rating scale, instead of the current 3-point scale, or by adding more discriminating items. Further factor-analytic studies with larger samples are needed before conclusions can be drawn regarding this scale's factor structure.

Psychological Reports. 2001 Dec Vol 89(3) 759-773

[025]
Ho, Ying-chyi

College students' meaning of life and its correlates: An empirical study of the concept of logotherapy.
Studied the sense of the meaning of life in 873 Chinese college students. Results show that the meaning of life was positively related to responsibility, self-transcendence, and time perception and was negatively related to powerlessness. Females showed more existential vacuum than males. Results support V. E. Frankl's (1981) concept of logotherapy in general.

Bulletin of Educational Psychology. 1987 May Vol 20 87-106

[026]
Itatsu, Hiromi

The relationship of self-acceptance to life attitude and hopelessness.
Studied the relationship of self-acceptance and self-evaluative behavior to attitudes toward life. Ss were 366 undergraduate students. Tests results were factor analyzed. The Self-Acceptance Scale (H. Itatsu, 1989), the Life Attitude Profile, the Life Attitude Scale (Itatsu, 1992) and the Hopelessness Scale were used.

Japanese Journal of Counseling Science. 1995 Mar Vol 28(1) 37-46

[027]
Jenerson-Madden, Dolores; Ebersole, Peter; Romero, Ana M.

Personal life meaning of Mexicans.
Neither the Purpose in Life Test nor the Meaning in Life Depth measure revealed significant differences in personal meaning depth between 97 1st generation Mexican adults (aged 28-49 yrs) in the US and matched groups of US White adults (aged 25-51 yrs). Regarding types of meaning in life, a higher percentage of Mexican Ss focused on relationships. The Mexicans' family focus was especially oriented toward helping their children grow regarding their education. White Ss chose religious belief more often than Mexicans as the most important type of meaning in life. Results challenge those more pessimistic about the condition of the world since only a few Ss from both groups stated that they saw life as meaningless.

Journal of Social Behavior & Personality. 1992 Jan Vol 7(1) 151-161

[028]
Jenks, Julie; Kahane, Jonathan; Bobinski, Virginia; Piermarini, Tina

The relationship between perceived college student satisfaction and goal-directedness.

Administered the College Student Satisfaction Questionnaire and Purpose in Life Test to 292 college seniors to determine the correlation between the 2 tests. Measures of satisfaction, which included "compensation," "working conditions," "recognition," "social life," and "quality of education," were correlated with goal-directedness. The hypothesis dealing with total satisfaction and its relationship to goal-directedness was significantly supported. Results also support hypotheses concerned with the male and White samples, but not those for the female, non-White, graduate-, and nongraduate-study-orientation groups.

Measurement & Evaluation in Guidance. 1979 Jan Vol 11(4) 225-229

[029]
Kahana, Eva; Lawrence, Renee H.; Kahana, Boaz; Kercher, Kyle; Wisniewski, Amy; Stoller, Eleanor; Tobin, Jordan; Stange, Kurt

Long-term impact of preventive proactivity on quality of life of the old-old.
This research explored the long-term benefits of engaging in proactive health promotion efforts among old-old residents of Sunbelt retirement communities to empirically test components of the Preventive and Corrective Proactivity (PCP) Model of Successful Aging. Specifically, we examined the contributions of exercise, tobacco use, moderate alcohol use, and annual medical checkups to multidimensional quality of life indicators of physical health, psychological well-being, and mortality. Data were obtained from a longitudinal study of adaptation to aging. Annual in-home interviews were conducted with 1000 older adults over a 9-year period. Whether health promotion behaviors at baseline predicted quality of life outcomes 8 years later was examined, controlling for the baseline outcome, sociodemographic variables, and, as an additional test, baseline health conditions. Exercise was predictive of fewer IADL limitations and greater longevity, positive affect, and meaning in life 8 years later.

Psychosomatic Medicine. 2002 May-Jun Vol 64(3) 382-394

[030]
Klcovanska, Eva; Masnicakova, Marta

Experiencing of existential meaningfulness of Slovak university students.
Presents the results of a study carried out with 154 undergraduates (aged 18-27 yrs). The aim of the study was to determine how much meaning Slovak students ascribe to their lives and to compare that to Czech students and Austrian populations. The authors used the logo-test—authored by V. E. Frankl's student, E. Lukas (1986). The 3-part questionnaire enables one to judge the level and the area at which man experiences meaningfulness of his life or, on the contrary, its void. Results show that 68% of the Ss had average or good level of experiencing meaningfulness. The influence of the Ss' father's education on the level of meaningfulness is briefly discussed.

Studia Psychologica. 1998 Vol 40(4) 271-276

[031]
Leontyev, Dmitry A.; Kalashnikov, Mikhail O.; Kalashnikova, Ol ga E.

The factor structure of the Purpose in Life Test.
Studied the factor structure of the Chinese translation of the Russian version of the Purpose in Life Test. Human Ss: 480 normal Chinese adults (students at 2 polytechnic institutes in

Hong Kong). Five components related to the meaning of life were obtained. Three of them reflected Ss' orientation towards life goals, processes, and results as possible sources of meaning, while the other 2 reflected aspects of locus of control.

Psikhologicheskiy Zhurnal. 1993 Jan-Feb Vol 14(1) 150-155

[032]
Levit, Robert A.

Meaning, purpose, and leadership.
Hypothesized that the motive force behind the influence of a leader is meaning and purpose, because if leaders are to clarify meaning and purpose for others, they themselves must have a greater-than-average sense of purpose and meaning. 60 executives completed the Purpose in Life test and the Leadership Effectiveness Analysis, which measured dimensions such as creating a vision, leadership style, and team playing. Ss who perceived themselves as leaders were characterized by a greater sense of purpose than those whose leadership perception was not as strong, thus supporting the hypothesis. There was a correlation between executives strong in their perception of their transformational leadership skills and their perceived purpose in life. These leaders are able to actualize this purpose and its foundational meaning to those who follow them through the common goals that characterize effectively led organizations.

International Forum for Logotherapy. 1992 Fal Vol 15(2) 71-75

[033]
Lindeman, Marjaana; Verkasalo, Markku

Meaning in life for Finnish students.
Reported on the relation of study content and the experience of meaning in life. Hypothesized that students faced with abstract and ill-defined problems in their studies and future work would find less meaning in their lives than would those who tackled more concrete and well-defined problems. Psychology students represented the field of work with ill-defined and abstract tasks. Firefighter trainees, nursing students and social work students represented fields of work with concrete and well-defined tasks. Ss completed the Life Regard Index. Results show that students' experience of life as meaningful seemed to increase as a function of concreteness in their education.

Journal of Social Psychology. 1996 Oct Vol 136(5) 657-649

[034]
Lipkina, A. I.

Personal meaning of learning factors for schoolchildren.
Studied the responses of 160 students in Grades 1-8 who, on assignments involving 1-2 hrs of work, were given marks 1 or 2 points below those they had given themselves. Ss' reactions showed that they evaluated their own work mostly in terms of the time spent on it, their general attitude toward it, and the intellectual effort expended (in terms of creativity or independent approaches to problem solving). The investment of mental effort in study is governed by self-actualization and self-assertion motives and is reinforced when personally meaningful results are obtained. At the same time, such results acquire meaning with ref-

erence to the opinions of meaningful others. These, when explicitly stated, provide the child with a feeling of competence and self-assuredness.

Voprosy Psychologii. 1983 Nov-Dec No 6 35-42

[035]
Magen, Zipora; Birenbaum, Menucha; Pery, Dvora

Experiencing joy and sorrow: An examination of intensity and shallowness.
Explores whether perceived human experience may be best typified by its intensity or by its joyous to sorrowful nature. The study examined students' most joyful and sorrowful experiences in terms of intensity (ranging from shallow to "peak") and in terms of content in three areas (with self, with external world, and interpersonally). The sample included two age groups (15-16.5 vs 20-25 yr olds) and used two questionnaires (the Positive Experience Questionnaire and the Negative Experience Questionnaire). In contrast with expectations, no age differences were found. In line with the hypotheses, consistency in the intensity level and content selection of experiences was revealed, irrespective of their joyous or sorrowful character. The results were interpreted to suggest that human experience is typically perceived along a continuum from intense-meaningful to shallow-empty rather than along a spectrum from happy-joyful to pained-sorrowful. The results also support V. Frankl's thesis that meaning exists under all circumstances. Further supported is the concept that people's experiences with other human beings, rather than with themselves alone or with the external world, are the most meaningful.

International Forum for Logotherapy. 1996 Spr Vol 19(1) 45-55

[036]
Martin, John D.; Martin, Elinor M.

The relationship of the Purpose in Life (PIL) Test to the Personal Orientation Inventory (POI), the Otis-Lennon Mental Ability Test scores, and grade point averages of high school students.
Determined the degree of correlation between the PIL and (a) the Time Competency (TC) scale of the POI, (b) the Innerdirected (I) scale of the POI, (c) IQ scores of 24 high school students who took the Otis-Lennon Mental Ability Test (Form L-M), and (d) Ss' GPA. The coefficients of correlation between scores on the PIL and (a) POI-TC, (b) POI-I, (c) Otis-Lennon Mental Ability Test, and (d) GPA were, respectively, .71, .69, .55, and .42 (all significant). It appears that a positive relationship exists between certain attributes of a self-actualizing person and the life style of the person who scores high on the PIL. One cannot, on the basis of this research, rule out the possibility that self-actualization and strong purpose in life are related secondarily through separate relationships with other variables.

Educational & Psychological Measurement. 1977 Win Vol 37(4) 1103-1105

[037]
Martinez Romero, Jose V.; Munton, Silvia M.; Payarola, Mario A.; Saenz, Adriana A.

Meaning crisis in affluent Argentina.
Assessed degree of inner meaning fulfillment by administering the Logotest to 44 male and 35 female affluent students (aged 16-18 yrs). Ss accepted the meaning factors of self-actualization, social aspects, and experiences (nature, art) but rejected service based on religious or political conviction and overcoming of distress as meaning factors. Ss with a score show-

ing very good inner meaning fulfillment found meaning in both work and family. In the medium-range group, males found meaning in studying for a career, and females valued family and maternity. Ss with a poor inner meaning fulfillment did not value specific occupations or well-being. Data support the view of V. E. Frankl (1964, 1970) that the search for meaning is relatively independent of external circumstances and that material comfort, success, and riches may work against this search.

International Forum for Logotherapy. 1990 Spr Vol 13(1) 7-14

[038]
McWilliam, Carol L.; Brown, Judith Belle; Carmichael, Janet L.; Lehman, Jocelyn M.

A new perspective on threatened autonomy in elderly persons: The disempowering process.
Explored factors other than medical condition and treatments that contributed to the discharge experiences of 12 rural and 9 urban patients (all Ss aged 68-84 yrs). Interpretive research methodology included document review, observation, and in-depth interviews of the 21 patients, 22 informal caregivers, and 117 professionals involved in the hospital and or home setting. Findings document a new perspective on how patients and professionals together contribute to the patient's threatened autonomy. Lack of clarity about goals, aspirations, and purpose in life and a generally negative frame of mind in the elderly combine with professional practice approaches to create a disempowering process. Faced with the biomedical orientation and paternalism of professionals, patients with a positive mindset and sense of direction and purpose in life did not experience threat to their autonomy.

Social Science & Medicine. 1994 Jan Vol 38(2) 327-338

[039]
Meier, Augustine; Edwards, Henry

Purpose-in-Life Test: Age and sex differences.
Assessed the relationship of age and sex differences to "meaning in life" by administering the Purpose-in-Life Test (PIL) and the Frankl Questionnaire (V. E. Frankl, 1966) to 200 randomly chosen nonpatient Ss divided into 5 age groups: 13-15, 17-19, 25-35, 45-55 and 65+ yrs, each composed of equal numbers of males and females. Age groups were found through analysis of variance to differ in PIL test scores, but no sex differences or age by sex interaction were found with respect to this dependent variable. The 2 youngest age groups were found to score significantly lower than the 3 older age groups, with the exception that the 13-15 age group did not differ from the 25-35 age group. No significant differences were found among the mean scores of the 3 older age groups.

Journal of Clinical Psychology. 1974 Jul Vol 30(3) 384-386

[cf. 395]
Moomal, Zubair

The relationship between meaning in life and mental well-being.

South African Journal of Psychology. 1999 Mar Vol 29(1) 36-41

[040]
Nackord, Ernest J.

A college test of logotherapeutic concepts.
Compared 8 male and 35 female 24-42 yr old high achievers (Group A) with 22 male and 30 female 18-36 yr old low achievers (Group B) on their scores on the Purpose in Life Test (PIL), 4 symptoms of neuroses, will to meaning vs will to pleasure and power, and creative, experiential, and attitudinal values. Ss were students in a nursing program. Results show that PIL differences between Group A and B Ss concerned responsibleness, future-orienta-tion, and personal meaning. Group A Ss rated meaning as a motivating force 4 times as high as Group B Ss. No significant difference was found in Ss' values.
International Forum for Logotherapy. 1983 Fal-Win Vol 6(2) 117-122

[041]
Niemi, Hannele

The meaning of life among secondary school pupils: A theoretical framework and some initial results.
Investigated secondary school pupils' concepts about the meaning of life using the theoret-ical framework proposed by V. E. Frankl's (1965, 1978) logotherapeutic theory. 394 Finnish secondary school students completed questionnaires consisting of numerous tests measur-ing Ss' concepts of their own life's purpose, significance, and meaningfulness. Values and attitudes were also assessed, and Ss evaluated the significance of school subjects for their own life's meaning. Results support Frankl's hypotheses. Ss reflected on the meaning of life, and 75% thought that such topics should be dealt with at school. The significance of most school subjects was evaluated to be slight in relation to life's purpose and meaning.
Research Bulletin, Department of Education, U. Helsinki. 1987 No 65 81

[042]
Nishita, Yukiko

Diverse life-styles and psychological well-being in adult women.
Clarified the effects of diverse life-style factors in adult women (aged 25-65 yrs) on multi-dimensional psychological well-being. Ss in Exp 1 were 241 female adults (mean age 45.1 yrs) in Japan. A theoretically grounded scale was constructed to measure psychological well-being. The scale consisted of 6 dimensions: self-acceptance, positive relations with others, autonomy, environmental mastery, purpose in life, and personal growth. Ss were adminis-tered the scale. The results show its reliability and validity. Ss in Exp 2 were 435 female adults (mean age 44.4 yrs) in Japan. Ss were administered questionnaires about life-style fac-tors in relation to scale dimensions of psychological well-being. The results show that: (1) participation in work and social activities affected psychological well-being in differentiat-ed ways, and social activity, which was rarely emphasized in the empirical literature, had an important effect on women's psychological well-being throughout adulthood; and (2) attainment of role performance was related differently to psychological well-being, depend-ing on the age of the Ss, and the quality of each role was important across each life cycle of the Ss.
Japanese Journal of Educational Psychology. 2000 Dec Vol 48(4) 433-443

[043]
Peacock, Edward J.; Reker, Gary T.

The Life Attitude Profile (LAP): Further evidence of reliability and empirical validity.
Administered the Life Attitude Profile (LAP) Form III to 38 college students (mean age 25 yrs) and 25 guidance counselors (mean age 44 yrs). Ss also completed a semantic differential measure of 6 life events. Following a 1-mo interval, the LAP was readministered to 32 students. The 7 LAP dimensions (Life Purpose, Existential Vacuum, Life Control, Death Acceptance, Will to Meaning, Goal Seeking, and Future Meaning to Fulfill) were shown to be internally consistent and stable over time. Evidence was also obtained for the empirical validity of a number of the LAP dimensions.
Canadian Journal of Behavioural Science. 1982 Jan Vol 14(1) 92-95

[044]
Rahman, Tania; Khaleque, Abdul

The purpose in life and academic behaviour of problem students in Bangladesh.
Examined whether there is any difference in the purposefulness of life or meaning in life between problem (identified as irregular in class attendance, nonattentive to class lectures and creating disturbances in the class, etc.) and normal students. 30 problem students (mean age 20 yrs) were compared with age-matched regular students in 1st and 2nd yr honors at Dhaka University with respect to a Purpose in Life (PIL) scale. Results showed that problem students had lower scores than the normal students. These scores differed significantly. It was concluded that the problem students showed such activities due to a lack of purpose in their lives, although it was granted that some causality probably runs in both directions. It is hypothesized that counseling may be helpful in order to improve such behavior.
Social Indicators Research. 1996 Sep Vol 39(1) 59-64

[045]
Reker, Gary T.

Logotheory and logotherapy: Challenges, opportunities, and some empirical findings.
Reviews studies that point to empirical ways through which some of the challenges and opportunities facing logotherapy and logotherapists can be met. The Life Attitude Profile—Revised (LAP—R) and the 16-item Sources of Meaning Profile (SOMP) are described. Responses from 300 adults (aged 16-93 yrs) to the original LAP showed the increase in life purpose with advancing age predicted by V. E. Frankl. In another study, 186 elderly Ss who took the LAP showed that Ss who aged successfully, with good health and psychological well-being, had higher scores of personal meaning. 103 elderly adults (aged 60-90 yrs) who completed measures of everyday stress, personal meaning, perceived well-being, self-esteem, and physical health showed that Ss high in personal meaning were not affected by stress. Responses from 360 adults who took both the LAP—R and the SOMP showed that Ss with meaning from sources transcending self found deeper meaning in life.
International Forum for Logotherapy. 1994 Spr Vol 17(1) 47-55

[046]
Reker, Gary T.; Fry, Prem S.

Factor structure and invariance of personal meaning measures in cohorts of younger and older adults.
The purpose of the present study was to examine the factor structure and factorial invariance of measures of personal meaning (i.e. the existential belief that life has purpose and coherence) in cohorts of younger and older adults. Samples of 163 young adults and 144 older adults completed six measures of personal meaning in life. Confirmatory factor analysis and multiple-groups confirmatory factor analysis was used to assess structure and structural invariance. The results show that a general second-order model of personal meaning best characterizes the factor structure of personal meaning of both younger and older adults. Factorial invariance across younger and older adults was demonstrated at the first-order factor level, but not at the second-order level. A test of age differences between the means of the six latent personal meaning factors revealed no significant differences, although there was a tendency for older adults to experience greater meaning in life. Implications for the use of personal meaning measures in cross-sectional and longitudinal research are discussed.
Personality & Individual Differences. 2003 Oct Vol 35(5) 977-993

[047]
Reker, Gary T.; Peacock, Edward J.

The Life Attitude Profile (LAP): A multidimensional instrument for assessing attitudes toward life.
Describes the development of LAP, a multidimensional measure designed to assess the degree of existential meaning and purpose in life and the strength of motivation to find meaning and purpose. Principle component factor analyses performed on the responses of 219 undergraduates to the 56-item, 7-point Likert scale resulted in the extraction of 7 primary dimensions of life attitudes (life purpose, existential vacuum, life control, death acceptance, will to meaning, goal seeking, and future meaning to fulfill) and 3 higher order factors. The normative data showed that males scored significantly higher on the death acceptance dimension and on the total LAP compared to females. Age was significantly related to a number of the LAP factors for males but not for females.
Canadian Journal of Behavioural Science. 1981 Jul Vol 13(3) 264-273

[048]
Reker, Gary T.; Peacock, Edward J.; Wong, Paul T.

Meaning and purpose in life and well-being: A life-span perspective.
300 men and women at 5 developmental stages—young adulthood (aged 16-29 yrs), early middle age (aged 30-49 yrs), late middle age (aged 50-64 yrs), young-old (aged 65-74 yrs), and old-old (aged 75+ yrs)—completed measures of life attitudes and well-being. Significant age differences were found on 5 life attitude dimensions: Life Purpose (LP), Death Acceptance (DA), Goal Seeking (GS), Future Meaning (FM), and Existential Vacuum (EV). LP and DA increased with age; GS and FM decreased with age; EV showed a curvilinear relationship with age. Significant sex differences were found for Life Control and Will to Meaning.
Journal of Gerontology. 1987 Jan Vol 42(1) 44-49

[049]
Ruini, Chiara; Ottolini, Fedra; Rafanelli, Chiara; Ryff, Carol; Fava, Giovanni Andrea

Italian validation of Psychological Well-being Scales (PWB).
(La validazione italiana delle Psychological Well-being Scales [PWB].)
The measurement of psychological well-being and positive functioning has important conceptual and methodological implications. The aim of this study was to present the Italian version of Carol Ryff' s Psychological Well-Being Scales (PWB) and to analyze their psychometric characteristics. PWB is a 84 item self-rating inventory, which consists of six scales which represent the six dimensions of psychological well-being: self-acceptance, autonomy, environmental mastery, personal growth, purpose in life and positive relations. It has been translated into Italian and administered to a sample of 415 people. Age differences are significant only in the environmental mastery and personal growth scales. People with high cultural level show significantly higher scores in purpose in life and personal growth. There are significant differences according to social class in autonomy, environmental mastery and self-acceptance, which, however, have been not replicated in the retest. The findings suggest that PWB presents good psychometric characteristics. It can be used also in Italy because it provides a complete evaluation of psychological well-being.
Rivista di Psichiatria. 2003 May-Jun Vol 38(3) 117-130

[050]
Ryff, Carol D.

Happiness is everything, or is it? Explorations on the meaning of psychological well-being.
Reigning measures of psychological well-being have little theoretical grounding, despite an extensive literature on the contours of positive functioning. Aspects of well-being derived from this literature (i.e., self-acceptance, positive relations with others, autonomy, environmental mastery, purpose in life, and personal growth) were operationalized. Three hundred and twenty-one men and women, divided among young, middle-aged, and older adults, rated themselves on these measures along with six instruments prominent in earlier studies (i.e., affect balance, life satisfaction, self-esteem, morale, locus of control, depression). Results revealed that positive relations with others, autonomy, purpose in life, and personal growth were not strongly tied to prior assessment indexes, thereby supporting the claim that key aspects of positive functioning have not been represented in the empirical arena. Furthermore, age profiles revealed a more differentiated pattern of well-being than is evident in prior research.
Journal of Personality & Social Psychology. 1989 Dec Vol 57(6) 1069-1081

[cf. 402]
Sappington, A. A.; Bryant, John; Oden, Connie

An experimental investigation of Viktor Frankl's theory of meaningfulness in life.
International Forum for Logotherapy. 1990 Fal Vol 13(2) 125-130

[051]
Scherler, H.R.; Lajunen, T; Gülgöz, S.

Comparison study of Finnish and Turkish university students on the Existential Scale.

This is a comparison study of Finnish and Turkish university students on the Existential Scale which is an instrument based on V. Frankl's Logotherapy, measuring aspects in relation to finding meaning in life. A total of 387 universiy students from Helsinki and Istanbul served as subjects. For each country, factor analyses, correlations of the Existential Scale with Rosenberg's Self Esteem Scale and the Neuroticism and Extraversion dimensions of the Eysenck Personality Questionnaire were conducted, and differences between the countries on the Existential Scale scores were investigated. A two factor solution was found for both countries, however the distribution of items into these factors was not the same. The Existential Scale scores correlated positively with the Self Esteem scores and negatively with the Neuroticism scores for both countries, yielding evidence supportive of the construct validity of the translated versions. Cultural differences were discussed to account for the difference between Finnish and Turkish scores on a subscale. The possibility of logotherapeutic concepts, as measured by the Existential scale, to be manifested differently in different cultures was pointed out. It was concluded that contextually sensitive methodological refinements were necessary for the meaningful use of the existential scale in therapeutic settings across cultures.

*The International Journal of Logotherapy and Existential Analysis / The Journal of the Viktor Frankl Institute. Volume 6, Number 2 (Fall/Winter 1998)**

[052]
Schulenberg, S. E.

A psychometric investigation of logotherapy measures and the OQ-45.2 in a non-clinical university population.
The purpose of this study was to expand the psychometric properties of four Logotherapy measures, namely the Purpose-in-Life test (PIL), the Life Purpose Questionnaire (LPQ), the Seeking of Noetic Goals test (SONG), and the Meaning in Suffering test (MIST) in order to better understand how they relate to one another and to a measure of psychological distress (the OQ-45.2). The sample was composed of 341 undergraduate students from a medium-sized Southern University. Correlations among the measures and subscales were all in the expected direction, and almost all correlations were statistically significant. The total scores of the measures were found to be internally consistent. Two subscales of the MIST were found to have questionable reliability. The PIL and the LPQ, both general measures of meaning, appear to have comparable psychometric properties, although the LPQ tended to be preferred by respondents in many respects.

Manuscript submitted for publication at the time of inclusion in bibliography (2004).

[053]
Shaughnessy, Michael F.; Evans, Robert

The meaningful personality.
Used the Purpose in Life test to examine the personality traits of individuals with "meaningful" or "healthy" characteristics in the context of V. Frankl's logotherapy. 214 college freshmen and 150 adults completed the Purpose in Life test. Ss who scored at the 85 percentile or above were administered the Sixteen Personality Factor Questionnaire (16PF). In the resulting sample of 54 students, certain personality traits predominated. High PIL Ss were on the average outgoing, emotionally stable, mature, conscientious, and responsible. Emotional stability and maturity were most often represented for Ss aged 18-20 yrs, where-

as emotional stability, assertiveness, and conscientiousness and responsibility were most often represented for Ss aged 20-30 yrs. Results were similar for older Ss (aged 30+ yrs).
International Forum for Logotherapy. 1987 Spr-Sum Vol 10(1) 46-49

[054]
Shek, Daniel T.

Reliability and factorial structure of the Chinese version of the Purpose in Life Questionnaire.
Administered a Chinese version of the Purpose in Life Test (PIL) to 2,140 secondary school students (aged 11-20 yrs) in Hong Kong. The PIL was found to have high internal consistency as a scale and high item-total correlations for most items. Five factors were abstracted from the scale: Quality of Life, Meaning of Existence, Death, Choice, and Retirement. By randomly splitting the total sample into 2 subsamples, high coefficients of congruence were found for 4 factors. Alternative analysis with a 2-factor solution showed that 2 general factors, Existence and Death, could be extracted.
Journal of Clinical Psychology. 1988 May Vol 44(3) 384-392

[cf. 422]
Shek, Daniel T.

Meaning in life and psychological well-being: An empirical study using the Chinese version of the Purpose in Life questionnaire.
Journal of Genetic Psychology. 1992 Jun Vol 153(2) 185-200

[055]
Shek, Daniel T.

Measurement of pessimism in Chinese adolescents: The Chinese Hopelessness Scale.
Administered the Chinese version of the Hopelessness Scale (C-HOPE) to 500 Chinese undergraduates to examine the psychometric properties of the scale. Ss were also administered measures of general health, state and trait anxiety, depression, self-esteem, purpose in life (PIL), existential well-being (EWB), and life satisfaction to examine the relationship between these measures and the C-HOPE. The C-HOPE had high internal consistency as a scale, and factor analysis showed that 3 factors were abstracted from the scale, namely, Hopelessness, Certainty about the Future, and Future Expectation. These factors were reliably reproduced in 2 random subsamples. While the C-HOPE correlated significantly with other measures of psychiatric symptoms and positive mental health, it correlated most highly with indices of PIL and EWB and it was specifically linked to depression rather than to anxiety.
Social Behavior & Personality. 1993 Vol 21(2) 107-119

[056]
Shek, Daniel T.

The Chinese Purpose-in-Life Test and psychological well-being in Chinese college students.
Administered the Chinese version of the Purpose-in-Life (PIL) test to 500 Chinese undergraduates, along with measures of psychological well-being (PWB) assessing psychiatric

symptoms and positive mental health. Results show that the total PIL test and 2 subscales, Quality of Existence and Purpose of Existence, correlated significantly with all measures of PWB. Relative to Purpose scores, Quality scores were more predictive of PWB. Ss with different existential statuses (defined by high vs low levels of Quality and Purpose) had different degrees of PWB. Findings imply that different aspects of meaning need to be distinguished when addressing the relationship between meaning and PWB.

International Forum for Logotherapy. 1993 Spr Vol 16(1) 35-42

[057]
Shek, Daniel T.; Hong, Eric W.; Cheung, Mary Y.

The Purpose In Life Questionnaire in a Chinese context.
Administered the Chinese version of the Purpose in Life Test to 480 postsecondary school students (aged 18-25 yrs) in Hong Kong. Factor analysis yielded the following factors: Quality of Life, Meaning of Existence, Answers to Existence, Constraint of Existence, and Future Existence Self-Responsibility. The mean total score of the Chinese Ss was comparatively lower than that reported for Western students by J. T. Crumbaugh

Journal of Psychology. 1987 Jan Vol 121(1) 77-83

[058]
Simmons, Dale D.

Purpose-in-Life and the three aspects of valuing.
Correlated the Purpose-in-Life Test designed to assess V. Frankl's (1973) concept of existential vacuum, with other measures of valuing competence, fulfillment in valuing, and value system content. Data from 99 undergraduates indicate that a sense of meaning in living is associated with a differential ability to make value judgments about the self but not about the external world, with present and anticipated future satisfaction but not with judged quality of past life, and with a relative emphasis upon responsible, intellectual self-control and a deemphasis on being cheerful and pleasant.

Journal of Clinical Psychology. 1980 Oct Vol 36(4) 921-922

[059]
Simmons, Dale D.

Identity achievement and axiological maturity.
Discusses the concept of axiological maturity and its function as a link between 3 aspects of valuing (competence, value system content, and fulfillment). It is proposed that axiological maturity would be reflected in identity status and that scores on the Identity Achievement Status Scale would be significantly related to a measure of valuing competence (the Defining Issues Test, designed to assess principled moral judgment), to a measure of valuing fulfillment (the Purpose-in-Life Test), and to the conjoint valuing of freedom and equality (as assessed by the content-oriented Rokeach Value Survey). Results of the administration of these measures to 99 university students indicate support for these predictions. Identity achievement was found to be associated with value competence and valuing fulfillment. Implications of the results on value and identity development are discussed.

Social Behavior & Personality. 1983 Vol 11(2) 101-104

[060]
Sink, Christopher A.; van Keppel, John; Purcell, Mark

Reliability estimates of the Purpose in Life and Seeking Noetic Goals tests with rural and metropolitan-area adolescents.
The Purpose in Life and Seeking Noetic Goals tests were administered to 198 rural Missouri and 659 metropolitan-area Washington high school students and readministered after an 8-week interval. The obtained test-retest and Cronbach alpha coefficients were largely consistent with earlier research using adult clinical samples.
Perceptual & Motor Skills. 1998 Apr Vol 86(2) 362

[cf. 133]
Takkinen, Sanna; Ruoppila, Isto

Meaning in life as an important component of functioning in old age.
International Journal of Aging & Human Development. 2001 Vol 53(3) 211-231

[061]
Taylor, Shelby J.; Ebersole, Peter

Young children's meaning in life.
When personal meaning was defined to them as that which in their whole life is most important to them, 26 1st graders were able to express that they had personal meaning in their lives.
Psychological Reports. 1993 Dec Vol 73(3, Pt 2) 1099-1104

[062]
Tena, Antonio; Rage, Ernesto; Virseda, Jose Antonio

The purpose in life of university youth: A descriptive study.
(Sentido de vida en jovenes universitarios: Estudio descriptivo.)
Studied the meaning of life and the purpose in life in a university population in Mexico. Ss were 159 male and 123 female students with a mean age of 21.46 yrs. The Purpose in Life Test and the Logo-Test (E. Lukas, 1963-1964) were administered. No significant differences related to age or field of study were found. The results indicate that females had more meaning in their lives, a stronger sense of freedom, and a greater sense that life is worth living compared to males. Ss who had undergone psychological treatment had less fear of death and had fewer suicidal ideas than Ss without this treatment.
Psicologia Contemporanea. 1999 Vol 6(2) 76-83

[063]
Van Ranst, Nancy; Marcoen, Alfons

Meaning in life of young and elderly adults: An examination of the factorial validity and invariance of the Life Regard Index.
The main question of the present investigation was whether the Life Regard Index (LRI) is an adequate instrument to study possible differences between young and elderly adults with regard to experienced meaning in life. Participants in this study were a group of 206 young adults (mean age 17.8 yrs) and 373 elderly adults (mean age 65.90 yrs). Ss completed a Dutch paper-and-pencil version of the LRI. The LISREL confirmatory factor analytic

model was used to test for the equivalence of measurement and of structure of the instrument. Results show that in both age groups the items of the LRI were found to be distributed to the 2 a priori dimensions of meaning in life, Framework and Fulfillment. Only the factor loadings of the Framework items were invariant across both groups. Neither the error of measurement, nor the structure of the underlying concept were equivalent for young and elderly adults. Young adults were found to experience less meaning in life than the elderly.

Personality & Individual Differences. 1997 Jun Vol 22(6) 877-884

[064]
Van Selm, Martine; Dittmann-Kohli, Freya

Meaninglessness in the second half of life: The development of a construct.
A new construct of meaninglessness in the 2nd half of life was presented. It was found that 4 theoretically based components of the construct of meaninglessness were expressed in the self- and life-descriptions of 95% of 153 Dutch independently living aged adults (aged 58-90 yrs). The self- and life-descriptions were assessed by a content analysis of Ss' answers on a sentence completion questionnaire for personal meaning (SELE). With respect to the content of the components of meaninglessness, a lack of goals and an impoverishment of meaning were responsible for most motivational meaninglessness. On the affective level, meaninglessness is far more characterized by dejection-related emotions, than by agitation-related emotions. Alienation from one's self, others, or society appeared to be characteristic for most of the cognitive component of meaninglessness. The self-evaluative component was mainly characterized by low self-esteem. A tentative explanation was presented for the differences in proportion of each of the components, pointing to the cumulative character of the construct itself.

International Journal of Aging & Human Development. 1998 Vol 47(2) 81-104

[065]
Vitola, Janice de Oliveira Castilhos

The third age: Motivational tendency and life sense.
(Terceira idade: Tendencia atualizante e sentido de vida.)
Studied motivation and attitudes about life in older adults. Human Ss: 50 male and female Brazilian old adults (aged 65-80 yrs). Data on sociodemographic variables and motivation and attitudes about life were obtained by questionnaire. Eight Ss were selected according to level of vital motivation for further study by semistructured interview. The results were evaluated using content analysis techniques according to age, sex, SES, educational level, marital status, number of children, motivation level, retirement and desire to survive, health or illness status, leisure activities, loss of family member, sense of life, spirituality, and affectional bonds. Test used: The Purpose in Life Test. Statistical tests were used.

Psico. 1998 Jan-Jun Vol 29(1) 63-88

[066]
Walters, Lynda H.; Klein, Alice E.

A cross-validated investigation of the Crumbaugh Purpose-in-Life test.
The Purpose in Life Test was factor analyzed and then cross-validated with 2 similar samples (349 and 404 Ss) of high school students. Although assumed to be unidimensional, the

test was found to contain 2 orthogonal dimensions: Despair and Enthusiasm.
Educational & Psychological Measurement. 1980 Win Vol 40(4) 1065-1071

[067]
Weinstein, Lawrence; Almaguer, Linda L.

"I'm bored"
The degree of existential meaning in life of 56 undergraduates at a small college was compared with previously obtained large-university students' Purpose in Life Test scores. Results show that Ss from a small college had feelings of boredom that were no different from those of students at large campuses. It is concluded that if students arrive at a campus without inherent motivation, they will view the prevailing environment in a purposeless manner.
Bulletin of the Psychonomic Society. 1987 Sep Vol 25(5) 389-390

[068]
Weinstein, Lawrence; Cox, Linda L.

College students are more bored than college faculty.
Compared the scores on the Purpose in Life Test of 78 undergraduates (aged 18-40 yrs) and 24 faculty (aged 25-58 yrs) at a secular college with those of 25 age-matched undergraduates and 12 faculty from a religious college.
Bulletin of the Psychonomic Society. 1989 Jan Vol 27(1) 69-70

[069]
Wells JN, Bush HA, Marshall D.

Purpose-in-life and breast health behavior in Hispanic and Anglo women.
Hispanic and Anglo women differ in their practice of breast health behavior. A likely factor is differences in purpose-in-life (PIL) that influence motivation to achieve goals. To determine the relationship between PIL and breast health behavior, the PIL Test was modified and translated into Spanish, and the Breast Health Behavior Questionnaire (BHBQ) was generated. Both Spanish and English versions of the PIL Test and the BHBQ were measured in 40 Spanish and 40 Anglo women ages 20 to 49. Cronbach's alpha for the PIL Test were .86 for the English version and .72 for the Spanish; Cronbach's alpha for the BHBQ were .78 for the English and .70 for the Spanish version. There was a significant relationship between PIL and breast health behaviors in Anglo women but not in Hispanic women. Findings suggest further study of PIL in Hispanic women and may indicate a need for teaching the benefits of self-regulation to maintain health.
Journal of Holistic Nursing. 2002 Sep;20(3):232-49

[070]
Welter, Paul

Childlike adults and meaning in life.
Constructed the Childlike Adult Inventory and administered it, along with the Purpose in Life Test, to 338 college students to examine the relationship between childlikeness and meaning. There was a significant correlation between the scores on the 2 instruments. Results indicate that childlike Ss had a greater purpose in life than nonchildlike Ss. Also, altruistic Ss were more childlike.
International Forum for Logotherapy. 1988 Spr-Sum Vol 11(1) 55-59

[071]
Wheeler, Robert J.; Munz, David C.; Jain, Ashish

Life goals and general well-being.
Examined whether Ss with high general well-being (WB) could be discriminated from Ss with low WB using their views of meaning, purpose, and life goals. 115 university students were divided into subgroups scoring high and low on WB, and differences in their life-goal orientation were estimated. Analysis indicated a significant relationship between general WB and particular aspects of life-goal orientation. Recognition of a framework of purpose, a perspective of progress, and a sense of commitment significantly differentiated between Ss scoring high and low in WB.

Psychological Reports. 1990 Feb Vol 66(1) 307-312

[072]
Wong, P. T. P., & Reker, G. T.

Stress, Coping, and Well-Being in Anglo and Chinese Elderly.
Stress, perceived well-being, and coping behaviours were studied comparing a sample of aging Chinese immigrants with Anglos. The Chinese sample found growing old a more stressful experience, reported lower psychological well-being, depended more heavily on external and palliative coping strategies, and felt less effective in coping as compared to the Anglo counterparts. External strategies included seeking social support from family and friends, and depending on religious coping. Some of the palliative strategies such as "trying to live with the problem" and "Engaging in meaningful activities" are aspects of existential coping (e.g., acceptance and meaning seeking). The finding supported the double jeopardy hypothesis of ethnic minority aging.

Canadian Journal on Aging. 1984. 4, 29-37.

[073]
Wong, P. T. P., & Weiner, B.

When People Ask "Why" Questions, and the Heuristics of Attributional Search.
Five experiments making use of a self-probe methodology in both simulated and real conditions demonstrated that individuals do engage in spontaneous attributional search. This search is most likely when the outcome of an event is negative and unexpected. Content analysis of attributional questions revealed two kinds of attributional search: Causal and existential. The former refers to the looking for causes of an outcome, while the latter refers to the examining the reason or purpose of an event (e.g., Why did this happen to me?). Results also showed that causal search is biased toward internality after failure but toward externality following success. This reverse of the oft-reported hedonic bias implicates the adaptive function of causal search. The data also revealed that the most commonly used heuristic in attributional search is to center on the locus and control dimensions of causality. The importance of heuristics in causal search and the advantages of the self-probe methodology employed in these investigations are discussed.

Journal of Personality and Social Psychology. 1981. 40, 650-663.

[074]
Wurst, Elisabeth; Maslo, Ruth

Mental health, personality, and existential resources: An empirical contribution from the perspective of existential analysis.
(Seelische Gesundheit—Personalitaet—Existentialitaet. Ein empirischer Beitrag aus existenzanalytischer Sicht.)
Studied interaction among mental health, personality characteristics, and existential resources. Human Ss: 211 normal male and female Austrian adults (aged 18-70 yrs)(predominantly high educational and professional levels). The Ss completed questionnaires assessing mental health; personality traits (e.g., purpose in life, self-esteem, autonomy, capacity for love); and existential resources (e.g., capacities for self-distancing, self-transcendence, freedom, and responsibility). Correlations among these measures were analyzed, and age and gender differences were determined. Tests used: The Trier Personality Questionnaire (P. Becker,1989) and the Existence Scale (A. Laengle and C. Orgler, 1991).
Zeitschrift fuer Klinische Psychologie, Psychiatrie und Psychotherapie. 1996 Vol 44(2) 200-212

[075]
Xu, Shulian; Wu, Zhiping; Wu, Zhenyun; Sun, Changhua; Zhang, Yao

Age differences of psychological well-being of Chinese adults.
Studied age differences in the psychological well-being of Chinese adults. 777 adults in 4 groups—young (aged 20-39 yrs, n=202), middle aged (aged 40-59 yrs, n=200), old (aged 60-74 yrs, n=203), and very old (aged 75 yrs and over, n=172)—completed Carol D. Ruff's scale (1989). The results show that the scale had satisfy reliability and discriminant validity. The 2 younger groups had higher scores in personal growth (PG) than the 2 older groups; the 3 relatively young groups had higher scores in purpose in life (PL) and positive relation with others (PRO) than the very old group. Middle aged and old groups had higher scores in environment control than the very old group; the very old group had higher scores in self-acceptance (SA). Males had higher scores in autonomy, PG, PL, and SA; females had higher scores in PRO. Influential factors in the young group included work, education, disease, mood; in middle aged group included work, marriage, and interpersonal relations; in the old group included mood and health; and in the very old group included mood, interpersonal relations, disease, education, and family relations. In comparison with American studies, Chinese participants had lower scores in PL and SA. The study concludes that psychological well-being is influenced by age.
Chinese Mental Health Journal. 2003 Vol.17 No.3

Sources and Depth of Meaning

[076]
Bar-Tur, Leora; Prager, Edward

Sources of personal meaning in a sample of young-old and old-old Israelis.
Sources of meaning in life were studied for 210 elderly Israelis, looking at the differences between the old-old (80 yrs old or older) and young-old (65-79 yrs old). Comparisons were made in 2 ways: between the old-old and young-old living in the community, and between the old-old living in the community and the old-old living in an institutional facility. The assumptions were that age would not be a differentiating factor in sources of meaning between the young-old and old-old in the community, but that meaning scores for old-old institutional dwellers would differ significantly from those of old-old community dwellers. Using the Sources of Meaning: Profile (SOMP) it was found that there were few significant differences between the young-old and old-old community dwellers. The findings did point to significant differences in sources and depth or "strength" of meaning between old-old community and institution dwellers. The findings are discussed with reference to adjustment to the institutional environment in general and to activity participation in particular.
Activities, Adaptation & Aging. 1996 Vol 21(2) 59-76

[077]
Bar-Tur, Liora; Savaya, Rivka; Prager, Edward

Sources of meaning in life in young and old Israeli Jews and Arabs.
Examined developmental, ethnic group and gender differences in sources of meaning in life among 362 younger (below 40 yrs) and older (60 yrs and over) Israeli Jewish and Arab women and men. The results of the Sources of Life Meaning Scale reveal the impact of ethnicity and age on most of the 10 sources of meaning, despite similarities in breadth of meaning manifested in the overall amount of meaning in life in all groups. The differences tended to vary according to age group, as more differences were apparent among the older respondents than among the younger ones. Gender had an effect on only 3 sources of meaning, suggesting that culture and age may overshadow gender differences.
Journal of Aging Studies. 2001 Sep Vol 15(3) 253-269

[078]
Batlle, Silvia; Aisenson, Diana

Teenagers: The meaning of work in the moment of change.
(Jovenes: el significado del trabajo frente a situaciones de cambio.)
Studied the relation of work meaning, seeking and obtaining employment, and personal goals among adolescents. Human Ss: 36 normal male and female Brazilian adolescents (secondary school students). Data on sociodemographic variables, meaning of work, and motivation were obtained by semistructured interview. The results were evaluated according to academic specialization, paternal educational level, paternal occupation and status, family support, family models for study and work, school support for finding work, school models of work, friends' comments and experience with work, general information about work,

future work and study plans, attitude toward work, work representation, perception, degree of autonomy granted by work, and importance of experience.

Acta Psiquiatrica y Psicologica de America Latina. 1998 Jun Vol 44(2) 161-167

[079]
Battista, Robert R.

Personal meaning: Attraction to sports participation.
Examined the personal meaning of sport participation among 50 female and 48 male racquetball club members (aged 18-61 yrs). Ss completed a questionnaire on which they identified and ranked personal factors associated with playing racquetball. Ss ranked enjoyment as the primary motive for participation. Men scored significantly higher on competition; however, women scored significantly higher on self-satisfaction, feedback, beauty in movement, and feeling together. There was an association for both sexes of active participation and athletic ability.

Perceptual & Motor Skills. 1990 Jun Vol 70(3, Pt 1) 1003-1009

[080]
Baum, Steven K.

Meaningful life experiences for elderly persons.
50 elderly adults (aged 70-96 yrs) from 2 settings were assessed for objective purpose scores as well as the sources of meaningful experiences. The noninstitutionalized Ss felt younger than their institutionalized peers, reported more meaningful life events, and had higher scores on the Purpose In Life test but did not differ from each other with respect to the events in life that were most meaningful. The categories that evolved included love and marriage, births, career education, separations divorce, and accidents illnesses deaths. No meaningful experiences (except accidents illnesses deaths) were reported by either group after age 40 yrs. The lack of meaningful experience in the 2nd half of life is addressed with respect to consequences for both institutionalized and noninstitutionalized elderly persons.

Psychological Reports. 1988 Oct Vol 63(2) 427-433

[081]
Baum, Steven K.; Stewart, Robert B.

Sources of meaning through the lifespan.
185 Ss (aged 17-96 yrs) completed several measures to assess the amount and origins of most meaningful events in a person's life. As assessed by a modification of the Purpose-in-Life Test, the amount of purpose did not vary with age or sex. The sources of meaning did not alter across time or sex. Themes of involvement emerged as the salient sources of meaning and included love, work, birth of children, independent pursuits, accidents, illnesses, deaths, separations, or divorces, and to a lesser extent major purchases. The common sources and their timing are discussed within the context of a lifespan developmental model.

Psychological Reports. 1990 Aug Vol 67(1) 3-14

[082]
Beutel, Ann M.; Marini, Margaret Mooney

Gender and values.
Examined gender differences in the fundamental value orientations of US high school sen-

iors between 1977-1991. The 3 measures of value orientation used included compassion, materialism, and meaning in life. There were substantial gender differences on all 3 measures. Female Ss were more likely than male Ss to express concern and responsibility for the well-being of others, less likely than male Ss to accept materialism and competition, and more likely than male Ss to indicate that finding purpose and meaning in life is extremely important. These differences are observed throughout the period from the mid-1970s to the early 1990s and show little sign of decreasing; they are evident across social class subgroups and cannot be explained by gender differences in religiosity or the perceived availability of social support.

American Sociological Review. 1995 Jun Vol 60(3) 436-448

[083]
Borges, Livia de Oliveira

Attributes and measurement of the meaning of work.
(Os atributos e a medida do significado do trabalho.)
Studied evaluative and descriptive attributes of work among Brazilian construction workers. Human Ss: 586 normal male and female Brazilian adults (mean age 31.3 yrs) (construction workers and furniture makers). Data on sociodemographic variables and evaluative and descriptive attributes of work were obtained by semistructured interview. Ss were presented with 58 descriptive and evaluative attributes of work and asked to rate each on a 4-point scale according to values (how it should be) and descriptive characteristics (how it actually is). A color scale was used for illiterate Ss. The results were evaluated according to evaluative and descriptive factors of financial independence and pleasure, work fairness, physical effort, social dignity, respect, social function, and psychosocial content. Test used: The Inventory of Work Significance (L. Borges, 1998). The factor structure of the instrument was determined. Factorial analysis and other statistical tests were used.

Psicologia: Teoria e Pesquisa. 1997 May-Aug Vol 13(2) 211-220

[084]
Brandtstaedter, Jochen; Meiniger, Christian; Graeser, Horst

Action resources and meaning resources: Developmental patterns and protective effects.
(Handlungs- und Sinnressourcen: Entwicklungsmuster und protektive Effekte.)
Perceived resources in four different domains (personal resources, social and material resources, biographical resources, religious and value-related resources) were assessed on a sample of 808 participants in the age range from 63-86 yrs. The resource domains show distinct and partly similar associations with personality traits such as extraversion or perceived control, but opposite regressions on age: Within the age-range studied, losses in personal action resources are accompanied by increases in meaning-related resources (religious and value commitments, life review). Moderated regression analyses furthermore indicate that the predictive weight of these resources for subjective life quality and well-being changes with age; moderating effects are suggestive of a compensatory relationship between "action" resources and "meaning" resources.

Zeitschrift für Entwicklungspsychologie und Pädagogische Psychologie. Vol 35. 1. 49-58

[085]
Burbank, Patricia M.

An exploratory study: Assessing the meaning in life among older adult clients.
Investigated factors perceived as meaningful (meaning framework) and the degree of fulfillment (meaning fulfillment) among 81 Ss (aged 63-88 yrs) using a symbolic interactionist
perspective. 89% of the Ss reported having something so important in their lives that it gave
their lives meaning. Of these 73 Ss, 60 specified items that gave life meaning. 57% of the
Ss listed relationships as most important to them. Service was important to 12%. Religion-
related items were most important for 13% of the Ss, while 10% reported activities as most
important. The remaining 8% were divided among the categories of living growth, home,
health, and learning. Most respondents reported a high degree of meaning fulfillment; however, 8 Ss stated their lives were meaningless.
Journal of Gerontological Nursing. 1992 Sep Vol 18(9) 19-28

[086]
Carney, John M.; Dobson, Judith E.; Dobson, Russell L.

Using senior citizen volunteers in the schools.
Evaluated the impact of an elementary school-based volunteer "grandparent" program on
140 students, 6 homeroom teachers, and 15 senior citizens. Volunteers' activities included
reading, storytelling, working with children individually and in groups, and otherwise
assisting the teacher. Results of pretest-postest analyses indicate that self-concept—measured by the Piers-Harris Children's Self-Concept Scale by E. V. Piers and D. B. Harris
(1984) given to 55 students—increased significantly for 3rd graders and nonsignificantly
for 4th and 5th graders. Teachers' subjective evaluations of student attitudes and interpersonal relations with volunteers were positive, and records showed fewer disciplinary actions.
Volunteers' scores on the Purpose in Life Scale by J. C. Crumbaugh and L. T. Maholick
(1981) increased pre- to posttest and were higher than norms. Participants' comments
showed that the program was well received.
Journal of Humanistic Counseling, Education & Development. 1987 Mar Vol 25(3) 136-143

[087]
Carr, Deborah

The fulfillment of career dreams at midlife: Does it matter for women's mental health?
Examines whether a women's mental health at midlife is affected by the degree to which her
earlier career aspirations have been fulfilled. Two dimensions of mental health are considered: depression and purpose in life (PIL). Based on data for 3,499 female respondents to
the Wisconsin Longitudinal Study, results indicate that women who have fallen short of
their earlier career goals suffer from lower levels of PIL and higher levels of depression, even
after controlling for social background, human capital, family, and health characteristics.
For PIL, the harmful effects of falling short of one's goal attenuate considerably when current family characteristics are controlled. For depression, the harmful effects of falling short
of one's goal decline considerably once health characteristics are considered. Although
women who aspire to be housewives evidenced lower levels of PIL at midlife than women
with work aspirations, this difference was not statistically significant once human capital
characteristics were controlled. Women who, at age 35, "did not know" what they hoped to

do in the future had significantly lower levels of PIL in their 50s, even after controlling for social background, human capital, family, and health characteristics.

Journal of Health & Social Behavior. 1997 Dec Vol 38(4) 331-344

[088]
Chamberlain, Kerry; Zika, Sheryl

Measuring meaning in life: An examination of three scales.
Evaluated the factor structure of 3 scales to measure meaning in life: a Purpose in Life (PIL) test, a Life Regard Index, and a Sense of Coherence scale. 194 women with at least 1 child under age 5 yrs and not employed outside the home served as Ss. Results suggest that meaning in life can be regarded as a multidimensional construct, with meaning able to be attained in different ways. Oblique factor solutions were accepted and higher-order analyses were conducted for all 3 scales. A general 2nd-order meaning in life dimension was identified only for the PIL test. It is suggested that this scale may be the best general measure of the construct.

Personality & Individual Differences. 1988 Vol 9(3) 589-596

[cf. 144]
Chambre, Susan M.

Is volunteering a substitute for role loss in old age? An empirical test of activity theory.

Gerontologist. 1984 Jun Vol 24(3) 292-298

[089]
D'Braunstein, Steven; Ebersole, Peter

Categories of life meaning for service organization volunteers.
34 university student volunteers in a service organization selected Growth as their central life meaning much more frequently than did a comparable group of 106 university student nonvolunteers. Results suggest that more effective recruitment of volunteers would emphasize not only service or helping possibilities of the volunteer position but also the potential for personal development.

Psychological Reports. 1992 Feb Vol 70(1) 281-282

[090]
Debats, Dominique Louis

Sources of meaning: An investigation of significant commitments in life.
Investigates, combining qualitative and quantitative research methods, the sources of meaning in life of young adult patients (aged 18-42 yrs old) and non-patients (18-26). In addition to the exploratory concerns, the current investigation tested the following three predictions: (a) relationships are the most frequent sources of meaning in life; (b) patients are less committed to their personal meanings than non-patients; and (c) participants' degrees of meaning in life, as operationalized with their scores on the Life Regard Index (LRI), are related to the degree of their commitment to their personal meanings. Findings from both the phenomenal and statistical analyses strongly support the predictions and generally confirm the clinical relevance of the meaning in life construct. Notably, the interpersonal dimension appears a critically relevant domain in the established differential effects in both

non-patients-patients and females-males comparisons. Implications for clinical practice and suggestions for future research are offered.

Journal of Humanistic Psychology. 1999 Fal Vol 39(4) 30-57

[cf. 013]
Debats, Dominique Louis; Drost, Joost; Hansen, Prartho

Experiences of meaning in life: A combined qualitative and quantitative approach.

British Journal of Psychology. 1995 Aug Vol 86(3) 359-375

[091]
DePaola, Stephen J.; Ebersole, Peter

Meaning in life categories of elderly nursing home residents.
Essays were gathered from 53 elderly, male and female nursing home residents (mean age 81 yrs) about the strongest meaning in their lives. A comparison group consisted of 36 elderly individuals, married an average of 52.9 yrs (average age 75.7 yrs). Ss completed the Meaning Essay Document assessment instrument. These elderly nursing home residents (mean length of residence 2.4 yrs) most often reported the category of family relationships as central, followed by pleasure and health. There was a significant difference between the type of meaning of the elderly nursing home residents and those of younger adults. An additional analysis found no significant difference between the nursing home residents and the group of golden anniversary control couples' meanings. Results indicate that elderly nursing home residents do not report an absence of meaning in their lives, and a sense of hopelessness does not prevail.

Journal of Aging & Human Development. 1995 Vol 40(3) 227-236

[092]
DePonti, E. C. M.; Lodewijks, J. G. L. C.; Roegels, N.

Study motives and learning styles among students at an older age.
(Studiemotieven en leerstijlen van studenten in het hoger onderwijs voor ouderen.)
Examined learning conceptions, motivational orientations, preferences regarding the way learning processes are regulated, and preferred learning activities in 88 senior and 1st-yr students enrolled in courses from different departments of Tilburg Learning profiles were measured by the Inventory of Learning Styles. Senior students' perspective on their studies was less influenced by the need to acquire useful knowledge and skills. Compared with 1st-yr students, seniors preferred to study in a meaning-oriented way, preferred external to self-regulated learning, perceived knowledge acquisition generally from a constructive position, and were stimulated mainly by genuine needs to know and understand.

Pedagogische Studien. 1997 Vol 74(3) 197-209

[093]
DeVogler, Karen L.; Ebersole, Peter

Categorization of college students' meaning of life.
Attempted to develop meaning-in-life categories that would have adequate interrater reliability and stability over time. Also of interest were the categories that college students endorsed and the number of students who reported no meaning in life. A pilot study was

used to develop appropriate categories. 100 undergraduates were asked to write about the 3 most meaningful things in their lives and then rank their written meanings in order of importance. Eight categories had adequate interrater reliability and stability over a 3-mo period. The "relationship" category was most often chosen followed by "service," "growth," "belief," "existential-hedonistic," "obtaining," "expression," and "understanding." Only 5% claimed life to have no meaning. (5 ref)

Psychological Reports. 1980 Apr Vol 46(2) 387-390

[094]
DeVogler, Karen L.; Ebersole, Peter

Adults' meaning in life.
96 30-80 yr olds were asked to write about, rank in order, and give an example of each of the 3 strongest meanings in their life. High interrater reliability (91% agreement) was achieved in categorizing the essays on meaning. Only 3% reported no meaning. The category of Relationships was most often reported followed by Belief, Health, Growth, Life Work, Service, and Understanding. The accompanying revisions as well as suggested modifications appear to be appropriate for describing categories of meaning across the adult life span.

Psychological Reports. 1981 Aug Vol 49(1) 87-90

[095]
DeVogler, Karen L.; Ebersole, Peter

Young adolescents' meaning in life.
116 13- and 14- yr-olds were asked to write about, rank in order of importance, and give an example of the 3 strongest meanings in their lives. The percentage of Ss seeming to understand what meaning in life was and able coherently to discuss their own was just as high as that found in older groups. The types of meaning reported differed sufficiently from those of college students and other older Ss to require 3 new categories (activities, school, and appearance). When only the most important meaning was tabulated, the category of Relationships received the highest percentage (67%).

Psychological Reports. 1983 Apr Vol 52(2) 427-431

[096]
DeVogler-Ebersole, Karen; Ebersole, Peter

Depth of meaning in life: Explicit rating criteria.
Attempted to develop a method of measuring meaning-of-life depth using judges' ratings of Ss in depth statements describing their meaning. Whether a significant proportion of Ss reported a feeling of meaningfulness, how many different types of meaning in life they reported, and what percentage of life meaning fell into each of the 8 categories previously developed by the present authors between 1980 and 1983 were investigated. In Exp I, 86 undergraduates were asked to report what gave them the greatest meaning in life and to provide examples explaining why. The authors rated the depth of the essays according to 5 guidelines. Results indicate that the depth criteria yielded high interrater reliability. Most Ss were satisfied with their meaning in life and reported having a relatively large number of meanings they thought were important to them. A 2nd experiment with 34 undergraduates and 2 independent outside judges was conducted to determine whether the high interrater

reliability would persist when outside judges rated the essays. Findings replicate the high interrater agreement obtained in the 1st experiment and emphasize the ease of use of the depth criteria, as the raters needed no special instruction in their use.

Psychological Reports. 1985 Feb Vol 56(1) 303-310

[097]
Dimitrijevic, Mirjana; Pavlovic, Bojana; Cirovski, Denise; Milosavljevic, Slavica; et al

Analiza motivacije za rad. A study of work motivation.
Studied orientation to work and the importance and satisfaction of needs as they relate to work productivity among 1,016 workers in a steel organization, using a battery of self-report questionnaires. Results indicate that only 68% of the Ss were more or less oriented to work. The most important needs emphasized by the Ss were security and social needs (65%), existential needs (46%), need for self-esteem and respect (33%), and self-actualization (28%). All examined needs were essentially frustrated during the work process, distracting Ss from fully concentrating on their work duties. A comparison of high- and low-productivity groups revealed significant differences in the Ss' orientation to work and the importance and satisfaction of different needs. It is suggested that motivational level has an effect on final work productivity.

Revija za Psihologiju. 1984 Dec Vol 14(1-2) 71-79

[098]
Dukes, Richard L.; Johnson, Ruth H.; Newton, Harvey

Long-term effects of travel and study: The Semester at Sea Program.
40 participants who spent a semester at sea were contacted 10 yrs after completion of a voyage to explore possible long-term effects of the travel-study experience. Ss responded to questions about outcomes of their semester at sea and completed the Purpose In Life Test. Ss maintained a global perspective and obtained high test scores. Those Ss who had become parents showed further discovery of meaning. The effect of the semester at sea is discussed within the context of a lifespan developmental model.

Psychological Reports. 1991 Apr Vol 68(2) 563-570

[099]
Ebersole, Peter; DePaola, Steve

Meaning in life categories of later life couples.
Gathered essay statements from 36 active married seniors (mean age 75.7 yrs) about the strongest meaning in their lives. Ss most often reported the category of relationships (within the family) as central, followed by health, and pleasure. A chi-square analysis showed a significant difference between the type of meanings of seniors and those of younger adults. Results are similar to those from a study by S. V. McCarthy of convalescent home seniors, with the exception that the latter group more strongly emphasized belief and deemphasized pleasure. The importance of relationships over the lifespan and the implications of the findings for disengagement theory are discussed.

Journal of Psychology. 1987 Mar Vol 121(2) 185-191

[100]
Ebersole, Peter; DeVogler, Karen L.

Meaning in life: Category self-ratings.
An earlier study reported development of a reliable scale for categorizing the content of meaning in one's life. The present study concentrated on validation of this scale by investigating whether 112 undergraduates would tend to place their own meanings in the same content categories as would an outside rater. 75% of the Ss' ratings agreed with those of the outside rater. Ss were also asked whether they thought that others knew of their meaning (56% answered affirmatively). A .42 correlation was found between the Ss' rating of their meaning depth and ratings done by an outside rater. Percentage of Ss having no meaning (5%) and the frequency distribution of the meaning categories were similar to the earlier study done by the authors, although the 21% of meanings placed in the miscellaneous category was much higher.
Journal of Psychology. 1981 Mar Vol 107(2) 289-293

[101]
Ebersole, Peter; DeVogler-Ebersole, Karen

Depth of meaning in life and literary preference.
In validating a self-rating scale of depth of meaning in life, a significant relationship was predicted and found between the scale and 109 undergraduates' preferences for certain literary passages that reflected varying degrees of meaning. Upon replication, the measures were again found to be significantly related for a sample of 76 undergraduates. Findings are discussed in terms of the scale's use to further knowledge about literary preferences.
Psychology: A Journal of Human Behavior. 1984 Vol 21(3-4) 28-30

[102]
Ebersole, Peter; DeVogler-Ebersole, Karen

Meaning in life of the eminent and the average.
Reviews selected research on meaning in life in conjunction with an analysis of the written meanings of (1) 25 famous people whose meanings had been solicited by the philosopher Will Durant (1932) and (2) 96 30-80 yr olds in research previously reported by the present authors. Contrary to theoretical statements that the current age is one of lack of meaning, almost everyone in both samples maintained that they did have a meaning to their existence, although a number of meanings from the latter group appeared to be relatively superficial. Regarding types of meanings, the evidence supports the category of relationships as being the most common meaning for the general population, although the most-cited meaning by Durant's group of eminent people was life work. It is concluded that depth of meaning in life was expressed in a more developed manner by famous Ss, suggesting that such people çan inspire and guide others who are less eminent to articulate more clearly and fully to themselves and others what might be considered to be most meaningful about their own lives.
Journal of Social Behavior & Personality. 1986 Jan Vol 1(1) 83-94

[103]
Ejaz, Farida K.; Schur, Dorothy; Noelker, Linda S.

The effect of activity involvement and social relationships on boredom among nursing home residents.
This study investigated the types of activities that nursing home residents participate in, and whether participation in group activities and quality of residents' social networks could explain reports of boredom. 175 cognitively alert nursing home residents (average age 79 yrs) participated in a 1 hr structured interview assessing boredom, participation in activities, physical and mental health, and social relationships both inside and outside of the nursing home. Results indicate that residents enjoyed both solitary activities (watching TV, reading) as well as group activities like parties, social programs, playing cards and other games. Further, boredom was not related to participation in group activities but rather to depression, negative interactions with social network members and, perhaps, with a lack of friendships with other residents. Findings indicate that the personal and mental health needs of residents should be given major consideration while designing group activities for residents.
Activities, Adaptation & Aging. 1997 Vol 21(4) 53-66

[104]
Guttmann, David

Logophilosophy for Israeli's retirees in the helping professions.
Examined the retirement lifestyles of 136 older Israeli health professionals based on 3 theories that suggest that people choose a lifestyle that may lead to satisfaction and self-actualization after retirement. Continuity theory holds that older people continue to have social and psychological needs similar to those of middle age that require social involvement. Development theory argues that there are role changes and transitions over the lifespan that are perceived as crisis or as opportunities for personal growth and experimentation that necessitate new activities. Disengagement theory holds that older people become less involved in social activities, interactions, and roles. Findings support the continuity theory for adaptation to old age.
International Forum for Logotherapy. 1984 Spr-Sum 7(1) 18-25

[105]
Halama, Peter

From establishing beliefs through pursuing goals to experiencing fulfillment: Examining the three-component model of personal meaning in life.
Meaning in life is generally considered as a multidimensional phenomenon. G. T. Reker and P. T. P. Wong's model of personal meaning postulates three components: cognitive, motivational and affective. In the present study, the interrelations between these components are analyzed on a sample of 168 university students (mean age 20 yrs). Personal Meaning Index (PMI) and dimension Framework from Life Regard Index - Revised (LRI-R) were used as measures for the cognitive component, Hope Scale and dimension Will Tenacity to Purpose from Test Noo-dynamic (TND) for the motivational component, and dimension Fulfillment from Life Regard Index - Revised (LRI-R) with Acceptance of life from Test Noo-dynamic for the affective component. The analysis with structural equation modeling

showed the important role of the motivational component, which acts as a partial mediator of influence between the cognitive and the affective component.

Studia Psychologica. 2002 Vol 44(2) 143-154

[106]
Hardcastle, Beverly

Midlife themes of invisible citizens: An exploration into how ordinary people make sense of their lives.
Interviewed 23 men and women (aged 35-45 yrs) with low-profile jobs such as prison inmates and guards, hospital cooks, laundry workers, custodians, resort maids, gardeners, bartenders, and bellmen to examine their values and the sources of meaning in their lives. The research approach incorporated interview, life study, and oral history methods, and mixed open-ended questions with formal inventories such as the Rokeach Value Survey, a self-anchoring scale, a self-esteem scale, and the Purpose in Life Test. Four common themes emerged from the group. All Ss were hopeful about their futures and most felt that their present life was better than their past. A majority saw their life as being strongly influenced by some painful and traumatic life event such as a divorce, death of a loved one, accident, drug addiction, or view of war. The women tended to select relational events when asked for their most significant life events, whereas the men chose public or personal events. All saw themselves as being responsible for their lives. The greatest contributions were the life stories themselves, reminding one of the need to see individuals in the rich context of their separate lives in order to appreciate the logic of their life themes.

Journal of Humanistic Psychology. 1985 Spr Vol 25(2) 45-63

[107]
Harlow, Lisa L.; Newcomb, Michael D.

Towards a general hierarchical model of meaning and satisfaction in life.
Compared latent variable models to describe relationships (RLs) among 25 measured variables concerned with the process and content of a meaningful and satisfying life. Using data from 739 young adult Ss, a 3rd-order hierarchical model was retained. At the 1st-order level were 9 interrelated primary factors: (1) Peer RLs, (2) Intimate RLs, (3) Family RLs, (4) Purpose in Life, (5) Meaninglessness, (6) Powerlessness, (7) Perceived Opportunity, (8) Work Satisfaction (STF), and (9) Health STF. Factors 5 and 6 related negatively to meaning and STF; the 7 remaining factors related positively. These 9 factors were explained by 3 2nd-order factors of RL STF, Perceptions of Purposeful Living, and Work and Health STF. The 2nd-order factors were related by a 3rd-order factor of Meaning and STF.

Multivariate Behavioral Research. 1990 Jul Vol 25(3) 387-405

[108]
Hedlund, Bonnie; Ebersole, Peter

A test of Levinson's mid-life re-evaluation.
Investigated a primary component of D. Levinson's (1978) mid-life transition stage, reevaluation of "the Dream" or one's meaning in life (MIL). Ss in the 3 all-male groups (pretransition, mid-life transition, and posttransition) were 35-39, 41-46, and 48-53 yrs old, respectively. A total of 156 Ss were interviewed concerning components of the transition related to reevaluation of MIL. Results show no significant differences in degree of reevaluation of

MIL among the 3 age groups. Further analysis suggested that rather than reevaluation of MIL being an age-related phenomenon, it may be related to important life events.
Journal of Genetic Psychology. 1983 Dec Vol 143(2) 189-192

[109]
Heliker, Diane; Chadwick, Audrey; O'Connell, Theresa

The meaning of gardening and the effects on perceived well being of a gardening project on diverse populations of elders.
This pilot pre- and post-test study sought to demonstrate the feasibility and effectiveness of horticulture therapy and the perceived meaning and outcome on well being of a structured gardening intervention on 2 groups of elders in 2 culturally diverse settings. The total sample of 24 volunteers (aged 63-90 yrs) participated in a 3-mo gardening project. The personal meaning framework and the instrumentation developed based on that framework was utilized. Paired t-tests demonstrated a significant improvement in psychological well being. Content analysis of a semi-structured interview elicited the meaning of gardening. Themes that emerged included Legacy of Gardening, Gardening as Spiritual Heating and Therapy, and Remembering a Favorite Tree.
Activities, Adaptation & Aging. 2000 Vol 24(3) 35-56

[110]
Hermans, Hubert J.

The meaning of life as an organized process.
Reports on 2 studies with 26 Ss (aged 19-56 yrs) that used a self-confrontation procedure with 4 types of life-meaning organization (self-enhancement, contact union with the other, and coexistence or absence of self-enhancement and contact union with the other) to assess the meaning of life. The meaning of life is viewed as a motivated story that is organized thematically into a composite whole through repeated acts of self-reflection. The subjective meaning of life is thus a part-whole experience, in which a particular part is influencing the whole more than other parts at a given time, implying that life meaning can change.
Psychotherapy: Theory, Research, Practice, Training. 1989 Spr Vol 26(1) 11-22

[cf. 026]
Itatsu, Hiromi

The relationship of self-acceptance to life attitude and hopelessness.
Japanese Journal of Counseling Science. 1995 Mar Vol 28(1) 37-46

[111]
Jonsson, Hans; Borell, Lena; Sadlo, Gaynor

Retirement: An occupational transition with consequences for temporality, balance and meaning of occupations.
The aim of this study was to explore retirement as an occupational transition. 29 Ss aged 66 yrs were interviewed and the data analysed using a comparative qualitative method. The analysis showed that a new temporal structure developed where the participants were gliding into a slower rhythm. Some occupations also changed meaning when they were performed in the new circumstances of retirement. A common pattern in the transition was to

go from one imbalance, where work took too much time in life, to another type of imbalance where some kind of regular commitment within retirement would have been preferable. The discussion relates the findings concerning meaning and rhythm to concepts in dynamic systems theory. The importance of regular commitments in life for experience of occupational balance and the changing perspective of the future are also discussed.

Journal of Occupational Science. 2000 Apr Vol 7(1) 29-37

[112]
Kalmar, Stephen S.

What logotherapy can learn from high school students.
Analyzes the issues expressed by high school students in essays submitted to the Viktor E. Frankl Merit Award contest. These concerns include the desire to search for and find personal identity, values, and goals; to achieve significance; to satisfy one's curiosity; and to acquire creative thinking, eternality, and responsiveness. Other concerns revolve around education, suffering, suicide, death, religion, love, and the past and future. It is maintained that these essays can be illuminating to logotherapists interested in understanding youths.

International Forum for Logotherapy. 1982 Fal-Win Vol 5(2) 77-84

[113]
King, Laura A.; Napa, Christie K.

What makes a life good?
Two studies examined folk concepts of the good life. Samples of college students (N = 104) and community adults (N = 264) were shown a career survey ostensibly completed by a person rating his or her occupation. After reading the survey, participants judged the desirability and moral goodness of the respondent's life, as a function of the amount of happiness, meaning in life, and wealth experienced. Results revealed significant effects of happiness and meaning on ratings of desirability and moral goodness. In the college sample, individuals high on all 3 independent variables were judged as likely to go to heaven. In the adult sample, wealth was also related to higher desirability. Results suggest a general perception that meaning in life and happiness are essential to the folk concept of the good life, whereas money is relatively unimportant.

Journal of Personality & Social Psychology. 1998 Jul Vol 75(1) 156-165

[114]
Kinnier, Richard T.; Kernes, Jerry L.; Tribbensee, Nancy E.; Puymbroeck, Christina M.

What eminent people have said about the meaning of life.
Two-hundred and thirty-eight quotations from 195 eminent people regarding their beliefs about the meaning of life were content analyzed. The main themes (in order of their frequency) are as follows: 'Life is to be enjoyed,' 'We are here to love and help others,' 'It is a mystery,' 'There is no cosmic meaning,' 'We are here to serve or worship God,' 'Life is a struggle,' 'We must make a contribution to society,' 'Our mission in life is to seek wisdom truth, and to become self-actualized,' 'We must create meaning for ourselves,' and 'Life is absurd or a joke.' Discussion focuses on the meaning of the results and implications for practice.

Journal of Humanistic Psychology. 2003 Win Vol 43(1) 105-118

[115]
Kroger, Jane

Identity processes and contents through the years of late adulthood.
Presents an overview of current identity research during late adulthood, including the themes of identity formation, revision, and maintenance. The author also discusses the extension of J. Marcia's (1967) identity status interview into the years of late adulthood, and suggests modifications for its use. On the basis of qualitative analyses of the life histories of 14 individuals (aged 65 yrs or more), identity exploration and commitment variables of late adulthood are identified. The author details the identity processes of reintegration, rebalancing, readjustment, refinement, and maintenance of continuity, and identifies the identity contents of life-style, family social network commitments, and life meanings as important domains of identity during late adulthood.
Identity. 2002 Vol 2(1) 81-99

[116]
Lapierre, Sylvie; Bouffard, Leandre; Bastin, Etienne

Personal goals and subjective well-being in later life.
With a sentence completion technique, 708 elderly participants (aged 65-90 yrs) expressed 15,027 personal aspirations. These goals were classified according to their motivational content in 10 major categories and their relationships with various aspects of subjective well-being were studied. Two goal profiles emerged from this analysis. Aspirations centered on self-preservation were associated with poor self-rated physical health, being burden by difficulties, lack of meaning to life, dissatisfaction with life, and negative expectations for the future. Aspirations of self-development and interest in the well-being of others were associated with feelings of well-being in later life. Development of meaningful personal goals was discussed as a new intervention approach with the elders.
International Journal of Aging & Human Development. 1997 Vol 45(4) 287-303

[117]
Laufer, William S.; Laufer, Edith A.; Laufer, Leopold S.

Purpose in life and occupational interest in a gerontological sheltered workshop.
Measured the concept of purpose-in-life and underlying occupational interests and aspirations of 25 men and 29 women (55-84 yrs old) in a gerontological sheltered workshop. The relationship among the Purpose-in-Life Test, Vocational Preference Inventory, Will-to-Live scale, and demographic information is explored. Findings indicate that the constructs Purpose-in-Life and Vocational Aspirations were poorly related for workshop participants.
Journal of Clinical Psychology. 1981 Oct Vol 37(4) 765-769

[118]
Lorenzen-Huber, Lesa

Self-perceived creativity in the later years: Case studies of older Nebraskans.
Examined the creative lives of 20 older Nebraskans (aged 64-92 yrs), using a single-factor, embedded case-study design. The 4 research areas were (1) patterns of creativity, (2) factors affecting creativity, (3) loci of control, and (4) new insights on creativity and aging. Results corroborated findings from recent research challenging the assumption of an inevitable

decline in creativity with age. Three patterns of creativity were found: up down up, rising, and consistent. Having time available was most important to creative expression in the later years. Locus of control did not affect patterns of creativity. Ss expressed their own insights and ideas about creativity and aging in response to an open-ended question. Creativity could help older adults find satisfaction in life, achieve developmental tasks, and find meaning in life.

Educational Gerontology. 1991 Jul-Aug Vol 17(4) 379-390

[119]
Marshall, Sheila K.

Do I matter? Construct validation of adolescents' perceived mattering to parents and friends.
Examined the construct validity of mattering to others, the development of the Mattering to Others Questionnaire (MOQ), and the effects of gender and age on the perceived mattering of mothers, fathers, and friends by adolescents and young adults. 110 undergraduate students (aged 17-25 yrs) and 532 high school students (aged 15-19 yrs) completed the MOQ concerning perceived mattering to parents and friends. Ss also reported self-esteem, relatedness to family and friends, purpose in life, and attention from parents and peers. Results show that all Ss perceived a stronger sense of mattering to their mothers than their fathers. Undergraduate Ss perceived themselves as mattering less to friends than fathers while adolescent Ss reported a sense of mattering less to fathers than to friends. Adolescent Ss perceived parental acceptance and support and joint decision-making as positively associated with mattering to parents.

Journal of Adolescence. 2001 Aug Vol 24(4) 473-490

[120]
McCarthy, S. Viterbo

Geropsychology: Meaning in life for adults over seventy.
25 72-99 yr old residents in a convalescent center were each rated by a confidante or close relative on the Life Satisfaction Index, a Likert-type scale of 6 categories, each with a description of a source of meaning in life. Ss rated relationships as the most important category followed closely by health; service and belief were given intermediate ratings; growth and life work were least important. For the 20 Ss who had ratings from respondents on all categories, a 1-way ANOVA for ratings across the 6 categories yielded a significant F ratio. Subsequent tests indicated only chance differences between relationships and health, but these 2 categories were significantly more important than all the remaining categories as sources for meaning in life.

Psychological Reports. 1983 Oct Vol 53(2) 497-498

[121]
McCarthy, S. Viterbo

Geropsychology: Meaning in life for Elderhostelers.
30 participants in a 1984 summer session for older learners, aged from 60 to 84 yrs, completed the Life Satisfaction Index from self and other perspectives. This Likert-type scale has 6 categories, each with a description of a source of meaning in life. For all Ss, a 1-way ANOVA for self-ratings across the 6 categories yielded a significant F ratio. All comparisons

between pairs from categories rated most important—relationships, health, service—and least important—belief, growth, life work—were significant. There were only chance differences, however, among paired combinations within categories rated most or least important. A 1-way ANOVA for the 26 Ss who rated all categories from the perspective of other also yielded a significant F ratio. Results correspond with earlier reports of other ratings: The order of categories from highest to lowest was relationships, health, service, belief, growth, and life work.

Psychological Reports. 1985 Apr Vol 56(2) 351-354

[cf. 195]
Meddin, Jacob Robert

Dimensions of spiritual meaning and well-being in the lives of ten older Australians.
International Journal of Aging & Human Development. 1998 Vol 47(3) 163-175

[122]
Mor-Barak, Michal E.

The meaning of work for older adults seeking employment: The Generativity factor.
This study is a theory-based examination of the meaning of work for older adults in a sample of 146 older job-seekers. It proposes 4 factors to the meaning of work: Financial, Personal, Social, and the Generativity factor. The Generativity factor, unique to older adults, refers to viewing work as a way to teach, train and share skills with younger generations. A factor analysis of a 16-item Meaning of Work Scale (MWS) supports the proposed factors. The results indicate ethnic and employment differences with respect to the meaning of work, but no gender differences. Significant differences were detected between older adult job-seekers who obtained a job within a year of job search and those who did not, with respect to the personal factor of the MWS and with respect to ethnicity. The findings indicate that jobs providing opportunities for transfer of knowledge and experience to younger generations may be of particular value for older adults.
International Journal of Aging & Human Development. 1995 Vol 41(4) 325-344

[123]
Neimeyer, Greg J.; Leso, John F.; Marmarosh, Cheri; Prichard, Shawn; et al

The role of construct type in vocational differentiation: Use of elicited versus provided dimensions.
Recent studies of vocational structure have demonstrated that experimentally provided vocational constructs are used in less complex, less differentiated ways than are Ss' personally elicited construct dimensions. The possible reasons underlying these differences are addressed in this 2-part study. Results of Study 1 supported significant differences between the use of elicited and provided constructs and ruled out 1 methodological artifact that may have accounted for these differences. Study 2 helped to isolate the personal meaningfulness of the elicited construct as an active agent that accounts for differences in the use of these vocational constructs. Findings of both studies document, for the 1st time, a means of increasing differentiation and converge to suggest the important role of personal meaning in vocational structure.
Journal of Counseling Psychology. 1992 Jan Vol 39(1) 121-128

[124]
Nicholson, Mary A.

Meaning in women's lives.
Examined, using 1-2.5 hr assessment sessions, the paths to meaning taken by 168 women (aged 29-56 yrs). Data support the hypothesis, formulated from logotherapeutic principles, that experiences of intimacy and autonomy in childhood in conjunction with an adult internal locus of control and adequate social support are related to meaning in women's lives. The acceptance of responsibility for one's fate is essential to the discovery of meaning, particularly when one transcends the self through trust and empathy of authentic human intimacy.

International Forum for Logotherapy. 1991 Spr Vol 14(1) 22-25

[125]
Nunner-Winkler, Gertrud

Finding an occupation and a meaning in life.
(Berufsfindung und Sinnstiftung.)
Examined the relationships among factors influencing occupational choice and finding meaning in life using interview data from 112 West German youths (ages 14-23 yrs). It was hypothesized that (1) a person's occupation is increasingly becoming the source of meaning in life, especially for younger people; (2) persons who are oriented toward the extrinsic factors of an occupation (i.e., salary, benefits, and working conditions) derive less meaning from their jobs than persons who are oriented toward intrinsic factors of an occupation (i.e., interest in the field); and (3) analysis of the development of occupational orientation will validate the concept of occupational maturity. Interviews were conducted with youths who had been referred by counselors at a state employment agency in Munich, West Germany for occupational aptitude evaluation. Interview topics included the meaning of life, occupational orientation, and moral development. Factor analysis of the interview data provided support for Hypotheses 1 and 2. It is recommended that Hypothesis 3 be reevaluated with Ss with previous work experience.

Koelner Zeitschrift fuer Soziologie und Sozialpsychologie. 1981 Apr Vol 33(1) 115-131

[126]
O'Connor, Kay; Chamberlain, Kerry

Dimensions of life meaning: A qualitative investigation at mid-life.
Examined how people's accounts of their experiences of life meaning are drawn from 4 key dimensions: (1) sources, (2) cognitive, motivational, and affective components, (3) breadth, and (4) depth. 38 mid-life adults (40-50 yrs old) were interviewed in depth about sources of meaning in their lives. Results indicate that all 4 dimensions are present in personal accounts of meaning. Six categories of sources were identified, all of which revealed cognitive, motivational and affective components. Accounts showed variation in breadth and depth of meaning, although the assessment of depth proved problematic. These results generally confirm G. T. Reker & P. T. P. Wong's (1988) structural model.

British Journal of Psychology. 1996 Aug Vol 87(3) 461-477

[127]
Pattakos, Alex

The Search for meaning in Government Service.
In the postmodern era, there are many formidable challenges facing public sector employment, such as retirement (including succession planning), recruitment, and retention.
Moreover, it has been suggested that civil service systems are broken and that the general
public views government employment with suspicion, ambivalence, and even disrespect.
Yet, it has also been suggested that questions dealing with the human quest for meaning at
work must necessarily receive their first expression in public sector organizations. Building
on Viktor Frankl's Logotherapeutic principle, the will to meaning, this article examines how
public employees actualize three categories of valuescreative, experiential, and attitudinalas
sources of authentic meaning in their work and as their primary motivation for achieving
high standards of performance. Empirically, it is based primarily on structured interviews
conducted between 1998 and 2003 with more than 200 reflective public servants in Canada
and the USA. Among the findings derived from these interviews are the following: (1) the
desire to make a difference through their work was cited repeatedly as the primary source
of meaning among government employees and officials; (2) public servants also derive
meaning from a wide range of their work-related human encounters; and (3) the operating
domain of contemporary government service offers plenty of opportunity for employees to
actualize attitudinal values in ways that bring authentic meaning to their work. The search
for meaning in government service can best be described as a process, not a product, and it
was found to increase in importance over time among all categories of public sector employ-
mentelected, appointed, and career civil service. In order to manage the public's business
effectively, efficiently, and equitably, it is suggested that the time has come to change the
way that government service is perceived and treated. In large part, the spirit of public
administration in the twenty-first century will depend on public servants who are driven by
a search for meaning and who seek a noble calling through government service.
Public Administration Review 2004 Vol 64, No 1. 106-112*

[128]
Prager, Edward

Exploring personal meaning in an age-differentiated Australian sample: Another look at
the Sources of Meaning Profile (SOMP).
Administered the Sources of Meaning Profile (SOMP) to 461 Australians, aged 18-91 yrs,
to ascertain what they consider to be the most and least important sources of meaning in
their lives. The study was based upon and compared with a Canadian study (G. T. Reker,
1988) of 298 Ss, aged 18-83 yrs, for which the SOMP instrument was developed. While
some age-related differences were found, there was considerable consistency in the ratings
across the Australian age cohorts, with only 5 of the 16 sources of meaning differing on the
basis of age. Across cultures, there were similar results between the Canadian and Australian
Ss, whose youngest and oldest respondent groups agreed that the most important sources of
personal meaning are in personal relationships, personal growth, meeting basic needs, participation in leisure activities, and the preservation of values and ideals. Theoretical implications and practical applications are discussed.
Journal of Aging Studies. 1996 Sum Vol 10(2) 117-136

[129]
Prager, Edward

Meaning in later life: An organizing theme for gerontological curriculum design.
Reviews some of the theoretical and empirical formulations of personal meaning in later life and reports on a study in which 198 Israeli men responded to the Sources of Personal Meaning in Life Profile (SOMP) to determine if there were significant differences between 4 age groups. 58 Ss were aged 25-39 yrs, 37 Ss were aged 40-59 yrs, 60 Ss were aged 60-79 yrs, and 43 Ss were aged 80-95 yrs. There were no statistically significant differences between the 3 oldest age groups in any one category of SOMP and no differences in total score between any of the age groups. The study supports a model suggesting that men's social worlds do not change significantly through the life course and that perceptions of sources of personal meaning are continuous in content and depth. The author argues that such findings represent a need to unify existing theoretical, empirical and clinical knowledge through the introduction of humanistic and phenomenological approaches to gerontology education.

Educational Gerontology. 1997 Jan-Feb Vol 23(1) 1-13

[130]
Prager, Edward

Men and meaning in later life.
To examine sources of meaning and differences in sources of meaning between young, middle-aged, old, and old-old males, the author interviewed 198 Israeli males, aged 25-95 yrs, using the Sources of Meaning Profile (G. T. Reker and B. Guppy, 1988). Findings generally pointed to considerable consistency between age groups, confirming a continuity model positing that men's gendered world does not appreciably change throughout the life course. However, the oldest male groups scored significantly higher than the youngest men in sources of meaning reflecting philosophical and humanistic orientations, suggesting an age-related self-transcendence and a change from the egocentric and self-preoccupied orientations of earlier years.

Journal of Clinical Geropsychology. 1998 Jul Vol 4(3) 191-203

[131]
Prager, Edward

Observations of personal meaning in sources for Israeli age cohorts.
Using the Sources of Meaning Profile (SOMP), an instrument developed to measure the sources of personal, present meaning in one's life, this descriptive study looks at what 296 Israelis (aged 18-91 yrs) consider to be the most and least important sources of meaning in their lives. Ss, regardless of age, viewed personal relationships, enduring values and ideals and meeting basic needs as being among the most important sources of meaning in their lives. Though the importance of religious activities tended to increase, albeit insignificantly, with age this source of meaning was ranked among the lowest in importance by all age groups. There was evidence of an increasing philosophic and humanistic life orientation in the later years, as manifested in the importance attached to areas of social, cultural and value concerns.

Aging & Mental Health. 1998 May Vol 2(2) 128-136

[cf. 206]
Porpora, Douglas V.

Personal heroes, religion, and transcendental metanarratives
Sociological Forum. 1996 Jun Vol 11(2) 209-229

[cf. 613]
Shapiro, Stewart B.

Development of a life-meaning survey.
Psychological Reports. 1976 Oct Vol 39(2) 467-480

[cf. 407]
Stanich, John; Oertengren, Ilona

The Logotest in Sweden.
International Forum for Logotherapy. 1990 Spr Vol 13(1) 54-60

[132]
Stolin, V. V.; Kalvinio, M.

Personal meaning: Structure and forms of representation in consciousness.
Analyzed different forms of representation of personal meanings in individual consciousness, using the TAT and semantic differential procedure. The TAT was used to reveal notions significant for particular Ss (e.g., work, parents, and self) as well as personal meanings that stand behind the notions. The semantic differential procedure was used to scale the notions as well as to specifically designate personal meanings and their antonyms. The notion of "meaning constructs" is presented, and a typology of them is suggested.
Vestnik Moskovskogo Universiteta - Seriya 14: Psikhologiya. 1982 Oct No 3 38-47

[133]
Takkinen, Sanna; Ruoppila, Isto

Meaning in life as an important component of functioning in old age.
Locates different measures of meaning in life within a multidimensional space of functioning in old age. Ss were 55 persons aged 75 and older who participated in laboratory tests, a medical examination, and interviews over a 3-yr period. Measures of meaning in life included a sense of meaning, a sense of coherence, and 4 indices derived from a life-line drawing (linearity, trend, and mean level in the past and in the future). Other measures of functioning were chronic diseases, disability, walking speed, self-rated health, and cognitive capacity. Also rated were social relationships, loneliness, depressive mood, activities, life satisfaction, and wisdom. Using multidimensional scaling, the authors created a 2-dimensional model of functioning (subjective vs. objective and psychosocial vs. physical). In the first, all the measures were located in the subjective half. The measures along the 2nd dimension varied considerably. Some of the measures of meaning (sense of coherence, life-line trend, and linearity) were located in the physical half, while others (sense of meaning, life-line mean level in the past) were in the psychosocial half. The life-line mean level in the future was located in the center of the dimension.
International Journal of Aging & Human Development. 2001 Vol 53(3) 211-231

[134]
Takkinen, Sanna; Ruoppila, Isto

Meaning in life in three samples of elderly persons with high cognitive functioning.
Examined the relationships between meaning in life and cognitive functioning (CF). The 78 Ss in Sample I were aged 82-87 yrs, in Sample II 182 Ss aged 83-92 yrs, and in Sample III 299 persons aged 65-69 yrs. The samples took part in interviews and cognitive tests in 1996-1997. Several interview questions together with the Sense of Coherence questionnaire were used to study the degree and content of meaning in life. CF was measured by Digit Span, Digit Symbol, and Word Fluency in Sample I and Mini-D in Samples II and III. Each sample was divided into the group of persons with high CF and the comparison group. The analysis showed no difference between the groups in the degree of meaning in life in any of the 3 samples. The content of meaning in life differed in the 2 groups: relationships were reported as a reason for meaning in life and a source of strength in life more often by the persons with high CF than by the comparison group. Moreover, those with high cognitive functioning reported that they had taken up a new activity that gave a sense of meaning in life after retirement more often than the comparison group. Death had positive meaning for the majority of the Ss and the groups did not differ in meaning of death.
International Journal of Aging & Human Development. 2001 Vol 53(1) 51-73

[135]
Takkinen, Sanna; Suutama, Timo; Ruoppila, Isto

More meaning by exercising? Physical activity as a predictor of a sense of meaning in life and of self-rated health and functioning in old age.
Examined the predictive value of physical activity for a sense of meaning in life and for self-rated health and functioning among 198 elderly persons in Finland born between 1904 and 1913. The Ss were interviewed at baseline in 1988 and followed up in 1996. The baseline interviews dealt with physical, psychological, and social functioning. The interview questions selected for the follow-up study dealt with the intensity of physical activity, meaning in and zest for life, and self-rated health and social functioning. Longitudinal models show that physical activity had a positive effect on both meaning in life and self-rated health and functioning
Journal of Aging & Physical Activity. 2001 Apr Vol 9(2) 128-141

[136]
Thomas, L. Eugene; Kraus, Patricia A.; Chambers, Kim O.

Metaphoric analysis of meaning in the lives of elderly men: A cross-cultural investigation.
Analyzed explicit and implicit metaphors as a means of determining personal meaning in the lives of 10 elderly English and 10 Indian men (all Ss aged 70+ yrs). Analysis of explicit metaphors indicated marked differences in their psychological worlds, with the English men being more privatized and stoic, and the Indian men expressing strong achievement concerns while remaining embedded in family and society. Analysis of the implied metaphors confirmed this picture, while indicating related underlying beliefs. The English protocols revealed an underlying nature metaphor, which appeared to reflect their attempt to find a sense of personal continuity missing in their lives. Nature metaphors were missing in the Indian sample; the image of building up, of completing duty to family and society, as well

as to God, was an underlying metaphor in their protocols. The uses of metaphor for getting at unarticulated assumptions is discussed.

Journal of Aging Studies. 1990 Spr Vol 4(1) 1-15

[137]
Torres Alvarez T.

Factors related to satisfaction with life in retired factory workers of rural origin
A descriptive study was conducted in late 1991 of factors determining the satisfaction with life of a group of retired Mexican factory workers of rural origin. Twenty retired workers at a steel plant in the state of Puebla were interviewed. Their ages ranged from 61 to 79 years. The study instruments included a questionnaire concerning sociodemographic data and the "Purpose in Life" test, a 20-item attitude scale designed to measure the degree to which the individual has found significance and purpose in life. Each respondent was also asked what currently gave greatest significance to his life, and to provide an example. The responses were classified into nine categories. The only variable significantly related to the degree of satisfaction with life was appreciation of the amount of the pension. Twelve of the men were found to be satisfied with life, seven were undecided, and only one was dissatisfied. The three categories of factors providing most significance to the lives of the workers were relationships with others, pleasurable or recreational activities, and service to others.

Temas Poblac. 1993 Apr;3(9):24-34. *

[138]
Triado, Carme; Martinez, Gerard; Villar, Feliciano

The role and importance of grandchildren for adolescent grandchildren.
(El rol y la importancia de los abuelos para sus nietos adolescentes.)
Studied the relationship of adolescents and grandparents from the perspective of adolescents and young adults. Ss included 272 male and female secondary school and university students (aged 14-20 yrs) in Spain. Data on sociodemographic variables and perception of importance of grandparents in their lives were obtained by questionnaire. A Spanish translation of the Grandparents Meaning Scale (N. Van Rast et al, 1995) was used. The results indicate that girls have a perception of being closer to grandparents than boys, older grandparents are perceived as having more conciliatory roles than younger grandparents, maternal grandparents are perceived as having positive roles, and paternal grandparents are perceived as having distant roles in the lives of adolescents and young adults. Correlation analysis and other statistical tests were used.

Anuario de Psicologia. 2000 Jun Vol 31(2) 107-118

[139]
Trice, Lucy Bland

Meaningful life experience to the elderly.
The purpose of the study was to identify the basic structure of an experience from life through which or during which the elderly derive the sense that life is meaningful, as a manifestation of the human spirit. A phenomenological methodology was used, with 11 participants (aged 65-87 yrs) being interviewed until common themes emerged. Protocols obtained from the interviews were analyzed according to the 7-step method developed by P. Colaizzi (1978). An exhaustive description of the meaningful experience was obtained, and

included 4 common themes. Findings suggest that an experience during which or through which an elderly person has the sense that life is meaningful is an experience during which the individual involved performs an activity perceived as needed by, helpful to or useful to another person or group. Implications for nursing practice are discussed.

Image: Journal of Nursing Scholarship. 1990 Win Vol 22(4) 248-251

[140]
Van Jaarsveld, S:; Shantall, T.

Finding meaning in the workplace.
Viktor Frankl (1959; 1967; 1969; 1970; 1978; 1984), the father of logotherapy, a meaning-oriented form of psychotherapy and counselling, postulated that a search for meaning is the primary motivational force in a person's life. If this postulation is true for life in general, it can be expected that this will also be true for a person's work life, since work forms an integral part of that person's life. The need to experience meaning in the workplace as a vital part of a productive and satisfying work life, has been virtually ignored in empirical studies in Organisational Behaviour (Keeva, 1999). The main objective of this study was to contribute to a greater understanding of the importance of finding meaning in the workplace by exploring whether a person's experience of meaning in the workplace could be positively changed by giving the person the opportunity to explore the meaning and importance of work in his or her own personal life, using the Socratic dialogue, the principal method of logotherapy. Ten research participants were selected from the corporate environment, using a "judgmental" sampling design. Pre- and post-tests, using the Purpose-in-Life test and the Life Purpose Questionnaire were used to determine whether the logotherapeutic intervention could result in a greater experience of meaning in the workplace. A statistical analyses of the test results plus a phenomenological analyses of the transcribed logotherapy sessions, proved that a significant shift in meaning orientation did in fact take place over the course of the logotherapeutic intervention. The study proved that a greater awareness and experience of meaning in work can change the individual's attitude towards work and also bring about a greater motivation and commitment to doing his or her work, not just as a means of earning a living wage, but as centrally part of a worthwhile and meaningful life. The findings of this study illustrate the need to take more serious note of the central role of meaning in worker satisfaction and productivity in corporate programmes seeking to enhance job performance and efficiency in the workplace.

Forum for Logotherapy 2004*

[141]
Van Ranst, Nancy; Marcoen, Alfons

Cognitive restructuring and personal meaning in young elderly.
(Cognitieve herstructurering en zingeving bij jongbejaarden.)
Tested the hypothesis that older adults who are more able to restructure cognitively will experience more meaning in their lives than peers who are less capable. Human Ss: 40 normal male and female Dutch adults (aged 60-65 yrs). Tests used: The Life Attitude Profile (G. T. Reker and E. J. Peacock, 1981), the Sources of Meaning Profile (Reker, 1988), and a cognitive restructuring measure designed ad hoc.

Psychologica Belgica. 1991 Vol 31(1) 53-65

[142]
Van Ranst, Nancy; Verschueren, Karine; Marcoen, Alfons

The meaning of grandparents as viewed by adolescent grandchildren: An empirical study in Belgium.
Examined the reasons adolescents value their grandparents using 563 adolescents and young adults in Belgium. The Grandparent Meaning Scale which probes 11 a priori dimensions of meaning, was completed by 147 early adolescents, 175 middle adolescents, and 241 late adolescents. Results show that adolescents generally find their grandparents important and feel close to them. Grandparents were valued primarily because they provide affection, reassurance of worth, and reliable alliance. Relational-affective and caregiving meanings were assigned more often to grandmothers whereas advising, teaching, and narrative roles were ascribed more frequently to grandfathers. Maternal grandparents were generally perceived as more important and closer than paternal grandparents. Early adolescents assigned more importance and meaning to their grandparents than middle and late adolescents. There were no differences between grandsons and granddaughters.
International Journal of Aging & Human Development. 1995 Vol 41(4) 311-324

[143]
Weenolsen, Patricia

Transcending the many deaths of life: Clinical implications for cure versus healing.
Outlines findings on loss and transcendence (LT) as metaphorical deaths and births, considers their relationship to life and self-meaning, and examines how they affect identity. 48 women (aged 25-67 yrs) participated in a study using the LT Life History Form (P. Weenolsen, 1988). Most of the Ss believed that life has meaning, but defined life meaning differently. Definitions fell into 4 categories: cosmic-specific, cosmic-general, individual-specific, and individual-general. Findings also show that the life review is an important, ongoing process for the majority of individuals. The case history of a 30-yr-old woman illustrates some of the LT findings and major principles.
Death Studies. 1991 Jan-Feb Vol 15(1) 59-80

Value Orientation and Pro-social Behavior

[cf. 519]
Addad, Moshe; Leslau, Avraham

Moral judgment and meaning in life.
International Forum for Logotherapy. 1989 Fal Vol 12(2) 110-116

[cf. 082]
Beutel, Ann M.; Marini, Margaret Mooney

Gender and values.
American Sociological Review. 1995 Jun Vol 60(3) 436-448

[144]
Chambre, Susan M.

Is volunteering a substitute for role loss in old age? An empirical test of activity theory.
Performed a secondary analysis of the Americans Volunteer—1974 survey (ACTION, 1975). Ss were 4,339 nondisabled, nonstudent volunteers age 60 and over. A comparison of data for these elderly Ss with those for the entire volunteer sample indicates that older Ss volunteered less often. For older Ss, retirees were less likely to volunteer than those still in the labor force, and homemakers tended to volunteer more frequently than retirees but less frequently than those still working. Ss who lived alone volunteered only slightly more often than those living with others; and married Ss more often did volunteer work than did unmarried Ss. Stepwise multiple regression analyses failed to provide support for 3 models based on activity theory: Educational achievement, age, gender, and labor force participation were significant predictors of volunteering. Results suggest that rather than responding to role loss, these elderly Ss may be continuing a pattern of behavior established earlier in life.
Gerontologist. 1984 Jun Vol 24(3) 292-298

[cf. 171]
Crandall, James E.; Rasmussen, Roger D.

Purpose in life as related to specific values.
Journal of Clinical Psychology. 1975 Jul Vol 31(3) 483-485

[cf. 089]
D'Braunstein, Steven; Ebersole, Peter

Categories of life meaning for service organization volunteers.
Psychological Reports. 1992 Feb Vol 70(1) 281-282

[cf. 287]
Farran, Carol J.; Keane-Hagerty, Eleanora; Salloway, Sandra; Kupferer, Sylvia; et al

Finding meaning: An alternative paradigm for Alzheimer's disease family caregivers.
Gerontologist. 1991 Aug Vol 31(4) 483-489

[cf. 289]
Farran, Carol J.; Miller, Baila H.; Kaufman, Julie E.; Donner, Ed; Fogg, Louis

Finding meaning through caregiving: Development of an instrument for family caregivers
of persons with Alzheimer's disease.
Journal of Clinical Psychology. 1999 Sep Vol 55(9) 1107-1125

[cf. 181]
Furrow, James L.; King, Pamela Ebstyne; White, Krystal

Religion and positive youth development: Identity, meaning, and prosocial concerns.
Applied Developmental Science. 2004 Jan Vol 8(1) 17-26*

[145]
Hall VP.

Bearing witness to suffering in AIDS: the testing of a substantive theory.
AIDS volunteerism, as a response by those affected by loss associated with HIV/AIDS, has
been described as an act of bearing witness. The theory "bearing witness to suffering in
HIV/AIDS," proposes that AIDS volunteerism assists individuals affected by loss to increase
their levels of hope, self-esteem, social support, and develop a sense of purpose in life (PIL).
The purpose of this descriptive research was to determine if AIDS volunteerism, hope, self-
esteem, and social support were predictive of PIL among individuals affected by loss from
HIV/AIDS. Path analysis was used to analyze data. Hope, social support, and self-esteem
were found to have significant positive effects on PIL and accounted for 66% of the total
variance. The results from this study will be used to further develop the theory of bearing
witness; this theory may be useful to develop and test interventions to relieve the suffering
experienced by individuals affected by HIV/AIDS.
Journal of the Association of Nurses in AIDS Care. 2003 Jul-Aug;14(4):25-36*

[cf. 186]
Hermans, Hubert J. M.; Oles, Piotr K.

The personal meaning of values in a rapidly changing society.
Journal of Social Psychology. 1994 Oct Vol 134(5) 569-579

[146]
Hermans, Hubert J. M.; Oles, Piotr K.

Value crisis: Affective organization of personal meanings.
Examined specific affective organization of the self in value crisis (VC). Whereas the self is
conceptualized as an organized system of personal meanings, VC is defined as a disorganization of this system. Personal meanings were investigated using a self-confrontation

method sensitive to the affective properties of personal meanings and their organization into a composite whole. Three groups of college students were compared: 14 Ss scoring high, 18 Ss scoring medium, and 16 Ss scoring low on the Value Crisis Questionnaire. High VC Ss had a lower level of intensity of affect referring to self-enhancement, a lower intensity level of affect referring to contact and union with the other, and a lower level of positive affect in comparison with other Ss. In addition, negative meanings were more generalizing in the self of Ss in VC, whereas positive meanings were more generalizing in the self system of Ss not in VC. Moreover, Ss in VC showed more discontinuity between their past and future than did Ss not in VC. Two idiographic case studies were presented to illustrate meaningful exceptions to the rule. It is concluded that VC is an "in-between state" involving the risk of disorganization of the self, but at the same time including opportunities for innovative self-development.

Journal of Research in Personality. 1996 Dec Vol 30(4) 457-482

[147]
Hitlin, Steven

Values as the core of personal identity: Drawing links between two theories of self.
Personal identity is an underanalyzed level of the self, often regarded erroneously as too idiosyncratic for proper social psychological analysis. The two dominant theories of self, identity theory and social identity theory, mention but rarely explicate the concept of personal identity. In this paper I address this gap by making two moves, one conceptual and one empirical. First, I argue that values are a cohesive force within personal identity. Conceptualizing values as the core of one's personal identity leads toward understanding the cohesion experienced among one's various social identities. In the second, empirical move (n=314 university students), I use measures of a key dimension along which values are arrayed (self-enhancement vs. self-transcendence) to illustrate how a values-based conception of personal identity influences the formation of a role identity. Specifically, theoretically relevant values along the self-enhancement self-transcendence dimension are significant predictors of the volunteer identity, even when previous measures of the identity are controlled. I conclude by discussing the utility of values for studying a level of the self often considered too ideographic for sociological analysis.

Social Psychology Quarterly. 2003 Jun Vol 66(2) 118-137

[cf. 291]
Kahana, Eva; Midlarsky, Elizabeth

Perspectives on helping in late life: Conceptual and empirical directions.
Academic Psychology Bulletin. 1983 Jun Vol 5(2) 351-361

[cf. 293]
Konstam, Varda; Holmes, William; Wilczenski, Felicia; Baliga, Shanteri; Lester, Jill; Priest, Rebecca

Meaning in the lives of caregivers of individuals with Parkinson's disease.
Journal of Clinical Psychology in Medical Settings. 2003 Mar Vol 10(1) 17-26

[cf. 295]
MacKinlay, Elizabeth

The spiritual dimension of caring: Applying a model for spiritual tasks of ageing.
Journal of Religious Gerontology. 2001 Vol 12(3-4) 151-166

[148]
Magen, Zipora; Aharoni, Rachel

Adolescents' contributing toward others: Relationship to positive experiences and transpersonal commitment.
Explored the interrelations between involvement in community service activities, level of expressed transpersonal commitment, and intensity of remembered positive experiences among adolescents. 134 10th-12th graders involved in community service activities and 126 of these Ss' peers who were not participating in such activities completed questionnaires measuring life aspiration, positive experiences, and extracurricular activities. Involved Ss expressed higher levels of transpersonal commitment and a higher intensity of positive experiences; the 2 variables were positively related for both groups. Results support the contention that the ability to experience happiness and meaning in life was greater among those who were willing to give of themselves to others.
Journal of Humanistic Psychology. 1991 Spr Vol 31(2) 126-143

[149]
Mayton, Daniel M., II; Peters, Danya J.; Owens, Rocky W.

Values, militarism, and nonviolent predispositions.
This study utilized written survey methodology to assess the relations between values, militarism, and nonviolent predispositions. Respondents (college students and high school students; aged 17-48 yrs old) completed two separate instruments during a single 45-min session. Although nonviolent predispositions are positively related to the self-transcendence value types of universalism (i.e., social justice, broadminded, a world at peace, wisdom, a world of beauty, unity with nature, wisdom, equality) and benevolence (i.e., helpful, forgiving, honest, loyal), militarism as defined by L. Nelson (1995) was hypothesized to be positively related to the self-enhancement value types of power (i.e., social power, wealth, preserving public image), achievement (i.e., successful, capable, ambitious), and hedonism (i.e., pleasure, enjoying life). Preliminary data support these relations.
Peace & Conflict: Journal of Peace Psychology. 1999 Vol 5(1) 69-77

[150]
Oles, Piotr K.

Value crisis: Measurement and personality correlates.
A 25-item Value Crisis Questionnaire (VCQ) was developed using a sample of 207 students. The correlation between the VCQ and the Purpose In Life test was .70, and the internal consistency of the VCQ was .90. The VCQ was also administered to an additional sample of 218 graduate students. Data suggest that value crisis is a combination of 4 symptoms: (1) difficulties in hierarchical organization of value systems, (2) sense of value loss, (3) disintegration of the valuing process, and (4) sense of value unrealization.
Polish Psychological Bulletin. 1991 Vol 22(1) 53-64

[151]
Orbach, Israel; Iluz, Ayala; Rosenheim, Eliyahu

Value systems and commitment to goals as a function of age, integration of personality, and fear of death.
Examined the relationship between age, integration of personality, and fear of death and 2 aspects of the meaning of life (content of values and degree of commitment). 30 18-25 yr olds, 30 34-45 yr olds, and 30 54-67 yr olds from different cultural origins and various levels of education were requested to rank order 8 types of values (understanding, relationship, service, belief, expression, obtaining, growth, and hedonism) and completed a questionnaire on the degree of commitment to the goal actualization. Results show that the late adulthood group differed from the other 2 groups in the content of meaning by shifting to a more spiritual set of values. Interpersonal relationship was the most important value for all groups. Content of meaning was also related to one's level of education. The degree of commitment to goals was affected by integration of personality, age, and gender.
International Journal of Behavioral Development. 1987 Jun Vol 10(2) 225-239

[152]
Shek, Daniel T. L.; Ma, H. K.; Cheung, P. C.

Meaning in life and adolescent antisocial and prosocial behavior in a Chinese context.
Administered the Chinese version of the Purpose in Life Test (C-PIL) to 790 Chinese secondary school students (aged 11-19 yrs), along with other instruments assessing their antisocial and prosocial behavior. Results show that the C-PIL and its subscales, Quality of Existence (QEXIST) and Purpose of Existence (PEXIST), correlated significantly with all measures of antisocial and prosocial behavior, with Ss having higher C-PIL scores showing less antisocial behavior and more prosocial behavior. Relative to QEXIST scores, PEXIST scores were more predictive of antisocial and prosocial behavior measures. Findings are consistent with V. E. Frankl's (1955, 1959) notion that meaning in life is intimately related to psychological symptoms as indexed by antisocial behavior. The data also suggest that purpose in life is associated with positive social behavior as indexed by prosocial behavior.
Psychologia: An International Journal of Psychology in the Orient. 1994 Dec Vol 37(4) 211-218

[153]
Schwartz, Shalom H.; Sagiv, Lilach; Boehnke, Klaus

Worries and values.
Investigated the relations of 1,441 individuals' (mean age 32.4 yrs) value priorities to their worries in 7 samples (college students, adults, and immigrants) from 4 cultural groups (Eastern and Western Germany, Israel, and Russia). A social-cognitive analysis suggests that value priorities influence worries by increasing attention to and perception of threats to valued goals. On this basis, the authors generate hypotheses relating 2 types of worries, micro (about self and its extensions) and macro (about society and world), to 10 types of values. As predicted, giving priority to self-transcendence values (universalism and benevolence) is associated with low micro and high macro worry, whereas giving priority to self-enhancement values (power, hedonism, and—to a lesser degree—achievement) is associated with high micro and low macro worry. Meaningful associations are also found for other values. Values account for substantially more variance in macro than in micro worries.
Journal of Personality. 2000 Apr Vol 68(2) 309-346

[154]
Weinstein, Lawrence; Xie, Xiaolin; Cleanthous, Charalambos C.

Purpose in life, boredom, and volunteerism in a group of retirees.
Examined the relationship between time spent in volunteerism and purpose of life and boredom proneness among 40 retirees using the Purpose of Life test and the Boredom Proneness Scale. Results show that Ss who volunteered more than 10 hrs per week scored significantly higher on the Purpose In Life test than those who volunteered 10 or fewer hrs per week. A significant negative correlation of -.75 was obtained between scores on purpose in life and boredom proneness.

Psychological Reports. 1995 Apr Vol 76(2) 482

Family and Relationships

[155]
Bevvino, Deborah L.; Sharkin, Bruce S.

Divorce adjustment as a function of finding meaning and gender differences.
Examined the relationship between finding meaning after divorce and subsequent adjustment. 119 volunteers in various stages of divorce completed the Constructed Meaning Scale, the Sense of Coherence Questionnaire (to measure their general disposition to see the world as meaningful), the Disentanglement subscale (emotional separation from former spouse) of the Fisher Divorce Adjustment Scale, and the Scales of Psychological Well-Being. The participants also responded to open-ended questions about their perceptions of the causes and consequences of their divorce. Seven variables (gender, education, initiator status, length of separation, disentanglement, sense of coherence, and meaning) were used to predict psychological well being following divorce. Using sequential multiple regression analysis, the study found meaning to add predictive power to psychological well-being over and above all other predictor variables. No gender differences were obtained for meaning or level of psychological well-being. However, women generated significantly more positive consequences of their divorce than did men. In addition, gender differences in the perception of the causes of divorce were consistent with previous research, with physical, emotional and psychological abuse only reported by women.
Journal of Divorce & Remarriage. 2003 Vol 39(3-4) 81-97

[156]
Lantz, James; First, Richard

Family treatment and the noetic curative factor.
Examined whether the insight-catharsis, interactional, structural, or noetic (existential) factor was important in the treatment of 20 families conducted by 4 family therapy practitioners, each representing a specific theoretical approach (e.g., psychoanalytic, structural). 27 family member participants chose the noetic factor as the most helpful.
International Forum for Logotherapy. 1987 Fal-Win Vol 10(2) 110-111

[157]
McCann, Joseph T.; Biaggio, Mary K.

Sexual satisfaction in marriage as a function of life meaning.
48 married couples completed the Purpose in Life Test (PIL), Personal Orientation Inventory (POI), a selfism scale, Sexual Interaction Inventory, and the Crowne-Marlowe social desirability scale. Findings show that Ss high on PIL and POI scores reported higher levels of sexual enjoyment. Egocentricity was positively correlated with dissatisfaction; however, this result was significant for females but not males. Although no relationship was found between personality factors in the female spouse and male enjoyment, male self-actualization, but not egocentricity, was indicative of female dissatisfaction.
Archives of Sexual Behavior. 1989 Feb Vol 18(1) 59-72

[158]
Okamoto, Kaori

On existential tendency for life and family satisfaction in modern college students.
Studied the tendency toward an existential vacuum, the validity and reliability of the
Purpose in Life Test and Seeking of Noetic Goal Test, and the relationship between family
satisfaction and purpose in life. 114 undergraduate students completed Japanese versions of
the Family Satisfaction Scale, the Purpose in Life Test, and the Seeking of Noetic Goal Test.
Japanese Journal of Family Psychology. 1990 Sep Vol 4(2) 83-95

[159]
Prasinos, Steven; Tittler, Bennett I.

The existential context of lovestyles: An empirical study.
Attempts to demonstrate empirically that the way in which one views love has a broad and
definable existential context. J. Lee's typology of 6 "lovestyles" was investigated in relation
to other phenomenological dimensions, including the fear of death (Death Anxiety Scale),
ego strength, self-esteem (Rosenberg Self-Esteem Scale), and the meaningfulness of life (Life
Regard Index). The lovestyles were also related to various self-ratings and demographic variables. 153 undergraduates responded to measures of lovestyle and the existential and demographic variables. Existential profiles were generated for each lovestyle. A canonical correlation procedure resulted in an equation that placed the lovestyles along an existential dimension broadly conceived of as "affirmativeness." The agapic and manic lovestyles were particularly prominent in that they seemed to occur within opposite existential contexts. The
agapic appeared as a giving and positive position and the manic as dependent and negative.
Journal of Humanistic Psychology. 1984 Win Vol 24(1) 95-112

[160]
Sallee, Dock T.; Casciani, Joseph M.

Relationship between sex drive and sexual frustration and purpose in life.
Investigated the relationship between one's sense of purpose in life and sexual attitudes and
behavior, using 30 female and 18 male college students. Ss were administered the Purpose
in Life Test (PIL), a sex drive and interest scale, and a sexual frustration and maladjustment
scale. Correlations were computed between the Ss' PIL scores and scores on each of the sex
scales. Results indicate no relationship between PIL scores and the scores on the sex drive
scale, whereas significant negative correlations were found between PIL scores and the sexual frustration scores for males and the combined group of males and females. The scores
on the PIL and the sexual frustration scale were not related to the Ss' sex. Results support
V. E. Frankl's (1955) theory that sexual frustration may be a manifestation of a more general existential frustration.
Journal of Clinical Psychology. 1976 Apr Vol 32(2) 273-275

[161]
Shek, Daniel T. L.

Marital quality and psychological well-being of married adults in a Chinese context.
1,501 married Chinese adults (aged 30-60 yrs) responded to the Chinese Dyadic
Adjustment Scale, the Chinese Kansas Marital Satisfaction Scale (C-KMS), and to tools for

assessing their psychological well-being and perceived health status. In canonical analyses of the link between marital adjustment and well-being, Ss with greater marital maladjustment (1) showed more psychiatric symptoms and midlife crisis symptoms, (2) had lower levels of purpose in life and life satisfaction, and (3) perceived their health as relatively poorer. Similar findings were obtained for the link between marital satisfaction as indexed by the C-KMS and the various indicators of well-being. Results suggest that the quality of the marital relation is closely related to the psychological well-being and adjustment of married adults in the Chinese culture.

Journal of Genetic Psychology. 1995 Mar Vol 156(1) 45-56

Meaning and Spiritual Quest

[cf. 220]
Acklin, Marvin W.; Brown, Earl C.; Mauger, Paul A.

The role of religious values in coping with cancer.
Journal of Religion & Health. 1983 Win Vol 22(4) 322-333

[162]
Akerberg, Hans

Noogenic and private-religious attitudes: Evaluation of a series of pilot studies on college pupils at the age of 16-sup-17.
(Noogena och privatreligioesa attityder. Evaluering av en serie pilotstudier utfoerda pa elever inom gymnasieskolans arskurs.)
Conducted 5 pilot studies to investigate "noogenic" and private-religious attitudes of students, aged 16-17 yrs, from 3 Swedish towns. Questionnaires, a purpose-in-life test, and various types of written composition were used. Results indicate that more than 60% of Ss were influenced by noogenic experiences in their overall responses to life. Many of the Ss indicated that private-religious views and attitudes were used to counteract these experiences; conventional religion and other attitudes were also cited as remedies.
Pedagogisk-Psykologiska Problem. 1984 Jun No 433 122

[163]
Black, Helen K.

Life as gift: Spiritual narratives of elderly African-American women living in poverty.
Fifty elderly African-American women, over 70 yrs of age, living in poverty were interviewed for a research project entitled, "Chronic Poverty and the Self in Later Life." Using 4 representative case studies from the 50 respondents, this article explores how their spirituality informs their ability to cope with poverty. A key theme emerging from the women's narratives is that their relationship with God, perceived as personal, reciprocal, and empowering, allows them to take an active and positive stance in viewing and interpreting the circumstances of their life. Their spirituality imbues their hardship with meaning, engenders self-esteem, keeps despair at bay, and grants hope for rewards both in this life and the next.
Journal of Aging Studies. 1999 Win Vol 13(4) 441-455

[164]
Bolt, Martin

Purpose in life and religious orientation.
Notes that G. W. Allport has stated that intrinsic religion, in contrast to its extrinsic opposite, "floods the whole life with motivation and meaning." The present study, with 52 undergraduates, using J. Crumbaugh's purpose-in-life test and the religious orientation scale of G. W. Allport and J. M. Ross, tested the hypothesis that the intrinsic experiences a sig-

nificantly higher sense of meaning in life than does the extrinsic. Results support the hypothesis with both the intrinsic and indiscriminately proreligious indicating a significantly greater sense of purpose in life than the extrinsic.

Journal of Psychology & Theology. 1975 Spr Vol 3(2) 116-118

[165]
Bondevik, Margareth; Skogstad, Anders

Loneliness, religiousness, and purpose in life in the oldest old.
Compared 2 groups of Norwegian people (80 yrs old and older) with respect to loneliness, religiousness, purpose in life (PIL), and age group. One group was living in nursing homes and one group in the community. There were no differences in loneliness identified between residence groups. Community residents 80-89 yrs old reported significantly higher loneliness scores than did the 90-105 yr olds. A majority of all Ss reported religion to be important, but age group comparisons yielded non-significant results. Residents living in the community reported significantly higher PIL scores than did residents in institutions. In addition, the community group of 90-105 yr olds reported significantly higher PIL scores than the age group of 80-89 yr olds. Analysis of variance showed significantly higher (negative) correlations between loneliness and PIL than between these phenomena and religiousness.

Journal of Religious Gerontology. 2000 Vol 11(1) 5-21

[166]
Brennan, Mark

Spirituality and psychosocial development in middle-age and older adults with vision loss. Examined the buffering effects of spirituality on stress resulting from vision status, health status, and from other significant life events as related to psychosocial development according to E. H. Erikson's 8-stage theory. Participants were middle-aged and older adults with recent vision loss who had applied for vision rehabilitation services (n=195; aged 45-64 yrs for middle-aged and 65+ yrs for older adults). The regression model included independent factors of sociodemographic variables, life stress measures (i.e., vision status, health status, and life experience ratings), mediating variables (i.e., spirituality, religiousness, and social support), and the outcome of psychosocial development. Spirituality was found to play a buffering role on the effects of negative life experience impact and control ratings. Vision impairment status did not appear to either promote or hinder psychosocial development.

Journal of Adult Development. 2002 Jan Vol 9(1) 31-46

[167]
Burris, Christopher T.; Jackson, Lynne M.; Tarpley, W. Ryan; Smith, Galadriel J.

Religion as quest: The self-directed pursuit of meaning.
Tested, in 4 studies, 2 assumptions (Quest is born out of existential struggle with tragedy and conflict. Quest reflects an autonomous, self-directing approach to religion that may be inimical to established religious traditions) regarding C. D. Batson's quest religious orientation. In Study 1, with 56 undergraduates, Ss read articles relating to religion and completed questionnaires. In Study 2, 150 state university and 138 evangelical Christian college students completed questionnaires. Results suggest that increases in quest were associated with experimentally induced confrontation with tragedy and with self-reported family conflict.

In Study 3, with 389 US and 179 Canadian college students, and Study 4, with 142 male and 165 female undergraduates, questionnaire results found quest to be linked to personal (nonaffiliated) religion and to variables suggestive of decreased social identification.

Personality & Social Psychology Bulletin. 1996 Oct Vol 22(10) 1068-1076

[168]
Byrd, Kevin R.; Lear, Delbert; Schwenka, Stacy

Mysticism as a predictor of subjective well-being.
Examined mysticism as a predictor of subjective well-being in 150 college students (mean age 20.7 yrs). Four measures of subjective well-being (Satisfaction with Life, Purpose in Life, Negative Affect, and Religious Satisfaction) were each hierarchically regressed on several previously studied control measures of religiousness, 3 measures of mysticism, and 2 interaction terms. For both Satisfaction with Life and Purpose in Life, R-sup-2 was significantly increased when the 3 mysticism measures were entered as a block subsequent to the control variables. When nonsignificant predictors were removed from the equations, the interaction of Extrovertive Mysticism (the experience of a unity to all things) * Religious Interpretation (the tendency to find sacred meaning in experiences) was positively associated with Satisfaction with Life. However, Extrovertive Mysticism was negatively associated with Satisfaction with Life. Religious Interpretation was associated with Purpose in Life and Religious Satisfaction. The authors conclude that mysticism may have an important and complex relationship to subjective well-being that cannot be reduced to previously studied religious variables.

International Journal for the Psychology of Religion. 2000 Vol 10(4) 259-269

[cf. 480]
Carroll, Jerome F. X.; McGinley, John J.; Mack, Stephen E.

Exploring the expressed spiritual needs and concerns of drug-dependent males in modified, therapeutic community treatment.

Alcoholism Treatment Quarterly. 2000 Vol 18(1) 79-92

[cf. 481]
Carroll, Stephanie

Spirituality and purpose in life in alcoholism recovery.

Journal of Studies on Alcohol. 1993 May Vol 54(3) 297-301

[169]
Cashwell, Craig S.; Woolington, V. Jeanne

The relationship of spirituality to cognitive and moral development and purpose in life: An exploratory investigation.
In this exploratory study of 152 undergraduate students (aged 18-29 yrs), the relationships among spirituality, cognitive and moral development, and existential sense of meaning were examined. Results suggest that no relationship exists between spirituality and cognitive development, but that spirituality is positively related to both moral development and pur-

pose in life. Findings support the idea that spirituality is available to all, regardless of cognitive developmental level.

Counseling & Values. 1998 Oct Vol 43(1) 63-69

[170]
Chamberlain, Kerry; Zika, Sheryl

Religiosity, life meaning and wellbeing: Some relationships in a sample of women.
Examined religiosity as a predictor of different components of psychological well-being, in the context of several measures of meaning in life, with 188 adult women. It is proposed that religiosity may show different relationships to the major well-being dimensions of life satisfaction, positive affect, and negative affect. Results demonstrate the religion-well-being relationship to be variable. The pattern of results was not consistent, with specific results finding direct (zero-order) and mediated, suppressed, or interactive (second-order) associations between religiosity and specific components of well-being, when life meaning was taken into account. The findings support earlier research (e.g., by R. A. Witter et al, 1985) in demonstrating that the religiosity-well-being relationship, where it does occur, is positive but small.

Journal for the Scientific Study of Religion. 1988 Sep Vol 27(3) 411-420

[171]
Crandall, James E.; Rasmussen, Roger D.

Purpose in life as related to specific values.
The 1st study, with 86 undergraduate volunteers, investigated relations between perceived meaning or purpose in life, as measured by the Purpose in Life Test (PIL), and the endorsement of specific values from Rokeach's Value Survey. The values of pleasure, excitement, and comfort were associated with low scores on the PIL. Results support V. E. Frankl's (1955) contention that a hedonistic approach to life contributes to an existential vacuum. The value of salvation was associated with relatively high scores on the PIL. Consistent with Frankl's views and research by J. C. Crumbaugh et al (1970), this suggested that a genuine, intrinsic religious orientation may help to foster greater perceived meaning and purpose in life. A 2nd study, with 71 psychology student volunteers, was designed to explore further the relation between the PIL and religious values. On the Intrinsic-Extrinsic Religious Orientation Scale, perceived purpose in life was found to correlate with an intrinsic religious orientation, but not with an extrinsic orientation.

Journal of Clinical Psychology. 1975 Jul Vol 31(3) 483-485

[172]
Dufton, Brian D.; Perlman, Daniel

The association between religiosity and the Purpose-in-Life test: Does it reflect purpose or satisfaction?
Explored the theory and research that suggests that conservative religiosity is associated with a sense of life purpose, as measured by the Purpose in Life Test (PLT). 116 female and 116 male undergraduates classified as nonbelievers, conservative believers, or nonconservative believers completed the PLT. Results show that the PLT consists of 2 factors, one reflecting life purpose and another, stronger factor reflecting life satisfaction. Conservative religiosity

was associated with high scores on the PLT as a whole, as well as on both purpose and life satisfaction items.

Journal of Psychology & Theology. 1986 Spr Vol 14(1) 42-48

[cf. 382]
D'Souza, Russell

Do patients expect psychiatrists to be interested in spiritual issues?

Australasian Psychiatry. 2002 Mar Vol 10(1) 44-47

[cf. 432]
Ellis, Jon B.; Smith, Peggy C.

Spiritual well-being, social desirability and reasons for living: Is there a connection?

International Journal of Social Psychiatry. 1991 Spr Vol 37(1) 57-63

[cf. 287]
Farran, Carol J.; Keane-Hagerty, Eleanora; Salloway, Sandra; Kupferer, Sylvia; et al

Finding meaning: An alternative paradigm for Alzheimer's disease family caregivers.

Gerontologist. 1991 Aug Vol 31(4) 483-489

[cf. 289]
Farran, Carol J.; Miller, Baila H.; Kaufman, Julie E.; Donner, Ed; Fogg, Louis

Finding meaning through caregiving: Development of an instrument for family caregivers of persons with Alzheimer's disease.

Journal of Clinical Psychology. 1999 Sep Vol 55(9) 1107-1125

[173]
Ferriss, Abbott L.

Religion and the quality of life.
Examined the relationship between religion and quality of life (QOL). Two QOL indicators, subjective and objective, are examined separately. Objective measures include longevity and the proportion of the population of a state professing a religious faith. The subjective measure is the general happiness of the US population as measured in the General Social Survey (1972-1996). Results show happiness to be associated with the frequency of attendance at religious services, with denomination preference, and with doctrinal preference. Happiness also is associated with certain religious-related beliefs: belief that the world is evil or good but not belief in immortality. In a discussion of these and other findings, hypotheses are suggested to explain and to further explore the effects of religion on QOL. Among the conclusions: Americans' conception of the "good life" rests heavily upon Judeo-Christian ideals; religious organizations contribute to the integration of the community, hence enhancing QOL; since frequency of attendance is imperfectly associated with QOL, other influences are at work; the doctrine of the religion may attract persons of happy disposition; and that religion may explain a purpose in life that fosters well-being.

Journal of Happiness Studies. 2002 Vol 3(3) 199-215

[cf. 314]
Florian, Victor; Snowden, Lonnie R.

Fear of personal death and positive life regard: A study of different ethnic and religious-affiliated American college students.
Journal of Cross-Cultural Psychology. 1989 Mar Vol 20(1) 64-79

[174]
Foley, Linda

Exploring the experience of spirituality in older women finding meaning in life.
Spirituality is a broad, multifaceted, multidimensional construct that appears to increase in importance with aging and may assist older adults in seeking meaning to life and responding to stressful life events. Research in the area of spirituality is lacking especially as it relates to older women. The purpose of this study was to explore spirituality in the lives of older women. A convenience sample of 210 older women (aged 61-102 yrs) completed the JAREL Spiritual Well-Being Scale. Overall, data analysis indicated that these women had a reasonably high level of spirituality. In addition, those women who described their health as good or excellent and had a college education had higher spirituality scores. In order to explore, describe and understand the experience of women's spirituality, further research is essential.
Journal of Religious Gerontology. 2000 Vol 12(1) 5-15

[175]
Francis, Leslie J.

The influence of personal prayer on purpose in life among catholic adolescents
The relationship between personal prayer and perceived purpose in life is explored among a sample of 674 12-16 year olds attending Catholic school who identified themselves as members of the Catholic church. The data demonstrate a sgnificant positive relationship between frequency of personal prayer and perceived purpose in life after controlling for individual differences in church attendance. Moreover, personal prayer was shown to be a stronger predictor of purpose in life than church attendance.
The Journal of Beliefs and Values. 1994. Vol (15):2. 6-9

[176]
Francis, Leslie J.

The relationship between bible reading and purpose in life among 13-15-year-olds.
The relationship between bible reading and perceived purpose in life is explored among a sample of 25,888 13-15 yr olds throughout England and Wales, alongside information about sex, age, personality, belief in God and church attendance. The conclusion is drawn that bible reading makes a small but unique contribution to promoting a sense of purpose in life among this age group.
Mental Health, Religion & Culture. 2000 May Vol 3(1) 27-36

[177]
Francis, Leslie J., Evans, Thomas, E.

The relationship between personal prayer and purpose in life among churchgoing and non-churchgoing twelve-to-fifteen-year olds in the UK.
The relationship between personal prayer and perceived purpose in life is explored among two samples of 12-15-year-olds. The first sample comprises 914 males and 5726 females who never attend church. The second sample comprises 232 males and 437 females who attend church most weeks. The data demonstrate a significant positive relationship between frequency of personal prayer and perceived purpose in life among both groups.
Religious Education. 1996. Vol.91:1. 9-21

[178]
Francis, Leslie J., Kaldor, Peter

The relationship between religion and purpose in life in an Australian population survey.
A random sample of 1021 adults in an Australian community survey provided data on purpose in life, religiosity and personality. The national data confirmed the results or previous studies on specialised populations by demonstrating that there is a positive relationship between religiosity and purpose in life after controlling for individual differences in personality. The data also suggested that the social dimension may be particularly important in understanding the psychological mechanism behind the observed relationship between religion and purpose in life.
Research in the Social Scientific Study of Religion. 2001. Vol.12. 53-63

[179]
French, Sarah; Joseph, Stephen

Religiosity and its association with happiness, purpose in life, and self-actualisation.
The aim of the present work was to test for an association between religiosity and happiness. 101 undergraduates (aged 18-49 yrs) completed the Francis Scale of Attitude Towards Christianity, the Depression-Happiness Scale (DHS), the Oxford Happiness Inventory (OHI), the Purpose in Life Test (PIL), and the Index of Self-Actualisation (ISA). It was found that higher scores on the Francis Scale were associated with higher scores on the DHS, the OHI, the PIL, and the ISA, providing evidence for a positive association between religiosity and these facets of subjective well-being. However, partial correlations suggested that the association between religiosity and happiness is a function of purpose in life.
Mental Health, Religion & Culture. 1999 Nov Vol 2(2) 117-120

[180]
Fry, P. S.

Religious involvement, spirituality and personal meaning for life: Existential predictors of psychological wellbeing in community-residing and institutional care elders.
Examined the unique and combined contribution of specific dimensions of religiosity, spirituality and personal meaning in life as predictors of well-being in samples of 180 community-residing and 160 institutionalized older adults (aged 60-90 yrs). The results showed that personal meaning, involvement in formal religion, participation in spiritual practices, importance of religion, degree of comfort derived from religion, sense of inner peace with

self, and accessibility to religious resources were significant predictors of well-being for the combined sample. The pattern of associations between well-being and the preceding psychosocial dimensions was, however, stronger for the institutionalized elders. The findings confirmed that existential measures of personal meaning, religiosity and spirituality contributed more significantly to the variance in well-being than did demographic variables or other traditional measures such as social resources, physical health or negative life events. The importance of existential constructs of religiosity, spirituality and personal meaning in helping older adults to transcend old age stresses and sustain well-being are discussed.

Aging & Mental Health. 2000 Nov Vol 4(4) 375-387

[181]
Furrow, James L.; King, Pamela Ebstyne; White, Krystal

Religion and positive youth development: Identity, meaning, and prosocial concerns.
The role of religious identity in positive youth development was examined in this study of personal meaning and prosocial concerns in adolescence. A structural equation model was tested on a sample of 801 urban public high school students. Participants responded to questionnaires assessing religious identity, personal meaning, and prosocial personality. Prototypical descriptors derived from Walker and Pitts's (1998) highly religious person concept were examined as a measure of religious identity. Findings demonstrate a positive relationship between religious self-understanding, personal meaning, and prosocial personality. Differences were noted in the relationship of personal meaning to prosocial personality across age and gender cohorts. The findings provide further support for considering religion as a developmental resource associated with personal meaning and a concern for others among youth.

Applied Developmental Science. 2004 Jan Vol 8(1) 17-26

[182]
Gerwood, Joseph B.; LeBlanc, Michael; Piazza, Nick

The Purpose-in-Life Test and religious denomination: Protestant and Catholic scores in an elderly population.
The Purpose in-Life Test (PIL) was administered to a group of 118 elderly persons from 3 senior citizen centers. Data were obtained on religious denomination. Results suggested that whether a person was Protestant or Catholic had no significant effect on PIL scores, with mean scores almost identical. What seemed to be important was how meaningful spirituality was to the person. Those who scored high on an index of spirituality also scored high on the PIL.

Journal of Clinical Psychology. 1998 Jan Vol 54(1) 49-53

[cf. 332]
Golsworthy, Richard; Coyle, Adrian

Spiritual beliefs and the search for meaning among older adults following partner loss.

Mortality. 1999 Mar Vol 4(1) 21-40

[183]
Halama, Peter

On the relationship between religiosity and life meaningfulness.
Both psychologists of religion and psychologists dealing with meaning in life confirm interaction between religiosity and life meaningfulness. This study deals with the question of
which dimensions or aspects of religion are related to a sense of life meaninglessness. 104
students of Catholic grammar schools (aged 17 to 19) were given a set of questionnaires
containing measures of meaningfulness (Personal Meaning Index and Life Meaningfulness
Scale) and different religiosity dimensions (internal, external, quest, significance, orthodoxy,
mature religiosity). Correlation analysis of religion dimensino scores and all individual items
with these dimensions with meaning measures showed that connecting religiosity with life
meaningfulness involves: considering religion as very important to one's own life, avtive
effort to transfer religious beliefs into daily behaviour and decisions, commitment to religious beliefs and activities, and receiving support and reassurance from religion.
Archives for the Psychology of Religion. 2003. 24. 218-233*

[184]
Hall, Beverly A.

Ways of maintaining hope in HIV disease.
Research in Nursing & Health. 1994 Aug Vol 17(4) 283-293

[185]
Hall, C. Margaret

Religion and aging.
Investigated the relationship between religion and aging, using life-history data from 500
families and national-cultural values. Central questions were the extent to which an individual can select beliefs that lead to a longer, more meaningful life and the special influence
that religion may have in enhancing aging. It is concluded that religion may be an effective
means to identify these concerns and improve the quality of life of older people
Journal of Religion & Health. 1985 Spr Vol 24(1) 70-78

[186]
Hermans, Hubert J. M.; Oles, Piotr K.

The personal meaning of values in a rapidly changing society.
Explored personal and subjective interpretations of general values using a self-confrontation
method. 53 psychology students were asked to interpret their personal experience of E.
Spranger's (1919, 1924) postulated set of values. Social, religious, and theoretical values had
a stronger capacity to evoke personal valuations than did political, economic, and aesthetic
values. Positive valuations were mainly connected with aesthetic, theoretical, social, and religious values, whereas many negative valuations concerned economic and political areas.
Political and theoretical values had higher levels of self-enhancement than of contact and
union. Aesthetic, religious, and social values typically evoked a coincidence of self-enhancement, contact, and union.
Journal of Social Psychology. 1994 Oct Vol 134(5) 569-579

[cf. 026]
Itatsu, Hiromi

The relationship of self-acceptance to life attitude and hopelessness.
Japanese Journal of Counseling Science. 1995 Mar Vol 28(1) 37-46

[187]
Jackson, Laurence E.; Coursey, Robert D.

The relationship of God control and internal locus of control to intrinsic religious motivation, coping and purpose in life.
Examined the relationships among the variables of God control, personal control, religious involvement, and coping in 98 18-68 yr old Black Baptists. Unlike most studies among White Ss, the measure of high God control correlated with high internal locus of control (LOC) on Rotter's Internal-External Locus of Control Scale. Also, using stepwise regression analyses and removing the variance due to demographic and religious participation variables, internal LOC but not God control predicted measures of coping skills and purpose in life. Both LOC and God control predicted intrinsic religious motivation.
Journal for the Scientific Study of Religion. 1988 Sep Vol 27(3) 399-410

[188]
Johnson, Martin A.; Mullins, Phil

Moral communities: Religious and secular.
Considers the extent to which community groups (social service clubs, professional organizations, churches) constitute "moral communities" (coherent social networks that support meaningful human relationships by fostering common attitudes, values, and practices). Questionnaire data were collected from 135 psychology students, 440 adults who were contacted at home, and 405 adults attending church in 1 of 12 congregations. Data show that for many Ss community groups constitute moral communities, that such groups differ in the intensity and frequency of moral community feelings, and that the religious congregation is more likely to inspire feelings of moral community than any other group. Feelings of moral community were significantly correlated with reduced feelings of mass society and increased feelings of self-esteem and of meaning and purpose in life.
Journal of Community Psychology. 1990 Apr Vol 18(2) 153-166

[cf. 237]
Kaczorowski, Jane M.

Spiritual well-being and anxiety in adults diagnosed with cancer.
Hospice Journal. 1989 Vol 5(3-4) 105-116

[189]
Kass, Jared D.; Friedman, Richard; Leserman, Jane; Zuttermeister, Patricia C.; et al

Health outcomes and a new index of spiritual experience.
Clinical observations suggesting a relationship between spiritual experiences, life purpose and satisfaction, and improvements in physical health led to the development of an Index of Core Spiritual Experience (INSPIRIT). Data from 83 medical outpatients (aged 25-72

yrs) showed the INSPIRIT to have a strong degree of internal reliability and concurrent validity when comparred with Ss' performance on the Religious Orientation Inventory. Multiple regression analyses of data from the Medical Symptom Checklist and the Inventory of Positive Psychological Attitudes to Life showed INSPIRIT to be associated with (1) increased life purpose and satisfaction and a health-promoting attitude and (2) decreased frequency of medical symptoms.

Journal for the Scientific Study of Religion. 1991 Jun Vol 30(2) 203-211

[190]
Klaas D.

Testing two elements of spirituality in depressed and non-depressed elders.
Depression is a common source of morbidity and mortality among elders in North America and has a significant impact on their quality of life. Meaning in life and self transcendence, indicators of spirituality, have been linked to the experience of well-being in the elderly. Nurses are challenged to find ways to tap these natural resources as a means of addressing the serious problem of depression in the aged. The purpose of this study was to compare patterns of depression, meaning in life and self-transcendence as measured in three instruments in a group of elders 75 years of age and older. The Geriatric Depression Scale, Purpose in Life Test and Self-Transcendence Scale were completed by 77 elders residing independently or semi-independently in one of three retirement communities. Significant negative relationships were found between depression and meaning in life, and between depression and self-transcendence. A significant positive relationship was found between meaning in life and self-transcendence. Demographic data further contributed to patterns of depression and well-being in this group. The study conclusions support the importance of meaning in life and self-transcendence for well-being in the elderly. Based on the study results, suggestions are offered about ways to enhance health and well-being in this cohort.

International Journal of Psychiatric Nursing Research. 1998 Sep;4(2):452-62. *

[191]
Klaassen, Derrick W.; McDonald, Marvin J.

Quest and identity development: Re-examining pathways for existential search.
This article examines key assumptions underlying quest as a mature religious orientation rooted in existential struggles. Quest is posited by C. D. Batson and his colleagues to be an inherently meaningful search in the face of life's challenges. Moreover, Quest is seen to operate across the lifespan independently of the developmental search for identity. Accordingly, quest's relationships with key variables should be mediated by personal meaning but not by identity development. P. T. P. Wong's Personal Meaning Profile and G. R. Adams's Extended Objective Measure of Ego Identity Status were used to explore mediation of the relationship between quest (as measured by the Quest scale) and spiritual well-being (as measured by the Spiritual Well-Being Scale [SWBS]). The Quest-SWBS relation was partially mediated by personal meaning and identity development in a sample of 160 Christian university students (aged 18-25 yrs). These results and their implications for quest are discussed in light of J. E. Marcia's identity status theory and Wong's model of personal meaning.

International Journal for the Psychology of Religion. 2002 Jul Vol 12(3) 189-200

[192]
Kulik, Agnieszka; Szewczyk, Leszek

Sense of meaning of life and the emotional reaction among young people pursuing different types of meditation.
In modern times two major modes of meditation prevail: the Christian and the Oriental
trend. Both forms have elements that are common but that also diverge. The question of
whether these forms can be combined and which of them carries meaning life was investigated. 28 young people (mean age 17 yrs) voluntarily pursuing the Christian form of meditation (Light - Life Movement) and 23 persons (mean age 17 yrs) pursuing the Oriental
form (Transcendental meditation) participated. The following methods were used in the
research: the "Purpose in Life Test," the "Hostility - Guilt Inventory," The Hopelessness
Scale and "The I.P.A.T. Anxiety Scale." Persons pursuing the Christian or the Oriental form
of meditation revealed no significant differences with regard to the intensity of the sense of
meaning of life. The basic difference between the groups appears in the type of answers
which refer to the attitude towards oneself and others. The study has revealed a distinct
decrease in aggressive tendencies, a higher level of anxiety, lower resistance towards frustra-
tions and a slight sense of hopelessness among the meditating subjects. It shows that both
forms of meditation exert a similar influence on the emotional reactions.
Studia Psychologica. 2002 Vol 44(2) 155-166

[cf. 241]
Landis, B. J.

Uncertainty, spiritual well-being, and psychosocial adjustment to chronic illness.
Issues in Mental Health Nursing. 1996 May-Jun Vol 17(3) 217-231

[193]
MacDonald, Douglas A.; Holland, Daniel

Spirituality and boredom proneness.
Using data obtained from 296 university undergraduate students (aged 17-48 yrs), standard
regression analyses were calculated for men and women separately to examine the relation
of spirituality, defined multidimensionally as per the Expressions of Spirituality Inventory
(ESI), to boredom proneness as measured by the Boredom Proneness Scale (BPS). Results
reveal that spirituality significantly predicts boredom proneness scores. Semipartial correlations indicate that the facet of spirituality known as Existential Well-Being is the only significant predictor of boredom proneness for both sexes while ESI Cognitive Orientation to
Spirituality was significant for women only. ESI dimensions explicitly tapping religiousness,
spiritual experience and paranormal beliefs were not found to reliably or uniquely contribute to the prediction of boredom proneness. The findings involving ESI Existential
Well-Being are consistent with extant research showing a negative relation between boredom and meaning and purpose in life.
Personality & Individual Differences. 2002 Apr Vol 32(6) 1113-1119

[cf. 295]
MacKinlay, Elizabeth

The spiritual dimension of caring: Applying a model for spiritual tasks of ageing.
Journal of Religious Gerontology. 2001 Vol 12(3-4) 151-166

[194]
McHoskey, John W.; Betris, Terri; Worzel, William; Szyarto, Chris; Kelly, Kristen; Eggert, Tammy; Miley, Jenny; Suggs, Travis; Tesler, Adam; Gainey, Nikki; Anderson, Harmony

Relativism, nihilism, and quest.
Examined similarities and differences between relativism and nihilism by examining their relations with C. D. Baton's quest religious orientation. 90 college students (aged 17-40 yrs) completed questionnaires that assessed relativism, nihilism, quest, and interest in religion. As predicted, relativism was positively associated with quest total score, and all 3 of the quest subscales (existential, doubt, openness), and nihilism was negatively associated with quest. The results are consistent with the identification of similarities between relativism and nihilism, as they were positively correlated in this study. However, it is suggested that relativism and nihilism represent distinctly different approaches to constructing personal meaning in the face existential vacuum.
Journal of Social Behavior & Personality. 1999 Sep Vol 14(3) 445-462

[195]
Meddin, Jacob Robert

Dimensions of spiritual meaning and well-being in the lives of ten older Australians.
Examined how 10 prominent older Australians (7 male and 3 female; aged 65 yrs and older) impart a sense of spiritual meaning to their lives. The study is a secondary analysis of published interviews conducted by C. Jones on the Australian Broadcast Corporation's radio program, "The Search for Meaning." The interviews explicitly address issues of personal meaning. The findings reported in this article focus mainly upon nonroutine or spiritual aspects of meaning. The topics addressed are global sense of meaning, altruistic behavior, transcendent experiences, life review, and wisdom. Acquiring knowledge emerges as a global life purpose; altruistic behavior is prevalent; transcendent experiences are reported with frequency; life review and wisdom underscores both a sense of coherence and the continuity of personal characteristics over the life span, and a decidedly optimistic orientation toward human nature. The impression gained is one of older persons with an integrated and often deep and spiritual orientation toward their lives.
International Journal of Aging & Human Development. 1998 Vol 47(3) 163-175

[cf. 297]
Mickley, Jacqueline Ruth; Pargament, Kenneth I.; Brant, Curtis R.; Hipp, Kathleen M.

God and the search for meaning among hospice caregivers.
Hospice Journal. 1998 Vol 13(4) 1-17

[cf. 298]
Millison, Martin; Dudley, James R.

Providing spiritual support: A job for all hospice professionals.
Hospice Journal. 1992 Vol 8(4) 49-66

[cf. 249]
Moadel, Alyson; Morgan, Carole; Fatone, Anne; Grennan, Jennifer; Carter, Jeanne;
Laruffa, Gia; Skummy, Anne; Dutcher, Janice

Seeking meaning and hope: Self-reported spiritual and existential needs among an ethnically-diverse cancer patient population.
Psycho-Oncology. 1999 Sep-Oct Vol 8(5) 378-385

[197]
Molcar, Carol C.; Stuempfig, Daniel W.

Effects of world view on purpose in life.
Examined the association of 201 US undergraduate and graduate students' worldviews with their sense of purpose in life. Ss completed the Purpose in Life Test, and a measurement of worldviews. Ss ascribing to worldviews based on belief in a personal God tended to have more purpose in life than other Ss. Purpose in life comprised 2 factors, one involving satisfaction with general goals and meaning in life, and the other dealing with excitement in day-to-day living. The personal monotheism Ss had significantly higher purpose-in-life scores on the 1st factor than did Ss for whom a personal transcendent Being was irrelevant, but the groups did not differ significantly on the 2nd factor.
Journal of Psychology. 1988 Jul Vol 122(4) 365-371

[198]
Morris, Harold C.; Morris, Lin M.

Power and purpose: Correlates to conversion.
163 volunteer Ss from psychology courses were given the Rokeach Dogmatism Scale, the Purpose in Life Test, an irrelevant verbal task with 2 accompanying questions, and questions concerning conversion and power need. Converts (religious and otherwise) and nonconverts were identified within the S sample. It was hypothesized that (a) converts would attribute a purposeful pattern even to an irrelevant task that was lacking in any inherent discoverable pattern, (b) the convert group would demonstrate more need for self-structuring power than the nonconverts would, and (c) the converts would be more dogmatic than the nonconverts. Other issues including frustration, defensiveness, and suggestibility are discussed. Results suggest that converts have a greater tendency to need and express a purpose in what they experience. Converts and nonconverts did not differ in their need to know what the solution was to the irrelevant verbal task (no solution was actually available). This suggests that they did not differ on task performance justification. A convert was found to be more likely to express a desire for access to a source of great power to "get himself together." The need for closeness to a power source is connected to a need for self-structuring. The converts were found to be more dogmatic than the nonconverts.
Psychology: A Journal of Human Behavior. 1978 Nov-Dec Vol 15(4) 15-22

[199]
Mountain, Deborah Ann; Muir, Walter J.

Spiritual well-being in psychiatric patients.
Examined the spiritual well-being and religious practices, beliefs and psychological morbidity of 41 psychiatric patients compared to control groups of 40 patients with chronic
medical conditions and 39 community controls attending their GP. General Health
Questionnaire-28 (GHQ-28), the Spiritual Well-Being Scale (consisting of religious and
existential well-being subscales) and an open-ended Religious Survey Questionnaire were
personally administered to the groups and information was supplemented by case note data.
Although there were no differences between the groups on the measure of overall Spiritual
Well-Being or on the subscale of Religious Well-Being, the psychiatric group scored lower
on the Existential Well-Being subscale and had higher scores on the GHQ-28. The psychiatric group had increased frequency of private religious behavior (praying and reading the
Bible) which were thought to be coping strategies. Existential Well-Being of the whole sam-
ple was positively correlated to religious beliefs and to religious practice.
Irish Journal of Psychological Medicine. 2000 Dec Vol 17(4) 123-127

[200]
Niekludow, Katarzyna

World outlook and feeling of sense and satisfaction with life.
(Poglad na swiat a poczucie sensu i zadowolenia z zycia.)
Studied the relationship between world view and satisfaction with life. 120 male and
female university students aged 20-24 yrs in Poland were administered a Polish questionnaire on faith (in the forces determining the fate of the world and individuals, in a just vs
unjust world, and in human beings), the Purpose in Life Test, the Satisfaction with Life
Scale (E. Diener et al, 1985), and the Scale of Basic Emotions (B. Wojciszke et al, 1998).
The results support hypotheses regarding the positive relationship between (1) faith in
human beings and in a just world and (2) feelings of the worth of life and satisfaction
with life. Lack of faith correlated negatively with feelings of the worth of life and satisfaction with life. The effect of faith in God on these feelings is examined with reference to
data in the published literature.
Psychologia Wychowawcza. 2000 Mar-Jun Vol 43(2-3) 157-171

[cf. 151]
Orbach, Israel; Iluz, Ayala; Rosenheim, Eliyahu

Value systems and commitment to goals as a function of age, integration of personality,
and fear of death.
International Journal of Behavioral Development. 1987 Jun Vol 10(2) 225-239

[201]
Paloutzian, Raymond F.

Purpose in life and value changes following conversion.
The Purpose in Life Test (PIL) and the Rokeach Value Survey were completed by 91 undergraduates. There were 4 groups of religious converts: less than 1 wk, for 1 mo, up to 6 mo,
and 6 mo or longer. Two groups of nonconverts served as controls. Converts scored higher

on the PIL than nonconverts. New converts showed a sharp rise in PIL scores, which dropped to the control level for the 1-mo group, and rose back to and stabilized at an intermediately high level within 6 mo after conversion. A general sense of values was related to a higher sense of purpose. Values given relatively more weight by S high in PIL were salvation and being clean. Values given relatively more weight by S low in PIL were comfort, happiness, freedom, and mature love. Item analysis of the PIL revealed that fear of death declined continually following conversion. Both emotionally and cognitively toned items contributed to PIL total scores.

Journal of Personality & Social Psychology. 1981 Dec Vol 41(6) 1153-1160

[202]
Paloutzian, Raymond F.; Jackson, Steven L.; Crandall, James E.

Conversion experience, belief system, and personal and ethical attitudes.
Two studies assessed the relation between type of religious belief system ("ethical" vs "born again" Christianity), type of conversion experience (sudden vs gradual vs unconscious), and 4 attitudinal dependent variables: the Purpose in Life Test, Social Interest Scale, Intrinsic-Extrinsic Religious Orientation Scale, and the Short Dogmatism Scale. 84 college students served as Ss in Exp I, and 177 adults of varying ages were Ss in Exp II. The same basic pattern of results was obtained for both studies. Born-again Christians were significantly more intrinsically motivated in their religious beliefs and higher in social interest than ethical Christians. Sudden converts were significantly more intrinsic in religious orientation than unconscious converts. Professed Christians scored significantly higher on the Purpose in Life Test and Social Interest Scale than professed non-Christians. Findings suggest that it is useful to classify Christians according to type of belief and type of conversion experience. A deep religious commitment seemed to be accompanied by a sense of meaning in life, greater concern for the welfare of others, and a more dogmatic way of thinking.

Journal of Psychology & Theology. 1978 Fal Vol 6(4) 266-275

[cf. 510]
Pardini, Dustin A.; Plante, Thomas G.; Sherman, Allen; Stump, Jamie E.

Religious faith and spirituality in substance abuse recovery: Determining the mental health benefits.

Journal of Substance Abuse Treatment. 2000 Dec Vol 19(4) 347-354

[203]
Pargament, Kenneth I.; Smith, Bruce W.; Koenig, Harold G.; Perez, Lisa

Patterns of positive and negative religious coping with major life stressors.
Used exploratory and confirmatory factor analyses to identify positive and negative patterns of religious coping methods, develop a brief measure of these religious coping patterns, and examine their implications for health and adjustment. Participants were 296 church members (mean age 59.3 yrs) coping with the Oklahoma City bombing, 540 college students coping with major life stressors, and 551 elderly hospitalized patients (aged 55-97 yrs) coping with serious medical illnesses. A 14-item measure of positive and negative patterns of religious coping methods (called Brief RCOPE) was constructed. The positive pattern consisted of religious forgiveness, seeking spiritual support, collaborative religious coping, spiritual connection, religious purification, and benevolent religious reappraisal. The negative

pattern was defined by spiritual discontent, punishing God reappraisals, interpersonal religious discontent, demonic reappraisal, and reappraisal of God's powers. As predicted, people made more use of the positive than the negative religious coping methods. Furthermore, the 2 patterns had different implications for health and adjustment.

Journal for the Scientific Study of Religion. 1998 Dec Vol 37(4) 710-724

[204]
Plante, Thomas G.; Yancey, Scott; Sherman, Allen; Guertin, Mira

The meanings and correlates of spirituality: suggestions from an exploratory survey of experts.
There has been an increasing interest in spirituality among health care professionals over the last several decades. Specialists in the areas of trauma, grief, and death and dying have been among those who have shown particular interest in religious and spiritual issues. Recent efforts to distinguish religiosity from spirituality have stimulated inquiries into the changing meanings of these dimensions. Drawing on prior and parallel works, the authors created a questionnaire and asked for responses to it from convenience samples of experts in death studies (n = 22) and spiritual studies (n = 13). Our findings are suggestive of possible lines of convergence and divergence. Both groups considered themselves to be spiritual but not religious, and there was consensus that the meaning of the term spirituality is currently changing. There was also general agreement that spiritual experiences are meaningful learning opportunities and that spiritual individuals tend to be more hopeful and to experience more meaning or purpose in life than their nonspiritual peers. The themes most strongly associated with spirituality in both groups were charity, community or connectedness, compassion, forgiveness, hope, meaning, and morality. Future research should be directed toward clarifying what people mean by "spiritual" and how they experience and express this dimension of their lives.

Death Studies. 1999 Sep;23(6):521-8.

[205]
Plante, Thomas G.; Yancey, Scott; Sherman, Allen; Guertin, Mira

The association between strength of religious faith and psychological functioning.
Examined the relationship between religious faith and psychological functioning in 3 groups totaling 342 university students in diverse educational and geographic settings including a private West Coast Catholic college (sample 1), a Southern public state university (sample 2), and a Southern private Baptist college (sample 3). Participants completed several self-report measures. Strength of religious faith was significantly associated with optimism and experiencing meaning in life among sample 1. Results from sample 2 suggest that strength of religious faith was significantly associated with coping with stress, optimism, experiencing meaning in life, viewing life as a positive challenge, and low anxiety. Strength of religious faith was significantly associated with viewing life as a positive challenge and self-acceptance among sample 3. Although modest correlations surfaced, results suggest that strength of religious faith is associated with several important positive mental health benefits among college students.

Pastoral Psychology. 2000 May Vol 48(5) 405-412

[206]
Porpora, Douglas V.

Personal heroes, religion, and transcendental metanarratives.
Suggests that the study of heroes is important because heroes are one indicator of who we
are and what we stand for. That is partly what motivates the recent attention to the media's
identification of heroes. Yet while the media represent a very visible aspect of culture, who
individuals privately cite as their heroes is, although less visible, just as much a part of who
we are as a culture. Accordingly, the author reports on findings from 2 telephone surveys
conducted in Philadelphia that, among other questions pertaining to the meaning of life,
asked 627 adults whether they had any heroes and if so who those heroes were. The tendency to identify with heroes was found to be related to transcendental concerns with the
meaning of life and to religiosity. Overall, the pattern of findings discloses an unstudied
dimension of cultural disenchantment.
                                         Sociological Forum. 1996 Jun Vol 11(2) 209-229

[cf. 366]
Prager, Edward; Solomon, Zahava

Perceptions of world benevolence, meaningfulness, and self-worth among elderly Israeli
holocaust survivors and non-survivors.
                    Anxiety, Stress & Coping: An International Journal. 1995 Vol 8(4) 265-277

[cf. 322]
Rasmussen, Christina H.; Johnson, Mark E.

Spirituality and religiosity: Relative relationships to death anxiety.
                              Omega: Journal of Death & Dying. 1994 Vol 29(4) 313-318

[207]
Robbins, Mandy, Francis, Leslie J.

Religion, personality, and well-being : The relationship between church attendance and
purpose in life
A sample of 517 first-year, undergraduate students attending an Anglican College in Wales
completed the purpose-in-life scale (PILS) together with the short-form Revised Eysenck
Personality Questionnaire (EPQR) and a measure of church attendance. After controlling
for individual differences in personality, the data demonstrate a significant positive correlation between church attendance and scores on the PILS. A growing body of evidence indicates that attendance at religious services tends to promote the psychological well-being of
college students.
                              Journal of Research on Christian Education. 2000. Vol.9:2. 223-238

[208]
Shek, D. T.

Meaning in life and adjustment amongst midlife parents in Hong Kong.
Studied the relationship between intensity of meaning, as measured by the Chinese version
of the Purpose in Life Test (PIL), and adjustment in a sample of 90 midlife Chinese parents

(aged 30-60 yrs). The PIL was internally consistent and had high test-retest reliability. Ss who had lower PIL scores had higher levels of psychiatric morbidity, midlife crisis symptoms, and life dissatisfaction and perceived their health as relatively poorer. Higher levels of life meaning were associated with better perceived relationships with children, higher levels of marital adjustment and satisfaction, and more positive perceptions of the value of children.

International Forum for Logotherapy. 1994 Fal Vol 17(2) 102-107

[209]
Showalter, Shelley M.; Wagener, Linda Mans

Adolescents' meaning in life
Examined how religious children and adolescents differ in their self-reports of meaning in life compared to adolescents previously studied by K. L. DeVogler and P. Ebersole (1983). It was expected that adolescents in a Christian community more frequently attribute their meaning in life to beliefs than would adolescents in the non-Christian population. 81 11-14 yr olds from a religious summer camp reported commitment to a belief as their strongest personal meaning more frequently than any other category when reported in a free-response essay format, whereas no adolescents in the previous study reported belief as their strongest meaning.

Psychological Reports. 2000 Aug Vol 87(1) 115-126

[210]
Soderstrom, Doug; Wright, E. Wayne

Religious orientation and meaning in life.
Tested the general hypothesis that a mature religious commitment should aid youth in their search for meaning in life. A questionnaire was given to 427 college freshmen and sophomores in 6 midwestern colleges. Results indicate that intrinsically motivated Ss, committed Ss, and true believers had significantly higher Purpose in Life Test mean scores than did extrinsically motivated Ss, uncommitted Ss, and unbelievers. The results also indicate that religious integration (moral commitment paired with spiritual commitment) is indicative of meaning in life. It is concluded that a mature religious commitment should aid youth in their search for meaning in life.

Journal of Clinical Psychology. 1977 Jan Vol 33(1) 65-68

[cf. 423]
Springer MB, Newman A, Weaver AJ, Siritsky N, Linderblatt C, Flannelly KJ, Naditch B, VandeCreek L.

Spirituality, depression, and loneliness among Jewish seniors residing in New York City.
*Journal of Pastoral Care and Counselling. 2003 Fall;57(3):305-18**

[211]
Stones, Christopher R.

Personal religious orientation and Frankl's will-to-meaning in four religious communities.
72 Ss (average age 24 yrs) in 4 religious communities in Johannesburg, South Africa—the Jesus People, the Hare Krishna Devotees, the Maharaj Ji Premies, and a Catholic priest com-

munity—were given the Purpose in Life Test, its complementary scale (Seeking-of-Noetic-Goals Test), and the Religious Orientation Scale. Data confirm the hypotheses that as a function of integration into any one of these groups, individuals' lives take on greater meaning and purpose and that the motivation to seek meaning decreases. Results also indicate that members' personal religious orientations become more intrinsic.

South African Journal of Psychology. 1980 Vol 10(1-sup-2) 50-52

[212]
Stones, Christopher R.; Philbrick, Joseph L.

Purpose in life in South Africa: A comparison of American and South African beliefs.
Administered the Purpose in Life Test to 100 English-speaking South African Ss, who were later to become members of discrete religiously oriented groups, to test the hypothesis that Ss would receive substantially lower scores prior to their group affiliation than comparable American samples. Results confirmed the hypothesis. It is suggested that the presence of maladjustment might be accounted for in terms of the existential crisis brought about through the rapid and substantial cultural change.

Psychological Reports. 1980 Dec Vol 47(3, Pt 1) 739-742

[cf. 266]
Strang, Susan; Strang, Peter

Spiritual thoughts, coping and "sense of coherence" in brain tumour patients and their spouses.

Palliative Medicine. 2001 Mar Vol 15(2) 127-134. *

[cf. 305]
Strang Susan; Strang Peter; Ternestedt B.M.

Spiritual needs as defined by Swedish nursing staff

Journal of Clinical Nursing. 2002 Jan;11(1):48-57. *

[213]
Stuckey, Jon C.

Faith, aging, and dementia: Experiences of Christian, Jewish, and non-religious spousal caregivers and older adults.
Research consistently documents positive relationships among religion, spirituality, and outcomes related to well-being. The purpose of this study was to determine the degree to which spousal dementia caregivers and other older adults rely on religion and spirituality as coping resources. A total of 52 Christian, Jewish, and non-religious dementia caregivers - as well as matched comparison groups of non-caregivers - were interviewed. Qualitative data analysis yielded both common themes among the three religious groups as well as themes of distinction. The findings suggest that the search for meaning and purpose during stressful life events knows no religious or spiritual borders. Even among the non-religious and non-spiritual, purpose and meaning were found in other areas, including in caring for others, in friendships, or simply in the aesthetic joys of life.

Dementia: The International Journal of Social Research & Practice. 2003 Oct Vol 2(3) 337-352

[cf. 276]
Warner-Robbins, Carmen G.; Christiana, Nicholas M.

The spiritual needs of persons with AIDS.
Family & Community Health. 1989 Aug Vol 12(2) 43-51

[214]
Watson, P. J.; Morris, Ronald J.; Hood, Ralph W.

Quest and identity within a religious ideological surround.
307 undergraduates evaluated items from the Quest Scale of the Religious Life Inventory
(C. D. Batson and W. L. Ventis, 1982), which was developed to offer an alternative to the
Religious Orientation Inventory. For a group with an intrinsic commitment, a number of
items proved to be antireligious in their implications while one was proreligious. This
intrinsic interpretation of Quest also predicted relative mental health, including superior
identity formation, and this was especially true for intrinsic Ss themselves. For no other type
was the self-definition of Quest as robustly or as discriminatively linked to psychological
well-being. The original Quest Scale was tied to poorer self-functioning. Overall, these data
demonstrate the importance of measuring not just personal beliefs but the personal meaning of those beliefs as well.
Journal of Psychology & Theology. 1992 Win Vol 20(4) 376-388

[215]
Watson, P. J.; Morris, Ronald J.; Hood, Ralph W., Jr.; Milliron, J. Trevor; Stutz, Nancy L.

Religious orientation, identity and the quest for meaning in ethics within an ideological
surround.
Controversies in the religious orientation literature may reflect the unavoidable influences
of ideology in research of the psychology of religion. Support for this possibility was
observed when religious intrinsicness was associated with the idealism and antirelativism of
an absolutist ethical position. Quest Scales given to 679 Ss (mean age 19.96 yrs) were
incompatible with this absolutist search for meaning in ethics. Quest Scales also predicted
identity confusion, were associated with a disinterest in religion, and included items that
were evaluated as antireligious by individuals with an intrinsic religious commitment. In
short, intrinsicness defined an idealistic and antirelativistic religious identity, whereas Quest
pointed toward other ethical and antireligious ideologies that were more vulnerable to identity confusion. Overall, these data confirmed once again that ideological factors may play a
crucial role in the contemporary social scientific study of religion.
International Journal for the Psychology of Religion. 1998 Vol 8(3) 149-164

[216]
Weinstein, Lawrence; Cleanthous, Charalambos C.

A comparison of protestant ministers and parishioners on expressed purpose in life and
intrinsic religious motivation.
11 Protestant ministers (aged 32-52 yrs) and 38 parishioners (aged 28-90 yrs) completed
the Purpose in Life Test and the Hoge Test of Degree and Type of Religion. Ministers scored
higher than did their parishioners, which suggests that the ministers had found meaning in
their lives through their religious beliefs, while parishioners were still searching for such

meaning. Results suggest that as expressed intrinsic religious motivation increases, so does meaning in life, which supports V. E. Frankl's (1975) contention that a mature involvement with a religious group increases purpose in life.

Psychology: A Journal of Human Behavior. 1996 Vol 33(1) 26-29

[217]
Weinstein, Lawrence; de Man, Anton; Almaguer, Linda

Purpose in life as a function of religious versus secular beliefs.
Scores of 20 Catholic and 25 Mennonite undergraduates on the Purpose in Life Test were not significantly different. When scores of Mennonites were compared with previously obtained   scores of Dominican Sisters, Protestants, Recent Converts, and Seculars, the Mennonites' scores indicated significantly less meaning in life than each of the other groups. There was a significant difference between the Dominican Sisters and the Catholics. Findings are discussed in terms of the contention that religious belief strengthens the conviction to live a full and meaningful life.

Perceptual & Motor Skills. 1988 Aug Vol 67(1) 335-337

[218]
Wright, Loyd S.; Frost, Christopher J.; Wisecarver, Stephen J.

Church attendance, meaningfulness of religion, and depressive symptomatology among adolescents.
Self-administered questionnaires were completed by 208 male and 243 female 9th-12th graders. The instrument used contained the Beck Depression Inventory (BDI) and items to determine the participant's gender, frequency of church attendance, and meaningfulness of one's religion. Based on social support research and the writings of Jung (1932, 1933) and V. Frankl (1959), it was predicted that those who attended church frequently and those who viewed their religions as providing meaning for their lives would have lower BDI scores than their classmates. The findings supported these predictions.

Journal of Youth & Adolescence. 1993 Oct Vol 22(5) 559-568

[219]
Zainuddin, Roquiya

A factor-analytic study of spirituality.
Explored the factors of spirituality using the 9-dimensional test of spirituality developed by D. N. Elkins et al (1988) with 219 Ss (aged 24-60 yrs). The 9 dimensions of spirituality, namely, Transcendence, Meaning and purpose in life, Mission in life, Sacredness of life, Material values, Altruism, Idealism, Awareness of the tragic, and Fruits of spirituality, were found to cluster around 2 factors: the value dimension and the experiential dimension of spirituality.

Indian Journal of Clinical Psychology. 1993 Sep Vol 20(2) 88-92

Meaning in Suffering:
The Homo Patiens

Chronic Diseases and Disabilities

[220]
Acklin, Marvin W.; Brown, Earl C.; Mauger, Paul A.

The role of religious values in coping with cancer.
Tested the hypothesis that religious intrinsic values and perceptions of the meaningfulness
of life would enhance coping and well-being during the course of a life-threatening illness.
Data from 26 20-76 yr old cancer patients and 18 18-61 yr old noncancer medical patients
show that higher levels of attributed life meaning were positively related to intrinsic religious orientation and negatively related to despair, anger-hostility, and social isolation in the
cancer patients. Data from the noncancer patients were characterized by positive correlations between transcendent meaning, religious orientation, and denial. Perceived life threat
as a differentiating variable of the 2 groups is discussed.
Journal of Religion & Health. 1983 Win Vol 22(4) 322-333

[221]
Anderson, S.; Elizabeth H.

Personality, appraisal, and adaptational outcomes in HIV seropositive men and women.
A cross-sectional exploratory design was used to assess the relationships of personality, SES,
and appraisal with functional and emotional outcomes in 77 men and 50 women with HIV
infection. Multiple regression analysis showed that, among men, SES moderated the negative relationship between self-esteem and disruption in usual activities. Consistent with R.
Lazarus and S. Folkman's (1984) cognitive theory of stress, appraisal of HIV threat mediated the negative relationship between self-esteem and mood disturbance for men and
women, and the positive relationship between self-esteem and purpose in life for women.
Appraisal did not mediate between personality variables and disruption in usual activities or
life satisfaction for men or women.
Research in Nursing & Health. 1995 Aug Vol 18(4) 303-312

[222]
Bechtel, G.A.

Purpose in life among gay men with HIV disease.
Positive purpose in life (PIL) has been shown to influence health maintenance, facilitate
recovery from illness, and enhance psychological well-being. Among persons diagnosed
with human immunodeficiency virus (HIV) disease, PIL has received minimal attention.
This study used a convenience sample of 67 men who had a diagnosis of acquired immunodeficiency syndrome (AIDS) or who participated in high-risk sexual behavior associated

with HIV disease to measure PIL. Integrating qualitative data into the final analysis contributed to a greater understanding of PIL among persons with HIV disease and those at high risk for the disease. Results of the study demonstrated a significantly lower PIL score for men with AIDS. PIL scores were negatively correlated with religious beliefs for the group, and these scores were not influenced by the interval since the AIDS diagnosis. Men with HIV disease are often isolated and withdrawn from society and appear to lack clear meaning for existence.

Nursingconnections. 1994 Winter;7(4):5-11. *

[223]
Bowes, Denise E.; Tamlyn, Deborah; Butler, Lorna J.

Women living with ovarian cancer: Dealing with an early death.
The authors' intent to explore the emotion of anger in women living with ovarian cancer revealed a basic social concern of "dealing with an early death." The findings of this grounded theory study also identified the core variable of "finding meaning in life" as assisting the 9 female Ss (aged 36-70 yrs) in dealing with an early death. The categories of hope and physical wellness influenced the women's search for meaning after a diagnosis of ovarian cancer. Several action and interactional coping strategies were identified as positive coping behaviors. The consequences of finding meaning in life was a perception of well-being defined by the women as satisfaction with their lives. Conversely, an inability to find meaning in life resulted in feelings of despair. The women's perceptions of well-being were not static and could fluctuate as they lived with ovarian cancer. Implications for further research and practice are discussed.

Health Care for Women International. 2002 Mar Vol 23(2) 135-148

[cf. 166]
Brennan, Mark

Spirituality and psychosocial development in middle-age and older adults with vision loss.
Journal of Adult Development. 2002 Jan Vol 9(1) 31-46

[cf. 285]
Cheng Lai, Alice; Salili, Farideh

Stress and social support in parents whose children are hepatitis B virus (HBV) carriers: A comparison of three groups in Guangzhou.
International Journal of Psychology. 1997 Vol 32(1) 43-55

[224]
Christ, Grace H.; Siegel, Karolynn; Sperber, Diane

Impact of parental terminal cancer on adolescents.
Describes psychological and emotional concerns of 120 adolescents (aged 11-17 yrs) during a parent's terminal cancer. Compared to younger children, the adolescents' greater cognitive and empathic capacities allowed them to be more aware of losses and of the parent's physical and emotional pain. Parental illness also precipitated conflict around issues of developmentally appropriate separation. Problems and concerns that characterized adolescents' reactions to a parent's deteriorating condition included empathy for the parent's suf-

fering and guilt. The capacity to use intellectual defenses, search for meaning and deeper understanding, and seek help were potent coping abilities. Contrary to the prevailing view, most of the adolescents coped with stress without resorting to severe acting out.

American Journal of Orthopsychiatry. 1994 Oct Vol 64(4) 604-613

[cf. 595]
Coward, Doris D.

Self-transcendence and emotional well-being in women with advanced breast cancer.

Oncological Nursing Forum. 1991 Jul;18(5):857-63*

[cf. 596]
Coward, Doris D.

Meaning and purpose in the lives of persons with AIDS.

Public Health Nursing. 1994 Oct;11(5):331-6*

[225]
Deeks A.A.; McCabe M.P.

Well-being and menopause: an investigation of purpose in life, self-acceptance and social role in premenopausal, perimenopausal and postmenopausal women.
OBJECTIVES: Many studies have investigated anxiety and depression during the menopausal transition. However, there is little understanding of positive aspects of well-being among menopausal women. This paper reports on two studies which investigated how menopausal stage and age accounted for how women felt about their purpose in life, self-acceptance and social role. METHOD: In Study One, 304 women from a community sample completed structured questionnaires which included questions relating to demographic background and two subscales of the Psychological Well-being Inventory: purpose in life and self-acceptance. In Study Two, 203 participants from Study One returned a follow-up structured questionnaire related to purpose in life and social role. RESULTS: Study One found that the effects of age group and menopausal group could not be separated: All women felt they would be more positive about these well-being measures in the future than they had been in the past and at present. Study Two found that women who were perimenopausal and postmenopausal did not feel as positive about their role/s in life as premenopausal women, regardless of their age. CONCLUSIONS: The results suggest that the menopause may indicate to women that their role/purpose in life is changing. It is important that any understanding of the menopause incorporate psychosocial aspects of women's lives. Further longitudinal studies are needed to explore well-being factors and the menopause.

Quality of Life Research: An International Journal of Quality of Life Aspects of Treatment, Care & Rehabilitation. 2004 Mar;13(2):389-98.*

[226]
Devi; Radha

Vocational rehabilitation: Purpose-in-life, need achievement and security.
Studied 30 vocationally rehabilitated orthopedically handicapped persons (OHPs) and 30 nonrehabilitated OHPs matched for age, sex, nature of handicap, and socioeconomic status

(SES) in relation to their purpose in life, need for achievement, and security-insecurity feelings. Vocationally rehabilitated OHPs had significantly more purpose in life than nonrehabilitated OHPs; no significant differences were found between the groups on the other 2 factors.

Indian Journal of Applied Psychology. 1985 Jan-Jul Vol 22(1-2) 53-56

[227]
Elmberger, Eva; Bolund, Christina; Luetzen, Kim

Transforming the exhausting to energizing process of being a good parent in the face of cancer.
Examined the balancing of disease and parenting issues by females who have been treated for breast cancer. Nine females (aged 38-50 yrs) with children (aged 4-23 yrs) living at home at time of diagnosis completed interviews. Six Ss were single and primarily responsible for the care of their children. The main emerging theme of Ss' experiences was transforming the exhausting to energizing process in being a good parent in the face of cancer. Other issues included facing the reality of cancer, finding meaning in life, and recognizing the need for information and support. Dealing with children's reactions seemed to be most difficult for single mothers. Findings suggest a need for family counseling in this type of situation, with special attention paid to the single parent with cancer.

Health Care for Women International. 2000 Sep Vol 21(6) 485-499

[228]
Erlen, Judith A.; Mellors, Mary Pat; Sereika, Susan M.; Cook, Christa

The use of life review to enhance quality of life of people living with AIDS: A feasibility study.
Explored the use of life review in a sample of 20 people living with AIDS (PLWA) through a randomized controlled trial of its effectiveness in decreasing depressive symptoms and in increasing self esteem, quality of life, and purpose in life. Compared to the control group, the treatment group (80% male, mean age 43.7 yrs) had an improved overall quality of life and self-esteem over 12 mo, less depressive symptoms over 12 mo, and a greater purpose in life at 3 mo. The effects that were seen were mainly small to medium effects. The findings from this feasibility study suggest the potential value of life review to enhance quality of life, purpose in life, and self-esteem, and to decrease depressive symptoms in PLWA. Further research is needed with a larger sample and with other groups such as PLWA experiencing virologic failure.

*Quality of Life Research: An International Journal of Quality of Life Aspects of Treatment,
Care & Rehabilitation. 2001 Vol 10(5) 453-464*

[229]
Fife, Betsy L.

The measurement of meaning in illness.
Presents a scale that operationalizes the concept of meaning as it is constructed within the context of life-threatening illness. Development of the scale is based on a symbolic interactionist perspective. The Constructed Meaning Scale consists of 8 statements that refer to the impact of the illness on the individual's sense of identity, interpersonal relationships, and the individual's sense of what the future holds. The reliability and validity of the scale were examined with 422 persons with a variety of types of cancer at various points during the

disease. Results showed empirical evidence of the scale's reliability and validity. Meaning was found to be predicted by social support and specific coping strategies and to be predictive of personal control, body image, and psychological adjustment.

Social Science & Medicine. 1995 Apr Vol 40(8) 1021-1028

[230]
Giorgi, Bruno

The Belfast Test: A new psychometric approach to logotherapy.
Discusses the Belfast Test, a 20-item questionnaire designed to measure Ss' difficulty in finding meaning to circumstances beyond their control (e.g., death, disease) and in actualizing creative values to overcome problems such as war and discrimination. Discussion focuses on the relation of this measure to the logotherapeutic perspectives on existential frustration and alienation and to other instruments designed to measure the degree to which an individual experiences a sense of meaning and purpose in life.

International Forum for Logotherapy. 1982 Spr-Sum Vol 5(1) 31-37

[231]
Hall, Beverly A.

Ways of maintaining hope in HIV disease.
Examined the experiences and hopes of 8 males and 2 females (aged 28-39 yrs) in Clinical Category C (AIDS), Stage IV of HIV disease, utilizing N. Denzin's 1989 interpretative interactionism. Ss were interviewed from 1 to 3 times for 45 min to 2 hrs. Interviews and analysis revealed interpretations of the illness and how Ss maintained hope while coping with end-stage HIV; segments of actual interviews are presented. Results indicated that hope was maintained by beliefs in miracles, religion, involvement in work or vocations, and support of family and friends. Miracles could be either religious, physical, or medical; religion served as a vehicle to better understanding and acceptance of the impending death. Work or vocation served as a force to keep the Ss going, as did family and friend support which also served as a major force for spirituality and hope. Many Ss tried to find personal meaning and perspective in the suffering.

Research in Nursing & Health. 1994 Aug Vol 17(4) 283-293

[232]
Henrion, Rosemary

PIL Test on cancer patients: Preliminary report.
Administered the Purpose-In-Life (PIL) Test to 10 male cancer patients (aged 50-75 yrs) whose disease was in remission. Most Ss indicated that they were taking life 1 day at a time, and their scores indicated a lack of clear purpose in life. The author recommends the integration of E. Kubler-Ross's (1969) 5 stages of grief with logotherapeutic principles in treating cancer patients who lack meaning in their lives. This integration may help patients find meaning while they are suffering.

International Forum for Logotherapy. 1983 Spr-Sum Vol 6(1) 55-59

[233]
Meier, H.

Meaning and Illness
Examined the meaning fulfilment and the experience of hope in 11 chronically ill patients. Patients with high personal meaning scores had significantly heightened coping resources and tended to be less depressed.

Krankenbetreuung. 1982 July. Vol 10 (2) 32-34

[234]
Hoen, Beth; Thelander, Mary; Worsley, Jill

Improvement in psychological well-being of people with aphasia and their families: Evaluation of a community-based programme.
The York-Durham Aphasia Centre, a community-based program for people with aphasia and their families, offers long-term support and service at any time post-stroke or head injury. The current study assessed improvement in psychosocial well-being in the clients and their family members as a measure of program effectiveness. 35 clients (31-90 yrs old) were administered Ryff's Psychological Well-Being Scale twice, 6 mo apart. Time post-stroke ranged from 1 to more than 20 yrs. 12 family members also self-administered the scale twice. Results show that aphasic clients were able to complete the scale with little difficulty. Both clients and family members showed positive change in 5 of 6 dimensions of psychological well-being (e.g., self-acceptance, purpose in life, personal growth). This improvement in both groups may be related to the direct attention the program gives to psychosocial well-being and communication, the overall environment of the center, and the test administration itself. The positive change in these aphasic clients suggests that improvement in psychological well-being is possible regardless of time post-stroke and age.

Aphasiology. 1997 Jul Vol 11 (7) 681-691

[235]
Jahoda, Andrew; Cattermole, Martin

Activities of people with moderate to severe learning difficulties: Living with purpose or just killing time?
Examined the activities of residents living in hospitals and hostels. 12 people with moderate to severe learning difficulties living in hospitals and 12 people living in community based hostels were compared through observations. The findings demonstrate that the participants played an active part in determining their own lifestyles. A number of more active hospital participants dealt with the unstimulating functional regime by attempting to create a social niche for themselves. A number of less active participants coped with the hospital environment by withdrawing into themselves and engaging in stereotypical behavior to mark the passing of time. The participants in the hostel tended to occupy a peripheral status as the least able people in the hostels and day centers. They often had to seek staff support for activity or turned inwards.

Disability & Society. 1995 Jun Vol 10(2) 203-219

[236]
Jirapaet, Veena

Factors affecting maternal role attainment among low-income, Thai, HIV-positive mothers.
This phenomenological study used content analysis of interview data to explore factors affecting maternal role attainment in a convenience sample of 39 low-income, Thai, HIV-positive mothers (aged 18-40 yrs) selected for their successful adaptation. All mothers reported feeling comfortable in their maternal roles and achieved greater than 80% of the total score on the Maternal Behavioral Questionnaire. In-depth interviews were conducted regarding the life experience of the mothers. Results reveal the mothers' uses of internal and external resources to attain their maternal roles. Six factors were identified: (1) setting a purpose for life, that is, to raise the infant; (2) keeping secrets from others; (3) a feeling of normalization; (4) having good quality of support from others; (5) having hope for an HIV cure; and (6) receiving accessible, pleasant health services that protect anonymity regarding HIV status. Results suggest that nurses can promote maternal role attainment by supporting the mothers' management style.
Journal of Transcultural Nursing. 2001 Jan Vol 12(1) 25-33

[237]
Kaczorowski, Jane M.

Spiritual well-being and anxiety in adults diagnosed with cancer.
Measured the relationship between spiritual well-being (SWB) and state-trait anxiety (STA) in 144 adults diagnosed with cancer. Ss completed the State-Trait Anxiety Inventory and a spiritual well-being scale by R. F. Paloutzian and C. W. Ellison (1982). There was a consistent inverse relationship between SWB and STA, regardless of gender, age, marital status, diagnosis, group participation, and length of time since diagnosis. In some Ss, meaning and purpose in life was more closely related to anxiety than was a relationship with a higher being.
Hospice Journal. 1989 Vol 5(3-4) 105-116

[238]
Kass, Jared D.; Friedman, Richard; Leserman, Jane; Caudill, Margaret; et al

An inventory of positive psychological attitudes with potential relevance to health outcomes: Validation and preliminary testing.
Describes the validation of the Inventory of Positive Psychological Attitudes that has potential relevance to health outcomes and its preliminary testing wih chronic pain patients. The inventory taps 2 attitudinal domains: (1) life purpose and satisfaction and (2) self-confidence during potentially stressful situations. It also provides a total score. The inventory scales, developed using factor analysis in 2 studies involving 372 adult outpatients and 312 university students, were found to have a strong degree of internal reliability and concurrent validity. Preliminary testing with 228 outpatients suggested that positive change on these scales correlated with positive changes in the health status of chronic pain patients.
Behavioral Medicine. 1991 Fal Vol 17(3) 121-129

[239]
Khatami, Manoochehr

Logotherapy for chronic pain.
Describes a 1-yr follow-up study of 23 adults who had participated in a multimodal treatment program for chronic pain. Significant decreases in pain, depression, anxiety, somati-
zation, hostility, and analgesic ingestion were found without symptom substitution at 1 yr
for full completers of the program, while partial completers showed significant reductions
in only pain and depression.
International Forum for Logotherapy. 1987 Fal-Win Vol 10(2) 85-91

[240]
King, Gillian; Cathers, Tamzin; Brown, Elizabeth; Specht, Jacqueline A.; Willoughby,
Colleen; Polgar, Janice Miller; MacKinnon, Elizabeth; Smith, Linda K.; Havens, Lisa

Turning points and protective processes in the lives of people with chronic disabilities.
In this qualitative study, the authors examined the nature of resilience in people with chronic disabilities. 15 people with disabilities (aged 30-50 yrs) identified the factors that helped
or hindered them at major turning points, and the triggers and resolutions to these turning
points. Turning points were emotionally compelling experiences and realizations that
involved meaning acquired through the routes of belonging, doing, or understanding the
self or the world. The major protective factors were social support, traits such as perseverance and determination, and spiritual beliefs. Three new protective processes were identified: replacing a loss with a gain (transcending), recognizing new things about oneself (self-
understanding), and making decisions about relinquishing something in life (accommodat-
ing). These protective factors, processes, and ways in which people with disabilities draw
sense and meaning in life have important implications for service delivery.
Qualitative Health Research. 2003 Feb Vol 13(2) 184-206

[241]
Landis, B. J.

Uncertainty, spiritual well-being, and psychosocial adjustment to chronic illness.
Assessed spiritual well-being (SW-B) as an internal coping resource to buffer the effects of
uncertainty on psychosocial adjustment among 94 persons (aged 21-65 yrs) with diabetes
mellitus. Ss completed the Mishel Uncertainty in Illness Scale, Community Form; the
Spiritual Well-Being Scale; the Psychosocial Adjustment to Illness Scale; and the Participant
Survey. Findings indicate that uncertainty has a strong relationship with psychosocial
adjustment. A strong significant relationship was also found between SW-B and psychosocial adjustment; as SW-B increased, problems related to living with a chronic illness
decreased. Furthermore, SW-B had a significant inverse relationship with uncertainty, indicating that uncertainty decreased when SW-B increased. Findings suggest that SW-B may
be an important internal resource for persons forced to adjust to uncertainty related to long-
term health problems such as diabetes mellitus.
Issues in Mental Health Nursing. 1996 May-Jun Vol 17(3) 217-231

[cf. 294]
Li Cheng, Alice; Ma, Cui; Zheng, Hongbo

Preschool hepatitis B children and parenting stress: A comparison of three groups of parents in Guangzhou, China.
Chinese Mental Health Journal. 1994 Oct Vol 8(5) 213-216

[242]
Liu, S.J.

The construction and evaluation of the reliability and validity of a life attitude scale for elderly with chronic disease.
The elderly with chronic diseases face numerous impacts which influence their life attitudes. The purpose of this study was to construct, and evaluate the reliability and validity of a life attitude scale for elderly with chronic disease. Initially, the 27 items of the Life Attitude Scale were constructed by in depth interview of 48 elderly with chronic diseases. Then, the construct validity was established by factor analysis with 663 samples. Six factors: Congeniality of Family Life, Life Meaning, Dignity of Life, Struggle with Adversities, Hollow Existence, and Destiny to Life, which included 20 items, explained 59.7% of total variances. Content validity was found to be well established by 6 experts. Correlation of inter-rater reliability among 6 data collectors was 0.96. Cronbach's alpha of internal consistency was above 0.89 for 148 samples. Correlation of test-retest reliability was above 0.87 for 37 samples with 2-week interval. This study presents what the Taiwan elderly with chronic diseases are undergoing and their views on life and its value. There are highly culture-based and philosophy-based knowing about life attitude of elderly with chronic disease in Taiwan, and it is imperative to inspire nurses to promote the quality of spiritual care for elderly with chronic disease.
Journal of Nursing Research. 2001 Jun;9(3):33-42

[243]
Lo, Shih-lin

The effects of coping with "uncontrollable situation" on life attitude. A comparison of people with and without disabilities.
Compared ways of coping with uncontrollable life situations, and the relationship between coping style and attitude toward life in people with and without disabilities. Ss were 147 physically disabled children, adolescents, and adults (aged 10 and older) and 194 194 normal children, adolescents, and adults (aged 10 and older). Ss were administered a questionnaire on their attitudes toward life and were asked to complete stories about how a disabled person and an elderly person coped with living alone. Factor analysis was performed. The Life Attitude Profile and the Hopelessness Scale (A. T. Beck et al, 1974) were used.
Journal of Educational Psychology. 1993 Sep Vol 41(3) 284-292

[244]
Lyon, Debra E.; Younger, Janet B.

Purpose in life and depressive symptoms in persons living with HIV disease.
Examined relationships among purpose in life, HIV disease severity, demographic variables and depressive symptoms in people living with HIV disease. Ss were 123 adults (mean age

37 yrs) recruited from an urban infectious disease clinic. Ss completed a self-administered questionnaire, including a sociodemographic tool, the Center for Epidemiologic Studies Depression Scale and the Purpose in Life Scale. Concurrent severity of HIV disease measures included HIV RNA viral load, CD4+ T-lymphocyte count, and the Revised HIV Medical Symptom Scale. Results show that depressive symptoms were greater and purpose in life was lower for the HIV patients than for normative samples. Purpose in life was a stronger predictor of depressive symptoms than was HIV disease severity. It is concluded that since purpose in life was more important than laboratory markers of disease progression for predicting depressive co-morbidity, there is a need for routine assessment of depressive symptoms in people living with HIV.

Journal of Nursing Scholarship. 2001 Vol 33(2) 129-133

[245]
Mansell, Jim; Elliott, Teresa; Beadle-Brown, Julie; Ashman, Bev; Macdonald, Susan

Engagement in meaningful activity and "active support" of people with intellectual disabilities in residential care.
Forty-nine adults with learning disabilities living in 13 small staffed homes in England were studied as part of larger projects in 1997 and again in 2000. A pre-test/post-test comparison group design was used to assess differences in staff implementation of "active support," service user engagement in meaningful activities and adaptive behaviour. Homes which adopted active support showed significantly increased engagement in meaningful activity and adaptive behaviour between 1997 and 2000. A comparison group showed no significant change.

Research in Developmental Disabilities. 2002 Sep-Oct Vol 23(5) 342-352

[246]
Mayers, Aviva M.; Khoo, Siek-Toon; Svartberg, Martin

The Existential Loneliness Questionnaire: Background, development, and preliminary findings.
Describes the background and development of a new measure of existential loneliness, the Existential Loneliness Questionnaire (ELQ). Specifically, the authors analyzed the items of the preliminary version of the ELQ (ELQ-P) using methods based on item response theory (the Rasch model) and examined the convergent and discriminative validity of the ELQ in a sample of 47 HIV-infected women (aged 22-48 yrs). Item analysis produced an ELQ version consisting of 22 items that were internally consistent and performed well in measuring an underlying construct conceptualized as existential loneliness. In addition, the ELQ discriminated well between symptomatic and asymptomatic HIV-infected women. The ELQ correlated strongly with measures of depression, loneliness not identified as existential and purpose-in-life and moderately strongly with a measure of hopelessness. Holding constant depression scores, the correlation between the ELQ and loneliness not identified as existential was significantly attenuated. Limitations of the study include the small sample size, which precluded an analysis of the dimensional structure of the ELQ.

Journal of Clinical Psychology. 2002 Sep Vol 58(9) 1183-1193

[247]
McFadden, Susan H.; Ingram, Mandy; Baldauf, Carla

Actions, feelings, and values: Foundations of meaning and personhood in dementia.
V. Frankl's (e.g., 1984) writings on the sources of meaning in human life are compared to emergent views on personhood in older individuals with dementing illnesses. An ethnomethodological study of a community based residential facility (CBRF) with two sections, each housing about 10 persons, revealed meaning in residents' actions, feelings, and expressions of values. These individuals showed it is possible to retain what Frankl called "tragic optimism" despite cognitive deterioration. Through active engagement with their environments and with one another, a wide range of expressed emotions including happiness and humor, and caring sensitivity toward others, these elders showed that given a supportive environment, dementia does not destroy meaning. These observations form the basis of suggestions for pastoral care and ministry with people with dementia.
Journal of Religious Gerontology. 2000 Vol 11(3-4) 67-86

[248]
Mellors, Mary Pat; Erlen, Judith A.; Coontz, Phyllis D.; Lucke, Kathleen T.

Transcending the suffering of AIDS.
Examined how patients with AIDS (PWAs) transcend the emotional and physical suffering of their illness. Content analysis of the interviews of 5 PWAs (aged 39-54 yrs) resulted in 3 main themes: creating a meaningful life pattern, connectedness, and self-care. The results of this study provide presumptive evidence that PWAs can transcend the suffering associated with a life-threatening illness and live meaningful and productive lives. Nurses who anticipate actual and potential growth in PWAs will be able to validate such experiences and feelings and encourage further development.
Journal of Community Health Nursing. 2001 Dec Vol 18(4) 235-246

[249]
Moadel, Alyson; Morgan, Carole; Fatone, Anne; Grennan, Jennifer; Carter, Jeanne; Laruffa, Gia; Skummy, Anne; Dutcher, Janice

Seeking meaning and hope: Self-reported spiritual and existential needs among an ethnically-diverse cancer patient population.
Using a self-report needs assessment survey, the present study examined the nature and prevalence of spiritual and existential needs reported by 248 ethnically diverse, urban cancer patients (aged 18-85 yrs), and the association between spiritual existential needs and sociocultural, demographic, and medical characteristics. Results show that patients wanted help in overcoming fears, finding hope, talking about peace of mind, finding meaning in life and spiritual resources, as well as someone to talk to about the meaning of life and death. The greatest need for spiritual existential support was seen among non-college educated Hispanic patients, and the least need for spiritual support was seen among White patients. Patients lacking a significant partner were shown to have greater needs, and proximity to diagnosis was related to greater spiritual existential needs also. Implications for the development and delivery of spiritual existential interventions in a multi-ethnic oncology setting are discussed.
Psycho-Oncology. 1999 Sep-Oct Vol 8(5) 378-385

[250]
Mohr, David C.; Dick, Leah P.; Russo, David; Pinn, Jodi; Boudewyn, Arne C.; Likosky, William; Goodkin, Donald E.

The psychosocial impact of multiple sclerosis: Exploring the patient's perspective.
This study examined subjective patient experiences of the psychosocial consequences of multiple sclerosis (MS). Fifty patients were interviewed regarding the effects MS had on their lives and interpersonal relationships. These statements were collated and administered with a 5-point Likert scale to 94 MS patients. The responses were subjected to factor analysis. Three areas of subjective patient experience of the psychosocial consequences of MS emerged: demoralization, benefit-finding, and deteriorated relationships. Of particular interest was benefit-finding, which included a deepening of relationships, enhanced appreciation of life, and an increase in spiritual interests. Although benefit-finding was related to adaptive coping strategies such as positive reappraisal and seeking social support, it was unrelated to depression and was related to higher levels of anxiety and anger. These findings indicate that benefit-finding is a substantial and poorly understood part of the illness experience for MS patients.

Health Psychology. 1999 Jul Vol 18(4) 376-382

[251]
Nagata, K.

A study of logotherapy for chronic low back pain patients
DHEA-S (dehydroepiandrosterone sulfate) has many roles in human body as comprehensive vital power, whose metabolite is urine 17-KS-S (abbreviated S), having function of anti-cortisol. The metabolite of cortisol is urine 17-OHCS (abbreviated OH). DHEA-S is produced not only in adrenal glands but in brain. In order to examine the effects of logotherapy, urine S and OH were examined. Subjects were chronic low back pain patients treated by loxoprofen sodium (NSAID). In Group 1 (n = 11) logotherapy was not added, but in Group 2 (n = 10) it was added. Before the treatment, both groups showed low S and high OH. After 3 weeks, Group 2 showed higher S and lower OH than Group 1. After 18 weeks, 4 cases (40%) were relapsed in Group 2, and 10 (90.9%) were in Group 1 (p < 0.05). Group 2 was divided into 2 groups; relapsed group (n = 4) and non-relapsed group (n = 6). S, OH, S/OH were examined between 2 groups of Group 2 and Group 1. Relapsed group of Group 2 and Group 1 showed lower S and higher OH than non-relapsed group of Group 2. [Discussion] Logotherapy is a method to activate comprehensive human vital power. This is the mechanism through stimulating and activating human brain function.

Seishin Shinkeigaku Zasshi. 2003;105(4):459-67.*

[252]
Nekolaichuk, Cheryl L.; Jevne, Ronna F.; Maguire, Thomas O.

Structuring the meaning of hope in health and illness.
Describes a conceptual model for hope that captures the personal meaning of this construct within the context of health and illness. A research tool was created based on the semantic differential technique. This questionnaire was distributed to a sample of 550 people, consisting of a healthy adult subsample of 146 Ss, a subsample of 159 Ss with chronic and life-threatening illness, and a subsample of 206 nurses. 39 Ss were not classified within these 3 subsamples, dut to missing data or ineligible subsample criteria. The Ss ranged in age from

18-84 yrs. A multidimensional structure for the concept, Hope, was identified using principal components analysis. Three primary factors defined this structure: personal spirit (personal dimension), risk (situational dimension), and authentic caring (interpersonal dimension). Personal spirit, a dominant factor, is characterized by a holistic configuration of hope elements, revolving around a core theme of meaning. Risk is primarily a predictability factor, targeted with an underlying component of boldness. The authentic caring factor has a substantial credibility component, linked with the theme of comfort. This integrative model deepens our understanding of the experience of hope within health and illness at the theoretical, clinical, and methodological levels.

Social Science & Medicine. 1999 Mar Vol 48(5) 591-605

[253]
Nelson, Jenenne P.

Struggling to gain meaning: Living with the uncertainty of breast cancer.
Explored the uncertainty experiences of 9 women (aged 38-69 yrs) with breast cancer. Hermeneutic phenomenology and photographic hermeneutics were used to study uncertainty in the breast cancer trajectory in the Ss between 2-6 yrs posttreatment for breast cancer. Five themes of uncertainty were uncovered. Living with the vicissitude of emotions of uncertainty was a powerful aspect of uncertainty. The presence of support during uncertainty influenced the Ss' perceptions and interpretations. Uncertainty challenged the Ss to learn new ways of being in the world. Reflection of self in the world had a powerful effect on the Ss' uncertainty experiences. To deal with the uncertainty, the Ss had to understand their disease and put it into a broader and meaningful life perspective. Implications for nursing theory and practice are provided.

Advances in Nursing Science. 1996 Mar Vol 18(3) 59-76

[254]
Northouse, Peter G.; Northouse, Laurel L.

Communication and cancer: Issues confronting patients, health professionals, and family members.
Reviews the literature (over 200 clinical papers and research studies) published between 1966 and 1986 that focuses on communication dimensions of the cancer experience. The review analyzes communication issues from 3 perspectives: the patient, the health professional, and the family. The literature indicates that the major communication issues for patients are related to maintaining a sense of control, seeking information, disclosing feelings, and searching for meaning. For health professionals, the primary communication issues center on imparting information, communicating hope, and sharing control. Major issues facing family members pertain to the concealment of feelings, acquiring information, and coping with helplessness. A methodological critique of the literature is also provided.

Journal of Psychosocial Oncology. 1987 Fal Vol 5(3) 17-46

[255]
O'Connor, Brian P.; Vallerand, Robert J.

Psychological adjustment variables as predictors of mortality among nursing home residents.
Mortality over a 4-year period was examined in relation to self-esteem, depression, life sat-

isfaction, and meaning in life in a nonclinical sample of 129 intermediate-care nursing home residents. Survival was associated with the psychological adjustment variables, and the effect persisted after statistically controlling for age, sex, and physical health. Self-evaluations (self-esteem and depression) were stronger predictors of mortality than were general life evaluations (life satisfaction and meaning in life). Comparisons with previous studies suggest conditions under which psychological variables are likely to be associated with mortality.

Psychology & Aging. 1998 Sep Vol 13(3) 368-374

[256]
Ota, Tomoko; Tanaka, Koji

Relation between the patient's quality of life (QOL) and social support.
Conducted 2 surveys to determine (1) the conditions of patients' quality of life (QOL) and (2) the relationship between QOL and social support. Human Ss: 35 male Japanese old adults (mean age 72.3 yrs) (prostate cancer) (outpatients) (Survey 1). 49 normal male Japanese old adults (mean age 72.9 yrs) (control group) (Survey 1). 17 Japanese old adults (mean age 79.4 yrs) (prostate cancer) (outpatients) (Survey 2). 23 male and female Japanese old adults (mean age 83.2 yrs) (institutionalized) (rehabilitation patients) (Survey 2). The role of family support in QOL was assessed in Survey 1, and the effect of lifestyle and self-esteem on QOL was assessed in Survey 2. Tests used: The State-Trait Anxiety Inventory, the Health Identity Test, the Purpose in Life Test, and a 10-item measure of self-esteem (S. Suga, 1984).

Journal of Health Psychology. 1997 Vol 10(1) 12-22

[257]
Parry, Carla

Embracing uncertainty: An exploration of the experiences of childhood cancer survivors.
Using in-depth qualitative interviews, the author explores the paradoxical meanings and impact of uncertainty in the lives of 23 long-term survivors (aged 17-29 yrs) of childhood cancer. The findings suggest that although uncertainty can be a source of distress, it can also be a catalyst for growth, a deepened appreciation for life, greater awareness of life purpose, development of confidence and resilience, and optimism. The results suggest that uncertainty is a dialectic phenomenon located within larger contexts of both stress and coping, and psychospiritual growth.

Qualitative Health Research. 2003 Feb Vol 13(2) 227-246

[258]
Pettipher, Charlotte; Mansell, Jim

Engagement in meaningful activity in day centres: An exploratory study.
Observational measures of client engagement and staff-client contact were taken of 33 clients attending a day center for adults with mental handicap. A low ability group (LAG) was engaged in constructive activity for 22%, a middle ability group (MAG) for 46%, and a high ability group (HAG) for 66% of the observations. In a 5-hr day, LAG Ss were engaged for 66 min, MAG Ss for 2 hrs 18 min, and HAG Ss for 3 hrs 18 min. The most common disengagement code for the HAG was "inactivity" and for the MAG and LAG

"waiting." Relationship between client ability group and engagement level was also found by A. G. Crisp and P. A. Sturmey.

Mental Handicap Research. 1993 Vol 6(3) 263-274

[259]
Plach, Sandra K.; Heidrich, Susan M.; Waite, Ruth M.

Relationship of social role quality to psychological well-being in women with rheumatoid arthritis.
Examined the mediating and moderating effects of women's social role quality on the psychological well-being of women with rheumatoid arthritis (RA). 156 women with a diagnosis of RA (aged 39-87 yrs) completed self-report measures of arthritis history, physical health, psychological well-being, and role quality. Hierarchical multiple regression analyses indicated that role quality mediated the effects of physical health on depression and purpose in life, moderated the effects of health on depression, and moderated the effects of pain on purpose in life. Women in poor health with high role quality were significantly less depressed than women in poor health with poor role quality. Women with high levels of pain and high role quality had more purpose in life than women with high levels of pain and low role quality. Despite difficulties with their physical health, women who had high role quality had higher levels of psychological well-being. Findings from this study may aid in the development of meaningful interventions to help women with RA manage their daily lives to optimize well-being.

Research in Nursing & Health. 2003 Jun Vol 26(3) 190-202

[260]
Plahuta, Janice M.; McCulloch, B. Jan; Kasarskis, Edward J.; Ross, Mark A.; Walter, Rhoda A.; McDonald, Evelyn R

Amyotrophic lateral sclerosis and hopelessness: Psychosocial factors.
Examined the relationship of psychosocial factors to the presence of hopelessness among patients with amyotrophic lateral sclerosis (ALS). 136 ALS patients (aged 26-83 yrs) completed interviews regarding the 4 psychosocial factors of health locus of control (HLC), purpose in life (PIL), satisfaction with social support, and the degree to which spiritual beliefs help a patient cope with illness. Results show that HLC and PIL were significant predictors of hopelessness among ALS patients. Other factors, including socioeconomic and demographic variables, variables measuring length and severity of illness, social support satisfaction, and degree to which spiritual beliefs help to cope with ALS were not significant predictors of hopelessness.

Social Science & Medicine. 2002 Dec Vol 55(12) 2131-2140

[cf. 612]
Salmon P, Manzi F, Valori RM.

Measuring the meaning of life for patients with incurable cancer: the life evaluation questionnaire (LEQ).

European Journal of Cancer. 1996 May;32A(5):755-60*

[261]
Schnoll, Robert A.; Knowles, James C.; Harlow, Lisa

Correlates of adjustment among cancer survivors.
Examined demographic, clinical, and psychosocial correlates of adjustment among a sample of cancer survivors (83 females and 26 males, mean age 60.3 yrs). Analyses concerning demographic and clinical variables indicated that being married, having a high income and level of education, and a positive perception of one's health was related to higher levels of adjustment; female survivors and survivors of breast cancer (versus prostate cancer) also reported higher levels of sexual adjustment. Analyses concerning psychosocial predictors of adjustment indicated that survivors who reported higher levels of social support, optimism, and meaning in life, and lower levels of avoidant-type coping exhibited better adjustment. A prediction model of adjustment indicated strong empirical support for a model depicting higher psychosocial adjustment as a function of higher levels of social support and meaning in life and lower levels of avoidant-type coping behaviors. Overall, the findings offer important information for understanding variables associated with adaptation to a cancer diagnosis and provide support for the usefulness of clinical services for survivors that provide social support, minimize the use of avoidant-type coping and help them attain a sense of meaning from their illness.
Journal of Psychosocial Oncology. 2002 Vol 20(1) 37-60

[262]
Schultz, Ronald C.

Purpose in life among spinal cord injured males.
Examined the relationship between spinal cord injury (SCI) and purpose in life as measured by a purpose in life (PIL) test. 54 males were involved in the study: 15 university students with SCIs, 19 nondisabled university students, and 20 nonstudents with SCIs at a Veterans Administration medical center. Comparisons between groups were generally nonsignificant, but lower scores were found for paraplegic individuals. In addition, religious conviction was found to be significantly related to PIL scores for Ss with SCIs.
Journal of Applied Rehabilitation Counseling. 1985 Sum Vol 16(2) 45-47, 51

[263]
Smith, Bruce W.; Zautra, Alex J.

Purpose in life and coping with knee-replacement surgery.
The study reported in this article examined the role of a sense of purpose in life in recovery from total knee-replacement surgery in 59 older people (mean age 67.3 yrs). Participants completed questionnaires two weeks before, four weeks after, and six months after surgery. Regression analyses predicted health at six months from purpose in life, controlling for initial health and age, education, and gender. The results revealed that purpose in life was directly related to better mental health and indirectly related, through active coping, to better physical health. The findings support the efforts of occupational therapists to increase purposeful habits of living.
Occupational Therapy Journal of Research. 2000 Fal Vol 20(Suppl1) 96S-99S

[264]
Starck, Patricia L.

Rehabilitative nursing and logotherapy: A study of spinal cord injured clients.
Administered the Purpose in Life Test (PILT) and the Noetic Goals Test to 25 spinal cord-injured (SCI) Ss to determine whether promoting successful coping behaviors enhance rehabilitation. Results indicate that SCI Ss were no different from the general population in feelings about meaning and purpose in life, although there were discrepancies between Ss' answers and observations made of Ss. There was a significant drop in PILT scores from pre- to posttesting for the control group. This may be because the PILT triggered reflective thinking and raised awareness about lack of meaning and purpose in life or because Ss gave false high scores on the pretest and more realistic scores posttest. Although there was no significant difference for the experimental group in pre- and posttest scores, nearly half the Ss showed a gain in scores over the study period. The use of logotherapy in rehabilitation nursing for clients with SCI is promising.
International Forum for Logotherapy. 1981 Fal-Win Vol 4(2) 101-109

[265]
Starck, Patricia L.

Patients' perceptions of the meaning of suffering.
99 26-86 yr old patients with physical or mental pathology were administered a test of meaning in suffering (MIST), a demographic profile, and a nurse-client interaction evaluation. It was assumed that (1) Ss' beliefs about suffering affected coping ability and adaptation, (2) suffering provided opportunities by which to achieve greater appreciation of life, (3) meaning was found in suffering by the sufferer, and (4) the nursing role included assisting sufferers in coping. The 3 most frequent diagnoses were psychiatric, cardiovascular, and gastrointestinal disturbances. Ss with cancer were more optimistic, while Ss with medical breathing problems perceived themselves as suffering more. Perception of suffering without meaning was greatest in Ss with psychiatric problems, whereas Ss undergoing surgery perceived their suffering as most meaningful. MIST results revealed that most Ss believed that suffering had meaning and that some good came from it. Assessment of nurse-client interactions showed that Ss had a positive attitude toward discussing their suffering experiences.
International Forum for Logotherapy. 1983 Fal-Win Vol 6(2) 110-116

[266]
Strang, Susan; Strang, Peter

Spiritual thoughts, coping and "sense of coherence" in brain tumour patients and their spouses.
When a person is diagnosed with a life-threatening disease, existential questions are easily triggered. The aims of this study were to explore to what extent brain tumour patients and their next of kin were able to cope, understand, and create meaning in their situation, to explore whether spirituality could be supportive, and to analyse whether these concepts are related to A. Antonovsky's concept of sense of coherence. 20 patients and 16 of their kin took part in interviews. A content and context analysis was performed using a hermeneutic approach. The authors found that comprehensibility was to a large extent constructed by the patient's own thoughts and theories, despite an insecure situation. Manageability was achieved by active information-seeking strategies, by social support and by coping.

Meaningfulness was central for quality of life and was created by close relations and faith, as well as by work. A crucial factor was whether the person had a 'fighting spirit' that motivated him or her to go on. Sense of coherence as a concept can explain how exposed persons handle their situation. In its construction, sence of coherence integrates essential parts of the stress coping model (comprehensibility, manageability) and of spirituality (meaning).

Palliative Medicine. 2001 Mar Vol 15(2) 127-134

[267]
Taylor, E.J.

Factors associated with meaning in life among people with recurrent cancer.
Attribution theory proposes that negative or unexpected events challenge one's sense of meaning. The purpose of this correlational, cross-sectional study was to determine what factors were associated with the sense of meaning in life among people with recurrent cancer. A convenience sample of 74 subjects completed six survey instruments, including the Purpose in Life (PIL) Test, Symptom Distress Scale, Enforced Social Dependency Scale, and Psychosocial Adjustment to Illness Scale, as well as two surveys developed by the author to assess aspects.of the search for meaning, and demographic and illness variables. Significant negative Pearson correlations were found between sense of meaning and the following variables: symptom distress, social dependency, and length of time since diagnosis of recurrence. Adjustment to illness was associated with a clear sense of meaning. Analysis of variance indicated that married subjects had significantly higher PIL Test scores than single subjects. In concert, these factors accounted for 38% of the variance in sense of meaning. These findings empirically demonstrate that the sense of meaning is integrally associated with the physical and psychosocial effects of illness and suggest that oncology nurses must understand how to care for those who search for meaning.

Oncological Nursing Forum. 1993 Oct;20(9):1399-405*

[268]
Tellez Vargas, Hector

**The meaning of life in paraplegic former policemen: A phenomenological approach.
(El sentido de la vida en ex-policias paraplejicos. Enfoque fenomenologico.)**
Studied perceived quality of life among paraplegic former policemen with service-related central nervous system (CNS) injuries caused by firearms. Human Ss: Nine male Colombian adults (aged 22-58 yrs) (medullar injury) (former policemen) (2 mo to 24 yrs in paraplegic state). Using V. Frankl's (e.g., 1965, 1978, 1982) existential framework, Ss' perceptions of quality of life were assessed via standardized testing using the Purpose of Life Test by J. C. Crumbaugh and L. T. Maholick (1968), a self-report measure, and a semistructured interview.

Revista Latinoamericana de Psicologia. 1991 Vol 23(3) 401-416

[269]
Thomas, James M.; Weiner, Elliot A.

Psychological differences among groups of critically ill hospitalized patients, noncritically ill hospitalized patients, and well controls.
Examined differences on 9 psychological measures among groups of 25 critically ill hospitalized patients, 25 noncritically ill hospitalized patients, and 25 normal well controls. The

instruments used were the Purpose in Life Test, the Fundamental Interpersonal Relations Orientation-Behavior test, and 2 listening measures on which eye-blink rates were recorded. 4 multivariate discriminate function analyses were performed to determine those variables that discriminated groups of Ss. The critically ill group expressed (a) more "purpose in life," (b) an increased need for affection and inclusion, (c) a decreased "wanted control" from others, and (d) an increased rate of eye blinks in response to disease-related material. The critically ill group appeared to be psychologically unique, since there was little difference between the results of the other 2 S groups.

Journal of Consulting & Clinical Psychology. 1974 Apr Vol. 42(2) 274-279

[270]
Thompson, Nancy J.; Coker, Jennifer; Krause, James S.; Henry, Else

Purpose in life as a mediator of adjustment after spinal cord injury.
Objective: Determine how purpose in life influences adjustment after spinal cord injury (SCI). Study Design: Cross-sectional survey with mediation analysis. Subjects: 1,391 adults with traumatic SCI 1 or more years prior. Main Outcome Measure: Ladder of Adjustment (N. M. Crewe & J. S. Krause, 1990). The Purpose in Life scale (PIL: .J. C. Crumbaugh, 1968), the Zuckerman-Kuhlman Personality Questionnaire (M. Zuckerman, D. M. Kuhlman, J. Joireman, P. Teta, & M. Kraft, 1993), and the Multidimensional Health Locus of Control scale (K. A. Wallston, B. S. Wallston, & .R. DeVellis, 1978) were assessed. Results: PIL mediated between most measures and adjustment. Conclusions: Logotherapy is effective in strengthening purpose in life. Its use with persons with SCI may improve their adjustment and quality of life.

Rehabilitation Psychology. 2003 May Vol 48(2) 100-108

[271]
Thompson, Suzanne C.

The search for meaning following a stroke.
Tested predictions from cognitive theories of adjustment to victimization in 40 stroke patients and 40 caregivers (aged 21-81 yrs). A substantial proportion of Ss reported searching for a cause, asking themselves "Why me?" and finding meaning in the event. Analysis revealed that finding meaning had the positive effects proposed by a cognitive approach. Concern with the selective incidence of the event was associated with poorer adjustment, but being able to identify a cause was related to more positive outcomes. Ss who held themselves responsible for the stroke were more poorly adjusted.

Basic & Applied Social Psychology. 1991 Mar Vol 12(1) 81-96

[272]
Tomich, Patricia L.; Helgeson, Vicki S.

Five years later: A cross-sectional comparison of breast cancer survivors with healthy women.
Examined the psychological well-being and general quality of life of breast cancer survivors 5 yrs following diagnosis. 164 females (aged 33-81 yrs) diagnosed with and surgically treated for Stage I, Stage II, or Stage III breast cancer 5 yrs previously completed an intervention consisting of peer group discussion, education, or both. Ss completed interviews concerning assumptions about the world and themselves, meaning in life, spirituality, and qual-

ity of life. Results show that Ss perceived the world as benevolent and just, and that finding purpose in life was important. Cancer survivor Ss viewed the world as significantly less controllable and more random than did healthy control Ss, but reported more benefit from their experience. Ss who were searching for meaning in life displayed poorer mental functioning, less positive affect, and more negative affect.

Psycho-Oncology. 2002 Mar-Apr Vol 11(2) 154-169

[273]
Vaughan, Susan M.; Kinnier, Richard T.

Psychological effects of a life review intervention for persons with HIV disease.
Evaluated a life review intervention for persons with HIV disease. 27 adults (aged 28-56 yrs) with HIV disease (16 had been diagnosed with AIDS) were randomly assigned to 1 of 3 conditions: a group life review intervention (n = 8), a traditional support group (n = 9), or a waiting list (n = 10). Using a pre-post design, Ss were compared on psychological measures of optimism, self-esteem, purpose in life, coping ability, psychological distress, and death anxiety. Although analyses revealed no significant differences between the interventions, statistical trends and Ss' written evaluations favored the life review intervention. Attrition was a significant problem. Discussion focuses on the special problems encountered in conducting psychological intervention research with an HIV-positive population.

Journal of Counseling & Development. 1996 Nov-Dec Vol 75(2) 115-123

[274]
Vickberg, Suzanne M. Johnson; Bovbjerg, Dana H.; DuHamel, Katherine N.; Currie, Violante; Redd, William H.

Intrusive thoughts and psychological distress among breast cancer survivors: Global meaning as a possible protective factor.
Previous research has consistently demonstrated a positive association between intrusive thoughts about stressful experiences and psychological distress. The strength of this relation, however, has varied considerably across studies. To examine the possibility that an individual's sense of global meaning (i.e., the existential belief that one's life has purpose and order) may moderate the relation between intrusive thoughts and psychological distress, the authors conducted telephone assessments of 61 women (aged 30-81 yrs) who had survived breast cancer. Results confirmed that the frequency of intrusive thoughts was positively related to psychological distress. Global meaning, moreover, moderated the relation between intrusive thoughts and psychological distress consistent with the authors' hypotheses. Among Ss with lower global meaning, more frequent intrusive thoughts were associated with higher psychological distress. No association was found between intrusive thoughts and psychological distress among those Ss with higher global meaning.

Behavioral Medicine. 2000 Win Vol 25(4) 152-160

[275]
Vickberg, Suzanne M. Johnson; Duhamel, Katherine N.; Smith, Meredith Y.; Manne, Sharon L.; Winkel, Gary; Papadopoulos, Esperanza B.; Redd, William H.

Global meaning and psychological adjustment among survivors of bone marrow transplant.
Examined global meaning (belief that life has purpose and coherence) and psychological adjustment in survivors of bone marrow transplantation (BMT) for treatment of chronic or

acute leukemia. 85 17-59 yr old survivors of BMT participated in a telephone interview. Regression analyses demonstrate that after controlling for physical functioning, stressor severity, and gender, global meaning was inversely related to global psychological distress and BMT-related psychological distress (PTSD-like symptoms related to cancer treatment). Global meaning was also positively related to mental health aspects of quality of life such as emotional and social functioning. It is concluded that global meaning may be an important factor in the psychological adjustment of BMT survivors.

Psycho-Oncology. 2001 Jan-Feb Vol 10(1) 29-39

[276]
Warner-Robbins, Carmen G.; Christiana, Nicholas M.

The spiritual needs of persons with AIDS.
Examines the role of spirituality in patient care for persons with acquired immune deficiency syndrome (AIDS). It is not uncommon for persons with AIDS to be drawn even closer to their spiritual beliefs, as was shown in a survey of 24 AIDS patients. Ss noted beliefs in a caring, higher power; the value of life; the importance of support from religious laypersons and close friends; living an ethical life; the importance of facing death; and the presence of an inner peace in identifying a meaning to their lives.

Family & Community Health. 1989 Aug Vol 12(2) 43-51

[277]
Whitney, C.M.

Maintaining the square. How older adults with Parkinson's disease sustain quality in their lives.
In this article, the author's objective is to uncover the common practices that help sustain quality in the lives of older adults with Parkinson's disease. Interpretive phenomenology was the method used to gather and analyze the stories of six men and six women with idiopathic Parkinson's disease. The results show a constitutive pattern of Maintaining the Square. Five relational themes, including Learning How, Accepting Limitations, Seeking Knowledge, Engaging in Meaningful Experiences, and Living for Today, emerged from the participants' stories. The participants' ability to sustain continuity in their lives indicates their successful maintenance of the square. By identifying markers of continuity, they are able to maintain quality in their lives. As nurses, we can promote continuity in the lives of our patients if we take the time to learn what gives them meaning and purpose in life and then facilitate ways to help them maintain this connection.

Journal of Gerontolical Nursing. 2004 Jan;30(1):28-35*

[278]
Wineman, Nancy M.

Adaptation to multiple sclerosis: The role of social support, functional disability, and perceived uncertainty.
Tested a path model depicting the relationships among social support, functional disability, perceived uncertainty, and psychosocial adaptation in 38 men and 80 women (aged 22-67 yrs) with multiple sclerosis. Data were collected during an interview using standardized instruments and a semistructured format. 35% of the variance in depression and 33% of the variance in purpose-in-life, respectively, were explained by age, sex, social status, and the

perceived supportiveness and unsupportiveness of social network interactions. The perceived supportiveness of interactions was directly related to purpose-in-life but not to depression. Both the direct path between the perceived unsupportiveness of interactions and adaptation and the indirect one through perceived uncertainty were related to depression and to purpose-in-life. Functional disability had a direct effect on adaptation.

Nursing Research. 1990 Sep-Oct Vol 39(5) 294-299

[279]
Xuereb, Mary Carmen; Dunlop, Rosemary

The experience of leukemia and bone marrow transplant: Searching for meaning and agency.
This qualitative study examines the experience of haematological cancer as described by ten people who have been through leukaemia or lymphoma and a bone marrow transplant. The focus is on the interaction of these participants with this challenging experience and the meaning it had for them. The descriptions of their thoughts, feelings and actions as they negotiated the period from diagnosis to treatment and survival reveal that these people brought both the present values in their life, as well as a life-long pattern of dealing with adversity, into their confrontation of a life-threatening illness. Issues of personal meaning and agency (the capacity to act and control valued aspects of one's life) were found to be paramount. These results are then discussed with a view to their implications for patient care.

Psychooncology. 2003 Jul-Aug Vol 12(5) 397-409

[280]
Zebrack BJ, Chesler MA.

Quality of life in childhood cancer survivors.
The successful treatment for children with cancer has greatly increased the survival rates for these young people compared to children diagnosed with cancer 30 years ago. These new medical realities direct attention to the psychosocial consequences of successful treatment and subsequent survival. In this paper, quality of life in 176 childhood cancer survivors (age 16-28) is assessed using a survey instrument designed for cancer survivors. In addition, the instrument is evaluated for its utility with this population. Survivors indicate that symptoms often associated with treatment are at a minimum but that other long-term effects like fatigue, aches, and pain negatively impact quality of life. They rate themselves high on happiness, feeling useful, life satisfaction and their ability to cope as a result of having had cancer but their hopefulness is tempered by uncertainty. Whereas the salience of spiritual and religious activities appears to be low, having a sense of purpose in life and perceiving positive changes as a result of cancer are associated with positive quality of life. A lower valence of physical concerns reflects the vitality and positive life outlook of a young population.

Psychooncology. 2002 Mar-Apr;11(2):132-41.

The Caregiver's Perspective

[281]
Amenta, Madalon M.

Death anxiety, purpose in life and duration of service in hospice volunteers.
Examined levels of death anxiety and purpose in life in relation to competence in 42 screened, trained, and experienced hospice volunteers (mean age 45 yrs). The 18 Ss who left the program between 4 and 11 mo after starting and the 24 who worked 1 yr or more differed significantly in their scores on the Purpose in Life Test and the Death Anxiety Scale. The persisters scored higher on purpose in life and lower on death anxiety. These results should prove useful in the delineation of the characteristics of the good hospice worker as well as supplying a basis for developing more definitive selection procedures for hospice volunteers. Hospice programs are suggested as a source of cross-sectional samples of adults for gathering more data about these scales.
Psychological Reports. 1984 Jun Vol 54(3) 979-984

[282]
Amenta, Madalon M.

Traits of hospice nurses compared with those who work in traditional settings.
Compared 36 hospice nurses with 35 nurses who were working in traditional settings. Data from a battery of five tests (Templer Death Anxiety Scale, Purpose in Life, Shneidman "You and Death" Questionnaire, Myers- Briggs , Cattell 16PF) revealed the hospice nurses to be significantly more assertive, imaginative, forthright , free-thinking and independent than their colleagues, who scored lower than the norms. The nurses in traditional settings exhibited a stronger preference than both hospice nurses and norms for the practical and no-nonsense in their approach to life. They were also more conventional and comfortable with structure. These data suggest a useful basis for hospice staff selection procedures as well as further study of the hospice as a setting evocative of autonomous professional nursing practice.
Journal of Clinical Psychology. 1984 Mar;40(2):414-20.

[283]
Amenta, Madalon M.; Weiner, Arlene W.

Death anxiety and purpose in life in hospice workers.
Investigated the relationship between death anxiety and purpose in life in 98 hospice workers (aged 21-79 yrs) using the Death Anxiety Scale and the Purpose in Life Test. The Pearson product-moment correlation was -.34. Those exhibiting higher purpose in life scored lower on death anxiety.
Psychological Reports. 1981 Dec Vol 49(3) 920

[284]
Carlisle, Caroline

The search for meaning in HIV and AIDS: The carers' experience.

Explored informal caregivers' experiences and search for meaning in caring for people living with HIV and AIDS. A grounded theory approach was taken, with data collected during 43 in-depth interviews and participant observation with 20 caregivers. Analysis of transcribed interviews suggests that caregivers felt that it was important to have control over the emphasis that HIV had within their lives and to develop an attitude that put the virus in perspective. Getting involved in HIV and AIDS work outside of the immediate caregiving relationship was evident. The motivation for this was in part a reaction to prevailing societal views on HIV and in part altruistic, in that it provided further meaning for the caregiving experience. This study suggests that finding meaning in caregiving is a powerful way to achieve a balance between the costs of caregiving and personal reward.

Qualitative Health Research. 2000 Nov Vol 10(6) 750-765

[285]
Cheng Lai, Alice; Salili, Farideh

Stress and social support in parents whose children are hepatitis B virus (HBV) carriers: A comparison of three groups in Guangzhou.
Compared the moderating effect of social support on parental stress variables and mental health among parents of hepatitis B virus (HBV) children in a special kindergarten, parents of HBV children who stayed at home, and parents of normal kindergartners. All families lived in Guangzhou, in southern China. After a 1-hr interview, 90 mothers (aged 25-43) of 3-7 yr olds in the 3 groups were administered the General Health Questionnaire, the Global Assessment of Recent Stress Scale (M. W. Linn, 1985), the Purpose in Life Questionnaire (J. C. Crumbaugh, 1968), and the Interview Schedule for Social Interaction. Descriptive analysis, correlation analysis, and ANOVAs were performed. Parents of HBV children who attended school or stayed at home reported significant social isolation. Parents of healthy kindergartners reported the highest levels of overall social support. Implications for primary care intervention are examined.

International Journal of Psychology. 1997 Vol 32(1) 43-55

[cf. 382]
D'Souza, Russell

Do patients expect psychiatrists to be interested in spiritual issues?

Australasian Psychiatry. 2002 Mar Vol 10(1) 44-47

[286]
Ernzen, Florence

Healing and growing as a logotherapist.
Examined logotherapists' views concerning ways to aid their personal healing and development process. Logotherapists completed questionnaires concerning spiritual and physical exercises, inspirational authors, and how students, colleagues, and clients helped in their personal healing and development process. The responses of 10 logotherapists are provided in table form.

International Forum for Logotherapy. 2001 Spr Vol 24(1) 13-15

[287]
Farran, Carol J.; Keane-Hagerty, Eleanora; Salloway, Sandra; Kupferer, Sylvia; et al

Finding meaning: An alternative paradigm for Alzheimer's disease family caregivers.
Proposes that existentialism may help explain how persons might grow and find meaning through their caregiving experiences. Existentialism is described as a theoretical perspective that focuses on finding meaning through suffering. Data are reported from an interview study of 94 dementia family caregivers (aged 30-78 yrs). Ss expressed existential themes as they described their caregiving experience. Data suggest that caregivers can respond to their caregiving experience by making personal choices about life and caregiving, by valuing positive aspects of the caregiving experience, and by searching for provisional and ultimate meaning. An existential framework seems to provide an alternative paradigm for understanding the caregiving experience.

Gerontologist. 1991 Aug Vol 31(4) 483-489

[288]
Farran, Carol J.; Miller, Baila H.; Kaufman, Julie E.; Davis, Lucille

Race, finding meaning and caregiver distress.
Investigated the relationship between race, finding meaning (as a positive psychological resource variable), and the outcomes of caregiver depression and global role strain among 77 African American and 138 White spouse caregivers (mean age 71.1 yrs) of persons (mean age 74.7 yrs) with dementia. In-home structured interviews were conducted. Results show finding provisional meaning had a direct negative relationship with depression and global role strain. Although African American caregivers were less likely to report depression and role strain, there was no interaction by race in the process influencing caregiver distress.

Journal of Aging & Health. 1997 Aug Vol 9(3) 316-333

[289]
Farran, Carol J.; Miller, Baila H.; Kaufman, Julie E.; Donner, Ed; Fogg, Louis

Finding meaning through caregiving: Development of an instrument for family caregivers of persons with Alzheimer's disease.
Developed and tested a measure primarily designed to assess positive aspects and ways that caregivers find meaning through their experience of caring for a person with dementia. The measure has 3 subscales: Loss/Powerlessness (identifies aspects of caregiving); Provisional Meaning (identifies how caregivers find day-to-day meaning); and Ultimate Meaning (identifies philosophical/religious/spiritual attributions associated with the experience of caregiving. Exp 1 focused on establishing validity of the measure using criterion measures that had a clear existential base, and Exp 2 focused on establishing validity with stress/adaptation measures commonly used in caregiver research. In Exp 1, 46 home-based dementia caregivers (mean age 65.53 yrs) completed a series of questionnaires. In Exp 2, 215 spouse caregivers (mean age 71.67 yrs) completed specific caregiver stress/adaptation measures. Results support the use of the Finding Meaning Through Caregiving Scale as a measure of both positive and more difficult aspects that caregivers may experience while caring for a person with dementia. The scale was found to be a reliable and valid method of assessing caregivers' feelings of loss and powerlessness and their perceptions of how they find provisional and ultimate meaning.

Journal of Clinical Psychology. 1999 Sep Vol 55(9) 1107-1125

[290]
Kannady, Grace

Rethinking logotherapy training needs.
Conducted a survey of members of the Mid-America Institute of Logotherapy to gather information about the training interests and needs of respondents. The data for 55 Ss suggested a diversity of training needs. A major finding was one of omission, suggesting that the audience for logotherapy in the US is highly homogeneous. It is concluded that all social classes and ethnic groups are not involved equitably in the logotherapy community. Six recommendations for logotherapy training are offered.
International Forum for Logotherapy. 1994 Fal Vol 17(2) 96-101

[291]
Kahana, Eva; Midlarsky, Elizabeth

Perspectives on helping in late life: Conceptual and empirical directions.
Discusses a program of research regarding altruism and helping in late life. A series of field experiments is reviewed that considered helping behavior by Ss of varying ages (18-85 yrs), as well as situational factors that facilitate helping. A survey of residents of senior housing sites is also presented that explored the prevalence, salience, and personal meaning of helping by the elderly. The findings from these methodologically diverse studies indicate that helping is an important and prevalent aspect of social interactions of older persons, and that altruistic as well as exchange-based motives for helping are manifested by the elderly. Data underscore the importance of contributory roles in late life and indicate that altruism is a life span developmental phenomenon.
Academic Psychology Bulletin. 1983 Jun Vol 5(2) 351-361

[292]
Kahn, David L.; Steeves, Richard H.; Benoliel, Jeanne Q.

Nurses' views of the coping of patients.
Interactive interviews with 26 graduate students of nursing were analyzed to elicit explanations of the meaning of coping. The 1st idiom represented a view of coping as a rational, cognitive problem-solving response to illness. The nurses attributed, and thus valued, this view to science. In the 2nd idiom, the nurses spoke of coping as permeated with values that contrasted with the prior view of coping as a rational process. In the final idiom, the nurses spoke of coping as courage: They told stories of patients who had faced existential situations with strength and will. The focus of this idiom was on issues of spirituality, struggle, personal meaning, and acceptance.
Social Science & Medicine. 1994 May Vol 38(10) 1423-1430

[293]
Konstam, Varda; Holmes, William; Wilczenski, Felicia; Baliga, Shanteri; Lester, Jill; Priest, Rebecca

Meaning in the lives of caregivers of individuals with Parkinson's disease.
This study explores the contribution of finding meaning in general and finding meaning specific to caregiving as potentially important explanatory variables in predicting well-being in caregivers of individuals with Parkinson's disease. Fifty-eight caregivers (mean age 66.6

yrs) of individuals diagnosed with Parkinson's disease were provided self-report question-naires to assess well-being and meaning (general and specific), Results showed a significant proportion of the variance of positive affect (PASS) and negative affect (DYS) related to well-being, as assessed by the Multiple Affect Adjective Checklist—Revised. Purpose and Existential Vacuum (two subtests of the Life Attitude Profile—Revised used to assess general meaning) predicted well-being. Purpose predicted 41.8% of the variance related to PASS; Existential Vacuum predicted 30.8% of the variance related to DYS. Meaning related specifically to caregiving (Finding Meaning Through Caregiving Scale) did not explain any additional variance. Our results suggest that finding meaning, beyond meaning specifically associated with caregiving, is the key to understanding well-being among caregivers of individuals with Parkinson's disease.

Journal of Clinical Psychology in Medical Settings. 2003 Mar Vol 10(1) 17-26

[294]
Li Cheng, Alice; Ma, Cui; Zheng, Hongbo

Preschool hepatitis B children and parenting stress: A comparison of three groups of parents in Guangzhou, China.
Investigated the stress of parents of preschool children infected by the hepatitis-B virus (HBV). Ss were 30 parents whose 4-6 yr old preschool children with HBV stayed at home, 30 parents whose 4-6 yr old preschool children with HBV were in a special health kindergarten, and 30 parents whose 4-6 yr old preschool children were in an ordinary kindergarten. Ss' family environment, mental health status, stress caused by events of happiness or sadness, styles of coping with stress and purpose in life were compared among groups. The Parents Life Investigation Questionnaire (D. T. L. Shek et al, 1987) was used.

Chinese Mental Health Journal. 1994 Oct Vol 8(5) 213-216

[295]
MacKinlay, Elizabeth

The spiritual dimension of caring: Applying a model for spiritual tasks of ageing.
This article describes a spiritual dimension of ageing using themes and a model for spiritual tasks of ageing, developed as a part of doctoral studies that examined spirituality amongst a group of independent-living older adults in Canberra and New South Wales. This model has been tested further and the model was confirmed through in-depth interviews of residents of nursing homes in the ACT. The first study identified six major spiritual themes from participant interviews. These were: ultimate meaning in life for each person, the way they responded to meaning, self-sufficiency versus despair, moving from provisional to final life meanings, relationship versus isolation in ageing and hope versus despair.

Journal of Religious Gerontology. 2001 Vol 12(3-4) 151-166

[cf. 038]
McWilliam, Carol L.; Brown, Judith Belle; Carmichael, Janet L.; Lehman, Jocelyn M.

A new perspective on threatened autonomy in elderly persons: The disempowering process.

Social Science & Medicine. 1994 Jan Vol 38(2) 327-338

[296]
Marks, Nadine F.; Lambert, James David; Choi, Heejeong

Transitions to caregiving, gender, and psychological well-being: A prospective U.S. national study.
Guided by a life course perspective, this study examined the effects of transitioning into caregiving activity for a child, spouse, parent, other relative, or nonkin associate on 9 dimensions of psychological well-being. Data came from adults ages 19-95, who were noncaregiver primary respondents in the National Survey of Families and Households in 1987-88 and who were followed up longitudinally in 1992-93 (N=8,286). Results from multivariate regression models confirm that the transition to caregiving for primary kin (i.e., a child, spouse, or biological parent) was associated with an increase in depressive symptoms. However in selected instances, caregiving was associated with beneficial effects (e.g., women who began to provide nonresidential care to a biological parent reported more purpose in life than noncaregiving women). Evidence regarding gender differences was inconsistent, varying across caregiving role relationship types
Journal of Marriage & Family. 2002 Aug Vol 64(3) 657-667

[297]
Mickley, Jacqueline Ruth; Pargament, Kenneth I.; Brant, Curtis R.; Hipp, Kathleen M.

God and the search for meaning among hospice caregivers.
Describes both religious and nonreligious appraisals of caregiving for a terminally ill patient and explores the relationship between these appraisals with situational outcomes, mental health outcomes, and spiritual health outcomes in the caregivers. 92 caregivers (aged 25-84 yrs) completed a questionnaire consisting of religious and nonreligious appraisals, general and religious outcomes, depression, anxiety, and purpose in life. Caregivers who appraised their situation as part of God's plan or as a means of gaining strength or understanding from God reported positive outcomes while caregivers who viewed their situation as unjust, as unfair punishment from God, or as desertion from God had low scores on mental and spiritual health outcomes. Religious appraisals made a significant and unique contribution to the prediction of situational outcomes and mental and spiritual health outcomes above and beyond the effects of nonreligious appraisals.
Hospice Journal. 1998 Vol 13(4) 1-17

[298]
Millison, Martin; Dudley, James R.

Providing spiritual support: A job for all hospice professionals.
Examined the spirituality of 117 hospice caregivers in their professional practice. Ss completed a questionnaire regarding their approaches to helping patients with their spiritual or religious needs. Ss considered themselves religious. Their attendance at religious services was high, and their feeling that religion is a source of strength and comfort was strong. Ss rated their own spirituality as stronger than their religiosity, which suggests that for some Ss, their spirituality was not attached to religion. Ss rated spirituality as important in their hospice work. However, only 39% of Ss routinely initiated discussion of patients' religious or spiritual needs during assessment. Patients' religion did not affect Ss' comfort in intervening with patients' spiritual concerns. Ss who were clergy used prayer, scripture reading, medita-

tion, religious spiritual readings, and aspects of ceremonial worship more than did nonclergy.

Hospice Journal. 1992 Vol 8(4) 49-66

[299]
Montgomery, Carol L.

The care-giving relationship: Paradoxical and transcendent aspects.
Interviewed 35 nurses to determine the nature of caring from the perspective of the caregiver's experience. What emerged from the interviews as an overriding theme of caring was the experience of spiritual transcendence. Spiritual transcendence was defined as experiencing oneself in relationship as a part of a force greater than oneself. This spiritual transcendence experience was critical, not only in terms of the nurse's satisfaction with caring, but also as an explanation of the paradox of distance and closeness. This formulation of the spiritual dimension of caring includes 3 properties: (1) the nature of connection, (2) the source of energy, and (3) the effect on the caregiver. These dimensions are explored and illustrated using quotes from the interviews.

Journal of Transpersonal Psychology. 1991 Vol 23(2) 91-104

[300]
Nagata H.; Ohta T.; Aoyama H.

Nursing practitioners' perception of inpatients' anxiety, self-esteem, purpose-in-life and health locus of control.
This study explored how nursing practitioners perceived inpatients' anxiety, self-esteem, purpose-in-life and multidimensional health locus of control. Seventy-three nurses, 60 third-year and 70 first-year nursing students, and 61 control students not majoring in nursing science estimated how inpatients rated these four psychological states. Their ratings were compared with those given by 121 inpatients. Findings showed that the nursing practitioners, as well as the control participants, overestimated inpatients' anxiety, while they underestimated their self-esteem and purpose-in-life. The inpatients' scores for internal locus of control were greater than their scores for the two types of external locus of control (powerful others and chance), and were also greater than the scores given by the nursing practitioners in estimating the patients' perception of internal locus of control. The findings indicate that inpatients have a more positive attitude toward themselves and their own lives, and hence much better mental health, than the nursing practitioners estimate they do.

Acta Med Okayama. 1998 Oct;52(5):271-8. *

[301]
Nagata H.; Ohta T.; Aoyama H.

Medical students' perception of inpatients' anxiety, self-esteem, purpose-in-life and health locus of control as compared with nursing practitioners'.
Medical students (fourth-year: n = 67; fifth-year: n = 63) estimated inpatients' feelings of anxiety, self-esteem, purpose-in-life, and multidimensional health locus of control. Their ratings were compared both with the ratings given by the 121 inpatients themselves and with those given by nursing practitioners (nurses and nursing students). Findings showed that the medical students overestimated inpatients' anxiety, while they underestimated the inpatients' purpose-in-life and internal health locus of control. Hence they underestimated,

as did the nursing practitioners, the inpatients' positive emotional states and their positive attitude toward their own lives. Fifth-year medical students, with clinical experience, rated the inpatients' score of chance health locus of control higher than did the fourth-year medical students, who had no clinical experience. These findings indicate that medical students, like nursing practitioners, are inclined to pay more attention to inpatients' weaknesses than to their strengths.

Acta Med Okayama. 1999 Jun;53(3):141-5. *

[cf. 396]
Nair, V.; Tiwari, S.; Wee, M.; Leong, S.F.; Sarjit, K.; Thavamani, Liew, C.S.

Quality of life survey among long-stay mentally ill patients: patient and staff perspectives.
Singapore Medical Journal. 1996 Oct;37(5):512-6. *

[cf. 254]
Northouse, Peter G.; Northouse, Laurel L.

Communication and cancer: Issues confronting patients, health professionals, and family members.
Journal of Psychosocial Oncology. 1987 Fal Vol 5(3) 17-46. *

[cf. 256]
Ota, Tomoko; Tanaka, Koji

Relation between the patient's quality of life (QOL) and social support.
Journal of Health Psychology. 1997 Vol 10(1) 12-22

[302]
Rhoades, Donna R.; McFarland, Kay F.

Caregiver meaning: A study of caregivers of individuals with mental illness.
Examined caregiver meaning in an agency-supported program. Ss were 61 individuals (aged 31-79 yrs) paid and supported by the South Carolina Department of Mental Health Homeshare program to provide care in their homes for individuals with severe mental illness. A structured questionnaire and interviews were used to develop categories and themes about caregiver meaning. Quantitative and qualitative analyses yielded 3 categories of caregiver meaning: other-directed-altruistic, self-directed-self-actualization, and existential-purpose in life. Caregivers most often referred to altruistic themes, with the most common one being "helping others." The next most common themes were "home and family" and "making a difference." Caregiving difficulties also were categorized. Social work implications are discussed.
Health & Social Work. 1999 Nov Vol 24(4) 291-298

[303]
Rhoades, Donna R.; McFarland, Kay F

Purpose in life and self-actualization in agency-supported caregivers.
The purpose of this study is to observe positive experiences of 85 paid caregivers for seriously, mentally ill individuals, especially the meaning or purpose it gives their lives and the

self-fulfilment or self-actualization that caregiving provides. Ss completed the Purpose in Life Test and the Personal Orientation Inventory. The caregivers in this study possessed a high purpose in life suggesting that caregiving may give meaning to life. Also, the caregivers of these individuals with severe, mental illness tend to be highly other-oriented (altruistic), an external focus that may decrease their own self-awareness. Thus, caregivers who provide continuous residential care may benefit from therapeutic interventions designed to reinforce self-care skills

Community Mental Health Journal. 2000 Oct Vol 36(5) 513-521

[304]
Stetz, Kathleen M.

The relationship among background characteristics, purpose in life, and caregiving demands on perceived health of spouse caregivers.
Examined the effect of personal meaning and the experience of caregiving on spouse care-giver health. 65 spouse caregivers (aged 30-90 yrs) of persons with advanced cancer were interviewed. Instruments included the Mishel Uncertainty in Illness Scale and measures of caregiving demands, role alterations, purpose in life, and general health perceptions. Sense of purpose in life and the caregiver's level of uncertainty were significant predictors of care-givers' health. A stonger sense of purpose in life was positively associated with perceived health. A higher level of caregiver uncertainty was negatively associated with health, which suggests the need for nursing interventions to assist caregivers in coping with their role.

Scholarly Inquiry for Nursing Practice. 1989 Sum Vol 3(2) 133-153

[305]
Strang Susan; Strang, Peter, Ternestedt, B.M.

Spiritual needs as defined by Swedish nursing staff.
A study was undertaken to describe how Swedish nursing staff at six different units characterize spiritual needs in a broad context, including both religious and existential issues. Another aim was to study whether there are any special groups of patients for whom these needs are considered to be of utmost importance. A questionnaire comprising two open-ended questions (the focus of the study) and six background questions was mailed to 191 nurses. Data were obtained from 141 nurses who worked on the oncology, palliative, neurological, neurosurgery and psychiatric units or in nursing homes. Data from the open-ended questions were analysed using content analysis and classified into three categories: (i) (general) spiritual issues, (ii) religious issues, and (iii) existential issues. Sub-categories of the latter were (a) meaning, (b) freedom, (c) isolation and (d) death, i.e. the four central issues in existentialism as previously defined by existential philosophers. A majority of the nurses only had limited theoretical knowledge about definitions. Nevertheless, their suggestions for improved spiritual and existential support contained essential elements that could be allocated to the three main categories. They had some difficulty distinguishing between spiritual and psychosocial care. According to the nurses, special groups of interest for spiritual and existential support were severely ill, dying persons and immigrants who actively practiced their religion. We conclude that there is a willingness to pay attention to spiritual and existential needs, but nurses still have difficulty defining what such care should include. The study revealed that nursing staff needed, and also made inquiries about, more education in order to deepen their knowledge.

Journal of Clinical Nursing. 2002 Jan;11(1):48-57.

[cf. 213]
Stuckey, Jon C.

Faith, aging, and dementia: Experiences of Christian, Jewish, and non-religious spousal caregivers and older adults.
Dementia: The International Journal of Social Research & Practice. 2003 Oct Vol 2(3) 337-352

[306]
Viswanathan, Ramaswamy

Death anxiety, locus of control, and purpose in life of physicians: Their relationship to patient death notification.
Investigated gender and specialty differences in death anxiety, locus of control, and purpose in life, and the influence of these variables on clinical behavior regarding death notification with 155 attending and house staff physicians (40 women). Ss completed the Death Anxiety Scale, Nowicki-Strickland Internal-External Control Scale for Adults, and the Purpose in Life Test. Women scored higher in death anxiety than men. Psychiatrists scored higher in death anxiety than surgeons. There was a trend for the internists to have scores indicating a more external locus of control. Purpose in life was inversely correlated with death anxiety and external locus of control. Death anxiety was related to the physicians' preferred mode of conveying the news of an unexpected patient death to the next of kin.
Psychosomatics: Journal of Consultation Liaison Psychiatry. 1996 Jul-Aug Vol 37(4) 339-345

[307]
Wilson, Sarah A.

The family as caregivers: Hospice home care.
Examined the experience of caring for a terminally ill person as described by family caregivers (CGs) and hospice staff. An ethnographic approach combined participant observation and semistructured interviews. Ss were 8 terminally ill patients (aged 50-90 yrs); their female spouses, daughters, or sisters; and 12 hospice staff members. Family members were able to cope with the caregiving role and find meaning in it through the process of (1) becoming a CG, which included choosing and sharing the role and fulfilling a moral obligation, and (2) "making it through," which involved keeping a journal, relying on spiritual beliefs, and taking one day at a time. Hospice staff assisted families in becoming CGs and making it through the CG role. A case example is presented of a patient who required more care than an elderly CG can provide.
Family & Community Health. 1992 Jul Vol 15(2) 71-80

[308]
Yamamoto-Mitani N, Ishigaki K, Kuniyoshi M, Kawahara-Maekawa N, Hasegawa K, Hayashi K, Sugishita C.

Impact of the positive appraisal of care on quality of life, purpose in life, and will to continue care among Japanese family caregivers of older adults: analysis by kinship type
PURPOSE: The impact of positive appraisal of care (PAC) on the caregiver's quality of life (QL), sense of purpose in life (sense of ikigai) and will to continue care was examined.
METHODS: Data were collected from 322 Japanese family caregivers of older adults who were using visiting nursing services through 21 facilities in the Tokyo metropolitan area, and

the prefectures of Shizuoka, Mie and Okinawa. RESULTS: The data were grouped by kinship type (husband or son, wife, daughter or daughter-in-law) and analyzed separately. From the multiple regression and logistic regression analyses, the following results were derived: 1) The PAC was not related to the physical QL regardless of the relationship type; 2) The relationship depended upon the relationship type: only the PAC was related to the mental QL among husband and son caregivers, both the PAC and the negative appraisal of care (NAC) were important among wives, only the NAC among daughters, and none of them among daughters-in-law; 3) Both the PAC and NAC were related to the sense of ikigai in all caregiver types except among husband and son caregivers, which showed no relationship between the NAC and sense of ikigai; 4) Both the PAC and NAC were related to will to continue care among son and husband caregivers, whereas only the PAC was among wives and daughters-in-law. Only the NAC was related among daughters. However, the difference across kinship type seems minimal for will to continue care. CONCLUSIONS: Understanding the PAC among family caregivers may be important in order to better assist them to improve their mental QL or sense of ikigai as well as to predict their continuation of caregiving at home. The impact of PAC varies depending on the kinship type, and it should be assessed separately with reference to this pariable to develop plans for appropriate assistance.

Nippon Koshu Eisei Zasshi. 2002 Jul;49(7):660-71 *

[309]
Yiu-kee, Chan; Tang, Catherine So-kum

Existential correlates of burnout among mental health professionals in Hong Kong.
Surveyed 132 mental health counselors, clinical psychologists, psychiatrists, psychiatric nurses, and social workers living in Hong Kong about existential aspects of burnout. Instruments included the Maslach Burnout Inventory, the Purpose in Life Test, and the Seeking of Noetic Goals Test. As hypothesized, purpose in life and motivation to seek purpose were significant existential correlates of burnout. Specifically, purpose in life was correlated with the personal accomplishment dimension of burnout, whereas motivation to seek purpose was related to the emotional exhaustion dimension. Of the 5 professional groups, psychiatric nurses experienced the highest level of depersonalization and psychiatrists had the lowest motivation to seek purpose in life. Results are discussed in terms of V. E. Frankl's (1959, 1985) existential theory.

Journal of Mental Health Counseling. 1995 Apr Vol 17(2) 220-229

[310]
Zeman, Iwona

Parental feeling of sense of life and acceptance of a disabled child.
(Poczucie sensu zycia u rodzicow a akceptacja niepelnosprawnego dziecka.)
Studied the level of acceptance of a disabled child among parents in Poland who differed in their level of satisfaction of the need for life's meaning. 27 parents of children with brain damage, Down's syndrome, autism, or mild, moderate, or severe mental retardation were interviewed and were administered the Purpose in Life Test. The results confirm the association between parents' feeling of the sense of life and their acceptance of a disabled child. Parents with a greater feeling of the sense of life were more accepting, but this feeling was generally below the expected level.

Psychologia Wychowawcza. 1999 Sep-Oct Vol 42(4) 340-349

Death and Mortality

[cf. 281]
Amenta, Madalon M.

Death anxiety, purpose in life and duration of service in hospice volunteers.
Psychological Reports. 1984 Jun Vol 54(3) 979-984

[cf. 283]
Amenta, Madalon M.; Weiner, Arlene W.

Death anxiety and purpose in life in hospice workers.
Psychological Reports. 1981 Dec Vol 49(3) 920

[311]
Baum, Steven K.; Boxley, Russell L.

Age denial: Death denial in the elderly.
Compared differences of perceived age and death anxiety levels in 301 elderly persons (mean age 75.5 yrs) who were divided into 3 groups: community residents who were actively involved in a group membership club (affiliated Ss), community residents who were inactive group members (community Ss), and institutionalized board-and-care level elders (institutionalized Ss). Ss were interviewed and administered a modified version of the Death Anxiety Scale, the Cornell Medical Index, the SCL-90, Rotter's Internal-External Locus of Control Scale, and the Purpose-In-Life Test. No relationship was found between age denial and death denial. Single Ss who were poorer in emotional health and felt more externally controlled appeared to manifest more death anxiety. Conversely, those Ss who were married, of sound emotional health, and who perceived themselves as internally controlled received lower death anxiety scores.
Death Education. 1984 Vol 8(5-6) 419-423

[312]
Bolt, Martin

Purpose in life and death concern.
The Purpose in Life Test (PIL), Death Anxiety Scale (DAS), and Diggory and Rothman's death questionnaire measuring the importance of 7 death concerns were administered to 78 undergraduates. The correlation between PIL and DAS scores was negative and significant, indicating that higher perceived purpose in life is associated with less fear of death. As predicted, PIL scores were significantly correlated with rankings of the specific death concern of having life's plans and projects end.
Journal of Genetic Psychology. 1978 Mar Vol 132(1) 159-160

[313]
Drolet, Jean-Louis

Transcending death during early adulthood: Symbolic immortality, death anxiety, and pur-

pose in life.
Developed a sense of symbolic immortality (SI) scale, based on the theory of R. J. Lifton (1979), and administered it to 136 university students (aged 19-39 yrs) to examine whether SI develops with age. The Death Anxiety Scale and the Purpose in Life Test were also administered. Established adults had a sense of SI and a purpose in life significantly stronger than those of young adults. They showed a negative correlation between death anxiety and purpose in life, while purpose in life correlated highly with the sense of SI. The premise that the sense of SI helps cope with the fear of death was supported.

Journal of Clinical Psychology. 1990 Mar Vol 46(2) 148-160

[314]
Florian, Victor; Snowden, Lonnie R.

Fear of personal death and positive life regard: A study of different ethnic and religious-affiliated American college students.
Investigated differences among college students from diverse ethnic and religious backgrounds in their fear of personal death and positive life regard. 280 American Ss from 6 ethnic groups (Chinese, Mexican, Vietnamese, Black, White/Christian, and White/Jewish) and 4 reported religions (Protestant, Catholic, Jewish, and Buddhist) filled out the Fear of Personal Death Scale developed by V. Florian and S. Kravetz and the Life Regard Index created by J. Battista and R. Almond. Results indicate that, compared with other ethnic groups, Vietnamese Americans received higher scores on certain aspects of the fear of personal death and lower scores on the Life Regard Index. Compared with other religious groups, Asian Americans of the Buddhist faith expressed higher concern over the consequences of death to family and friends and fear of punishment in the hereafter, and lower positive life regard. An expected relationship was found between fear of death and positive life regard, but only among White/Christians and Blacks.

Journal of Cross-Cultural Psychology. 1989 Mar Vol 20(1) 64-79

[315]
Gesser, G., Wong, P. T. P., & Reker, G. T.

Death attitudes across the life-span: The development and validation of the Death Attitude Profile (DAP).
Four orthogonal factors were identified by principal component factor analysis: Fear of Death/Dying, Approach-Oriented Death Acceptance, Escape-Oriented Death Acceptance, and Neutral Death Acceptance. Approach Acceptance is based on religious beliefs in Heaven and life after death. Escape acceptance is primary based on the desire to escape from the present life, because of the suffering and meaninglessness of human existence. Neutral acceptance based on a rational acceptance of one's own mortality. Theta estimates of the internal consistency of the factor scales ranged from fair (.60) to good (.89). An elderly sample ($n = 50$) showed less fear of death and more acceptance (all three kinds of acceptance) than the middle age ($n = 50$) and the young ($n = 50$) samples. As predicted, Fear of Death/Dying was negatively related to happiness, but positively related to hopelessness, whereas Escape-Oriented Death Acceptance was positively related to hopelessness, thus providing some evidence of concurrent validity of the DAP.

Omega. 1987. 18, 113-128.

[316]
Kastenbaum, Robert

The search for meaning: When a long life ends.
Discusses the search for meaning often related to death encounters, especially those involving elderly persons. Relevant questions of meaning that are raised in the following 3
vignettes are considered: a 60-yr-old female actress actually died on stage at the same time
as her character was supposed to; an elderly woman died alone at home and was not found
for several days; and a physically ill elderly man repeatedly attempted, although unsuccess-
fully, to commit suicide. The self other split, which is accentuated under complex and
ambiguous circumstances and during a crisis atmosphere; the Western tradition in which
the last scene is taken as significant commentary on the total life that was lived; the issue of
whether death threatens the most fundamental and precious values held by a person; and
the concept of murdering the past are discussed.
Generations: Journal of the American Society on Aging. 1987 Spr Vol 11(3) 9-13

[317]
Kuiken, Don; Madison, Gregory

The effects of death contemplation on meaning and purpose in life.
Investigated affective involvement during reflection on personal mortality in 20 undergraduates engaged in an age progression fantasy during which they imagined themselves gradu-
ally aging and eventually dying. Ss evaluated their fantasy experiences objectively or
attempted to find words or images that characterized their feelings. Compared with 14 Ss
in the objective evaluation condition, Ss in the affective involvement condition scored lower
on the Purpose in Life Test and on the rated meaningfulness of activities. Results indicate
that the effect of affective involvement during death contemplation is a distressing disengagement from previously meaningful pursuits. The role of this effect in long-term psychological change is discussed.
Omega: Journal of Death & Dying. 1987-1988 Vol 18(2) 103-112

[318]
Lo, Raymond S. K.; Woo, Jean; Zhoc, Karen C. H.; Li, Charlotte Y. P.; Yeo, Winnie;
Johnson, Philip; Mak, Yvonne; Lee, Joseph

Quality of life of palliative care patients in the last two weeks of life.
Quality of life (QOL) is the main consideration in caring for advanced cancer patients, yet
little is known about the QOL in the terminal phase. The present study profiled the QOL
of 58 advanced cancer patients (aged 17-86 yrs) during their last 2 wks of life using the
McGill QOL questionnaire-Hong Kong version. Patients provided ratings of QOL an average of 5.6 (median 6) days before death. Palliative care services were successful in maintaining the total QOL scare during the dying phase. The mean score was 7.0 of 10. Among
the various domains, the physical and existential domains scored relatively poorly at 5.9 and
6 of 10, respectively. The "worst physical symptom" and "meaning of life" were the individual items with the poorest scores. Compared with admission, there was statistically significant improvement in "worst physical symptom" and "eating" items, but deterioration in
the "physical well-being", "meaning of existence" and "satisfaction with oneself" items. In
conclusion, QOL evaluation during the terminal phase identifies important aspects requir-

ing improvement during the last 2 wks of life. Physical and existential domains of dying cancer patients needed more attention

Journal of Pain & Symptom Management. 2002 Oct Vol 24(4) 388-397

[319]
Moore, Robert J.; Newton, James H.

Attitudes of the life threatened hospitalized elderly.
Studied selected attitudes of a sample of 29 37-92 yr old (average age 68 yrs) life-threatened patients in the extended care unit of a Canadian hospital. Employing a clinical-quantitative strategy for attitude research, patients, patients' families, and staff (including those in the Terminal Care Unit) were interviewed concerning their feelings and attitudes toward aging, illness, and dying. Some findings were concerned with patient attitudes toward quality of health care over time, staff attitudes toward the effectiveness of other disciplines in meeting the needs of the patients, and patient-family attitudes toward their loved one's last wishes. Other findings were related to attitudes toward death, dying, aging, security, interpersonal communication, religious orientation, pain, and meaning in life. The role of denial as a predominant mode of coping with the reality of death is discussed.

Essence. 1977 Vol 1(3) 129-138

[320]
O'Brien, Sandra J.; Conger, Patricia R.

No time to look back: Approaching the finish line of life's course.
As part of a larger study (e.g., P. R. Conger and S. J. O'Brien, 1989) on the physical fitness and body composition of participants at senior's games, a qualitative exploration of personal life philosophy was undertaken to examine the cognitive makeup of 81 female and 108 male 55-86 yr old competitve and sport-involved elderly people. Content analysis of open-ended survey questions about life in review and future goals permitted insight into life orientation differences between men and women. Sport and physical recreation may be an important type of coping strategy for some elderly adults who find life meaning and a sense of achievement in challenging themselves physically. Beyond a general optimism in life orientation, uncertainties about the nature of the future left many Ss with a sense of urgency combined with specific short-term goal setting.

International Journal of Aging & Human Development. 1991 Vol 33(1) 75-87

[321]
Quinn, Patrick K.; Reznikoff, Marvin

The relationship between death anxiety and the subjective experience of time in the elderly.
Explored the relationship between level of death anxiety and sense of purpose in life and personal experience of time, while controlling for general anxiety and social desirability, in 145 women (aged 60-85 yrs). Ss completed a booklet of 6 questionnaires (the Templer Death Anxiety Scale, Purpose-in-Life Test, Time Metaphors Test, Ricks-Epley-Wessman Temporal Experience Questionnaire, State-Trait Anxiety Inventory, and Marlowe-Crowne Social Desirability Scale). Ss high in death anxiety expressed less sense of purpose in their lives, a sense that time is moving forward, a feeling of being harassed and pressured by the passage of time, a discontinuity and lack of direction in their lives, an inclination to pro-

crastinate and be inefficient in their use of time, and a disposition toward being inconsistent. The relationship between death anxiety and the other variables held even when controlling for general anxiety and social desirability.

International Journal of Aging & Human Development. 1985 Vol 21(3) 197-210

[322]
Rasmussen, Christina H.; Johnson, Mark E.

Spirituality and religiosity: Relative relationships to death anxiety.
To assess the relative contributions of spirituality and religiosity to levels of death anxiety, the Templer Death Anxiety Scale and the Spiritual Well-Being Scale were administered to 134 female and 74 male undergraduate and graduate students, aged 18-61 yrs. Results of stepwise multiple regression analyses reveal that spirituality had a significant negative relationship with death anxiety. As the degree of certainty with respect to life after death, greater levels of satisfaction with life, and greater feelings of purpose in life increased, levels of death anxiety decreased. No significant relationship was revealed between religiosity and death anxiety, but female Ss reported higher levels of death anxiety than did males. Findings suggest that the inconsistency in research findings concerning the relationship between religiosity and death anxiety may be accounted for by the variable of spirituality.
Omega: Journal of Death & Dying. 1994 Vol 29(4) 313-318

[323]
Rappaport, Herbert; Fossler, Robert J.; Bross, Laura S.; Gilden, Dona

Future time, death anxiety, and life purpose among older adults.
Administered the Rappaport Time Line, the Purpose-in-Life Test, and the Death Anxiety Scale to 58 residents (aged 52-94 yrs) of a church-affiliated retirement community. The study anticipated (1) a negative correlation between purpose in life and death anxiety, (2) a positive correlation between purpose in life and temporal extension into the future, (3) a negative correlation between death anxiety and temporal extension into both the past and the future, (4) a negative correlation between purpose in life and temporal density in the present, and (5) a positive correlation between death anxiety and temporal density in the present. Results confirm the 1st, 2nd, and 5th hypotheses, but no significant correlation was found either between death anxiety and temporal extension into the future or between purpose in life and temporal density in the present.
Death Studies. 1993 Jul-Aug Vol 17(4) 369-379

[324]
Rigdon, Michael A.; Epting, Franz R.

Reduction in death threat as a basis for optimal functioning.
Tested the hypothesis that a positive resolution of the issue of personal mortality enables a person to live a more intense, meaningful life, by inviting participation in selected death education experiences designed to produce a more positive death orientation and higher levels of psychological functioning. 96 undergraduates completed the Purpose in Life Test, the Collett-Lester Fear of Death Scale, and a threat index before and after completing a personal obituary, writing a farewell letter, or participating in a stress management exercise (control condition). Data fail to support the impact of death-related experiences on death orienta-

tion or optimal functioning. Females showed a more negative death orientation than did males, and religiosity was associated with a positive death orientation

Death Studies. 1985 Vol 9(5-6) 427-448

[cf. 612]
Salmon P, Manzi F, Valori RM.

Measuring the meaning of life for patients with incurable cancer: the life evaluation questionnaire (LEQ).

European Journal of Cancer. 1996 May;32A(5):755-60*

[325]
Van Ranst, N.; Marcoen, A.

Personal meaning in the elderly: Sources of meaning, well-being, coping, and death attitudes.
(Zinervaring bij ouderen: zingevingsbronnen, welbevinden, coping en houding tegenover de dood.)
Studied patterns of personal meaning among adults of various ages. Human Ss: 376 male and female Dutch middle-age, old, and very old adults (aged 48-88 yrs). Ss were administered 7 standardized questionnaires. Cluster analysis was performed. Tests used: The Sources of Meaning Profile (G. T. Reker, 1991), the Personal Meaning Index (Reker, 1989), the Life Satisfaction Index Form A, the Self-Rating Depression Scale, the Self-Judgment Questionnaire (H. M. Van der Ploeg et al, 1980), the Coping Orientations and Prototypes (P. T. Wong et al) and the Death Attitude Profile—Revised (Wong et al).

Tijdschrift voor Gerontologie en Geriatrie. 1996 Feb Vol 27(1) 5-13

[cf. 306]
Viswanathan, Ramaswamy

Death anxiety, locus of control, and purpose in life of physicians: Their relationship to patient death notification.

Psychosomatics: Journal of Consultation Liaison Psychiatry. 1996 Jul-Aug Vol 37(4) 339-345

[cf. 143]
Weenolsen, Patricia

Transcending the many deaths of life: Clinical implications for cure versus healing.

Death Studies. 1991 Jan-Feb Vol 15(1) 59-80

[326]
Zuehlke, Terry E.; Watkins, John T.

The use of psychotherapy with dying patients: An exploratory study.
A group of 6 male terminally ill patients received 6 sessions of psychotherapy. A 2nd group of 6 patients served as nontreated controls. At the conclusion of the treatment sessions, psychotherapy patients reported (using the Purpose in Life Test and Death Anxiety Scale) a significantly greater increase in willingness to admit and discuss death-related anxiety and in their perceived purpose in life than did the nontreated group. Clinical impressions indicat-

ed that patients who participated in psychotherapy perceived their treatment experience positively and appreciated the opportunity to explore their feelings about imminent death. Results offer considerable support for the usefulness of psychotherapy to help such patients cope with the emotional stress generated by their limited life expectancy.

Journal of Clinical Psychology. 1975 Oct Vol 31(4) 729-732

Bereavement

[327]
Danforth, Marion M.; Glass, J. Conrad, Jr.

Listen to my words, give meaning to my sorrow: A study in cognitive constructs in middle-age bereaved widows.
Examined how women widowed in midlife give meaning to the experience of loss in the process of grief resolution following the 1st yr of bereavement. Qualitative data were gathered from women between the ages of 51-56 yrs through interviews guided by critical reflection. Six themes emerged in the meaning-making process: emotional dissonance, identification of previously held assumptions, reflections on current life experiences—testing the assumptions, identification of self as survivor, changes in sense of self and ways of knowing, and changes in perspectives. Findings indicate that the crisis of loss challenged basic assumptions about self, relationships, and life options and initiated a need to find new perspectives that would incorporate loss and provide for meaningful life direction. Perspective transformation began to occur after the 1st yr following loss, when the initial crisis of survival and anguish had abated, and was most effectively achieved several years after the death. Implications are presented for the bereaved, practitioners who assist the bereaved, adult educators, and researchers
Death Studies. 2001 Sep Vol 25(6) 513-529

[328]
Davis, Christopher G.; Wortman, Camille B.; Lehman, Darrin R.; Silver, Roxane Cohen

Searching for meaning in loss: Are clinical assumptions correct?
Reviewed existing research that addresses the assumptions that (a) people confronting sudden, traumatic losses inevitably search for meaning, (b) over time most are able to find meaning and put the issue aside, and (c) finding meaning is critical for adjustment or healing. Additional evidence from a study of 124 parents coping with the death of their infant and a study of 93 adults coping with the loss of their spouse or child to a motor vehicle accident is also provided. Results of the studies indicate that (a) a significant subset of individuals do not search for meaning and yet appear relatively well-adjusted to their loss; (b) less than half of the respondents in each of these samples report finding any meaning in their loss, even more than a year after the event; and (c) those who find meaning, although better adjusted than those who search but are unable to find meaning, do not put the issue of meaning aside and move on. Rather, they continue to pursue the issue of meaning as fervently as those who search but do not find meaning. Implications for both research and clinical intervention are discussed.
Death Studies. 2000 Sep Vol 24(6) 497-540

[329]
Edmonds, Sarah; Hooker, Karen

Perceived changes in life meaning following bereavement.
Investigated whether positive aspects of bereavement exist. 49 undergraduates who recently experienced the death of a close family member completed measures of grief-related distress and existential meaning and answered open-ended questions regarding perceived changes in belief in God and life goals occurring as a result of their experience. A significant

inverse relationship emerged between grief and existential meaning. The majority of Ss reported a positive change in life goals; these Ss had significantly higher existential meaning than those who reported a negative change in goals. Those who experienced change (positive or negative) in belief in God had higher levels of grief than those who reported no change. Results suggest that positive changes are associated with bereavement and that grief itself may serve as an impetus for personal growth.

Omega: Journal of Death & Dying. 1992 Vol 25(4) 307-318

[330]
Florian, Victor

Meaning and purpose in life of bereaved parents whose son fell during active military service.
Tested the hypothesis that bereaved parents, following the loss of an adult son during military activity, would experience a deep sense of "existential vacuum" that is expressed through lack of meaning and purpose in life. 52 bereaved couples who had lost their son during military action and 50 controls who had not experienced loss of a son were given the Purpose in Life Test and a meaning in life scale. Findings confirm the hypothesis. Bereaved parents evaluated their health status as poorer compared with the control group. Recommendations are proposed to promote the well-being of bereaved parents.

Omega: Journal of Death & Dying. 1989-1990 Vol 20(2) 91-102

[331]
Fry, P. S.

The unique contribution of key existential factors to the prediction of psychological well-being of older adults following spousal loss.
This study examined the unique contribution of key existential factors to the prediction of psychological well-being of older adults following spousal loss. A number of measures to assess psychological well-being, sociodemographic standing, social resources, and religious and spiritual resources were administered to a volunteer sample of 188 widows and widowers (aged 65-87 yrs) to test the hypothesis that existential factors such as personal meaning, religiosity, and spirituality are more potent predictors of psychological well-being than sociodemographic, social support, and physical factors. A hierarchical regression analysis of the data supported the hypothesis that existential factors are major contributors to psychological well-being of older adults following spousal loss. Findings showed that widowers, compared to widows, scored lower on the measure of psychological well-being. Implications of the findings are discussed for practitioners working with bereaved spouses; suggestions for further research concerning bereavement and psychological well-being are made.

Gerontologist. 2001 Feb Vol 41(1) 69-81

[332]
Golsworthy, Richard; Coyle, Adrian

Spiritual beliefs and the search for meaning among older adults following partner loss.
This study explores the role played by spiritual beliefs in the process of meaning-making among older adults following the death of a partner. In-depth interviews were carried out with 9 participants (aged 53-78 yrs) who held Christian beliefs. Data were analyzed using interpretative phenomenological analysis to highlight both commonality and diversity with-

in the association between spiritual beliefs and structures of meaning. Participants' beliefs were diversely related to the creation of meaning for the loss and for the survivor's ongoing life. In more specific terms, these beliefs were implicated in discussions of support, ongoing relationships with the deceased, attributions of responsibility, the creation of explanations for the death, and hope for the future. Findings are considered in terms of existing bereavement literature and implications for therapeutic practice are examined.

Mortality. 1999 Mar Vol 4(1) 21-40

[333]
Hershberger, Paul J.; Walsh, W. Bruce

Multiple role involvements and the adjustment to conjugal bereavement: An exploratory study.
Examined the significance of multiple role involvements (RI) for positive adjustment to conjugal bereavement in 49 surviving spouses (aged 24-74 yrs). RI included roles as a parent, employee, friend, student, hobbyist, and participant in social, community, political, and religious organizations. The self-report behavioral measure of RI after bereavement was a better predictor of adjustment than was sex, age, time elapsed from spouse's death, educational attainment, income level, or religiosity. The number of RI was significantly and positively correlated with a sense of purpose in life. RI before the death of the spouse explained most of the variance in the number of current roles.

Omega: Journal of Death & Dying. 1990 Vol 21(2) 91-102

[334]
Hogan, Nancy S.; Schmidt, Lee A.

Testing the Grief to Personal Growth model using structural equation modeling.
Notes that the belief that loss can result in growth has been hypothesized for centuries. Yet, traditional grief theories have viewed grief work as a process of resolving grief and returning to normal. Formal conceptualizations of grief to growth models have been delineated by several grief theorists. The Grief to Personal Growth model represents one emergent perspective of the qualitative changes resulting from the loss of a loved one. The model delineates a pathway through grief that indicates the bereft experience despair and detachment followed by intrusive thoughts and later avoidance of intense preoccupation with grief. Social support is shown to facilitate the bereft as they reconstruct their lives and find new meaning in life. A second path indicates that some bereaved individuals become mired in grief and need help to proceed toward personal growth. The model was tested in a sample of 148 bereaved parents (mean age 49.17 yrs) using structural equation modeling as a method of theory testing. The results of testing this model are presented within a framework of theory testing as a mechanism to bridge the gaps between theory, practice, and research. Implications for practice are considered.

Death Studies. 2002 Oct Vol 26(8) 615-634

[335]
Levinson, Jay I.

Existential vacuum in grieving widows.
Examined the existential components of bereavement as related to V. E. Frankl's (published 1962-1969) existential vacuum. Participants were 30 widows (aged 28-76 yrs), whose

length of bereavement was 3-22 mo. Results are integrated with Frankl's concept of meaning in life and E. Kubler-Ross's (1969) concept of meaning in death into an existential model of bereavement to assist clinicians in understanding and treating those in mourning.
International Forum for Logotherapy. 1989 Fal Vol 12(2) 101-109

[336]
Martinson, Ida M.; Lee, Hae-Ok; Kim, Susie

Culturally based interventions for families whose child dies.
Explored cultural issues in family response to the death of a child from cancer and how nurses help families manage this situation. Interview results of 18 Korean families living in South Korea, 15 Chinese families living in Taiwan, and 22 American families whose child had died from cancer are reported. Results show that the impact of the child's death from cancer on the family has 4 broad aspects: the manifestations of grief, the experiences of support or nonsupport, the meaning of life and of death, and changes in attitudes. Illustrations are given of the similarities and differences among the American, Chinese, and Korean families in their responses.
Illness, Crisis & Loss. 2000 Jan Vol 8(1) 17-31

[337]
Murphy, Shirley A.; Johnson, L. Clark; Lohan, Janet

Finding meaning in a child's violent death: A five-year propective analysis of parents' personal narratives and empirical data.
Finding meaning in the death of a loved one is thought to be extremely traumatic when the circumstances surrounding the death are perceived to be due to negligence, is intentional, and when the deceased suffered extreme pain and bodily harm immediately prior to death. We addressed this assumption by obtaining personal narratives and empirical data from 138 parents 4, 12, 24, and 60 months after an adolescent's or young adult child's death by accident, suicide, or homicide. Using the Janoff-Bulman and Frantz's(1997) framework of meaning-as-comprehensibility and meaning-as-significance, the purposes were to identify the time course to find meaning, present parents' personal narratives describing finding meaning in their experiences, identify predictors of finding meaning, and compare parents who found meaning versus those who did not on five health and adjustment outcomes. The results showed that by 12 months postdeath, only 12% of the study sample had found meaning in a child's death. By 60 months postdeath, 57% of the parents had found meaning but 43% had not. Significant predictors of finding meaning 5 years postdeath were the use of religious coping and support group attendance. Parents who attended a support group were 4 times more likely to find meaning than non-attendees.
Death Studies. 2003 Jun Vol 27(5) 381-404

[338]
Parappully, Jose; Rosenbaum, Robert; van den Daele, Leland; Nzewi, Esther

Thriving after trauma: The experience of parents of murdered children.
Psychological literature on trauma usually focuses on pathology that results from trauma and pays little attention to positive outcomes. This article presents a phenomenological inquiry into the experiences of a profoundly traumatized group of people—parents whose son or daughter has been murdered—to assess if they were able to experience a positive out-

come resulting from their trauma and to identify associated processes and resources. Of 65 parents who volunteered, 16 (35-75 yrs old) were selected to complete a questionnaire and were given in-depth, semistructured interviews. The interview data, analyzed qualitatively, affirm positive outcomes for these parents. Four processes—acceptance, finding meaning, personal decision making, and reaching out to others in compassion-and six resources—personal qualities, spirituality, continuing bond with the victim, social support, previous coping experience, and self-care-facilitate a positive outcome.

Journal of Humanistic Psychology. 2002 Win Vol 42(1) 33-70

[339]
Pfost, Karen S.; Stevens, Michael J.; Wessels, Anne B.

Relationship of purpose in life to grief experiences in response to the death of a significant other.
40 undergraduates who had sustained the death of a relative or friend within the past 3 yrs completed the Purpose in Life Test and the Grief Experience Inventory. Ss who reported little meaning in their lives appeared to experience more intense anger in response to the death of a significant other than did Ss with high purpose. This relationship was not moderated by passage of time since the loss. Counselors may wish to help emotion-focused clients whose mourning processes center around anger and meaninglessness consider alternative ways of coping.

Death Studies. 1989 Jul-Aug Vol 13(4) 371-378

[340]
Robak, Rostyslaw W.; Griffin, Paul W.

Purpose in life: What is its relationship to happiness, depression, and grieving?
118 college students (mean age 21.5 yrs) completed Crumbaugh and Maholick's Purpose in Life test, the Depression-Happiness Scale, the Death Depression Scale, and the Texas Revised Inventory of Grief as well as a questionnaire with specific questions related to the Ss' "most recent loss of a significant person through death." Results indicate a strong positive relationship between purpose in life and happiness, and a negative correlation between life purpose and death depression. No relationship was noted between length of time since a death and purpose in life of the griever. The only gender difference found was a greater degree of death depression reported by women. It was also shown that one's relationship to the deceased predicts grief reaction, but not purpose in life. A simple self report of having "gotten over the loss completely" predicted a greater purpose in life, happiness, and lesser grief reaction.

North American Journal of Psychology. 2000 Vol 2(1) 113-119

[341]
Schwartzberg, Steven S.; Janoff-Bulman, Ronnie

Grief and the search for meaning: Exploring the assumptive worlds of bereaved college students.
Examined the impact of bereavement on 3 categories of basic assumptions: Benevolence of the World, Meaningfulness of the World, and Self-Worth. 21 undergraduates who had recently lost a parent and 21 matched controls (CTLs) completed a test battery that included the SCL-90, a locus of control scale, and a self-esteem scale. Ss also completed semi-

structured clinical interviews. Ss and CTLs differed significantly on measures of psychological functioning. Assumptions about meaning emerged as an important variable, in distinguishing between Ss and CTLs and in accounting for differences in Ss' grief responses. Compared with CTLs, Ss were significantly less likely to believe in a meaningful world. Within the S sample, the greater the Ss' ability to find meaning (i.e., make sense of the loss), the less intense their grief. (

Journal of Social & Clinical Psychology. 1991 Fal Vol 10(3) 270-288

[342]
Stevens, Michael J.; Pfost, Karen S.; Wessels, Anne B.

The relationship of purpose in life to coping strategies and time since the death of a significant other.
Investigated the relationship of experienced purpose in life to strategies used to cope with a loss resulting from death and the amount of time since the loss. 40 undergraduates (aged 18-38 yrs) completed an information sheet, the Purpose in Life Test, and the revised Ways of Coping Checklist. Ss who experienced low purpose in life reported using more emotion-focused coping strategies than did Ss with high purpose. Results are linked to the literature on emotion-focused coping and depression and are discussed in terms of assessment and preventive treatment of bereaved clients.

Journal of Counseling & Development. 1987 Apr Vol 65(8) 424-426

[343]
Talbot, Kay

Transcending a devastating loss: The life attitude of mothers who have experienced the death of their only child.
Measured 80 mothers' attitudes about life 5+ yrs after the death of their only child. Ss completed the Life Attitude Profile—Revised. The 5 highest and 5 lowest scoring Ss were interviewed in depth. Discriminant analysis of questionnaire responses revealed that 86% of the Ss were correctly classified by 7 variables as survivors (reinvestors in life) or as remaining in a state of perpetual bereavement. Four of these variables accounted for 39% of the variance in Ss' life attitude scores. Interview and questionnaire findings suggest that motherhood becomes an integral part of the self and to survive after the death of an only child it is necessary not to relinquish this construct, but to incorporate "mothering" into their new lives. A positive life attitude was an indicator of adaptation to this unique form of loss.

Hospice Journal. 1996 Vol 11(4) 67-82

[344]
Talbot, Kay

Mothers now childless: Survival after the death of an only child.
This study aimed to understand how the additional loss of the role of motherhood affects bereavement survival after the death of a child. The Life Attitude Profile-Revised and interviews were used to understand the life-world of 80 mothers whose only child (aged 3-21 yrs) died from accident or illness 5 or more yrs previously. The data produced descriptions of the qualitative difference between remaining in a state of perpetual bereavement and surviving to live life "alive" again. The findings suggest that motherhood becomes an integral part of the self and in order to survive this dual loss, it is necessary not to relinquish this

construct. Rather, it is important to find meaningful ways to continue "mothering" as part of a new, more integrated identity which acknowledges the child's death but also preserves the child's memory and honors the woman's past life as a mother.

Omega: Journal of Death & Dying. 1997 Vol 34(3) 177-189

[345]
Talbot, Kay

Mothers now childless: Structures of the life-world.
Utilized both qualitative and quantitative methods to examine what it means for mothers to survive the death of their only child. The article focuses on the findings from 10 in-depth interviews which delineate the life-world of 80 participant bereaved mothers. Implications for counselors and other professionals assisting bereaved mothers of only children are included.

Omega: Journal of Death & Dying. 1998 Vol 36(1) 45-62

[346]
Talbot, Kay

Mothers now childless: Personal transformation after the death of an only child.
Examined the impact of loss on human development and the factors associated with changes in personal identity experienced by 80 women whose only child had died. All participants completed a life attitude profile and 20 participants were interviewed. A phenomenological content analysis was performed on the transcribed, verbatim interview texts. Four factors were found to be common among those participants who felt they had survived their loss and changed in positive ways: (1) resolving a spiritual crisis brought about by the child's death; (2) making a conscious decision to survive; (3) reaching out to help others by volunteering or working in a helping profession; and (4) integrating what was learned from surviving the child's death into a new, more compassionate identity.

Omega: Journal of Death & Dying. 1998-1999 Vol 38(3) 167-186

[347]
Ulmer, Ann; Range, Lillian M.; Smith, Peggy C.

Purpose in life: A moderator of recovery from bereavement.
119 recently bereaved adults (aged 16-86 yrs) completed questionnaires assessing life purpose, reasons for living, the impact of bereavement, social support, and satisfaction with life. 25 of the Ss' loved ones had committed suicide. Purpose was associated with greater life satisfaction, stronger reasons for living, more social support, and less impact. Unexpectedly, Ss bereaved by suicide were not different from other cause of death groups on these measures. A high sense of meaning and purpose in life was also associated with better recovery from bereavement.

Omega: Journal of Death & Dying. 1991 Vol 23(4) 279-289

[348]
Uren, Tanya H.; Wastell, Colin A.

Attachment and meaning-making in perinatal bereavement.

The study examined the psychological impact of perinatal bereavement on 108 women, from a dual attachment and meaning-making perspective, both descriptively and predictively. The study hypothesized that grief acuity is a function of both attachment security (operationalized by A. Antonovsky's 1979 Sense of Coherence scale), and the ongoing search for meaning. Controlling for time post-loss, psychological distress and intrusive thoughts; sense of coherence and search for meaning significantly predicted current grief acuity. The findings supported the conceptualization of grief as an interpretive phenomenon, elicited by the loss of a primary attachment figure, thereby shattering core life purposes, and implicating the need to reinstate meaning.

Death Studies. 2002 Apr Vol 26(4) 279-308

[349]
Wagnild, Gail; Young, Heather M.

Resilience among older women.
This qualitative study was designed to identify and describe characteristics of successfully adjusted older women. The participants were 24 women (aged 67-92 yrs) who reported a recent major loss and were considered successfully adjusted as evidenced by social involvement in a senior center, a mid level to high level of morale and self-report. Using a grounded theory approach, 5 underlying themes were identified: equanimity, self-reliance, existential aloneness, perseverance and meaningfulness. These themes are thought to constitute resilience. Lateral grounding of the concept resilience is accomplished by comparison with philosophical writings of V. E. Frankl, B. Bettelheim, A. Frank, W. F. May and H. D. von Witzleben. Resilience is important in late life as a component of successful psychosocial adjustment.

Image: Journal of Nursing Scholarship. 1990 Win Vol 22(4) 252-255

[350]
Wheeler, Inese

The role of meaning and purpose in life in bereaved parents associated with a self-help group: Compassionate friends.
Explored the relationship of parental bereavement to meaning and purpose in life. The study attempted to (1) investigate the relationship of bereaved parents' perception of purpose in life and specific parent, child, death, and grief characteristics and (2) provide descriptive information on the role of meaning in parental bereavement. 203 bereaved parents who had lost a child from 1 mo to 40 yrs previously completed a questionnaire consisting of the Purpose in Life Test, a grief experience inventory, and questions on meaning. Results indicate that lower purpose in life for bereaved parents was related to less time since the death, loss by suicide, loss of an only child, and loss of more than one child. Data also indicate that a crisis of meaning may follow the death of a child.

Omega: Journal of Death & Dying. 1993-1994 Vol 28(4) 261-271

[351]
Wheeler, Inese

Parental bereavement: The crisis of meaning.
This descriptive study used qualitative methods to look at two aspects of the search for meaning in parental bereavement—the search for cognitive mastery and the search for

renewed purpose. 176 bereaved parents (aged 22-83 yrs) answered open-ended questions about the experience of their child's death and the meaning of their life since the death. For most parents, the child's death precipitated a severe crisis of meaning and initiated a search for meaning that involved both cognitive mastery and renewed purpose. Those parents who were able to find meaning in the death cited connections with people, the memory of the child, and positive gains resulting from the trauma. The great majority of parents believed that their lives since the death of the child had meaning. Meaning came from connections with people, activities, beliefs and values, personal growth, and connections with the lost child. Implications for grief counseling are discussed.

Death Studies. 2001 Jan-Feb Vol 25(1) 51-66

[352]
Yalom, Irvin D.; Lieberman, Morton A.

Bereavement and heightened existential awareness.
Examined whether bereavement, for some individuals, results in psychological shifts analogous to the positive changes reported by terminally ill patients. Differences in the degree of existential awareness and the consequences of such awareness on the course of bereavement were studied in 36 bereaved spouses (mean age 56.7 yrs) and 20 controls. Data suggest the presence of personal growth, a positive outcome of bereavement.

Psychiatry: Journal for the Study of Interpersonal Processes. 1991 Nov Vol 54(4) 334-345

Miscellaneous Conditions and Findings

[353]
Bearsley, Cate; Cummins, Robert A.

No place called home: Life quality and purpose of homeless youths.
Subjective quality of life (SQOL) has been reported to display remarkable resilience to objective circumstances. This is thought to derive from the capacity to interpret experience in positive ways, but is defeated by very adverse circumstances. This raises the question of whether such positive mental devices are able to adequately protect the SQOL of homeless youths, who typically face substantial objective trials. This study compares youths who are homeless or at risk of homelessness with youths living consistently with their families. 524 adolescents (aged 14-17 yrs) were administered questionnaires about their life attitudes. It was found that both the homeless and "at risk" youths reported significantly lower SQOL. These youths also reported lower levels of personal meaning than the control group, and higher existential vacuum. Of the variables measured, personal meaning provided the strongest prediction of SQOL, challenging theories that would predict choice responsibleness to provide the predominant contribution. Lack of differences in response between homeless and "at risk" youths suggests that subjective difficulties may precede homelessness rather than stem from it. A model is proposed to describe the possible factors involved in the maintenance and erosion of SQOL.
Journal of Social Distress & the Homeless. 1999 Oct Vol 8(4) 207-226

[354]
Biswas-Diener, Robert; Diener, Ed

Making the best of a bad situation: Satisfaction in the slums of Calcutta.
Eighty three people in the slums of Calcutta, India were interviewed, and responded to several measures of subjective well-being. The respondents came from one of three groups: Those living in slum housing (aged 18-70 yrs), sex workers (prostitutes) residing in brothels (aged 18-50 yrs) , and homeless individuals living on the streets (aged 18-75 yrs). They responded to questions about life satisfaction and satisfaction with various life domains, as well as to a memory recall measure of good and bad events in their lives. While the mean rating of general life satisfaction was slightly negative, the mean ratings of satisfaction with specific domains were positive. The conclusion is that the slum dwellers of Calcutta generally experience a lower sense of life satisfaction than more affluent comparison groups, but are more satisfied than one might expect. This could be due, in part, to the strong emphasis on social relationships and the satisfaction derived from them.
Social Indicators Research. 2001 Sep Vol 55(3) 329-352

[355]
Bonnin, Rodolfo; Brown, Chris

The Cuban diaspora: A comparative analysis of the search for meaning among recent Cuban exiles and Cuban Americans.
144 recent exiled Cubans (55 males and 49 females, aged 18-64 yrs) and 98 Cuban Americans (70 females and 28 males, aged 18-78 yrs) were compared on purpose in life,

well-being, and family dimension variables. Specifically, the authors examined (a) whether acculturation, family adaptability, and family cohesion predict purpose in life; (b) the relations among family dimension variables, acculturation, purpose in life, and U.S. residency; and (c) whether recent exiled Cubans and Cuban Americans differ on family adaptability, family cohesion, and purpose in life. Findings revealed that family adaptability, family cohesion, and acculturation were significant predictors of purpose in life. Furthermore, several of the variables under investigation were significantly related, in particular a significant relationship was found between purpose in life and the two family dimension variables for both groups. Finally, recent exiled Cubans as compared to Cuban Americans scored higher on family adaptability, purpose in life, and well-being.

Hispanic Journal of Behavioral Sciences. 2002 Nov Vol 24(4) 465-478

[356]
Czaja, Iwona

Sense of coherence and delayed consequences of post-traumatic stress in persons persecuted for political reasons in Poland in the years 1944-56.
(Poczucie koherencji a odlegle nastepstwa stresu pourazowego u osob represjonowanych w Polsce z przyczyn politycznych w latach 1944-56.)
Analyzed the relationship between the sense of coherence and delayed consequences of posttraumatic stress disorder (PTSD) in 100 male Ss (aged 59-79 yrs) who were persecuted for political reasons in Poland during the years 1944-1956. Ss were assessed using the following tests: the Sense of Coherence Questionnaire (K. Petrie & R. Brook, 1992); the PTSD-Interview (C. G. Watson, et al, 1991); the Beck Depression Inventory (A. T. Beck et al, 1979); the State-Trait Anxiety Inventory (C. D. Spielberger, 1979); the Purpose in Life Test (B. Mroz, 1993); the Psychological General Well-Being Index (H. J. Dupuy, 1984); and the Scale of Interpersonal Relationships (J. M. Stanik, 1994). The results indicate that the strength of sense of coherence was negatively correlated with Ss' level of anxiety, depression, and enmity syndrome, and positively correlated with Ss's meaning of life, psychological well-being, and social relationships. The results confirm the significance of sense of coherence in modifying experience of delayed consequences of PTSD in Ss.

Psychiatria Polska. 2001 Nov-Dec Vol 35(6) 921-935

[357]
de Oliveira, Tania Chalhub

Homeless children in Rio de Janeiro: Exploring the meanings of street life.
Assessed the feasibility of qualitative research with Brazilian homeless children and investigated the meanings they give to street life. This phenomenological study is based on open-ended interviews and observations with street children affiliated with a non-governmental organization that meets such needs as shelter, education, nutrition, medical assistance as compared with a group of 6 children who were living together on the sidewalks and not affiliated with any organization. The author also interviewed 4 social educators, 3 policemen, and 6 people who worked in the neighborhood. Interviews were usually informal and some were tape recorded. Results show 6 major themes: time-space relations, freedom, group protection, being a girl and being a child. The category of violence was found to overlap with all of the above categories.

Child & Youth Care Forum. 1997 Jun Vol 26(3) 163-174

[358]
Draucker, Claire Burke

Learning the harsh realities of life: Sexual violence, disillusionment, and meaning.
Explored how women find meaning in experiences of sexual violence committed by men close to them. Data were provided by 44 women (aged 18-64 yrs) who had participated in 1 of 3 studies on women's responses to sexual abuse and assault by intimate others. The women's explanations for the violence they experienced, discussions of how they made sense of the violence, and references to the meaning or purpose of the violence in their lives were analyzed using grounded theory methods. The women indicated that their victimizing experiences had taught them "the harsh realities of life"; that is, the world is violent and society tolerates and, in some cases, promotes violence against women. This lesson forced them to take it upon themselves to create a better life. This psychosocial process of "taking it upon oneself" involved 3 tasks: pursuing one's own safety, taking justice into one's own hand, and making something good out of something bad. By accomplishing these tasks, the women found meaning in their suffering.
Health Care for Women International. 2001 Jan-Feb Vol 22(1-2) 67-84

[359]
DuRant, Robert H.; Getts, Alan; Cadenhead, Chris; Emans, S. Jean; et al

Exposure to violence and victimization and depression, hopelessness, and purpose in life among adolescents living in and around public housing.
225 African-American adolescents (aged 11-19 yrs) living in or around public housing completed a battery of measures, including the Children's Depression Inventory, the Hopelessness Scale for Children, and the Purpose in Life scale. Depression was correlated with exposure to violence, family conflict (FC), and corporal punishment (CP) scales; perceived probability of being alive at age 25 yrs; SES of head of household; anticipated SES as an adult; and number of sexual partners (NSPs). Based on multiple regression analysis, CP, FC, educational level of head of household, and perceived probability of being alive at age 25 yrs explained 18% of the variation in depression. Unemployed head of household, FC, and CP explained 11% of the variation in the hopelessness scale. Unemployed head of household, CP, and NSPs explained 9.7% of the variation in purpose in life. Exposure to violence in the home was associated with psychological distress.
Journal of Developmental & Behavioral Pediatrics. 1995 Aug Vol 16(4) 233-237

[360]
Ebersole, Peter; Flores, Joan

Positive impact of life crises.
Gathered self-reports from 96 undergraduates on the amount of self-growth as a consequence of experiencing what they judged to be their most difficult life crises. Ss filled out an anonymous questionnaire that inquired about the most painful experience of their life, its long-term effect, and its impact on their personal life meaning (PLM). Ss also rated how positive or negative the painful experience ultimately turned out to be. It was found that 87% of those who rated the impact of long term crises positively reported a positive PLM change. This suggests that the cognitive changes induced by painful experiences present a means of evolving and strengthening PLM.
Journal of Social Behavior & Personality. 1989 Vol 4(5) 463-469

[cf. 021]
Halama, Peter

Dimensions of Life Meaning as Factors of Coping
Studia Psychologica. 2000. 42:4. 339-350

[361]
Jones, Lynne

Adolescent understandings of political violence and psychological well-being: A qualitative study from Bosnia Herzegovina.
The Harvard Trauma Questionnaire and Hopkins Symptoms Checklist (HSCL-25) were given to 337 13-15 yr olds who had lived through the recent war in Bosnia Herzegovina, on opposite sides of the conflict. A gender-balanced subsample of 40 adolescents was selected on the basis of their combined symptom scores, including equal numbers of high and low scorers from each side. A year of participant observation in two cities and in-depth interviews were conducted with the subsample to explore their understandings of the war and their subjective perceptions of their psychological well-being. Case studies are presented to show that the degree to which an adolescent engaged in searching for meaning (SFM) to the conflict is related to their psychological well-being. SFM did not appear to be protective. Less well adolescents in both cities were more engaged in SFM. Well adolescents appeared to be more disengaged. SFM appeared to be associated with sensitivity to the political environment, and feelings of insecurity about the prospect of a future war. The particular local context had an important effect in mediating the manner in which disengagement and engagement occurred. These data suggest that the more avoidant methods of coping with political violence warrant further investigation.
Social Science & Medicine. 2002 Oct Vol 55(8) 1351-1371

[362]
Lantz, Jim; Gregoire, Tom

Existential psychotherapy with Vietnam veteran couples: A twenty-five year report.
Asserts that existential psychotherapy with Vietnam combat veteran couples should include the treatment elements of holding, telling, mastering, and honoring the combat trauma pain. The authors describe these 4 treatment elements and provide a descriptive clinical study of this treatment approach with 53 Vietnam veteran couples treated between 1974-1999. All couples were provided marital therapy and completed the Purpose of Life Test (J. Crumbaugh and L. Maholick, 1966) and the Marital Relationship Perceptions Test (J. Lantz, 1974, 2000) at the beginning and end of treatment, and at a 6-mo to 1-yr follow-up interview. The results show that all 53 couples made good progress during treatment, as indicated by the self-report and marital adjustment measures.
Contemporary Family Therapy: An International Journal. 2000 Mar Vol 22(1) 19-37

[363]
Miller, Leonard E.; Adwell, Steven T.

Combating stress and burnout among correctional employees.
Surveyed the administrative, custodial, and program staff of 2 correctional institutions to determine the levels of stress and burnout experienced by Ss and to research the relation-

ship between the existential construct purpose in life and stress burnout. Results show stress burnout scores comparable to those found by F. E. Cheek (1983) in a national study. Purpose in life was significantly related to burnout, health, nutrition, physical exercise, and job satisfaction scores (Purpose in Life Test).

International Forum for Logotherapy. 1984 Fal-Win Vol 7(2) 112-117

[364]
Orbuch, Terri L.; Harvey, John H.; Davis, Susan H.; Merbach, Nancy J.

Account-making and confiding as acts of meaning in response to sexual assault.
Compared the interpretive and coping responses of female and male survivors of incest and female survivors of sexual assault by a nonrelative. 28 adults responded to a questionnaire that asked them to provide an account of the nature of an assault, the role of confidants in helping them cope with the assault, how they coped and tried to understand the assault over time, how they felt the assault affected their close relationships, and how they evaluated their current state of recovery. The results for male and female incest groups were similar in revealing great difficulty in coping and in having adult close relationships. These 2 groups showed more continuing lack of resolution than did the female nonfamilial survivors. The male group of incest survivors showed the greatest overall difficulty. Findings are discussed in terms of searching for meaning via account-making and confiding as ways of dealing with long-term major stressors.

Journal of Family Violence. 1994 Sep Vol 9(3) 249-264

[cf. 338]
Parappully, Jose; Rosenbaum, Robert; van den Daele, Leland; Nzewi, Esther

Thriving after trauma: The experience of parents of murdered children.
Journal of Humanistic Psychology. 2002 Win Vol 42(1) 33-70

[365]
Peacock, E. J., & Wong, P. T. P.

Anticipatory stress: The relation of locus of control, optimism, and control appraisals to coping.
This paper examined the locus of control beliefs and optimism as predictors of control appraisals and coping schemas associated with three different anticipatory stressful situations (employment decisions, teacher bias, and natural disaster). The 118 undergraduate participants completed measures of locus of control (Rotter I-E), optimism (Life Orientation Test) and control appraisals (Stress Appraisal measure) 2 weeks prior to completing the Inventory of Coping Schemas to report their coping strategies used in dealing with each stressor. Regression analyses indicated that optimism and locus of control we relatively independent predictors of control appraisals and that control appraisals were generally better predictors of coping than either locus of control of optimism. As expected, somewhat different patterns of significant predictors were obtained for the three stressors. Results are discussed in terms of the congruence model of effective coping, which predicts relations among control appraisals and coping for various types of stressful situations. Specifically, situational and preventive coping were significantly higher for the two controllable stressors than for the uncontrollable stressor, whereas existential and religious/spiritu-

al coping were significantly higher for the uncontrollable stressor than for the two controllable ones.

Journal of Research in Personality. 1996. 30, 204-222.

[366]
Prager, Edward; Solomon, Zahava

Perceptions of world benevolence, meaningfulness, and self-worth among elderly Israeli holocaust survivors and non-survivors.
Hypothesized that traumatic events may challenge and even disrupt basic individual assumptions about the world, including the perception of the world as a benevolent place, the meaningfulness of the world, and the self-worth of the individual. The cognitive schemata of 61 Israeli Holocaust survivors (mean age 68.3 yrs) were compared with those of 131 non-Holocaust controls (mean age 72.9 yrs). Multivariate ANOVA indicated a significant overall Holocaust effect on World Assumptions. Data implicate 2 of the 3 schemata studied: world benevolence and world meaning. Exposure to the Holocaust accounted for almost all the explained variance in the world benevolence scheme, while sociodemographic variables contributed almost all of the explained variance to world meaning and self-worth.

Anxiety, Stress & Coping: An International Journal. 1995 Vol 8(4) 265-277

[367]
Ryff, Carol D.; Essex, Marilyn J.

The interpretation of life experience and well-being: The sample case of relocation.
Social psychological theories of the self postulate mechanisms through which individuals interpret their life experiences to ensure positive self-evaluation. This framework was applied to a sample of 120 aging women (mean age 74.9 yrs) who had experienced community relocation. The authors measured their reasons for moving (push factors), reasons for selecting the new setting (pull factors), and interpretive mechanisms, including how they compared with others in their new setting, how they were viewed by significant others following the move, how their behaviors changed following relocation, and whether the above evaluations occurred in life domains central to their sense of self. Regression analyses showed that push-pull factors and interpretive mechanisms accounted for substantial variance in multiple aspects of psychological well-being, particularly environmental mastery, purpose in life, and positive relations with others.

Psychology & Aging. 1992 Dec Vol 7(4) 507-517

[368]
Ryff Carol D.; Keyes, C.L.; Hughes D.L.

Status inequalities, perceived discrimination, and eudaimonic well-being: do the challenges of minority life hone purpose and growth?
Considerable prior research has investigated links between racial/ethnic status and diverse aspects of mental functioning (e.g. psychological disorders, quality of life, self-esteem), but little work has probed the connections between minority status and eudaimonic well-being. Derived from existential and humanistic perspectives, eudaimonia describes engagement in life challenges and is operationalized with assessments of purpose in life, personal growth, autonomy, environmental mastery, self-acceptance, and positive relations with others. Using

Midlife in the United States (MIDUS), a national survey of Americans aged 25-74, plus city-specific samples of African Americans in New York City and Mexican Americans in Chicago, minority status was found to be a positive predictor of eudaimonic well-being, underscoring themes of psychological strength in the face of race-related adversity. Perceived discrimination was found to be a negative predictor of eudaimonic well-being, although such effects were gender-specific: it was women, both majority and minority, with high levels of discrimination in their daily lives whose sense of growth, mastery, autonomy, and self-acceptance was compromised.

*Journal of Health and Social Behavior. 2003 Sep;44(3):275-91**

[369]
Shek, Daniel T. L.

Meaning in life and sense of mastery in Chinese adolescents with economic disadvantage. Examines the relationship between meaning in life and sense of mastery in economically disadvantaged Chinese adolescents residing in Hong Kong. 229 Hong Kong Chinese adolescents with economic disadvantage responded to the Chinese version of the Existential Well-being Scale and the Mastery Scale. Results showed that there was a positive relationship between reported meaning in life and sense of mastery.

Psychological Reports. 2001 Jun Vol 88(3) 711-712

[370]
Silver, Roxane L.; Boon, Cheryl; Stones, Mary H.

Searching for meaning in misfortune: Making sense of incest.
A critical feature of many undesirable life events is that they often shatter the victim's perception of living in an orderly, meaningful world. Many authors have suggested that following such outcomes, the search for meaning is a common and adaptive process. The present study explored the validity of that claim by considering data from a recent study of 77 18-72 yr old women who were victimized as children: survivors of father-daughter incest. In the process, several central questions regarding the search for meaning are addressed. For example, how important is such a search years after a crisis? What are the mechanisms by which individuals find meaning in their negative outcomes? Does finding meaning in one's victimization facilitate long-term adjustment to the event? Findings indicate that to the extent that the search for meaning results in finding meaning in an undesirable event, it is likely to be an adaptive process. The authors maintain that the ruminations and cognitive rehearsal that accompany such a search serve an adaptive function in that they are likely to be the means by which individuals gain mastery over and make sense of their experience. However, finding meaning does not appear to terminate the search or the ruminations. Moreover, when after an extended period the search fails to bring understanding, the continuing process of searching and repeatedly ruminating appears to be maladaptive

Journal of Social Issues. 1983 Sum Vol 39(2) 81-101

[371]
Tweed, Sandra H.; Ryff, Carol D.

Adult children of alcoholics: Profiles of wellness amidst distress.
Investigated the psychological adjustment of adult children of alcoholics, using 114 such Ss and 125 demographically comparable adults from nonalcoholic families. The sample was

further divided into young- and middle-adult age groups (aged 18-24 yrs and 25-45 yrs, respectively) and men and women. Measures of psychological well-being and emotional distress included the Self-Rating Depression Scale, the Anxiety scale of the Jackson Personality Inventory, and the Purpose in Life Test. Results indicate that adult children of alcoholics did not differ from the comparison group on most of the measures. However, adult children of alcoholics scored significantly higher for anxiety and depression than did adults from non-alcoholic families. Findings are discussed in light of the need to implement future research that will explain the apparent variability in the psychological functioning of adult children of alcoholics.

Journal of Studies on Alcohol. 1991 Mar Vol 52(2) 133-141

[372]
Tedeschi, Richard G.; Calhoun, Lawrence G.

The Posttraumatic Growth Inventory: Measuring the positive legacy of trauma.
Describes the development of the Posttraumatic Growth Inventory (PTGI), an instrument for assessing positive outcomes reported by persons who have experienced traumatic events. This 21-item scale includes factors of New Possibilities, Relating to Others, Personal Strength, Spiritual Change, and Appreciation of Life. Three studies were conducted to develop the items and determine scale reliability, and concurrent and discriminant validity, and to examine construct validity. The Ss were 17-25 yr old college students. The studies indicated that the PTGI has good internal validity, acceptable test-retest reliability, and scores on the scale are approximately normally distributed. The results also indicated that women tend to report more benefits from traumatic events than do men, and persons who have experienced these events report more positive changes than do persons who have not experienced extraordinary events. The PTGI is modestly related to optimism and extraversion. The scale appears to have utility in determining how successful individuals, coping with the aftermath of trauma, are in reconstructing or strengthening their perceptions of self, others, and the meaning of events.

Journal of Traumatic Stress. 1996 Jul Vol 9(3) 455-472

[373]
Wan, Thomas T.; Odell, Barbara G

Major role losses and social participation of older males.
Examined the relative importance of major role losses experienced in widowerhood and retirement, personal characteristics, and prior level of participation as predictors of formal and informal social participation in old age. Data obtained from the Longitudinal Retirement History Survey (LRHS) of 6,603 males (aged 58-63 yrs) were analyzed. Stepwise regression analysis revealed that prior level of participation and personal characteristics such as SES and kin network size explained more variance in participation than major role losses considered alone or in conjunction with related deteriorative changes such as income loss. When the effects of these variables were simultaneously controlled, Ss with major role losses had lower levels of participation in formal organizations and in selected areas of informal activity than those without comparable losses. Examination of the cumulative effects of experiencing both major role losses exacerbated these results. Policy implications for preretirement education and programming are discussed.

Research on Aging. 1983 Jun Vol 5(2) 173-196

[374]
Williams, Nancy R.; Lindsey, Elizabeth W.; Kurtz, P. David; Jarvis, Sara

From trauma to resiliency: Lessons from former runaway and homeless youth.
This exploratory study presents findings on resiliency development in 5 former runaway
and homeless youth (aged 18-25 yrs). Subjected to chronic trauma, this unique population
lacked the protective factors other studies have associated with resiliency development. Five
young women were compared and contrasted in relation to the following questions: what
factors promote resiliency in runaway and homeless youth and how are resilient youth differentiated from their peers who continue to exhibit high risk behaviors? A multiple case
study design was used to explore themes that emerged from in-depth interviews with an
original sample of 22 former runaway and homeless youth. These themes included determination, meaning and purpose in life, self-care and readiness to accept help.
Journal of Youth Studies. 2001 Jun Vol 4(2) 233-253

[375]
Zika, Sheryl; Chamberlain, Kerry

Relation of hassles and personality to subjective well-being.
We examined three personality variables—locus of control, assertiveness, and meaning in
life—as possible moderators of the relation between stressors and subjective well-being.
Results from a sample of 160 students suggested that any moderating effects were not extensive and were mainly limited to the locus of control variable with female subjects.
Replication of the study on a sample of 120 community members found no significant
moderating effects. Chronic daily stressors (hassles) were found to have a direct effect on
well-being reports. Among the personality variables, meaning in life consistently predicted
positive well-being, and internal locus of control and assertiveness had direct but somewhat
less consistent effects. Consideration is given to possible explanations for the pattern of
results, and implications for the structure of well-being are discussed.
Journal of Personality & Social Psychology. 1987 Jul Vol 53(1) 155-162

PART II

PSYCHOPATHOLOGY

Meaning-Oriented

Psychopathology (General)

[376]
Addad, Moshe

Psychogenic neuroticism and noogenic self-strengthening.
Examined possible connections between meaning and life and extraversion in relation to psychogenic neuroticism and noogenic self-strengthening. 140 imprisoned criminals and 306 noncrimnals (all Ss aged 17-51 yrs) completed a measure of extraversion and neuroticism and the Purpose-in-Life questionnaire. The authors found that criminals with lower levels of neuroticism had higher scores on levels of meaning, suggesting that criminality itself may have contributed to the high meaning in life scores. Findings show a negative correlation between level of neuroticism and meaning in life scores. No correlation was found between Purpose-in-Life and level of extraversion. It is argued that criminals fill the existential vacuum with the substitute of criminality and that aspirations for power, control, or pleasure result in criminal behavior and become a substitute for meaning.
International Forum for Logotherapy. 1987 Spr-Sum Vol 10(1) 52-59

[cf. 005]
Balcar, Karel

Meaning in life, well-being, and health.
(Zivotni smysluplnost, dusevni pohoda a zdravi.)

Ceskoslovenska Psychologie. 1995 Vol 39(5) 420-424

[377]
Becker, Peter

Coping behavior and mental health.
(Bewaeltigungsverhalten und seelische Gesundheit.)
Investigated the structure of efficient coping behavior, defined as behavior chosen by mentally healthy people in stressful situations, among 60 elderly women, ages 51 to 75 yrs. Ss were selected to differ in their levels of mental health, which was assessed using a variety of strategies: (1) physician diagnosis; (2) interviews and observations conducted by psychologists, using 50 items from the California Q-Sort (J. Block, 1961); (3) a 38-item self-actualization questionnaire developed by the author; (4) the Purpose in Life Test (J. C. Crumbaugh and L. T. Maholick, 1972); and (5) 2 self-report scales developed by the author to assess neuroticism and intelligence. These assessments provided data on 12 mental health indicators. Ss' coping behaviors were assessed using both the stress coping questionnaire (Stresverarbeitungsfragebogen) developed by W. Janke, G. Erdmann, and W. Boucsein (1978) and a newly developed research strategy that requires Ss to describe their probable reactions to specific, stressful, daily situations. Results indicate that Ss differing in their levels of mental health also differ in some aspects of their reactions to stressful situations.

Results are discussed in terms of the findings of other investigators and with regard to implications for programs designed to promote coping competencies.

Zeitschrift fuer Klinische Psychologie. Forschung und Praxis. 1985 Vol 14(3) 169-184

[378]
Bond, M. J.; Feather, N. T.

Some correlates of structure and purpose in the use of time.
Reports findings from studies that used the Time Structure Questionnaire (TSQ), an instrument designed to measure the degree to which individuals perceive their use of time as structured and purposive. Results from 3 samples of university students showed that the TSQ has acceptable psychometric properties. They also showed that TSQ total scores were positively correlated with a sense of purpose in life, self-esteem, reported health, present standing and optimism about the future, Type A behavior, and more efficient study habits, and were negatively correlated with depression, psychological distress, anxiety, neuroticism, physical symptoms, hopelessness, and anomie. Perceived use of time also varied with role demands, such as whether a person was single or married, employed or unemployed, or a part-time or full-time student.

Journal of Personality & Social Psychology. 1988 Aug Vol 55(2) 321-329

[379]
Chaudhary, P. N.; Sharma, Umesh

Existential frustration and mental illness: A comparative study of purpose in life in psychiatric patients and normals.
The Purpose in Life Test was administered to 60 schizophrenic, 60 neurotic, and 60 normal males matched for age (18-32 yrs), education, and socioeconomic background. Results show that (a) the schizophrenic and neurotic Ss differed significantly from the normals with respect to possession of a purpose in life, and (b) the schizophrenics also differed significantly from the neurotics. Findings indicate the usefulness of the Purpose in Life Test for discriminating psychiatric patients from normals in an Indian population. It is suggested that the loss of a life purpose may cause existential frustration, anxiety, and despair, and in extreme form may result in neurotic or psychotic illness.

Indian Journal of Clinical Psychology. 1976 Sep Vol 3(2) 171-174

[380]
Cohen, Alex

The search for meaning: Eventfulness in the lives of homeless mentally ill persons in the Skid Row district of Los Angeles.
In the past two decades, the field of psychiatry has seen the once dominant psychoanalytic theories overtaken by biological explanations and approaches to severe mental illness. With this change in perspective, the significance of fantasies and delusions have been reduced to being merely symptoms of psychopathology rather than reflections of human needs and motivations. Using ethnographic evidence from a long-term research project, this paper explores one method by which mentally ill homeless individuals in the Skid Row district of Los Angeles attempted to wrest meaningful lives for themselves out of an environment that featured disaffiliation, violence, boredom, and extreme poverty.

Culture, Medicine & Psychiatry. 2001 Sep Vol 25(3) 277-296

[cf. 012]
Debats, Dominique L.

The Life Regard Index: Reliability and validity.
Psychological Reports. 1990 Aug Vol 67(1) 27-34

[381]
Debats, Dominique L.

Meaning in life: Clinical relevance and predictive power.
The clinical relevance of the meaning in life construct is examined by evaluating its ability to predict 114 patients' (aged 18-42 yrs) general and psychological well-being and their post- treatment functioning. Evidence is obtained for the notion that meaning in life (1) would affect both positive and negative aspects of well-being, (2) that it would be related to improvement during psychotherapy, and (3) that it would predict the outcome of psychotherapy, independently of patients' pre-treatment levels of well-being. Findings not only support the clinical relevance of the meaning in life concept, but they also favor the construct validity of the Life Regard Index, an instrument designed to measure the relevant construct. It is concluded that the neglected meaning in life issue deserves greater therapeutic and scientific consideration.
Journal of Clinical Psychology. 1996 Nov Vol 35(4) 503-516

[cf. 014]
Debats, Dominique L.; Van der Lubbe, Petra M.; Wezeman, Fimmy R.

On the psychometric properties of the Life Regard Index (LRI): A measure of meaningful life: An evaluation in three independent samples based on the Dutch version.
Personality & Individual Differences. 1993 Feb Vol 14(2) 337-345

[382]
D'Souza, Russell

Do patients expect psychiatrists to be interested in spiritual issues?
Reports on a pilot study surveying the spiritual attitudes and needs of patients with a psychiatric illness at the Centre of Excellence in Remote and Rural Psychological Medicine, Broken Hill Base Hospital, NSW. A questionnaire consisting of 6 questions was completed by 79 patients (aged 17-71 yrs). It was found that 79% of the patients rated spirituality as very important and 82% thought their therapists should be aware of their spiritual beliefs and needs. 69% of the patients reported that patients spiritual needs should be considered by the therapist in treating their psychological illness and 67% said that their spirituality helped them cope with their psychological pain. The majority of patients said spirituality was important to them and that they wanted their therapist to take their spiritual needs into consideration in the assessment and management of their illness.
Australasian Psychiatry. 2002 Mar Vol 10(1) 44-47

[cf. 599]
Dyck, Murray J.

Assessing logotherapeutic constructs: Conceptual and psychometric status of the Purpose in Life and Seeking of Noetic Goals tests.

Clinical Psychology Review. 1987 Vol 7(4) 439-447

[383]
Gonsalvez, Graig J.; Gon, Manjuli

A comparative study of purpose-in-life in psychopathological and normal groups.
Administered the Purpose-in-Life (PIL) Test to 30 schizophrenics, 30 psychoneurotics, 30 nonpatient college students, and 30 nonpatient seminarians. All Ss were aged 17-37 yrs. Each group with psychopathology exhibited significantly lower PIL scores than the nonpatient groups, but there were no significant differences in PIL scores between the 2 psychopathology groups or between the scores of the 2 normal groups. It is suggested that a pathological lack of purpose is a cause of the development of conventional psychopathological syndromes. Symptoms that differentiated the groups were the following: Schizophrenics and psychoneurotics had greater feelings of boredom, sameness, and routineness in daily living than did normals, and a negative self-image was more characteristic of the patients than of the normals.

Indian Journal of Clinical Psychology. 1983 Sep Vol 10(2) 211-218

[cf. 438]
Heisel, Marnin J.; Flett, Gordon L.

Purpose in Life, satisfaction with life, and suicide ideation in a clinical sample.

Journal of Psychopathology & Behavioral Assessment. 2004 Jun Vol 26(2) 127-135

[384]
Ilstad, Steinar; Jarle, Ivar

Work stress, purpose in life, and mental health.
(Jobbstress, hensikt med livet og mental helse.)
Studied the correlations between purpose in life (PIL), on 1 hand, and stress, strain, social support, and coping, on the other; and assessed the potential buffering effect of PIL between stress and various strain indicators (dissatisfaction with work, dissatisfaction with life as a whole, depression, low self-respect, concentration problems, and sleep disorders). Ss included 99 male and female Norwegian adults (aged 20-65 yrs) (engineers). Ss completed a questionnaire designed to measure the relevant factors. PIL's relationship to the concept of hardiness (commitment, control, and challenge), and facets of a general personal resistance resource also were assessed.

Tidsskrift for Norsk Psykologforening. 1993 Dec Vol 30(12) 1167-1173

[385]
Juros, Andrzej

Personality correlates of the feeling of the meaning of life.
(**Korelaty osobowosciowe poczucia sensu zycia.**)

Discusses the development, factor structure, construct validity, and reliability of the Purpose in Life Test. Correlations with the State Anxiety Scale of the State-Trait Anxiety Inventory, the Eysenck Personality Inventory, the Minnesota Multiphasic Personality Inventory (MMPI), and the Self-Rating Depression Scale are considered.
Roczniki Filozoficzne: Psychologia. 1984 Vol 32(4) 97-112

[386]
Kish, George B.; Moody, David R

Psychopathology and life purpose.
Hypothesized that psychopathology would be negatively correlated with a sense of meaning and purpose in life in 48 male patients in an alcohol dependency program. At the end of the 1st wk in the program, Ss completed the Shipley Institute of Living Scale for Measuring Intellectual Impairment; the Minnesota Multiphasic Personality Inventory (MMPI); the Life Purpose Questionnaire (R. Hablas and R. R. Hutzell, 1982); and the Existential Depression Scale (R. R. Hutzell and M. S. Peterson, 1985). Results indicate that a good sense of life purpose was accompanied by a lesser degree of psychopathology in Ss. Lack of meaning and purpose in life was related to a wide variety of psychological syndromes.
International Forum for Logotherapy. 1989 Spr Vol 12(1) 40-45

[387]
Kishida Y. ; Kitamura T.; Gatayama R.; Matsuoka T.; Miura S.; Yamabe K.

Ryff's psychological well-being inventory: factorial structure and life history correlates among Japanese university students.
The theoretical model of psychological well-being that encompasses six domains (self-acceptance, positive relations with others, autonomy, environmental mastery, purpose in life, and personal growth) was tested with a Japanese university student population (N = 574) using a Japanese translation of Ryff's 1989 Psychological Well-being Inventory. A factor structure similar to Ryff's original model emerged. Both depression and anxiety correlated only moderately with scores on some subscales of the inventory, suggesting the relative independence of these dimensions of psychological well-being and negative affectivity. With negative affectivity controlled, some early life experiences were significantly linked with psychological well-being: relationships with romantic partners were linked with greater autonomy and experiences which enhance self-esteem were liked with greater personal growth. Careful psychometric work on the Japanese version is required to use the scale; then a replication and extension of the present study would be feasible.
Psychological Reports. 2004 Feb;94(1):83-103

[388]
Labelle, Real; Alain, Michel; Bastin, Etienne; Bouffard, Leandre; Dube, Micheline; Lapierre, Sylvie

Well-being and psychological stress: Toward a hierarchical, cognitive-affective model in mental health.
(Bien-etre et detresse psychologique: Vers un modele hierarchique cognitivo-affectif en sante mentale.)
Studied the relation of psychological well-being, anxiety, depression, and stress in 278 male and female older adults (mean age 63.7 yrs) in Canada. Data on sociodemographic variables

and clinical and psychological symptoms were obtained by questionnaire. The State-Trait Anxiety Inventory, the Mental Status Scale (M. F. Folstein et al, 1975), the Geriatric Depression Scale (J. A. Yeasavage et al, 1983), the Self-Esteem Scale (M. Rosenberg, 1965), the Actualization Potential Measure (G. Leclerc et al, 1997), the Life Satisfaction Scale (E. Diener et al, 1985), and the Sense of Life Scale (C. D. Ryff, 1989) were administered. Factorial analysis and other statistical tests were used to analyze data. The results were used to develop a hierarchical, cognitive-affective model of mental health. The results indicate that state anxiety, trait anxiety, and depression are associated with psychological distress while self-esteem, self-actualization, life satisfaction, and meaning of life are associated with psychological well-being.

Revue Quebecoise de Psychologie. 2001 Vol 22(1) 71-87

[389]
Lantz, James E.

The noetic curative factor in group therapy.
In the rankings of 65 short-term, acute-care, psychiatric clients engaged in twice weekly group sessions during hospitalization (averaging about 8 Ss session), the noetic curative factor ("The group helped me find meaning in my life") was chosen most often as being the most important. Other curative factors frequently picked among the 1st 3 were universality, cohesiveness, and instillation of hope. It is suggested that these curative factors have an existential or noetic characteristic.

International Forum for Logotherapy. 1984 Fal-Win Vol 7(2) 121-123

[390]
Li, Han Z.; Browne, Annette J.

Defining mental illness and accessing mental health services: Perspectives of Asian Canadians.
Asian Canadians consistently underutilize mainstream mental health services. This study investigates how the definition and meaning of mental illness relates to barriers Asian Canadians find in accessing mental health services. Personal interviews were conducted with 60 Asian Canadians (mean age range 41-43 yrs) in a northern community in the province of British Columbia. Content analyses revealed six themes that defined a mental health problem: (1) feeling a lack of purpose in life, (2) feeling lonely, (3) difficulties understanding and dealing with a new environment, (4) high anxiety levels, (5) descriptions of mental health problems as somatic illnesses, and (6) perceptions of mental illness as serious and potentially not treatable. It was also found that poor English language ability and a lack of understanding of mainstream culture were major barriers to accessing mental health facilities. Findings of this study provide valuable insights concerning Asian immigrants' hesitancy to access and utilize mainstream mental health facilities. The many poignant personal anecdotes illustrate that the migration and adaptation processes can be painful and full of anguish.

Canadian Journal of Community Mental Health. 2000 Spr Vol 19(1) 143-159

[391]
Lindfors, Petra

Positive health in a group of Swedish white-collar workers.
C. D. Ryff's Psychological Well-being scales cover six dimensions of psychological well-being (Self-acceptance, Environmental mastery, Positive relations with others, Personal growth, Purpose in life, and Autonomy) and have been suggested as an adequate measure of positive psychological functioning. Apart from translating the scales to Swedish and examining the psychometric properties of the measure, the present study aimed to explore the relationships between the Ryff scales and the General Health Questionnaire, negative affectivity, and physical symptoms using self-ratings from 91 full-time employed women and men (aged 24-62 yrs). Given low internal consistency for the different dimensions of the Ryff scales, correlational analyses were based on a composite index. Analysis indicated negative relations between the Ryff index and other measures and are in line with prior findings showing that the index taps positive psychological functioning while other indices focus on negative functioning.
Psychological Reports. 2002 Dec Vol 91(3,Pt1) 839-845

[392]
Lukas, Elisabeth

A validation of logotherapy.
A theoretical structure of logotherapy is presented, based on a logotest developed by the present author (1969), which states that the human being possesses a noetic dimension. Premises include the following: The human being has 3 dimensions. In each dimension, the dependency on given circumstances is different. The 3 dimensions form an inseparable unit. No dimension must be disregarded in psychotherapy. The feedback mechanisms work differently in each dimension. For each dimension, the principle of homeostasis has a different validity. From these premises, it is suggested that psychotherapeutic practice can not be effective either with logotherapy alone or without logotherapy at all. Use of 4 logotherapeutic methods (modification of attitudes, paradoxical intention, dereflection, and appealing technique) in the treatment of 300 patients over 6 yrs is assessed.
International Forum for Logotherapy. 1981 Fal-Win Vol 4(2) 116-125

[393]
Opoczynska, Malgorzata

Identity Crisis in Schizophrenia and ways of overcoming it
This paper, based on the V.E.Frankl's logotherapy and the identity theory of D.P. McAdams, discusses the problem of identity crisis in schizophrenia and puts the question of the possibility of its reachievement after the active phase of this illness. The investigation of 30 case studies (applying mainly biographical methods and projective techniques) resulted in the conclusion that religious beliefs of persons suffering from schizophrenia may help them to find meaning of their own illness and make it easier for them to accept the illness and to integrate it with the rest of their life story. The study also showed that this help is not equally efficient in every case. That means, it is not enough to be a believer and to "use" the beliefs, if necessary, in order to understand the meaning of different events in life. The most important thing seems to be the way in which the reality, which is the object of one's beliefs,

is experienced, as the way in which one understands their life depends on how this reality is seen and understood.

The International Journal of Logotherapy and Existential Analysis / The Journal of the Viktor Frankl Institute. 1997: Volume 5, Number 2 (Fall/Winter 1997)*

[394]
Mee, Jeannie; Sumsion, Thelma

Mental health clients confirm the motivating power of occupation.
Most occupational therapists believe that engagement in meaningful occupation is fundamental to helping overcome the effects of disability. This paper describes the method and
one of the resulting themes of a study that investigated the value, related to personal meaning, of occupation from the perspective of people with enduring mental health problems.
Qualitative research methods were used in 2 mental health day service settings: a workshop,
where woodwork was provided as a medium for creative therapy, and a drop-in facility.
Clients were 39-61 yr olds with diagnoses of manic depression, psychotic depression, chronic anxiety, personality disorder, chronic depression, and schizophrenia. They were asked
about their motivation, their occupational experiences, and any benefits that engagement in
occupation might have had for them. Participant observation was undertaken over 10 sessions and 6 in-depth interviews were conducted. Occupation was identified as a means for
generating intrinsic motivation. By providing a sense of purpose and a structuring of time,
within an empowering environment, engagement in occupation was seen to be of value and
had personal meaning for the clients. The authors note the implications of their findings for
occupational therapy.

British Journal of Occupational Therapy. 2001 Mar Vol 64(3) 121-128

[395]
Moomal, Zubair

The relationship between meaning in life and mental well-being.
The aim of this study was to add and corroborate findings concerning the relationship
between meaning in life and mental well-being by examining the relationship between
meaning in life or its absence and the extent to which a non-clinical sample of 92 university students manifest pathological indicators. The hypothesis addressed is that meaning in
life is positively associated with mental well-being irrespective of the nature of the psychopathology. This hypothesis stems from an existential perspective on psychopathology
(and consequently psychotherapy) which holds that a sense of meaning in life is a vital element in providing coherence to an individual's worldview and hence to his her mental well-
being. Ss completed the Purpose in Life Test, the MMPI, and the revised Eysenck
Personality Questionnaire-Neuroticism Scale. Correlational analyses on data corroborated
that meaning in life is associated with a wide spectrum of conventional categories of psychopathology as well as with general neurosis. Statistically significant correlations were
established.

South African Journal of Psychology. 1999 Mar Vol 29(1) 36-41

[cf. 199]
Mountain, Deborah Ann; Muir, Walter J.

Spiritual well-being in psychiatric patients.
                    Irish Journal of Psychological Medicine. 2000 Dec Vol 17(4) 123-127

[396]
Nair, V.; Tiwari, S.; Wee, M.; Leong, S.F.; Sarjit, K.; Thavamani; Liew, C.S.

Quality of life survey among long-stay mentally ill patients: patient and staff perspectives.
In order to improve the quality of life of the chronically mentally ill patients, their treatment programmes must be individualised to address their multiple disabilities and social
impairment. The patient's perception of his quality of life (QoL) can be used as an organ-
ising framework for long-term care. Subjects in the study included staff and inpatients from
the 10 rehabilitation wards in New Woodbridge Hospital which offers a wide range of rehabilitation activities. Using subjective indices, patient and staff perception of patients' quality of life were compared across several life domains. Significant differences between the 2
groups were noted in areas including living conditions, relationship with others and sense
of purpose in life. Most patients found the new hospital a better place in terms of its physical comfort and the medical and psychiatric care received. The implications of these findings for improving existing care for our patients are discussed.
                    Singapore Medical Journal. 1996 Oct;37(5):512-6 *

[397]
Pearson, Paul R.; Sheffield, Brian F.

Purpose-in-Life and the Eysenck Personality Inventory.
In a study of 144 outpatient neurotics, the correlations between the Purpose-in-Life Test
and the Eysenck Personality Inventory (Form A) indicated that patients with a higher purpose in life are less neurotic and more sociable.
                    Journal of Clinical Psychology. 1974 Oct Vol 30(4) 562-564

[398]
Pearson, Paul R.; Sheffield, Brian F.

Purpose in life and social attitudes in psychiatric patients.
Administered the Purpose-in-Life Test and the Conservatism Scale to 84 male and 97
female psychiatric outpatients. For males purpose in life was related positively to
Conservatism, Idealism, Anti-hedonism, and Religion-puritanism, but only to Idealism and
Anti-hedonism for females.
                    Journal of Clinical Psychology. 1975 Apr Vol 31(2) 330-332

[399]
Pearson, Paul R.; Sheffield, Brian F.

Psychoticism and purpose in life.
Administered the Purpose in Life Test and the Eysenck Personality Questionnaire to 83
young female nurses. Purpose in life was significantly negatively related to psychoticism and

neuroticism and positively to extraversion. Results support the hypothesis that individuals high in psychoticism tend to have little purpose in life.

Personality & Individual Differences. 1989 Vol 10(12) 1321-1322

[400]
Raffi, Anna Rita; Rondini, Monica; Grandi, Silvana; Fava, Giovanni Andrea

The prodromal phase of bulimia nervosa.
(La fase prodromica della bulimia nervosa.)
Studied the relation of sociodemographic variables, life events, psychological factors, and prodromal symptoms of bulimia nervosa in 30 female adults (mean age 26.2 yrs) with bulimia nervosa (mean duration 6.3 yrs) and 30 female adults without bulimia nervosa (matched controls) in Italy. A modified version of the Clinical Interview for Depression, (E. S. Paykel, 1985), the Psychological Well-Being Scale (C. D. Ryff, 1989), and the Symptom Rating Scale were used. Statistical tests were used. The results show that most of the patients report prodromal symptoms, including anorexia, low self-esteem, depression, anhedonia, generalized anxiety, and irritability. The results also show that bulimia nervosa Ss, when compared to controls, report significantly more stressful life events; less psychological well-being in terms of autonomy, environmental mastery, personal growth, positive relationships, purpose in life, and self-acceptance; and more problems in terms of relaxation, contentment, and friendliness. Implications for assessing vulnerability to bulimia nervosa are considered.

Rivista di Psichiatria. 2000 Nov-Dec Vol 35(6) 270-275

[401]
Rangaswamy, K.

The experience of purpose-in-life by neurotics.
Administered the Purpose in Life Test (PLT) to 20 patients in each clinical category of anxiety neurosis, neurotic depression, neurotic hysteria, and hysteria. 30 normal controls matched for age (20-40 yrs), sex, education, and SES also completed the PLT. Results indicate that neurotics experienced less purpose in life than did controls, and the perceived purpose in life of depressives and hysterics was lower than that of the other neurotic groups. Implications for therapy are discussed.

Journal of Psychological Researches. 1982 May Vol 26(2) 73-75

[cf. 467]
Roehrig, Helmut R.; Range, Lillian M.

Recklessness, depression, and reasons for living in predicting suicidality in college students.

Journal of Youth & Adolescence. 1995 Dec Vol 24(6) 723-729

[402]
Sappington, A. A.; Bryant, John; Oden, Connie

An experimental investigation of Viktor Frankl's theory of meaningfulness in life.
Evaluates V. Frankl's (1962) theory that finding a sense of purpose in life is essential to physical health and psychological adjustment in 2 experiments with a total of 194 undergradu-

ates. Activities were assigned that were designed to increase perceived meaningfulness by helping Ss "give to the world" or "take from the world." Data suggest that these techniques were effective in increasing Purpose in Life Test scores. The availability of techniques for increasing meaningfulness makes possible the study of the causal role played by perceived meaningfulness in effective physical and psychological functioning.

International Forum for Logotherapy. 1990 Fal Vol 13(2) 125-130

[403]
Sheffield, Brian F.; Pearson, Paul R.

Purpose-in-life in a sample of British psychiatric out-patients.
Administered the Purpose-in-Life (PIL) Test to 363 male and female psychiatric outpatients, representing anxiety state, neurotic depressive, other neurotic, endogenous depressive, and personality disorders. Except for the category "other neuroses," the data indicate a general tendency for males to have higher PIL scores than females. The group with lowest PIL scores was that of females with personality disorder.

Journal of Clinical Psychology. 1974 Oct Vol 30(4) 459

[404]
Shek, Daniel T.

Mental health of secondary school students in Hong Kong: An epidemiological study using the General Health Questionnaire.
Assessed mental health status in 2,155 students (aged 11-20 yrs) in Hong Kong, using measures including the Chinese version of the General Health Questionnaire (GHQ), the Beck Depression Inventory, the Leeds Scales for the Self-Assessment of Anxiety and Depression, the State-Trait Anxiety Inventory, and the Purpose in Life Test. Results show that a significant proportion of Ss could be considered as psychologically at risk. Ss' mental health was related to personal (sex and age), school-related (grade, mode of attendance, and school type), and environmental (area and density) variables, and there was a significant relationship between GHQ scores and Ss' perceptions of parental treatment methods.

International Journal of Adolescent Medicine & Health. 1988 Jun-Sep Vol 3(3) 191-215

[405]
Shek, D. T.

Adolescent positive mental health and psychological symptoms: A longitudinal study in a Chinese context.
Examined the relationships between positive mental health (life satisfaction, self-esteem, purpose in life, and sense of hope) and general psychological symptoms in a sample of 378 Chinese adolescents (aged 12-16 yrs) at 2 time periods. Adolescents completed the Chinese versions of the General Health Questionnaire, the Life Satisfaction Scale, the Self-Esteem Scale, the Purpose in Life Scale, and the Hopelessness Scale. Parents completed a Parent Questionnaire containing instruments on the psychosocial adjustment and perceived family environment of the parents. Results showed that: (1) measures of positive mental health were concurrently related to general psychological symptoms at Time 1 and Time 2; (2) longitudinal and prospective analyses revealed that positive mental health and general psychological symptoms predicted each other across time; and (3) no obvious gender differences in the strengths of association between positive mental health and general psychological

symptoms were found. Multiple regression analyses further showed that relative to life satisfaction and hopelessness, self-esteem and purpose in life exerted a stronger influence on psychological morbidity over time.

Psychologia: An International Journal of Psychology in the Orient. 1998 Dec Vol 41(4) 217-225

[406]
Skrzynski, Wieslaw

Particular dimensions of time in the evaluation of neurotics with various degrees of a sense of purpose in life.
(Poszczegolne wymiary czasu w ocenie neurotykow o roznym stopniu poczucia sensu zycia.)
Examined 60 hospitalized neurotic patients and 60 normal individuals to determine the meaning of dimensions of time for persons with different degrees of the sense of purpose in life (PIL) and of different psychological health. Ss were grouped according to their degree of PIL measured by the Purpose in Life Test. Ss with low PIL were described as noogenic neurotics. Ss with high PIL were psychogenic neurotics. Ss also evaluated the concepts of past, present, and future on 10 bipolar adjective scales using the semantic differential technique. Results show that noogenic neurotics displayed the least accepting attitude toward all 3 dimensions of time. Their evaluations of the past and present were negative. Less intense disapproval of the future is postulated to be caused by their high concentration on present difficulties. Evaluations of psychogenic Ss were almost similar to those of normal Ss. It is suggested that in a person's existential space, the most important dimension of time is the present, including those elements of the past that coexist with it as meaningful and as nonaccepted. Results are relevant for therapy with neurotic patients. (8 ref)

Roczniki Filozoficzne: Psychologia. 1981 Vol 29(4) 203-214

[407]
Stanich, John; Oertengren, Ilona

The Logotest in Sweden.
Administered the Logotest and the Eysenck Personality Inventory (EPI) to 150 Ss (average age 39.4 yrs). Most Ss indicated that they perceived high inner meaning fulfillment with regard to social aspects and experiences, whereas few answered positively to overcoming distress. Parts I and III of the Logotest correlated positively, but not significantly, with the EPI neuroticism score, while Part II correlated positively and significantly with the neuroticism score. While revisions are suggested for Part I of the Logotest, Part II neatly covered the intrapsychic factors in 7 questions. Part III proved valuable despite its low correlation with the rest of the test.

International Forum for Logotherapy. 1990 Spr Vol 13(1) 54-60

[408]
Trzebiatowska IA, Gizinska D, Majkowicz M.

Purpose in life among schizophrenic patients during psychoeducation program – preliminary report
The article describe impact of psychoeducation on purpose in life, will of life, hope, delight

and satisfaction with life's attainments, relationship with family, health care and socio-economic situation among schizophrenic patients. There were no significant difference in on purpose in life hope and satisfaction with life's attainments, relationship with family, health care and socioeconomic situation. Patient after psychoeducation have significantly higher level of hope and delight.

Psychiatria Polska. 2002 Nov-Dec;36(6 Suppl):265-9. *

[409]
Yater, Stephanie M.; Klarman, Muriel

The effect on siblings of psychiatrically disturbed children by means of a questionnaire: A pilot study.
Administered to 60 7-28 yr old siblings of hospitalized psychiatrically disturbed youngsters a 62-item questionnaire that assessed 6 variables: anger, guilt, depression, withdrawal, identification, and search for meaning. A preponderance of the "search for meaning factor" is seen to suggest maturity of thinking in general. Thus, reactions of most siblings were found to be positive, hopeful, and interested. It is further suggested that the reaction of a sibling toward the hospitalized child could influence that patient's improvement.

Family Therapy. 1981 Vol 8(2) 141-148

[410]
Zika, Sheryl; Chamberlain, Kerry

On the relation between meaning in life and psychological well-being.
Investigated the relation between meaning in life and psychological well-being, using several meaning measures and both positive and negative well-being dimensions. 179 mothers (mean age 29 yrs) at home with small children and 129 elderly (mean age 69 yrs) completed 3 sets of questionnaires over 6 mo. Instruments included C. T. Viet and J. E. Ware's Mental Health Inventory and the Purpose in Life Test. A strong association was found between meaning in life and well-being. Meaning in life had a stronger association with positive than with negative well-being dimensions, suggesting the value of taking a salutogenic approach to mental health research.

British Journal of Psychology. 1992 Feb Vol 83(1) 133-145

Depression and Despair

[411]
Baron, Pierre; Hanna, Jayne

Egocentrism and depressive symptomatology in young adults.
Administered the Adolescent Egocentrism-Sociocentrism scale and the Beck Depression Inventory to 152 undergraduates. As predicted, Ss with high egocentrism showed significantly more depressive symptoms than those with low egocentrism. Results replicate those obtained by P. Baron with adolescents and suggest an association between egocentrism and depressive symptomatology across ages.
Social Behavior & Personality. 1990 Vol 18(2) 279-285

[412]
Baum, Steven K.; Boxley, Russell L.

Depression and old age identification.
308 persons (mean age 75.5 yrs) were selected from 3 settings to test the relationship between psychological depression and feeling "old." Ss were administered the Symptom Checklist-90, an age identification item, and several other measures of well-being (such as the Cornell Medical Index, Purpose-in-Life Test, and Rotter's Internal-External Locus of Control Scale). Results indicate that irrespective of age, persons who felt older were significantly more depressed and less healthy than their younger feeling counterparts. Multivariate level analysis further implicated personal meaning as a major correlate of depression.
Journal of Clinical Psychology. 1983 Jul Vol 39(4) 584-590

[cf. 378]
Bond, M. J.; Feather, N. T.

Some correlates of structure and purpose in the use of time.
Journal of Personality & Social Psychology. 1988 Aug Vol 55(2) 321-329

[cf. 575]
Brockner, Joel; Hjelle, Larry; Plant, Robert W.

Self-focused attention, self-esteem, and the experience of state depression.
Journal of Personality. 1985 Sep Vol 53(3) 425-434

[413]
De la Luz Ortega, Maria; Marvan, Maria Luisa

Depression and existential emptiness in women not in a profession.
(Depresion y vacio existencial en mujeres profesionales que no ejercen su profesion.)
Studied the relation of depression, profession and goal-seeking behaviors among 120 married Mexican women (aged 30-50 yrs). Data on sociodemographic variables, occupation, and goal-seeking attitudes were obtained by questionnaire. Results were evaluated accord-

ing to occupational status (working professionals, non-working professionals, working non-professionals, and non-working non-nonprofessionals), degree of depression, presence of an existential vacuum, and degree of goal-seeking behavior. Tests used: The Beck Depression Inventory, the Purpose in Life Test, and the Seeking of Noetic Goals Test. Higher levels of depression and existential vacuum, as well as lower goal seeking, were observed in Ss who didn't work outside the home. In contrast, professional Ss who were practicing their career demonstrated less depression and existential vacuum, as well as higher goal seeking. It is concluded that in spite of the problems that are implicated in developing as a housekeeper and worker, having a profession and practicing it is a stimulus to developing identity, autonomy, and independence.
Acta Psiquiatrica y Psicologica de America Latina. 1997 Jun Vol 43(2) 122-126

[cf. 359]
DuRant, Robert H.; Getts, Alan; Cadenhead, Chris; Emans, S. Jean; et al

Exposure to violence and victimization and depression, hopelessness, and purpose in life among adolescents living in and around public housing.
Journal of Developmental & Behavioral Pediatrics. 1995 Aug Vol 16(4) 233-237

[414]
Feather, N. T.; Bond, M. J.

Time structure and purposeful activity among employed and unemployed university graduates.
255 employed and 43 unemployed 1979-80 university graduates completed a questionnaire that included a self-esteem scale, the Beck Depression Inventory, and items designed to measure employment importance and the extent to which time was used in a structured and purposeful way. It was found that unemployed Ss were less organized and less purposeful in their use of time and reported more depressive symptoms when compared with the employed sample. In both groups, structured and purposeful use of time was positively associated with self-esteem and negatively associated with depressive symptoms. Correlations between employment importance and the use of time measures (total score, engagement, direction, structure, and routine) were negative for unemployed Ss and positive for the employed ones, indicating that employment importance functioned as a moderator variable. Females (n = 129) reported higher employment importance and more use of a routine but their self-esteem scores were lower than those of males (n = 169).
Journal of Occupational Psychology. 1983 Sep Vol 56(3) 241-254

[415]
Fenton, Fred R.; Cole, Martin G.; Engelsmann, Frank; Mansouri, Iradj

Depression in older medical inpatients.
Studied prevalence rates of major depressive disorder (MDE) among 215 inpatients (aged 65-74, 75-84, and 85+ yrs) and identified associations between demographic, social and clinical variables, and MDE. Ss were interviewed and assessed for orientation, memory, and concentration; daily functioning; mental disorders; and depression. Point prevalence rates of MDE were similar in the 3 age groups, 28%, 28%, and 24%, respectively. Rates among the 115 female Ss were over twice as high in age groups 65-74 and 75-84 yrs. The intensity of the MDEs detected was on average mild. Clinically meaningful statistical associations

were observed between psychological (absence of meaning in life and premorbid personality) and clinical (impaired ability to perform routine daily activities relating to self-care and previous consultation or treatment for an emotional problem) correlates.

International Journal of Geriatric Psychiatry. 1994 Apr Vol 9(4) 279-284

[416]
Garcia Pintos, Claudio C.

Depression and the will to meaning: A comparison of the GDS and PIL in an Argentine population.
Administered the Purpose in Life Test (PIL) and Geriatric Depression Scale (GDS) to 181 elderly residents of Buenos Aires. 75% of the Ss showed no depression, and the remaining 25% were divided between mild (22%) and severe depression (3%). There was a significant relationship between feelings of life satisfaction and no depression. 80% of the severely depressed Ss reported feelings of meaninglessness. It is asserted that the frustration of the natural "will to meaning" guides people to a feeling of life meaninglessness and existential vacuum which promotes the emergence of a geriatric depression. Spiritual causes of depression are also discussed.

Clinical Gerontologist. 1988 Spr-Sum Vol 7(3-4) 3-9

[cf. 577]
Greenberg, Jeff; Pyszczynski, Tom

Persistent high self-focus after failure and low self-focus after success: The depressive self-focusing style.

Journal of Personality & Social Psychology. 1986 May Vol 50(5) 1039-1044

[417]
Grygielski, Michal; et al

Meaning in life and hopelessness: Interrelationships and intergroup differences.
Analyzed the interrelationships between the feeling of meaning in life measured by The Purpose in Life Test (PILT) and the feeling of hopelessness measured by the Hopelessness Scale (HS), hypothesizing that a higher feeling of meaning in life should imply a lower feeling of hopelessness. It was predicted that age and existential situation differentiate people in terms of meaning in life and hope. 201 high school and university students, old-age pensioners, handicapped people, and ex-internees were tested. Testing was repeated 6 mo later with 112 Ss from the same group. A high negative correlation was found between feeling of meaning in life and feeling of hopelessness. Mean scores on the PILT were lowest for handicapped testees and old-age pensioners and highest for university students. Old-age pensioners and handicapped testees scored significantly higher than high school and university students on the HS. The 2nd testing revealed similar results. The substance of interrelations between feeling of meaning in life and feeling of hopelessness and between the former and the existential background are discussed.

Polish Psychological Bulletin. 1984 Vol 15(4) 277-284

[cf. 021]
Halama, Peter

Dimensions of life meaning as factors of coping
                              Studia Psychologica. 2000. 42:4. 339-350
[cf. 436]
Harlow, Lisa L.; Newcomb, Michael D.; Bentler, P. M.

Depression, self-derogation, substance use, and suicide ideation: Lack of purpose in life as a mediational factor.
                              Journal of Clinical Psychology. 1986 Jan Vol 42(1) 5-21

[cf. 146]
Hermans, Hubert J. M.; Oles, Piotr K.

Value crisis: Affective organization of personal meanings.
                              Journal of Research in Personality. 1996 Dec Vol 30(4) 457-482

[cf. 384]
Ilstad, Steinar; Jarle, Ivar

Work stress, purpose in life, and mental health.
(Jobbstress, hensikt med livet og mental helse.)
                              Tidsskrift for Norsk Psykologforening. 1993 Dec Vol 30(12) 1167-1173

[cf. 580]
Ingram, Rick E.; Lumry, Ann E.; Cruet, Debra; Sieber, William

Attentional processes in depressive disorders.
                              Cognitive Therapy & Research. 1987 Jun Vol 11(3) 351-360

[cf. 581]
Ingram, Rick E.; Smith, Timothy W.

Depression and internal versus external focus of attention.
                              Cognitive Therapy & Research. 1984 Apr Vol 8(2) 139-151

[cf. 582]
Ingram, Rick E.; Wisnicki, Kathleen

Situational specificity of self-focused attention in dysphoric states.
                              Cognitive Therapy & Research. 1999 Dec Vol 23(6) 625-636

[418]
Kinnier, Richard T.; Metha, Arlene T.; Keim, Jeanmarie S.; Okey, Jeffrey L.; et al

Depression, meaninglessness, and substance abuse in "normal" and hospitalized adolescents.

In a partial replication of the L. L. Harlow et al study, the relationships between depression, meaninglessness, suicide ideation, and substance abuse were examined in 2 samples of adolescents: 48 high school students and 113 patients in 2 psychiatric hospitals. All Ss were aged 12-18 yrs. Correlational analyses indicated that the high school students who viewed themselves negatively, were depressed, or who had found little meaning in their lives, were more likely to consider suicide and to abuse drugs. Regression and structural modeling analyses uncovered a strong mediational relationship between purpose in life with the precursor of depression and the consequence of substance abuse.

Journal of Alcohol & Drug Education. 1994 Win Vol 39(2) 101-111

[cf. 386]
Kish, George B.; Moody, David R.

Psychopathology and life purpose.

International Forum for Logotherapy. 1989 Spr Vol 12(1) 40-45

[cf. 190]
Klaas D.

Testing two elements of spirituality in depressed and non-depressed elders.

International Journal of Psychiatric Nursing Research. 1998 Sep;4(2):452-62. *

[cf. 388]
Labelle, Real; Alain, Michel; Bastin, Etienne; Bouffard, Leandre; Dube, Micheline; Lapierre, Sylvie

Well-being and psychological stress: Toward a hierarchical, cognitive-affective model in mental health.
(Bien-etre et detresse psychologique: Vers un modele hierarchique cognitivo-affectif en sante mentale.)

Revue Quebecoise de Psychologie. 2001 Vol 22(1) 71-87

[cf. 447]
Lester, David; Badro, Souhel

Depression, suicidal preoccupation and purpose in life in a subclinical population.

Personality & Individual Differences. 1992 Jan Vol 13(1) 75-76

[cf. 244]
Lyon, Debra E.; Younger, Janet B.

Purpose in life and depressive symptoms in persons living with HIV disease.

Journal of Nursing Scholarship. 2001 Vol 33(2) 129-133

[cf. 449]
Malone, Kevin M.; Oquendo, Maria A.; Haas, Gretchen L.; Ellis, Steven P.; Li, Shuhua; Mann, J. John

Protective factors against suicidal acts in major depression: Reasons for living.
American Journal of Psychiatry. 2000 Jul Vol 157(7) 1084-1088

[cf. 246]
Mayers, Aviva M.; Khoo, Siek-Toon; Svartberg, Martin

The Existential Loneliness Questionnaire: Background, development, and preliminary findings.
Journal of Clinical Psychology. 2002 Sep Vol 58(9) 1183-1193

[cf. 394]
Mee, Jeannie; Sumsion, Thelma

Mental health clients confirm the motivating power of occupation.
British Journal of Occupational Therapy. 2001 Mar Vol 64(3) 121-128

[cf. 557]
Michelson, Larry K.; Bellanti, Christina J.; Testa, Sandra M.; Marchione, Norman

The relationship of attributional style to agoraphobia severity, depression, and treatment outcome.
Behaviour Research & Therapy. 1997 Dec Vol 35(12) 1061-1073

[cf. 586]
Mor, Nilly; Winquist, Jennifer

Self-focused attention and negative affect: A meta-analysis.
Psychological Bulletin. 2002 Jul Vol 128(4) 638-662

[cf. 587]
Nix, Glen; Watson, Cheryl; Pyszczynski, Tom; Greenberg, Jeff

Reducing depressive affect through external focus of attention.
Journal of Social and Clinical Psychology, 14 (Spring), 36-52

[419]
Oakley, Linda Denise; Kane, Janet

Personal and social illness demands related to depression.
Surveyed currently recently treated and repeatedly treated depression patients to ascertain their experience of negative personal and social experiences that they relate to their depression, and to determine whether or not these negative experiences might be stable or persistent. The Demands of Illness Inventory (DOII) Personal Meaning and Social Relationships subscales and standard measures of depression, stress, and support were completed by 131 adults (mean age 45.9 yrs) with a history of repeated treatment for depres-

sion. 49 adults (mean age 34.5 years) currently and recently treated for depression completed the illness demands and depression measures 3 times in 8 wks. The DOII subscales showed adequate internal consistency and construct validity. High depression was associated with more intense and higher numbers of illness demands, but illness demands related to depression showed stability despite current recent treatment.

Archives of Psychiatric Nursing. 1999 Dec Vol 13(6) 294-302*

[cf. 255]
O'Connor, Brian P.; Vallerand, Robert J.

Psychological adjustment variables as predictors of mortality among nursing home residents.

Psychology & Aging. 1998 Sep Vol 13(3) 368-374

[420]
Phillips, W.M.

Purpose in life, depression, and locus of control.
Parallel to Frankl's theory of the search for meaning, which posits the separateness but intertwining of the psychological and existential realms, the Purpose In Life Test (PIL) has been found to have a low to moderate relationship with most conceptually related psychological measures. Extending separate correlational studies of the PIL with depression and locus of control, the current study inspected the relationship of individual PIL items to groups formed according to Zung Self-Rating Depression Scale and Rotter Internal-External Locus Of Control scores. One-hundred thirty-four Ss were split into four groups: Depressed external, depressed internals, nondepressed externals, and nondepressed internals. Although ungrouped correlational analysis of PIL items revealed only seven significant relationships with depression and two with locus of control, multiple discriminate analysis was successful in correctly classifying depressed externals about three-fourths of the time, and the overall "hit rate" for the four groups was above 60%. In addition to further validating the interaction of purpose in life with related psychological and social expectancy variables, results indicated a compounding effect between depression and external perception of reinforcement control with PIL scores in general, and two items (#4, 12) in particular, which appear to reflect the experience of current congruent involvement between the individual and his world.

Journal of Clinical Psychology. 1980 Jul;36(3):661-7.

[421]
Prager, Edward; Bar-Tur, Leora; Abramowici, Ilana

The Sources of Meaning Profile (SOMP) with aged subjects exhibiting depressive symptomatology.
Examines the correlation between depressive symptomatology and the importance the aged patient assigns to various sources of life meaning. The 16-item Sources of Meaning Profile (SOMP) was administered to 37 Israeli Ss (mean age 73.62 yrs) diagnosed as evidencing depressive symptomatology, and their meaning scores were compared with those of 4 other groups comprised of 310 Israelis and Australians with no known depressive symptomatology. The magnitude of meaning scores, an indicator of how important or unimportant a source of meaning was for the individual, was strongly and negatively correlated with

depressive symptomatology, as measured by the Beck Depression Inventory. Meaning scores correctly discriminated between "normal" and "depressed" Ss in almost 90% of the cases. The evaluative and therapeutic utility of the SOMP, as a phenomenologically grounded self-assessment of "current being," is briefly discussed.

Clinical Gerontologist. 1997 Vol 17(3) 25-39

[cf. 588]
Pyszczynski, Tom; Greenberg, Jeff

Evidence for a depressive self-focusing style.

Journal of Research in Personality. 1986 Mar Vol 20(1) 95-106

[cf. 589]
Pyszczynski, Tom; Hamilton, James C.; Herring, Fred H.; Greenberg, Jeff

Depression, self-focused attention, and the negative memory bias.

Journal of Personality & Social Psychology. 1989 Aug Vol 57(2) 351-357

[cf. 466]
Rietdijk, Eveline A.; van den Bosch, Louisa M. C.; Verheul, Roel; Koeter, Maarten W. J.; van den Brink, Wim

Predicting self-damaging and suicidal behaviors in female borderline patients: Reasons for living, coping, and depressive personality disorder.

Journal of Personality Disorders. 2001 Dec Vol 15(6) 512-520

[cf. 340]
Robak, Rostyslaw W.; Griffin, Paul W.

Purpose in life: What is its relationship to happiness, depression, and grieving?

North American Journal of Psychology. 2000 Vol 2(1) 113-119

[cf. 467]
Roehrig, Helmut R.; Range, Lillian M.

Recklessness, depression, and reasons for living in predicting suicidality in college students.

Journal of Youth & Adolescence. 1995 Dec Vol 24(6) 723-729

[cf. 590]
Sakamoto, Shinji

A longitudinal study of the relationship of self-preoccupation with depression

Journal of Clinical Psychology. 1999 Jan Vol 55(1) 109-116

[cf. 591]
Sakamoto, Shinji; Tomoda, Atsuko; Iwata, Noboru; Aihara, Waka; Kitamura, Toshinori

The relationship among major depression, depressive symptoms, and self-preoccupation.
Journal of Psychopathology & Behavioral Assessment. 1999 Mar Vol 21(1) 37-49

[cf. 403]
Sheffield, Brian F.; Pearson, Paul R.

Purpose-in-life in a sample of British psychiatric out-patients.
Journal of Clinical Psychology. 1974 Oct Vol 30(4) 459

[cf. 404]
Shek, Daniel T.

Mental health of secondary school students in Hong Kong: An epidemiological study using the General Health Questionnaire.
International Journal of Adolescent Medicine & Health. 1988 Jun-Sep Vol 3(3) 191-215

[cf. 055]
Shek, Daniel T.

Measurement of pessimism in Chinese adolescents: The Chinese Hopelessness Scale.
Social Behavior & Personality. 1993 Vol 21(2) 107-119

[422]
Shek, Daniel T.

Meaning in life and psychological well-being: An empirical study using the Chinese version of the Purpose in Life questionnaire.
2,150 Chinese secondary school students (aged 11-20 yrs) completed the Chinese version of the Purpose in Life questionnaire (CPIL) and other instruments assessing psychiatric symptoms and positive mental health such as the State-Trait Anxiety Inventory and the Beck Depression Inventory. Total CPIL and its 2 subscales, Quality of Existence (QEXIST) and Purpose of Existence (PEXIST), correlated significantly with all measures of psychological well-being. Relative to PEXIST scores, QEXIST scores were found to be more predictive of psychological well-being. Ss with different existential status (defined by high vs low levels of QEXIST and PEXIST) were associated with different degrees of psychological well-being
Journal of Genetic Psychology. 1992 Jun Vol 153(2) 185-200

[423]
Springer, M.B.; Newman, A.; Weaver, A.J.; Siritsky, N.; Linderblatt, C.; Flannelly. K.J.; Naditch B.; VandeCreek, L.

Spirituality, depression, and loneliness among Jewish seniors residing in New York City.
This article reports the results of research that examined a randomized group of 118 Jewish seniors who were clients of one of three Jewish social service agencies in New York City. They were interviewed by four Clinical Pastoral Education residents at the Jewish Institute

for Pastoral Care. During the interview, participants were asked to respond to the questions contained in the Brief Depression Scale, Version 3 of the UCLA Loneliness Scale, and the Index of Core Spiritual Experience—INSPIRIT. A statistically significant positive correlation was found between the depression and loneliness scores, r(116) = .56, p < .001. Spirituality was not correlated with either of these scales. Both depression and loneliness were significantly higher among women, among people who had physical impairments and those who had been victims of Nazi persecution. Depression and loneliness were inversely related to participants' ability to venture out of their house and to their relationship with their families. Having a sense of meaning or purpose in life was also inversely related to depression and loneliness. Spirituality tended to be higher among women, those participants, with more years of religious education, and those with physical impairments, but only the gender effect was statistically significant.

Journal of Pastoral Care and Counselling. 2003 Fall;57(3):305-18*

[424]
Stewart, Jonathan W.; Mercier, Mary A.; Quitkin, Frederic M.; McGarth, Patrick J.; et al

Demoralization predicts nonresponse to cognitive therapy in depressed outpatients.
39 Ss (aged 21-58 yrs) meeting Diagnostic and Statistical Manual of Mental Disorders-III (DSM-III) criteria for nonmelancholic major depression or dysthymic disorder were treated with cognitive therapy. Demoralization, as measured by items from the Beck Depression Inventory, the Hopelessness Scale, and the Dysfunctional Attitudes Scale, was assessed before and after treatment. After cognitive therapy, 20 Ss were considered responders (51%), although 3 quickly relapsed (44% responded and maintained). Nonresponders had significantly higher pretreatment demoralization scores than did responders. Results suggest that high levels of demoralization may predict poor response of depression to cognitive therapy, although the small sample size precluded differentiation of demoralization from hopelessness

Journal of Cognitive Psychotherapy. 1993 Sum Vol 7(2) 105-116

[cf. 062]
Tena, Antonio; Rage, Ernesto; Virseda, Jose Antonio

The purpose in life of university youth: A descriptive study.
(Sentido de vida en jovenes universitarios: Estudio descriptivo.)
Psicologia Contemporanea. 1999 Vol 6(2) 76-83

[cf. 371]
Tweed, Sandra H.; Ryff, Carol D.

Adult children of alcoholics: Profiles of wellness amidst distress
Journal of Studies on Alcohol. 1991 Mar Vol 52(2) 133-141

[cf. 594]
Wood, Joanne V.; Saltzberg, Judith A.; Neale, John M.; Stone, Arthur A.; et al

Self-focused attention, coping responses, and distressed mood in everyday life.
Journal of Personality & Social Psychology. 1990 Jun Vol 58(6) 1027-1036

[cf. 218]
Wright, Loyd S.; Frost, Christopher J.; Wisecarver, Stephen J.

Church attendance, meaningfulness of religion, and depressive symptomatology among adolescents

Journal of Youth & Adolescence. 1993 Oct Vol 22(5) 559-568

Suicide

[425]
Chan, David W.

Reasons for living among Chinese adolescents in Hong Kong.
279 secondary school students (aged 12-19 yrs) in Hong Kong responded to the Chinese version of the Reasons for Living Inventory (M. M. Linehan, 1985). The importance of these reasons could be adequately described by 5 dimensions interpreted as Positive Values and Self-Efficacy, Optimism, Family Concerns, Concerns for Social Disapproval, and Suicidal Fears. These dimensions corresponded closely to the original subscales of the inventory. Implications of the importance of gender and age group differences in endorsing coping beliefs, rather than fears, in times of crisis are discussed. Boys generally tended to attach greater importance to reasons related to self-efficacy, while girls were more motivated by fears related to the suicidal act and the consequence of suicide and to social disapproval.
Suicide & Life-Threatening Behavior. 1995 Fal Vol 25(3) 347-357

[426]
Chiles, John A.; Strosahl, Kirk D.; Ping, Zheng Yan; Michael, Mark C.; et al

Depression, hopelessness, and suicidal behavior in Chinese and American psychiatric patients.
Compared 37 patients in the People's Republic of China and 46 patients in the US who presented with suicidal thinking or behavior. Ss completed a suicidal intent scale, the Beck Depression Inventory, the Beck Hopelessness Scale, a suicidal thinking scale, and a reasons for living inventory. Hopelessness, reasons for living, and suicidal efficacy showed none of the expected relationships with suicidal intent among the Chinese Ss, but the 2 groups were similar on many variables theoretically related to suicidality. Chinese Ss were less likely to communicate suicidal intent and rated suicide as less effective at solving problems. Findings illustrate different cultural approaches to suicidal behavior.
American Journal of Psychiatry. 1989 Mar Vol 146(3) 339-344

[cf. 522]
Cole, David A.

Validation of the Reasons for Living Inventory in general and delinquent adolescent samples.
Journal of Abnormal Child Psychology. 1989 Feb Vol 17(1) 13-27

[427]
Connell, David K.; Meyer, Robert G.

The Reasons For Living Inventory and a college population: Adolescent suicidal behaviors, beliefs, and coping skills.
Assessed the suicidal behavior of 205 undergraduates. Ss were categorized into 4 groups: never suicidal, brief suicidal ideation, serious suicidal ideation, and parasuicidal. They also answered questions about why they would not choose suicide, on the Reasons for Living

Inventory (RFLI) of M. M. Linehan et al. Depression, hopelessness, and social desirability scales also were completed. A significant difference existed between suicidal and nonsuicidal Ss on the RFLI, specifically on the factors of Survival and Coping Beliefs, Responsibility to Family, and Moral Objections. Hopelessness and depression were correlated positively and significantly with suicidal behavior. Social desirability was high among Ss who were not suicidal and declined as suicidal behaviors became more severe.

Journal of Clinical Psychology. 1991 Jul Vol 47(4) 485-489

[428]
Durak, A; Yasak-Gultekin, Y.; Sahin, N. H.

Validity and reliability of the Reasons for Living Inventory.
(Insanlari yasama baglayan nedenler? Yasami surdurme nedenleri envanterinin (YSNE) guvenirligi ve gecerligi.)
The purpose of this study was to check the validity and reliability of the YSNE (Reasons for Living Inventory) for Turkish populations. A pilot study was conducted to adapt the inventory for the Turkish culture. As a result, 40 new items were added to the original inventory developed by Linehan et al ((1983). The new inventory, which consisted of 87 items, was given to a sample of 230 subjects. The study showed that the inventory is a reliable and valid scale for the Turkish culture.

Teurk Psikoloji Dergisi. 1993 Vol 8(30) 7-19

[429]
Dyck, Murray J.

Positive and negative attitudes mediating suicide ideation.
Both the presence of negative expectancies and the absence of positive reasons to live have been offered as partial explanations for why individuals consider suicide. The independent viability of these 2 explanations was evaluated in 3 studies that explored whether the Hopelessness Scale and the Reasons for Living Inventory by M. Linehan et al measured different constructs. 329 undergraduates and 31 cognitive therapy outpatients participated. Results indicate distinct nomological nets for the measures of "hopelessness" and "reasons for living." Suicide intent is related to both positive and negative attitudes, and these in turn are both associated with personality dimensions.

Suicide & Life-Threatening Behavior. 1991 Win Vol 21(4) 360-373

[430]
Edwards, Melanie J.; Holden, Ronald R.

Coping, meaning in life, and suicidal manifestations: Examining gender differences.
Life meaning and coping strategies were investigated as statistical predictors of suicidal manifestations in a sample of 298 university undergraduates (aged 18-25 yrs). Participants completed measures of hopelessness, sense of coherence, purpose in life, coping for stressful situations, suicide ideation, prior suicide attempts, and self-reported likelihood of future suicidal behavior. Moderated multiple regression techniques examined the incremental validity of life meaning by coping interactions for predicting each suicide variable separately by gender. The interaction of sense of coherence and emotion-oriented coping made a unique, significant contribution to the statistical prediction of all suicide variables for women. For men, the interaction between sense of coherence and emotion-oriented coping contributed

significantly to the statistical prediction of suicide ideation. All interactions remained significant when hopelessness was statistically controlled.

Journal of Clinical Psychology. 2001 Dec Vol 57(12) 1517-1534

[431]
Ellis, Jon B.; Hirsch, Jameson K.

Reasons for living in parents of developmentally delayed children.
Identified adaptive characteristics that may or may not be present in parents of children with developmental delays. 49 children (aged <1-29 yrs), with disabilities ranging from mild to severe, and their parents, served as Ss. Parents were asked to rate the severity of their child's disability, answer several questions regarding length of time since they were informed about their child's problem, and provide limited demographic information. Parents also completed The Reasons for Living Inventory - an inventory developed to measure a range of beliefs and expectancies thought to be important in differentiating suicidal and nonsuicidal persons. Data analyzed via 4 (severity of disability) * 2 (gender of child) * 2 (single or 2-parent home) ANOVA revealed no significant differences between men and women, or between individuals in 1 -parent vs 2-parent households. The authors suggest that the experience of having a disabled child may help to strengthen adaptive characteristics and, possibly, reduce the risk of suicide.

Research in Developmental Disabilities. 2000 Jul-Aug Vol 21(4) 323-327

[432]
Ellis, Jon B.; Smith, Peggy C.

Spiritual well-being, social desirability and reasons for living: Is there a connection?
To explore the relationships between spirituality, social desirability, and reasons for living, 100 undergraduates completed the Reasons for Living Inventory (RFL; M. Linehan et al), the Spiritual Well-Being Scale (SWBS; C. Ellison), and the Marlowe-Crowne Social Desirability Scale. Positive correlations were found between religious well-being and the total RFL score and Moral Objections subscale and between existential well-being and several RFL scales. Results indicate that the RFL Moral Objections subscale tapped the same type of beliefs as did the SWBS religious well-being subscale. There also appeared to be a strong relationship between the adaptive cognitive beliefs that people reported as reasons for not considering suicide and their existential beliefs. This emphasizes the need for careful assessment of individual needs and beliefs when dealing with suicidal individuals.

International Journal of Social Psychiatry. 1991 Spr Vol 37(1) 57-63

[433]
Gutierrez, Peter M.; Osman, Augustine; Kopper, Beverly A.; Barrios, Francisco X.

Why young people do not kill themselves: The Reasons for Living Inventory for Adolescents.
Assessed the reliability, validity, and predictive power of a new measure, the Reasons for Living Inventory for Adolescents (RFL-A; Osman et al, 1998). A group of 206 (101 boys and 105 girls) adolescent psychiatric inpatients completed the RFL-A, Minnesota Multiphasic Personality Inventory for Adolescents (Butcher et al, 1992), and a packet of self-report measures. Additional information about the patients including diagnosis and suicide status were obtained from their medical records. It was determined that the RFL-A

is a valid and reliable measure of adolescent suicide risk potential. Additionally, the RFL-A possesses better predictive power than the Beck Hopelessness Scale (Beck, Weissman, Lester, & Trexler, 1974). A discussion of the clinical and research utility of the RFL-A is included along with suggestions for future research.

Journal of Clinical Child Psychology. 2000 Jun Vol 29(2) 177-187

[434]

Gutierrez, Peter M.; Osman, Augustine; Kopper, Beverly A.; Barrios, Francisco X.; Bagge, Courtney L.

Suicide risk assessment in a college student population.
A group of 211 students at a midwestern university completed the Suicidal Behaviors Questionnaire (M. M. Linehan & S. L. Nielsen, 1981), Adult Suicidal Ideation Questionnaire (W. M. Reynolds, 1991a), Multi-Attitude Suicide Tendency Scale (I. Orbach et al., 1991), Beck Helplessness Scale (A. T. Beck, A. Weissman, D. Lester, & L. Trexler, 1974), and the Reasons for Living Inventory (M. M. Linehan, L. J. Goodstein, S. L. Nielsen, & J. A. Chiles, 1983) to determine if this group of commonly used self-report measures can distinguish between individuals with high and low levels of suicidal ideation and history of self-harmful behaviors. Exploratory principal-axis factor analysis resulted in an interpretable 2-factor solution accounting for 36.2% of the variance in suicidality. Support for convergent validity of the chosen measures was also found. It appears that rapid, accurate assessment of university student suicide risk is possible. Implications for reduction of suicide risk in this segment of the population are discussed.

Journal of Counseling Psychology. 2000 Oct Vol 47(4) 403-413

[435]

Gutierrez, Peter M.; Osman, Augustine; Barrios, Francisco X.; Kopper, Beverly A.; Baker, Monty T.; Haraburda, Cheryl M.

Development of the Reasons for Living Inventory for Young Adults.
Assessment of the reliability, validity, and predictive power of the Reasons for Living Inventory for Young Adults (RFL-YA) is described. A series of 3 studies, involving a total of 1,186 Ss, was conducted at 2 Midwestern universities to develop initial items for this new measure, refine item selection, and demonstrate the psychometric properties of the RFL-YA. The theoretical differences between the RFL-YA and the College Student Reasons for Living Inventory (CS-RFL) are discussed. Although the 2 measures were not directly compared, it appears that the RFL-YA has greater specificity for exploring aspects of the protective construct and may be more parsimonious than the CS-RFL. Principal-axis factor analysis yielded a 5-factor solution for the RFL-YA accounting for 61.5% of the variance. This 5-factor oblique model was confirmed in the final phase of investigation. Alpha estimates for the 5 subscales ranged from .89-.94. Concurrent, convergent-discriminant, and criterion validity also were demonstrated. The importance of assessing protective factors in addition to negative risk factors for suicidality is discussed. Directions for future research with the RFL-YA also are discussed.

Journal of Clinical Psychology. 2002 Apr Vol 58(4) 339-357

[436]
Harlow, Lisa L.; Newcomb, Michael D.; Bentler, P. M.

Depression, self-derogation, substance use, and suicide ideation: Lack of purpose in life as a mediational factor.
Examined a theoretical model of adolescent behavior that hypothesizes that depression and self-derogation may lead to a lack of purpose in life, which, in turn, may lead to suicide ideation and substance use. Confirmatory factor analyses and structural equation procedures were used to examine the model, using data from 211 male and 511 female 19-24 yr olds on measures such as the Purpose in Life Test and the Center for Epidemiologic Studies Depression Scale. The model adequately accounted for the data, although there were some important differences between the sexes. In response to depression and self-derogation, males were more apt to turn to drugs and alcohol, whereas females considered suicide. Conversely, in response to feelings of meaninglessness or a lack of purpose in life, females appeared to turn to substance use, whereas males reacted with thoughts of suicide.
Journal of Clinical Psychology. 1986 Jan Vol 42(1) 5-21

[437]
Hasegawa A, Fujiwara Y, Hoshi T, Shinkai S.

Regional differences in ikigai (reason(s) for living) in elderly people—relationship between ikigai and family structure, physiological situation and functional capacity
The purpose of this paper is a) to make a comparative study of the existence of ikigai (reason(s) for living) in elderly people and its relevance to their family structure, physiological situation and functional capacity in both rural areas and metropolitan suburban areas, and b) position basic research into the structure of ikigai in the near future, by clarifying several related factors, from which the concept of ikigai may be defined. The meaning of the word "ikigai" in Japanese is difficult to express exactly, and specialists in gerontology have varying definitions. If ikigai were translated from Japanese into English, it could be "reason(s) for living", "self-actualization", "meaning of life" and/or "purpose in life". In this paper, ikigai is used to mean "feeling of being alive now and/or individual motivation for living". As of October 2000, we studied 1,544 people aged 65 years and over living in town Y of Niigata Prefecture (rural area), and as of January 2001, we studied 1,002 people in the same age group in town H of Saitama Prefecture (metropolitan suburban area). The above investigations revealed the following characteristics:—(a) Regarding the percentages of persons having or not having ikigai, there were no significant differences between the rural area and the metropolitan suburban area. (b) In both areas, the 3 factors of self-rated level of health, intellectual activeness and social roles, were associated with having ikigai. (c) In the rural area, the family structure was strongly associated with having ikigai, but gender or generation were irrelevant. (d) In the metropolitan suburban area, the hospitalization experience of men was strongly associated with ikigai. Furthermore, there was a strong correlation with generation. In this regard, while the contents of ikigai are seldom examined in detail, clarification of the structure of ikigai should be worked out in the next stage of the study, using covariance structure analysis. In addition the development of concrete plans to promote ikigai by municipal organs could be beneficial.
Nippon Ronen Igakkai Zasshi. 2003 Jul;40(4):390-6. *

[438]
Heisel, Marnin J.; Flett, Gordon L.

Purpose in Life, satisfaction with life, and suicide ideation in a clinical sample.
This study examined the role of purpose in life and satisfaction with life in protecting
against suicide ideation in a clinical psychiatric sample. Forty-nine psychiatric patients completed self-report measures of suicide ideation, purpose in life, satisfaction with life, neuroticism, depression, and social hopelessness. Zero-order correlations indicated significant
associations between suicide ideation and the various predictors, in the hypothesized directions. Regression analyses illustrated that purpose in life and satisfaction with life accounted for significant additional variability in suicide ideation scores above and beyond that
accounted for by the negative psychological factors alone. Purpose in life also mediated the
relation between satisfaction with life and suicide ideation and moderated the relation
between depression and suicide ideation. These findings demonstrate the potential value of
attending to both resilience and pathology when building predictive models of suicide
ideation and of attending to key existential themes when assessing and treating suicidal individuals.
Journal of Psychopathology & Behavioral Assessment. 2004 Jun Vol 26(2) 127-135

[439]
Hirsch, Jameson K.; Ellis, Jon B.

Differences in life stress and reasons for living among college suicide ideators and non-
ideators.
For students, depression, hopelessness, and suicidal behaviors may be more common than
for peers not attending college, due to increased demands and higher levels of perceived
stress. Individuals with less well developed adaptive characteristics may also be more sus-
ceptible to such influences. 203 undergraduates (132 women, 71 men) were administered
a Suicide Ideation Question- naire, a Life Experience Survey, and the Reasons for Living
Inventory (RFL). ANOVA's revealed ideators as having higher levels of life-stress and lower
RFL total score than non-ideators. Women scored higher than men on several RFL subscales, including: Survival and Coping Beliefs, Child Related Concerns, and RFL total
score.
College Student Journal. 1996 Sep Vol 30(3) 377-386

[440]
Ivanoff, Andre; Jang, Sung Joon; Smyth, Nancy J.

Clinical risk factors associated with parasuicide in prison.
Identified risk factors associated with parasuicide among 130 male inmates in a state prison,
by testing a proposed model of the ability of current clinical and background variables to
predict parasuicide during incarceration. Psychiatric history, symptomatology, and psychological functioning variables (i.e., hopelessness, depression, reasons for living) affected parasuicide directly and indirectly through their contribution to suicidal ideation. Among Ss
with histories of alcohol abuse, however, hopelessness was a less significant predictor of
parasuicide, thus suggesting that interaction effects may warrant more attention.
International Journal of Offender Therapy & Comparative Criminology. 1996 Jun Vol 40(2)
135-146

[441]
Ivanoff, Andre; Jang, Sung Joon; Smyth, Nancy J.; Linehan, Marsha M.

Fewer reasons for staying alive when you are thinking of killing yourself: The Brief
Reasons for Living Inventory.
Developed a brief form of the Linehan Reasons for Living Inventory (LRLI) appropriate for
clinical use and examined the predictive validity of this measure, named the Brief Reasons
for Living Inventory (BRFL), to distinguish suicidal from nonsuicidal prison inmates. 130
male inmates (mean age 26 yrs) completed an interview battery that included the LRLI, the
Beck Depression Inventory (BDI), the Beck Hopelessness Scale (BHS), and the Scale for
Suicidal Ideation. Results indicate that the 12-item BRFL was as good as either the BDI or
the BHS at predicting suicidality among inmates. In addition, the BRFL tapped the same
set of adaptive beliefs and expectations as the LRLI in a much shorter time. Further study
is needed to validate the BRFL with different institutionalized and other populations as well
as to assess its ability to discriminate suicide ideators from those engaging in overt suicidal
behavior.
Journal of Psychopathology & Behavioral Assessment. 1994 Mar Vol 16(1) 1-13

[cf. 524]
Jackson, Javel

Outcome research with high-risk inmates.
Behavior Therapist. 2003 Jan Vol 26(1) 215-216

[442]
Jobes, David A.; Mann, Rachel E.

Reasons for living versus reasons for dying: Examining the internal debate of suicide.
The Reasons for Living vs. Reasons for Dying Assessment (D. A. Jobes and G. A. Bonanno,
1995) was used to obtain suicidal outpatients' top 5 reasons for living and for dying (RFL
and RFD), respectively. 49 suicidal university counseling center patients (aged 17-40 yrs)
provided 173 RFL and 145 RFD responses. These responses were organized into 8 RFL
coding categories and 9 RFD coding categories. Two coders trained in the RFL RFD coding system showed high levels of interrater reliability. Chi-square results for RFL and RFD
coding categories showed that the coding categories were not equally salient to these suicidal patients.
Suicide & Life-Threatening Behavior. 1999 Sum Vol 29(2) 97-104

[443]
Kinkel, R. John; Bailey, Charles W.; Josef, Norma C.

Correlates of adolescent suicide attempts: Alienation, drugs and social background.
Examined drug and alcohol use together with social background variables to determine
their relationship to adolescent suicide attempts. 2,631 adolescents (aged 12-18 yrs) were
surveyed using self-report methods. It was found that young women, farm residents, and
drug users were more likely to report a suicide attempt. Women who were frequent alcohol
users and heavy users of marihuana were more prone to a suicide attempt than were males.

Extreme pessimism and failure to find meaning in life proved to be important factors in identifying Ss at risk for suicide.

Journal of Alcohol & Drug Education. 1989 Spr Vol 34(3) 85-96

[444]
Kirkpatrick-Smith, Joyce; Rich, Alexander R.; Bonner, Ronald; Jans, Frank

Psychological vulnerability and substance abuse as predictors of suicide ideation among adolescents.
Extended the stress-vulnerability model of suicidal behavior among college students proposed by R. Bonner and A. Rich with 613 high school students (328 females and 285 males). Ss completed self-report measures of life stress, depression, hopelessness, reasons for living, loneliness, alcohol and drug use, and suicidal ideation. In stepwise multiple regressions, 4 variables emerged as significant predictors of suicidal ideation: depression, hopelessness, few reasons for living, and problem substance use. The linear combination of these variables accounted for 52% of the variance in suicide ideation scores. The substance abuse variable accounted for variance in ideation scores independent of the other factors.

Omega: Journal of Death & Dying. 1991-1992 Vol 24(1) 21-33

[445]
Kralik, Kathleen M.; Danforth, Walter J.

Identification of coping ideation and strategies preventing suicidality in a college-age sample.
286 undergraduates, self-identified as having no past suicidal ideation, mild ideation, severe ideation, or having attempted suicide, completed a reasons for living inventory (RLI), a similarly derived instrument for age-specific coping cognitions, and a scale of coping strategies for diminishing suicidality. The factor structure of the RLI was confirmed on this college-age population. It appears to be relevant in suggesting pertinent preventive cognitions among these Ss. Patterns of similarities and differences in mechanisms were identified. Having social attachments, engaging in problem-solving and coping ideation, and reliance on religious convictions distinguished mild from serious ideators. Serious ideators differed from attempters in the relative effectiveness that having social attachments has on preventing suicide behavior.

Suicide & Life-Threatening Behavior. 1992 Sum Vol 22(2) 167-186

[446]
Labelle, Real; Lachance, Lise; Morval, Monique

Validation of a French-Canadian version of the Reasons for Living Inventory.
(Validation d'une version canadienne-francaise du Reasons for Living Inventory.)
Discusses the French-Canadian version of an exceptional psychometric instrument in suicidology, the Reasons for Living Inventory (RFL). The Francophone version of RFL is characterized by the simplicity and clarity of its administration procedures, both for adults and adolescents, and the reliability of its findings. Described here is a pre-test administered to 300 full-time Francophone students at the University of Montreal (92 males, 208 females, median age 22.3 yrs). Study results include, in addition to the acceptable reliability of the indices of this psychometric instrument, a factorial structure comparable to that

of the American original, together with the negative correlations between the majority of subscales and the 1988 Anglophone Scale for Suicide Ideation (SSI).

Science et Comportement. 1996 Vol 24(3) 237-248

[447]
Lester, David; Badro, Souhel

Depression, suicidal preoccupation and purpose in life in a subclinical population.
Administered the Purpose in Life Test (PLT) and the Beck Depression Inventory to 120 undergraduates; Ss were also asked about previous suicide attempts or ideas. Scores from the PLT predicted current and previous suicidal preoccupation. For current suicidal preoccupation, both PLT scores and depression scores contributed to the regression equation. For previous suicidal ideation and threats, only PLT scores contributed to the regression equations.

Personality & Individual Differences. 1992 Jan Vol 13(1) 75-76

[448]
Linehan, Marsha M.; Goodstein, Judith L.; Nielsen, Stevan L.; Chiles, John A.

Reasons for staying alive when you are thinking of killing yourself: The Reasons for Living Inventory.
65 adults generated 72 distinct reasons for not committing suicide; these were reduced to 48 by factor analyses performed on 2 additional samples, and the items were arranged into the Reasons for Living Inventory (RFL), which requires a rating of how important each reason would be for living if suicide were contemplated. In addition, factor analyses indicated 6 primary reasons for living: Survival and Coping Beliefs, Responsibility to Family, Child-Related Concerns, Fear of Suicide, Fear of Social Disapproval, and Moral Objections. The RFL was then given to 2 additional samples, 197 Seattle shoppers (mean age 36 yrs) and 175 psychiatric inpatients (mean age 31 yrs). Both samples were divided into several suicidal (ideators and parasuicides) and nonsuicidal groups. Separate multivariate ANOVAs indicated that the RFL differentiated suicidal from nonsuicidal Ss in both samples. In the shopping-center sample, the Fear of Suicide scale further differentiated between previous ideators and previous parasuicides. In the clinical sample, the Child-Related Concerns scales differentiated between current suicide ideators and current parasuicides. In both samples, the Survival and Coping, the Responsibility to Family, and the Child-Related Concerns scales were most useful in differentiating the groups.

Journal of Consulting & Clinical Psychology. 1983 Apr Vol 51(2) 276-286

[449]
Malone, Kevin M.; Oquendo, Maria A.; Haas, Gretchen L.; Ellis, Steven P.; Li, Shuhua; Mann, J. John

Protective factors against suicidal acts in major depression: Reasons for living.
Over 30,000 people a year commit suicide in the US. The authors hypothesized that "reasons for living" might protect or restrain patients with major depression from making a suicide attempt. 84 inpatients with major depression (aged 18-80 yrs) were assessed for depression, general psychopathology, suicide history, reasons for living, and hopelessness. 45 had attempted suicide and 39 had not. The depressed patients who had not attempted suicide expressed more feelings of responsibility toward family, more fear of social disapproval, more moral objections to suicide, greater survival and coping skills, and a greater fear of sui-

cide than the depressed patients who had attempted suicide. Scores for hopelessness, subjective depression, and suicidal ideation were significantly higher for the suicide attempters. Reasons for living correlated inversely with the combined score on these measures, considered an indicator of "clinical suicidality." Neither objective severity of depression nor quantity of recent life events differed between the 2 groups. Results suggest that during a depressive episode, the subjective perception of stressful life events may be more germane to suicidal expression than the objective quantity of such events.

American Journal of Psychiatry. 2000 Jul Vol 157(7) 1084-1088

[450]
McLaren, Suzanne; Hopes, Lisa M.

Rural-urban differences in reasons for living.
The suicide rate in Australia is cause for concern, especially the increase in attempted and completed suicides in rural and regional locations. The present study examined reasons for choosing not to commit suicide as a function of residential location. The study involved 655 Victorian residents (mean age 42.71 yrs) from 4 population-based strata; urban, regional city, regional town, and rural. Results from the Reasons for Living Inventory revealed significant differences as a function of residential location. Overall, residents in rural locations reported having significantly more to live for than their urban counterparts. Further analysis of 6 reasons for living (child, family, moral, social, coping and death-related concerns) showed a pattern whereby residents in rural locations reported having the most to live for, followed by regional residents, and urban residents who reported having the least to live for. These findings are in contrast to increase of suicide rates in rural areas, and highlight the need for a greater understanding of the mechanisms underlying suicidal behavior.

Australian & New Zealand Journal of Psychiatry. 2002 Oct Vol 36(5) 688-692

[451]
Miller, Jill S.; Segal, Daniel L.; Coolidge, Frederick L.

A comparison of suicidal thinking and reasons for living among younger and older adults.
A cross-sectional design was used to examine age-related differences in suicidal thinking and reasons for living among 82 younger (aged 17-34 yrs) and 82 older (aged 60-95 yrs) adults. Ss completed completed the Beck Scale for Suicide Ideation and the Reasons for Living Inventory. Findings indicated that older adults do not manifest suicidal ideation differently than younger adults. However, there do appear to be some age-related differences in reasons for not committing suicide. Compared to the younger group, the older group reported moral objections and child-related concerns as stronger reasons for not committing suicide. An implication is that the identification of specific reasons that deter individuals from committing suicide, may be clinically useful and provide some assistance in suicide prevention efforts.

Death Studies. 2001 Jun Vol 25(4) 357-365

[452]
Moore, Sharon L.

A phenomenological study of meaning in life in suicidal older adults.
The purpose of this hermeneutical phenomenological study was to explore how older adults who were suicidal experienced meaning in their lives. 11 64-92-yr-olds were selected from

inpatient psychiatric units where they had been voluntarily admitted for the treatment of depression and suicidal ideation. These Ss were interviewed about their subjective experiences of feeling suicidal. Data were analyzed using M. van Manen's (1990) method of hermeneutical analysis. Three main themes evolved as characteristic of the fundamental thematic structure of the Ss' experiences of meaning. These themes were conceptualized under a broader theme of alienation, a theme which was characterized by broken connections with individuals and meaningful activities. The question of meaning in life for these Ss was reflected not only from the perspective of meaningfulness, but also from the viewpoint of meaninglessness. Their narratives contribute to a deepened understanding of what it is like to be old, suicidal, and to feel like life has no meaning and purpose.

Archives of Psychiatric Nursing. 1997 Feb Vol 11(1) 29-36

[453]
Neyra, Carmen J.; Range, Lillian M.; Goggin, William C.

Reasons for living following success and failure in suicidal and nonsuicidal college students.
61 college students who were relatively high or low suicide ideators participated in a computer task on which half got bogus success feedback and the other half got bogus failure feedback. Both groups then completed the Reasons for Living (RFL) Inventory of M. M. Linehan et al. Analyses indicated main effects for suicide on overall RFL and 4 of the 6 RFL subscales. Although there were no main effects for success vs failure, an interaction showed that in the failure condition, low suicidal Ss were significantly higher than high suicidal Ss in overall RFL. Suicidal individuals may need interventions to help them avoid potential failure or to bolster their coping mechanisms.

Journal of Applied Social Psychology. 1990 Jun Vol 20(11, Pt 2) 861-868

[454]
Oquendo, Maria A.; Baca-Garcia, Enrique; Graver, Ruth; Morales, Miguel; Montalvan, Viviana; Mann, J. John

Spanish adaptation of the Reasons for Living Inventory.
The Reasons for Living Inventory (RFL) is an instrument to measure a range of beliefs potentially important as reasons for not committing suicide. There is no Spanish version of this instrument. The adaptation process includes translation, back-translation, review of both versions, and application of the resulting instrument to a bilingual sample from the target population. This process allows for assessment of the equivalence between the English and Spanish version of the RFL in three stages: linguistic equivalence, conceptual equivalence, and scale equivalence. The sample in this study included 29 bilingual psychiatric outpatients. The most important aspects of the adaptation, conceptual and scale equivalence, are adequate in this Spanish version of the RFL. The adaptation of the RFL is ready to be used in Spanish-speaking populations.

Hispanic Journal of Behavioral Sciences. 2000 Aug Vol 22(3) 369-380

[455]
Orbach, Israel; Mikulincer, Mario; Gilboa-Schechtman, Eva; Sirota, Pinhas

Mental pain and its relationship to suicidality and life meaning.
Shneidman (1996) proposed that intense mental pain is related to suicide. Relatedly, Frankl

(1963) argued that the loss of life's meaning is related to intense mental pain. The first goal of this research was to test Shneidman's proposition by comparing the mental pain of suicidal and nonsuicidal individuals. Meaning in life and optimism are the polar opposites of suicidality and hopelessness, and the examination of these variables in relation to mental pain was undertaken to provide a test of Frankl's proposition. In two studies, a relationship between a newly developed measure of mental pain-the Orbach & Mikulincer Mental Pain Scale, 2002 and suicidal behavior and life meaning were examined. Results confirmed both propositions. Implications for the study of mental pain and suicide are discussed.

Suicide & Life-Threatening Behavior. 2003 Fal Vol 33(3) 231-241

[456]
Osman, Augustine; Gifford, Jody; Jones, Teresa; Lickiss, Laura; et

Psychometric evaluation of the Reasons for Living Inventory.
Examined the factor structure and psychometric properties of the Reasons for Living Inventory (RFL) in a sample of college students with a range of suicidal ideation and behaviors. An exploratory factor analysis of the 48-item RFL extracted 6 factors, similar to those described by Linehan et al. All coefficients alpha and item-subscale correlations were adequate. Additional nonclinical normative data are presented. Multivariate analysis of variance (MANOVA) identified 3 significant discriminant functions for group separation. Correlational analyses provided information about the relationships between the RFL and other self-report measures of suicide risk and general psychopathology. Three RFL subscales were useful in predicting suicide risk and general psychopathology. Limitations and future research issues are discussed.

Psychological Assessment. 1993 Jun Vol 5(2) 154-158

[cf. 609]
Osman, Augustine; Jones, Keith; Osman, Joylene R.

The Reasons for Living Inventory: Psychometric properties.

Psychological Reports. 1991 Aug Vol 69(1) 271-278

[457]
Osman, Augustine; Kopper, Beverly A.; Linehan, Marsha M.; Barrios, Francisco X.; Gutierrez, Peter M.; Bagge, Courtney L.

Validation of the Adult Suicidal Ideation Questionnaire and the Reasons for Living Inventory in an adult psychiatric inpatient sample.
This study investigated the factor structure of the Adult Suicidal Ideation Questionnaire (ASIQ) and the Linehan Reasons for Living Inventory (LRFI) in a sample of 205 adult psychiatric inpatients. Confirmatory factor analyses provided moderate support for the construct validity of each instrument. Coefficient alphas for the ASIQ (.98) and LRFL (.93) were high. In addition, a range of different clinical cutoff points was derived for each instrument. Both instruments were also better than chance in differentiating between the suicide attempter and psychiatric control groups. High ASIQ and low LRFL scores were significantly associated with scores on selected Minnesota Multiphasic Personality Inventory-2 Content scales. The analyses also indicated that only the ASIQ added to the symptoms of hopelessness and negative affect in differentiating between the suicide attempter and psy-

chiatric control groups. Results suggest that both instruments may be useful screening tests for suicidal behavior in psychiatric long-term care inpatient samples.

Psychological Assessment. 1999 Jun Vol 11(2) 115-123

[458]
Osman, Augustine; Kopper, Beverly A.; Barrios, Francisco X.; Osman, Joylene R.; et al

The Brief Reasons for Living Inventory for adolescents (BRFL-A).
This study modified and evaluated the psychometric properties of the Reasons for Living Inventory (RFL) in samples of adolescents. Internal consistency reliability, corrected item-total scale correlation, and exploratory factor analysis procedures were used with a mixed sample of 260 adolescents to identify 14 items for the brief version of the RFL (BRFL-A). Confirmatory factor analyses provided support for the five-factor oblique structure of the BRFL-A in a psychiatric inpatient sample with a range of suicidal behaviors. Reliabilities of the BRFL-A subscales were satisfactory. Four of the five subscales differentiated between suicidal and nonsuicidal adolescents. Significant correlations were found between three BRFL-A subscales and several suicide indices. Convergent-discriminant validity was examined by correlating the BRFL-A subscales with the Minnesota Multiphasic Personality Inventory—Adolescents (MMPI-A) Content Scales. Limitations of the study are discussed.

Journal of Abnormal Child Psychology. 1996 Aug Vol 24(4) 433-443

[459]
Osman, Augustine; Downs, William R.; Kopper, Beverly A.; Barrios, Francisco X.; Baker, Monty T.; Osman, Joylene R.; Besett, Tricia M.; Linehan, Marsha M.

The Reasons for Living Inventory for Adolescents (RFL-A): Development and psychometric properties.
Reports on the development and initial psychometric properties of a 32-item self-report inventory, the Reasons for Living Inventory for Adolescents (RFL-A). The RFL-A is designed to focus on adaptive factors that are relevant in the assessment of adolescent suicidal behavior. Participants were nonclinical and clinical adolescents, ages 14-18 yrs. In Phase 1, exploratory and confirmatory factor analyses was used to identify 5 correlated factors: Future Optimism, Suicide-Related Concerns, Family Alliance, Peer Acceptance and Support, and Self-Acceptance. In Phase 2, the 5-factor oblique model was cross validated in a different group of adolescents recruited from 2 high schools. In addition, evidence was examined for convergent, discriminant, and construct validities. The coefficient alpha indices for the RFL-A total and scales were satisfactory. In Phase 3, additional evidence of reliability and validity was evaluated using samples of high school and psychiatric inpatient adolescents. The results suggest that the RFL-A is a short, reliable, and valid measure that is potentially useful in the assessment of adolescent suicidal behavior.

Journal of Clinical Psychology. 1998 Dec Vol 54(8) 1063-1078

[460]
Pilecka, Barbara

Selected personality predictors of renewed suicide attempts in young people.
Examined the relationship between the Minnesota Multiphasic Personality Inventory (MMPI) Hysteria (Hy) scale and renewed suicide attempts and assessed the personality traits that correlate with heightened Hy scores. 50 male and 90 female patients (aged 15-25

yrs) in a therapy club for suicide attempters completed the MMPI, the IPAT Anxiety Scale Questionnaire, the Purpose in Life Test, and the Beck Depression Inventory. There were significantly more renewed suicide attempts in Ss with high than with low Hy scores. Ss with high Hy revealed excessive concentration on their health, depression, difficulties in adjustment, high anxiety, self-aggression, and a weak sense of purpose in life. Women showed significantly higher projection of aggression and tendencies toward uncontrolled aggressive outbursts.

Polish Psychological Bulletin. 1985 Vol 16(2) 99-108

[461]
Pinto, Aureen; Whisman, Mark A.; Conwell, Yeates

Reasons for living in a clinical sample of adolescents.
The psychometric properties and validity of the Reasons for Living (RFL) Inventory were examined in 253 psychiatrically hospitalized adolescents (aged 13-18 yrs), identified as suicide ideators, suicide attempters, and psychiatric controls. Confirmatory factor analysis suggested that the original RFL factors did not provide a good fit; exploratory factor analysis identified 5 factors, of which 3 were identical with the original RFL factors. Factor scores differentiated suicidal from non-suicidal adolescents and attempters from ideators. Correlational analyses indicated that RFL factors were associated with suicidal ideation, depression, and hopelessness, and predicted unique variance in suicidal ideation over that accounted for by depression and hopelessness. Findings provide support for the RFL as a sound measure for clinical and research assessment in adolescents.

Journal of Adolescence. 1998 Aug Vol 21(4) 397-405

[462]
Range, Lillian M.; Hall, Derek L.; Meyers,

Factor structure of adolescents' scores on the Reasons for Living Inventory.
The Reasons for Living Inventory (RFL) has been shown to be reliable and valid for adults. To ascertain its factor structure and internal consistency for adolescents, 128 high school students (aged 14-17 yrs) and 145 college students below age 20 yrs completed it. A 6-factor solution to a principal components factor analysis followed by varimax rotation accounted for 53.6% and 49.8%, respectively, of the variance in the 2 groups. For both groups, Cronbach alphas were strong for all subscales except Moral Objections, which was unsatisfactory. Means were higher than those of adults who reported never considering suicide. A Goodness of Fit Index was poor, suggesting that the factors in teens' reasons for living are different from adults. The overall RFL score appears to be a reasonable instrument for adolescents to use, and a low score should be taken as particularly troublesome.

Death Studies. 1993 May-Jun Vol 17(3) 257-266

[463]
Range, Lillian M.; Penton, Susan R.

Hope, hopelessness, and suicidality in college students.
For 206 unscreened undergraduates, scores on coping beliefs and hope, rather than those on hopelessness or other reasons for living, were most related to scores on suicidality. Thus, for these Ss, facilitating their hopefulness may bolster their coping, thereby discouraging

suicidality. Correlations with scores on subscales of the Reasons for Living Inventory support validity of the Hope Scale for suicide study in nonclinical groups.

Psychological Reports. 1994 Aug Vol 75(1, Pt 2), Spec Issue 456-458

[464]
Range, Lillian M.; Stringer, Traci A.

Reasons for living and coping abilities among older adults.
In the present study, 79 (55 women, 22 men, 2 unknown) older adults (mean age 60.6 yrs) recruited from churches, retirement groups, and relatives of college psychology students, completed the Reasons for Living (RFL) and the Cope inventories. Overall coping was significantly positively correlated with total reasons for living, although the low correlation suggests that the constructs are moderately unique. Further, coping was positively correlated with two RFL subscales, Survival and Coping Beliefs, and Child-Related Concerns. Women were higher than men in total reasons for living, but not significantly different in coping abilities. Older women may underrate their ability to cope. An implication is that suicide prevention strategies should target men and bolster their cognitive deterrents to suicide.

International Journal of Aging & Human Development. 1996 Vol 43(1) 1-6

[465]
Rich, Alexander R.; Bonner, Ronald L

Concurrent validity of a stress-vulnerability model of suicidal ideation and behavior: A follow-up study.
Conducted a follow-up study to test the concurrent validity of the authors' (1987) stress-vulnerability model of suicidal ideation and behavior, using 202 college students. Ss completed self-report measures of life stress, loneliness, depression (Self-Rating Depression Scale), dysfunctional cognitions, reasons for living, hopelessness, current suicide ideation, and predictions of future suicide probability. Multiple-regression analysis indicated that 30% of the variation in suicide ideation scores could be accounted for by the linear combination of negative life stress, depression, loneliness, and few reasons for living. The linear combination of current suicide ideation, hopelessness, dysfunctional cognitions, and few reasons for living explained 56% of the variance in self-predicted future suicide probability. Results support the proposed model.

Suicide & Life-Threatening Behavior. 1987 Win Vol 17(4) 265-270

[466]
Rietdijk, Eveline A.; van den Bosch, Louisa M. C.; Verheul, Roel; Koeter, Maarten W. J.; van den Brink, Wim

Predicting self-damaging and suicidal behaviors in female borderline patients: Reasons for living, coping, and depressive personality disorder.
Examined whether reasons for living predict self-damaging and suicidal behaviors, the associations of reasons for living with coping strategies and depressive personality disorder (PD), and the unique predictive validity of reasons for living in a multivariate predictor model. Reasons for living (RFL), coping strategies, and depressive personality disorder were measured at baseline in 38 patients (aged 20-49 yrs) who met Diagnostic and Statistical Manual of Mental Disorders-IV (DSM-IV) criteria for borderline personality disorder (BPD).

Frequency of self-damaging and suicidal behaviors in the 6-month period following base-line was measured prospectively at 3- and 6-month follow-ups. The RFL has only one sub-scale that predicts parasuicidal behaviors (i.e. Survival and Coping Beliefs [SCB]   ). Participants who scored low on this subscale were 6.8 times more likely to exhibit self-dam-aging and suicidal behaviors in the follow-up period than their high-scoring counterparts. However, SCB was substantially correlated with the coping strategies "reassuring thoughts," "active coping," and "palliative reaction pattern," as well as with depressive personality traits. In a multivariate model, the predictive power of SCB appeared to be accounted for by reassuring thoughts and depressive PD.

Journal of Personality Disorders. 2001 Dec Vol 15(6) 512-520

[467]
Roehrig, Helmut R.; Range, Lillian M.

Recklessness, depression, and reasons for living in predicting suicidality in college stu-dents.
Assessed recklessness, depression, and reasons for living in college students to see if reck-lessness would account for unique variance in suicidality. Ss completed a battery of instru-ments, including the Sommerfeldt-Clark Adolescent Experience Scale, the Self-Rating Depression Scale, and the Scale for Suicide Ideation. The Sommerfeldt-Clark Suicidal Tendencies subscale accounted for the most variance in suicidality. Further, this scale was moderately internally consistent and had adequate validity. Recklessness was not a compo-nent of suicidality among these nonclinical older adolescents but may be a factor in clinical or younger samples of adolescents.

Journal of Youth & Adolescence. 1995 Dec Vol 24(6) 723-729

[468]
Sahin, Nesrin H.; Batiguen, Ayseguel Durak; Sahin, Nail

Reasons for living and their protective value: A Turkish sample.
Investigated the various reasons for living which are protective against depression and lone-liness, variables frequently associated with suicide. 232 urban youth and adults (aged 14-45) from Turkey completed the Reasons for Living Inventory, Beck Depression Inventory, Offer-Loneliness Scale, and Ways of Coping Inventory and answered questions about life satisfaction and future expectations. Results indicate that Ss with more optimism toward life were less prone to depression and loneliness. In this Turkish sample, females were signifi-cantly more optimistic, a finding divergent from the international literature to date. Cultural factors and related contradictory findings in the West are discussed (e.g., moral religious values).

Archives of Suicide Research. 1998 Vol 4(2) 157-168

[469]
Strosahl, Kirk; Chiles, John A.; Linehan, Marsha

Prediction of suicide intent in hospitalized parasuicides: Reasons for living, hopelessness, and depression.
Examined the risk prediction efficiency of the Survival and Coping Beliefs subscale of the Reasons for Living Inventory, Beck Hopelessness Scale, Beck Depression Inventory, and the Life Experiences Survey with 51 newly hospitalized parasuicides (aged 14-46 yrs). The index

of suicidal potential chosen for this study was suicide intent as measured by Beck's Suicide Intent Scale. Regression analyses indicated that the Survival and Coping Beliefs subscale emerged as the single most important predictor of suicide intent. Classification analyses showed that neither hopelessness nor survival and coping beliefs were accurate at classifying low- or high-intent parasuicides. Factors contributing to the efficacy of survival and coping beliefs as a risk prediction index are discussed, as is the false-negative dilemma in suicide risk assessment and prediction.

Comprehensive Psychiatry. 1992 Nov-Dec Vol 33(6) 366-373

[cf. 062]
Tena, Antonio; Rage, Ernesto; Virseda, Jose Antonio

The purpose in life of university youth: A descriptive study.
(Sentido de vida en jovenes universitarios: Estudio descriptivo.)
Psicologia Contemporanea. 1999 Vol 6(2) 76-83

[470]
Westefeld, John S.; Badura, Amy; Kiel, Jeffrey T.; Scheel, Karen

The College Student Reasons for Living Inventory: Additional psychometric data.
Provides additional data on the properties and validity of the College Student Reasons for Living Inventory [CS-RLI]. In particular, the authors were interested in the utility of the CS-RLI in predicting suicidal risk among 175 female and 57 male college students. The examination of gender data was also of interest. Results show that the female sample had a significantly higher mean score than the male sample, indicating that females endorsed the reasons for living choices more strongly than the males. Significant differences were also found in levels of suicidal risk. In terms of suicidal risk, 87% of the Ss indicated that they never think about suicide, and 13% indicated that they think about it occasionally. Ss self-reporting greater suicidal risk had a lower mean CS-RLI score than those at the lower level of suicidal risk, indicating that students with a greater level of suicidality had fewer reasons for living.

Journal of College Student Development. 1996 May-Jun Vol 37(3) 348-350

[471]
Westefeld, John S.; Cardin, Denise; Deaton, William L.

Development of the College Student Reasons for Living Inventory.
Two studies evaluated the College Student Reasons for Living Inventory (CSRLI) of M. M. Linehan et al. In Study 1, 125 college students generated 84 (reduced to 46) "reasons for living" items. Six factors were extracted: (1) survival and coping beliefs, (2) college and future-related concerns, (3) moral objections, (4) responsibilities to friends and family, (5) fear of suicide, and (6) fear of social disapproval. Factors 1 and 3-6 reflected the themes of Linehan et al, but Factor 2 was unique to college students. In Study 2, 208 college students evaluated the CSRLI. Results indicate that the CSRLI holds promise as an instrument to predict suicidal risk in college students.

Suicide & Life-Threatening Behavior. 1992 Win Vol 22(4) 442-452

[472]
Westefeld, John S.; Scheel, Karen; Maples, Michael R.

Psychometric analyses of the College Student Reasons for Living Inventory using a clinical population.
87 clients (aged 18-43 yrs) presenting for counseling at a large, comprehensive university counseling center completed the College Student Reason for Living Inventory and several additional instruments as a means of gathering data concerning the utility of the CSRLI. Results indicate that the CSRLI is a useful tool for prediction of suicidal risk among college students.

Measurement & Evaluation in Counseling & Development. 1998 Jul Vol 31(2) 86-94

Substance Abuse and Addictions

[473]
Adams, Scot L.; Waskel, Shirley A.

Comparisons of Purpose in Life scores between alcoholics with early and later onset.
No significant differences were found on Purpose in Life Test scores of 33 early-onset
(before age 40 yrs) and 27 late-onset alcoholic men (all Ss aged 60+ yrs) in alcoholic treatment centers. Differences were found between the late-onset group and 38 early-onset alcoholics studied by J. C. Crumbaugh (1968) as well as an older nonalcoholic group of 20 men
tested by A. Meier and H. Edwards.
Psychological Reports. 1991 Dec Vol 69(3, Pt 1) 837-838

[474]
Amodeo, Maryann; Kurtz, Norman; Cutter, Henry S.

Abstinence, reasons for not drinking, and life satisfaction.
Examined the reasons given for not drinking by abstinent alcoholics with varying lengths of
sobriety. A reasons for not drinking scale was tested, as well as the Purpose in Life
Questionnaire and Life Satisfaction Scale. Ss were 60 34-55 yr old males from a VA population. Ss with less education and Ss treated in a detoxification setting were more likely to
endorse negative reasons for not drinking. Ss with short and long abstinence had a higher
level of life dissatisfaction than Ss with moderate periods of abstinence. Purpose in life, life
satisfaction, and reasons for not drinking were important measures of progress in treatment
and movement through phases of recovery.
International Journal of the Addictions. 1992 Jun Vol 27(6) 707-716

[475]
Arimond, Juergen-Peter; Kammer, Daniele

**Existential frustration, value convergence, and depression as predictors of outcome and
dropout in inpatient treatment of alcoholism.**
(Existentielle Frustration, Wertangleichung und Depressivitaet als Praediktoren von
Therapieverlaufsbeurteilung und Therapieabbruch bei stationaerer
Alkoholismusbehandlung.)
Studied the role of existential frustration, depression, and value convergence as predictors
of therapeutic outcomes to test the utility of L. Festinger's cognitive dissonance theory
and V. E. Frankl's (1982, 1984) logotherapy in predicting value convergence between
inpatient alcoholics and their therapists. Ss were 9 therapists (mean age 33 yrs) (therapists) and 51 of their alcoholic clients (mean age 41 yrs). Questionnaire data on existential frustration, depression, and value convergence were analyzed in relation to therapist
and patient ratings of group therapy processes and outcomes and in relation to treatment
dropout rates. Several instruments were used, including German versions of the Rokeach
Value Survey by M. Rokeach, the Logo-Test by E. S. Lukas (1986), and the Beck
Depression Inventory.
Zeitschrift fuer Klinische Psychologie. Forschung und Praxis. 1993 Vol 22(3) 276-290

[476]
Bammer, Gabrielle; Weekes, Sue

Becoming an ex-user: Insights into the process and implications for treatment and policy.
Interviewed 18 adult ex-users of heroin about stopping heroin use, the role of treatment, and their views on a proposal to make heroin available in a controlled manner as a new treatment option. Factors involved in stopping dependent heroin use included "hitting rock bottom" or a less intense crisis such as the death by overdose of someone close, falling in love, wanting to be a good parent, geographical relocation, and wanting to avoid becoming caught up with the police or going to jail. Other factors included maturing out or becoming sick of the lifestyle, finding a new purpose in life or developing a new lifestyle, dealing with past hurts, and the support of family, friends, other ex-users and professionals. Ss saw therapeutic communities as having both advantages and disadvantages as a way out of heroin use, and were evenly divided in supporting the controlled availability of heroin and the potential benefits and problems of such treatment.

Drug & Alcohol Review. 1994 Vol 13(3) 285-292

[477]
Bonebright, Cynthia A.; Clay, Daniel L.; Ankenmann, Robert D.

The relationship of workaholism with work-life conflict, life satisfaction, and purpose in life.
This study examined the differences between 2 types of workaholics (enthusiastic and nonenthusiastic workaholics) and nonworkaholic workers (work enthusiasts, relaxed workers, unengaged workers, and disenchanted workers) with respect to work-life conflict, life satisfaction, and purpose in life in a sample of 171 salaried employees of a high technology organization. Results differed for the 2 types of workaholics, supporting the importance of continued differentiation of workaholic types. Nonenthusiastic workaholics were found to have significantly more work-life conflict and significantly less life satisfaction and purpose in life than 3 of the 4 types of nonworkaholics. Enthusiastic workaholics were found to have significantly more life satisfaction and purpose in life than nonenthusiastic workaholics and significantly more work-life conflict than 3 of the 4 nonworkaholics. Implications for career planning and counseling are discussed.

Journal of Counseling Psychology. 2000 Oct Vol 47(4) 469-477

[478]
Brown, Janice M.; Ashcroft, Francesca G.; Miller, William R.

Purpose in life among alcoholics: A comparison of three ethnic groups.
Ethnic variability in perceived purpose in life and spirituality was measured in a group of 100 alcohol dependent male inpatients (aged 23-66 yrs). The sample was composed of Caucasian (38%), Hispanic (37%), and American Indian (25%) hospitalized alcoholics. Analysis of variance tests revealed significant differences on the Purpose in Life (PIL) instrument. Follow-up tests indicated that American Indians endorsed higher levels of purpose in life than either of the other 2 groups. Controlling for 4 alcohol severity covariates failed to obviate the effect of ethnicity on PIL scores, suggesting important ethnic differences in this construct.

Alcoholism Treatment Quarterly. 1998 Vol 16(3) 1-11

[479]
Cameron, Douglas; Thomas, Mark; Madden, Sarah; Thornton, Christine; Bergmark, Anders; Garretsen, Henk; Terzidou, Manina

Intoxicated across Europe: In search of meaning.
Explored a method of defining and quantifying the state of drunkenness in 5 different cities in Europe. Groups of clinical or research workers in alcohol problems in Edinburgh, Leicester, Stockholm, Rotterdam, and Athens wrote down all the words they could think of in their own language which meant "drunk." They then arranged these words on a spectrum from most positive to most negative and quantified the "top ten" words in terms of intensity of intoxication. All words were then sorted into 5 categories: psychological (any amount of alcohol and extreme amounts of alcohol), behavioral (any and extreme), and post hoc. Results showed the technique to be reliable. All these drinking cultures have a rich language to describe states of intoxication and it was possible to quantify and compare them. Three groups (English, Dutch, and Swedish) defined the most severe states of intoxication predominantly in behavioral terms. The Swedish group had the largest number of words describing drunkenness as the behavior induced by any level of ingested alcohol. The Scots and the Greeks used psychological definitions but the Scots also acknowledged that becoming severely intoxicated can be the consequence of attempting to get into a new psychological state, but overdoing it.
Addiction Research. 2000 Vol 8(3) 233-242

[480]
Carroll, Jerome F. X.; McGinley, John J.; Mack, Stephen E.

Exploring the expressed spiritual needs and concerns of drug-dependent males in modified, therapeutic community treatment.
200 18-65 yr old males admitted into 1 of 2 innercity residential substance abuse treatment programs were evaluated for spirituality religious concerns with the Substance Abuse Problem Checklist (J. F. X. Carroll, 1983). Results indicated considerable levels of religious spiritual needs and concerns for residents of both a Philadelphia and New York City modified therapeutic community program. Implications of these needs are identified and considered. The Substance Abuse Problem Checklist is appended.
Alcoholism Treatment Quarterly. 2000 Vol 18(1) 79-92

[481]
Carroll, Stephanie

Spirituality and purpose in life in alcoholism recovery.
Examined the relationship between spirituality and recovery from alcoholism. Spirituality was defined as the extent of practice of AA Steps 11 and 12 and was measured by a Step Questionnaire developed for this study. Step 11 suggests prayer and meditation, and Step 12 suggests assistance of other alcoholics. It was postulated that the extent to which Steps 11 and 12 were practiced would be positively correlated with the extent of purpose in life reported by 100 AA members. Positive correlations between practice of Step 11 and purpose in life scores and between Step 11 and length of sobriety were found. Number of AA meetings attended was significantly correlated with purpose in life scores and length of sobriety
Journal of Studies on Alcohol. 1993 May Vol 54(3) 297-301

[482]
Cisler, Ron A.; Zweben, Allen

Development of a composite measure for assessing alcohol treatment outcome:
Operationalization and validation.
This article operationally describes and empirically validates a composite outcome measure
developed for use in a multisite alcohol treatment matching study. Using empirically based
clinical guidelines to establish alcohol consumption and alcohol-related problems criteria,
1,726 Ss were classified as (1) abstinent, (2) moderate drinking without problems, (3) heavy
drinking or problems, or (4) heavy drinking and problems at intake and at 3, 6, 9, 12, and
15 mo postintake. Ss with poorer composite outcome also had poorer outcomes related to
quantity and frequency of alcohol consumption, alcohol-related problems, serum gamma-
glutamyltranspeptidase and other nonalcohol-related measures assessing psychiatric dysfunction, psychosocial functioning, and purpose or meaning in life. Differences in the present composite measure relative to other categorical measures used in research to date and
the potential for incorporating nonalcohol-specific variables into composite measures are
discussed.
Alcoholism: Clinical & Experimental Research. 1999 Feb Vol 23(2) 263-271

[483]
Coleman, Sandra B.; Kaplan, J. Doreene; Downing, Robert W.

Life cycle and loss: The spiritual vacuum of heroin addiction.
40 heroin addicts (mean age 28.05 yrs), 40 psychiatric outpatients (mean age 29.47 yrs),
and 31 college students were given an extensive interview and test battery to determine the
incidence of loss of family members and significant others and Ss' perception of their families' religious values and orientation to life's meaning and purpose. Results indicate that the
incidence of death differed significantly across groups and that addicts had a distinct orientation to death, were more suicidal, and had more premature and bizarre death experiences.
During childhood they had more family separations, and they tended to develop a distinct
pattern of continuously separating from and returning to their families. They were less likely to have a clearly defined purpose in life. A subset of parents from each group was also
interviewed and tested, and results support the theory of the intergenerational transmission
of behavior
Family Process. 1986 Mar Vol 25(1) 5-23

[484]
Crumbaugh, James C.

The Seeking of Noetic Goals Test (SONG): A complementary scale to the Purpose in Life
Test (PIL).
Describes the development of a new attitude scale, the Seeking of Noetic Goals Test
(SONG), to measure the strength of motivation to find meaning in life; the test was
designed to complement the Purpose in Life Test (PIL), which measures the degree to which
meaning has been found. Both instruments were designed from the orientation of V. E.
Frankl's (1955, 1959) logotherapy, which holds the "will to meaning" to be the strongest
human motivation. Ss were: Group 1 "abnormal," 128 logotherapy patients, 30 methadone
patients, and 262 alcoholics; Group 2 "normal," 19 seminary students, 64 mixed college
students, and 123 female college freshmen. (Subgroup fractionations were studied inde-

pendently.) Results support a predicted moderate negative correlation with the PIL and statistically significant construct validity in separating normal from abnormal populations. PIL-SONG combinations in the prediction of therapeutic outcome support the usefulness of the SONG as a supplementary instrument. The predicted differences are small, but in the expected direction.

Journal of Clinical Psychology. 1977 Jul Vol 33(3) 900-907

[485]
Edwards, Griffith; Brown, David; Oppenheimer, Edna; Sheehan, Margaret; et al

Long term outcome for patients with drinking problems: The search for predictors.
Reviews previous work on prediction of outcome among patients with drinking problems and presents results of a 10-yr follow-up of a group of 99 married male alcoholics. Ss were recruited into the research cohort between 1968-1970. At time of original contact, the Eysenck Personality Inventory was administered. At or just after the 10th anniversary of intake, a personal follow-up interview was conducted on 68 of the 81 surviving patients. Also administered at this time were the Purpose in Life Inventory, the Eysenck Personality Questionnaire, and a test which gave a measure of maximum experience of alcohol dependence at any stage in the individual's drinking career (T. Stockwell et al, 1979). A predictive approach of running individual intake variables against a range of outcome variables revealed little of significance, and actual drinking behavior could not be predicted at all. However, when outcome was measured in terms of dimensions deriving from a principal components analysis, some significant predictors were found that bear differentially on the 2 components.

British Journal of Addiction. 1988 Aug Vol 83(8) 917-927

[486]
Guttmann, David; Cohen, Ben-Zion

Excessive behaviors and meaning-in-life among the active elderly in Israel
What role does meaning-in-life play in the prevalence of excessive behavior patterns among active Israeli aged? Are such behaviors new, that is, developed after retirement, or do they manifest a continuation of previous life-style patterns? What other factors affect these behaviors? Exploration of these questions is necessitated by the fact that between 1960 and 1980 the elderly population in Israel has grown threefold, while the general population increased by only seventy percent. Moreover, the recent influx of immigrants from the former Soviet Union contains a large proportion of elderly people, placing an ever increasing demand on the Israeli health care and social welfare systems. The above questions were investigated in a sample of 148 active elderly living in the community with a shortened form of the Purpose-in-Life test. Excessive behaviors studied were medication abuse, alcohol consumption, smoking, and gambling. Subjects were participants at four retired persons' clubs operated by the municipal authorities in the city of Haifa. These four clubs were chosen to represent neighborhoods with differing socioeconomic levels and ethnic compositions in which attendees live. Data were collected by trained interviewers and recorded on a prepared schedule, which contained items on the demographic, familial, physical, and economic conditions in the past (age 50) and at present. Additional information was sought on their use of medications, consumption of alcohol, smoking, and gambling. Findings indicated that the overall prevalence of excessive behaviors in this sample was lower than expected. Meaning-in-Life had a positive correlation (eta=.63) with these behaviors.

However, it is not clear from the causal order whether these behaviors affect meaning-in-life, or whether they are affected by it. This finding needs further study with different samples and in different settings to ascertain its applicability to other elderly populations. From the additional findings it appears that excessive behaviors are associated with life style changes, even when these changes are for the better. Continuity in life style contributed to meaning-in-life, as did a secular outlook on life, economic situation and current level of health. A negative association found between meaning-in-life and religiousness needs further study as well. The results offer further confirmation of the importance of Frankl's concept of meaning.

The International Journal of Logotherapy and Existential Analysis / The Journal of the Viktor Frankl Institute. 1:2 Autumn 1993*

[487]
Harlow, Lisa L.; Mitchell, Kimberly J.; Fitts, Sherri N.; Saxon, Susan E.

Psycho-existential distress and problem behaviors: Gender, subsample, and longitudinal tests.
Examined gender differences and the nature of relationship between psycho-existential distress and problem behavior across 2 diverse subsamples of community and continuing-education women, as well as the longitudinal links across a 1-yr period. 602 college students (mean age age 19.86 yrs), 321 subsample from the wider community, 224 continuing-education females (aged 18-77 yrs) completed self-report questionnaire that measured psycho-existential distress (PED) and problem behavior variables such as self-derogation, meaning in life, substance use, and AIDS-risk behavior. The results indicate that for both male and female, and for both college and wider communities, a confidence of PED and other problem behaviors can occur. Individuals who are not able to successfully alleviate feelings of distress are more apt to engage in a number of problem behaviors such as substance abuse.

Journal of Applied Biobehavioral Research. 1999 Vol 4(2) 111-138

[cf. 436]
Harlow, Lisa L.; Newcomb, Michael D.; Bentler, P. M.

Depression, self-derogation, substance use, and suicide ideation: Lack of purpose in life as a mediational factor.

Journal of Clinical Psychology. 1986 Jan Vol 42(1) 5-21

[488]
Hutzell, Robert R.

Logoanalysis for alcoholics.
Presents findings from 2 studies designed to expand on data obtained by J. C. Crumbaugh and G. L. Carr (1979) on the use of logoanalysis (LA) in the treatment of inpatient alcoholics. Exp I assessed the overall sense of life meaning direction purpose of patients who had completed an alcohol dependency treatment program. 30 Ss in a subsequent assessment and rehabilitation program were examined on the basis of having participated in 7-20 LA sessions while in the original program or of not having participated in any LA sessions. Both groups were administered the Existential Depression subscale of the MMPI; Ss who completed LA reported higher scores on feelings of life meaning purpose than Ss who did not complete LA. Exp II sought to determine whether LA produced changes in patients' alco-

hol abuse behaviors. Ss had completed the alcohol treatment program within a 5-mo peri-od and were divided into 3 groups of 23—those who had missed 2 or fewer LA sessions (mean age 46.6 yrs), those who had attended 2 or fewer sessions (mean age 45.3 yrs), and those who had not participated (mean age 44.2 yrs). On a follow-up questionnaire, LA Ss again showed more positive results, displaying a greater likelihood of behavior change toward future quality sobriety than non-LA Ss.

International Forum for Logotherapy. 1984 Spr-Sum 7(1) 40-45

[489]
Hutzell, Robert R.; Finck, Willis C.

Adapting the Life Purpose Questionnaire for use with adolescent populations.
Examined the potential use of the Life Purpose Questionnaire (LPQ) among 2 groups of 100 high school students (aged 14-18 yrs). Ss were members of drug alcohol support groups; controls were other students. Two items were omitted from the 20-item LPQ, orig-inally designed for institutionalized geriatric individuals. 42% of the Ss, and 23% of the controls, scored below the average LPQ scores for meaning in life. The results suggest that the LPQ can be a useful measure of the degree of life-meaning in adolescents.

International Forum for Logotherapy. 1994 Spr Vol 17(1) 42-46

[490]
Hutzell, R. R.; Peterson, T. J.

Use of the Life Purpose Questionnaire with an alcoholic population.
Examined the potential use of the Life Purpose Questionnaire (LPQ) for assessing life meaning sensed by alcoholic patients. Correlations between scores of the LPQ and the more complicated Purpose-in-Life Test (PIL) were significant for 3 separate alcoholic groups totaling 220 Ss (aged 22-69 yrs). Groups 1 and 2 were administered the LPQ within an ini-tial logoanalysis session and the PIL for homework. Group 3 was administered the LPQ and PIL as part of a testing battery. It is concluded that the LPQ can be used with alcoholics in order to obtain a quick and readily understandable measure of the individual's sense of life meaning..

International Journal of the Addictions. 1986 Vol 21(1) 51-57

[491]
Iso-Ahola, Seppo E.; Crowley, Edward D.

Adolescent substance abuse and leisure boredom.
Examined the relationship between substance abuse, leisure boredom, and leisure partici-pation in 39 adolescent substance abusers (SAs) and 81 non-SAs (aged 15-18 yrs). SAs had a tendency to participate more frequently in leisure activities in general, and physical recre-ation activities in particular. Nonetheless, SAs were significantly more bored with leisure than non-SAs. Results are interpreted as evidence that SAs have a personality predisposition toward sensation seeking and a low tolerance for constant experience. If leisure activities fail to satisfy their need for optimal arousal, leisure boredom results and drugs may be used as an alternative. Findings also suggest that an experiential approach in treating adolescent SAs may be better than traditional cognitive and didactic approaches.

Journal of Leisure Research. 1991 Vol 23(3) 260-271

[492]
Jacobson, George R.; Ritter, Daniel P.; Mueller, Lynn

Purpose in life and personal values among adult alcoholics.
Ideas of purpose and meaning in life, religious or spiritual values, belief in a higher power, and related constructs often play an important role in traditional alcoholism rehabilitation approaches, but very few data are available. In the present study, 49 males and 8 females in a 30-day inpatient treatment program for alcoholics were given the Purpose in Life (PIF) test and the Allport-Vernon-Lindzey Study of Values (SOV) shortly after admission to the hospital and again just before discharge. Results indicate (a) significant increases in PIL scores; (b) no significant dissimilarities between alcoholics and normals on the SOV; and (c) significant correlations between PIL and the Aesthetic and Religious scales of the SOV on the 2nd administration only. Results are discussed in terms of future directions for research and implications for treatment.
Journal of Clinical Psychology. 1977 Jan Vol 33(1) 314-316

[493]
Johnson, Thomas J.

College students' self-reported reasons for why drinking games end.
Previous research has noted that drinking game participation is associated with increased risk of negative alcohol-related consequences. The current study examined the reasons that students give for how drinking games end and or why students elect to quit playing. Ss were 53 men (mean age 20.24 yrs) and 90 women (mean age 19.56 yrs). Both men and women identified other people quitting and deciding that they have had enough to drink as the most important single item reasons for quitting play. Principal components analysis using a list of 20 reasons identified six factors, four of which contained overlapping items: Conformity Boredom; Interpersonal Competition; Sexual Contact; Excessive Consumption; Interpersonal Conflict; and External Circumstances. The factors correlated in a theoretically meaningful fashion with measures of alcohol consumption and consequences and personality. Conformity Boredom reasons and External Circumstances reasons were least associated with negative alcohol-related consequences. Many students apparently play until they get too drunk or too sick to continue. Understanding how games end may offer clues to designing skills training or other prevention interventions to reduce harm associated with drinking games.
Addictive Behaviors. 2002 Jan-Feb Vol 27(1) 145-153

[494]
Kern, P.

Ideas and Opinions of Addicts about Everyday Concepts.
(Vorstellungen und Ansichten von Suchtkranken zu Begriffen des täglichen Lebens.)
This study shows that patients suffering from substance abuse disorders have a deep and ongoing concern about existential questions. Their existential quest is shown to be independent of sex, age, education or religious affiliation. An expanded therapy plan – complementary to more conventional primary therapy -, based on the principles of V.E. Frankl's logotherapy is shown to have a lasting and positive influence on patients.
The International Journal of Logotherapy and Existential Analysis / Journal of the Viktor Frankl Institute.. 1993 Vol 1, No 1 (Spring 1993)

[cf. 418]
Kinnier, Richard T.; Metha, Arlene T.; Keim, Jeanmarie S.; Okey, Jeffrey L.; et al

Depression, meaninglessness, and substance abuse in "normal" and hospitalized adolescents.
Journal of Alcohol & Drug Education. 1994 Win Vol 39(2) 101-111

[495]
Kinnier, Richard T.; Metha, Arlene T.; Okey, Jeffrey L.; Keim, Jeanmarie

Adolescent substance abuse and psychological health.
Tested the hypothesis that adolescents who occasionally used drugs would exhibit psychologically healthier characteristics than adolescents who had been frequent users or complete abstainers. 161 adolescents (aged 12-18 yrs) recruited from a public urban high school and 2 psychiatric facilities completed measures of self-esteem, depression, purpose in life, and drug use. The relationship between substance use and psychological health was linear. Increasing drug use was associated with an increase in depression, a decrease in self-esteem, and a deterioration of purpose in life.
Journal of Alcohol & Drug Education. 1994 Fal Vol 40(1) 51-56

[cf. 444]
Kirkpatrick-Smith, Joyce; Rich, Alexander R.; Bonner, Ronald; Jans, Frank

Psychological vulnerability and substance abuse as predictors of suicide ideation among adolescents.
Omega: Journal of Death & Dying. 1991-1992 Vol 24(1) 21-33

[496]
Klingemann, Harald K.

The motivation for change from problem alcohol and heroin use.
A 1988 study in Switzerland on spontaneous remission from substance abuse identified 60 practically treatment-free remitters. While 14 of the 30 alcohol cases reduced their consumption almost to abstinence, all but 2 heroin remitters stopped their consumption altogether. Qualitative analysis of the life histories led to a typology of the autoremission process. Motivation to change, implementation of the decision, and maintenance and negotiation of a new identity or meaning in life represent the 3 major stages. This study focuses on the 1st stage and the role of negative vs positive experiences in changes in alcohol or heroin consumption. The quantitative description is discussed in the context of a model of the decision-making process from cognitive psychology. Methodological drawbacks (e.g., recall problems) of this exploratory study are discussed.
British Journal of Addiction. 1991 Jun Vol 86(6) 727-744

[497]
Kolton, Marilyn S.; Dwarshuis, Louis

The role of volunteers in innovative drug treatment programs.
Studied 72 innovative drug programs for youth. The research methodology included retrieval conferences and extensive questionnaires on 35 essential program components.

Motivations for volunteering were also studied. Findings indicate volunteers' motivations include (a) learning about the drug scene, (b) vicarious experiencing, (c) seeking personal meaning, (d) wanting psychological help, (e) being a helper, (f) contributing professional skills, and (g) performing a parental role. Screening procedures and training are used to determine what motivation is acceptable. The extensive involvement of volunteers is an encouraging demonstration of ways to tap community resources.

Drug Forum. 1974 Vol 4(1) 39-45

[498]
Koski-Jaennes, Anja; Turner, Nigel

Factors influencing recovery from different addictions.
Examined environmental and behavioral factors that play a role in the recovery from addictive behaviors. Two primary questions were asked: To what extent the factors influential in resolving addictive behaviors and the means of maintaining the change differ by addictions, and to what extent the former factors predict the latter? 76 Ss (aged 25-76 yrs) who had managed to resolve their addiction and maintain the change for more than 3 yrs were recruited by newspaper ads. The sample included addictions to alcohol, multiple substances, nicotine, binge eating, and other, which included sex, gambling and benzodiazepine. The mean time of recovery was 9.3 yrs. Two types of factor analyses were used to define factors that played a role in resolving the problem and in maintaining the change. Seven change factors and 4 maintenance factors were supported by both methods. The change factors were: Tiring Out, Love, 12 Steps, Revival, Family, Social Consequences, and Peer Group change. The maintenance factors were: Self-Control, Professional Treatment, 12 Steps and Spirituality, as well as Social and Cognitive Coping. Significant addiction-related differences appeared in 4 change factors and 3 maintenance factors, thus displaying the differing routes to recovery in different addictions.

Addiction Research. 1999 Dec Vol 7(6) 469-492

[499]
Kosviner, A.; Hawks, D.

Seven attitude scales used in assessing cannabis use amongst students.
Five attitude scales, previously developed by the authors in studies of cannabis use among British university students, were administered to 830 university students. The scales measured political orientation, permissive-restrictiveness, puritan ethic, parental congruence, and extra-intrapunitiveness. In addition, a checklist concerned with degree of social and political activity, a modified version of the Purpose in Life Test, Srole's Anomie Scale, and the shortened form of the Eysenck Personality Inventory were used. Item loadings on the main factor in each scale and overall correlations between the scales are given. It is intended that these scales will provide a broader social psychological framework in which to consider attitudes and behavior toward cannabis.

Drug & Alcohol Dependence. 1976 Jun Vol 1(5) 339-348

[500]
Little G.L.; Robinson, K.D.

Effects of moral reconation therapy upon moral reasoning, life purpose, and recidivism among drug and alcohol offenders.

40 incarcerated DWI offenders and 62 drug offenders who were treated with Moral Reconation Therapy were assessed with respect to levels of moral reasoning, their perceived purpose in life, and subsequent recidivism. Analysis showed that, as clients progress in the program, levels of moral reasoning and purpose in life increase significantly. Level of moral reasoning appears to increase with clients' completion of therapeutic steps. Preliminary recidivism data on 103 male and female inmate-clients who have participated in an after-care program using the therapy appear encouraging.

Psychological Reports. 1989 Feb;64(1):83-90.

[501]
March, Ali; Smith, Leigh; Piek, Jan; Saunders, Bill

The purpose in life scale: Psychometric properties for social drinkers and drinkers in alcohol treatment.
The aim of the present research was to further investigate (a) the structure of the Purpose in Life test (PIL) using confirmatory factor analytic techniques, (b) the reliability of PIL scores, and (c) the validity of the PIL. Participants were 357 social drinkers (not in alcohol treatment) and 137 treatment drinkers (in alcohol treatment). With the exclusion of 3 items, a unidimensional measurement model for the PIL provided an adequate fit for social and treatment drinkers. Model invariance analysis indicated that 6 of 17 PIL items had different pattern coefficients for the two groups of drinkers. The 17 items of the PIL demonstrated good measurement reliability for both groups of drinkers and good criterion-related validity.

Educational & Psychological Measurement. 2003 Oct Vol 63(5) 859-871

[502]
Majer, John M.

Assessing the logotherapeutic value of 12-step therapy.
Evaluated the logotherapeutic value of treating chemically dependent persons by 12-step fellowships such as Alcoholics Anonymous (AA) and Narcotics Anonymous (NA). 29 adults from a chemical dependency treatment facility participated in a 12-step treatment program that included group counseling, full time employment vocational training, and assessment through a battery of tests and questionnaires. Test scores for Ss at the beginning of treatment were compared with those at the end of treatment. Data indicate that the longer the commitment to AA or NA, the greater the likelihood of finding meaning in life. Thus, although Ss were confronted with unavoidable suffering during therapy, their perception of it was likely altered in a meaningful way.

International Forum for Logotherapy. 1992 Fal Vol 15(2) 86-89

[503]
Minehan, Janet A.; Newcomb, Michael D.; Galaif, Elisha R.

Predictors of adolescent drug use: Cognitive abilities, coping strategies and purpose in life.
Investigated whether purpose in life and coping skills mediate the relationship between cognitive abilities and polydrug use among adolescents. 144 junior high and high school students (aged 12-17 yrs) completed questionnaires concerning crystallized and fluid intelligence, coping strategies, purpose in life, and polydrug use. Results show that the relationship between crystallized intelligence and alcohol use was mediated by purpose in life. Older

age predicted higher cognitive abilities, stronger coping strategies, more polydrug use, and less purpose in life. Cognitive abilities predicted less cigarette and illicit drug use, existential confusion predicted more illicit drug use, and cognitive approach skills predicted more polydrug use. Coping skills did not mediate the relationship between cognitive abilities and drug use.

Journal of Child & Adolescent Substance Abuse. 2000 Vol 10(2) 33-52

[504]
Newcomb, Michael D.; Bentler, P. M.; Fahy, Bridget

Cocaine use and psychopathology: Associations among young adults.
Examined the association between cocaine involvement and measures of psychopathology in a general community sample of 221 males and 518 females (aged 19-24 yrs). There were no sex differences in level of cocaine involvement or on associations between cocaine use and psychopathology. There were several small relationships between cocaine use and several indicators of psychopathology (increased sleep disturbance, decreased panic and phobia symptoms, lack of purpose in life, and increased psychotic proneness). It is concluded that the severe psychopathology associated with cocaine use often cited in the literature results from using clinic or treatment samples or chronic abusers and that such strong associations are not apparent in the general population of young adults with relatively brief cocaine use careers.

International Journal of the Addictions. 1987 Dec Vol 22(12) 1167-1188

[505]
Newcomb, Michael D.; Harlow, L. L.

Life events and substance use among adolescents: Mediating effects of perceived loss of control and meaninglessness in life.
Examined the possible mediating influences of perceived loss of control and meaninglessness interposed between the experience of stressful life events and the use of drugs. Uncontrollable stress (negative life change events) was assumed to create a sense of loss of control that engendered a decreased level of meaning in life. This meaninglessness in life, experienced as distressful and uncomfortable, is then treated or medicated with various drug substances. This model was tested in 2 studies with independent samples of adolescents (one sample of 376 high school and college students collected by the Rutgers University and the other sample of 640 high school students collected by the University of California, Los Angeles [UCLA]). The Rutgers sample was cross-sectional, whereas the UCLA sample provided longitudinal data. Results support the hypothesis that perceived loss of control and meaninglessness mediate the relation between uncontrollable stress and substance use. In the Rutgers data, the association between stress and drug use was accounted for by the mediating constructs; no direct path was necessary to explain the relation between stress and general drug use. However, in the UCLA data there remained a direct influence of uncontrollable stress on substance use after accounting for the significant impact of the mediating constructs.

Journal of Personality & Social Psychology. 1986 Sep Vol 51(3) 564-577

[506]
Newcomb, Michael D.; Vargas-Carmona, Jennifer; Galaif, Elisha R.

Drug problems and psychological distress among a community sample of adults:
Predictors, consequences, or confound?
The prospective relationships between psychological distress and drug problems (e.g., alcohol, marijuana, and cocaine) were examined in a community sample of 470 adults (aged 28-32 yrs). Results addressed 3 theories—self medication self-derogation, impaired functioning, and general deviance—to explain the relationship between drug use and psychological distress. Although the latent construct of Polydrug Problems was largely unaffected by Psychological Distress and generally had no effect on Psychological Distress, several specific effects emerged. Providing support for the impaired-functioning theory, adults who abused drugs early on experienced later impaired functioning, anxiety, suicidal ideation, psychoticism, hostility, and decreased purpose in life 4 yrs later. Providing support for both the self-medication and self-derogation theories, those who experienced aspects of psychological distress (e.g., dysphoria, suicidal ideation) reported drug problems 4 yrs later.
Journal of Community Psychology. 1999 Jul Vol 27(4) 405-429

[507]
Nicholson, Thomas; Higgins, Wayne; Turner, Paul; James, Susan; et al

The relation between meaning in life and the occurrence of drug abuse: A retrospective study.
Conducted an epidemiological, retrospective study to compare personal meaning in life (e.g., V. Frankl, 1959) between a group of 49 individuals (mean age 29.4 yrs) receiving inpatient treatment for drug abuse and a group of 49 matched, non-drug-abusing controls (mean age 29.1 yrs). All Ss completed the Purpose in Life Test and Life Attitude Profile—Revised. With both instruments, the inpatient drug-abusing Ss were found to have significantly lower levels of meaning in life. Results suggest that drug treatment and primary prevention programs should consider giving some attention toward life meaning issues in their intervention strategies.
Psychology of Addictive Behaviors. 1994 Mar Vol 8(1) 24-28

[508]
Noblejas de la Flor, M. Angeles

Meaning levels and drug-abuse therapy: An empirical study.
Evaluated the meaning levels of the participants of a Spanish logotherapeutic drug abuse rehabilitation program to address the relationship between addiction and existential frustration from 2 points of view: (1) comparison of a drug addicted sample with a non-drug-addicted sample and (2) study of inner meaning fulfillment at 3 stages of a therapeutic educational program. Two hypotheses, drug addiction is linked with existential frustration; and elimination of drug problems is related to a significant improvement in meaning of life, were assessed. 125 Ss were administered 2 logotherapy tests: the Purpose in Life test (PIL) and the LOGO test (E. Lukas, 1986). The PIL was used to assess meaning and the LOGO test was used to assess existential frustration. 841 Ss used to obtain Spanish norms for both tests were used as the "normal" sample. 33 Ss who completed the program several years prior were also considered. Statistical analyses of the results support both hypotheses
International Forum for Logotherapy. 1997 Spr Vol 20(1) 46-51

[509]
Orcutt, James D.

Contrasting effects of two kinds of boredom on alcohol use.
Examined 2 distinctive types of boredom identified in an earlier survey by the author and
L. K. Harvey (1983) and related them to drinking behavior in 30 male and 62 female
undergraduates. Ss completed a questionnaire designed to measure boredom. A scale of existential boredom (e.g., frequency of boredom and a lack of purpose in life) was found in
multiple regression analyses to have a strong, positive relationship to frequency of alcohol
use among males. A scale measuring interpersonal boredom (e.g., boredom with "small talk"
vs feelings of "happiness with people") was inversely related to quantity of alcohol con-
sumed by both males and females. Findings suggest that the mundane situational experience of boredom has important consequences that are worthy of further sociological investigation.
Journal of Drug Issues. 1984 Win Vol 14(1) 161-173

[510]
Pardini, Dustin A.; Plante, Thomas G.; Sherman, Allen; Stump, Jamie E.

Religious faith and spirituality in substance abuse recovery: Determining the mental
health benefits.
Examined the relationship between religious faith, spirituality, and mental health outcomes
in individuals recovering from substance abuse. 236 recovering alcoholics or drug addicts
(mean age 37.1 yrs) completed questionnaires. Results show that Ss reported high levels of
religious faith and religious affiliation, but chose to rate themselves as being more spiritual
than religious. Higher levels of religious faith and spirituality were associated with increased
coping, greater resilience to stress, an optimistic life orientation, greater perceived social
support, and lower levels of anxiety. It is concluded that the core belief systems and behaviors associated with religious faith and spirituality are related to positive mental health outcomes among recovering individuals.
Journal of Substance Abuse Treatment. 2000 Dec Vol 19(4) 347-354

[511]
Scheier, Lawrence M.; Botvin, Gilbert J.

Purpose in life, cognitive efficacy, and general deviance as determinants of drug abuse in
urban Black youth.
The conceptual appropriateness of social-psychological theories of drug use with minority
youth has rarely been tested empirically. In addition to normative developmental transitions
associated with adolescence, minority youth may encounter sociopolitical and economic
hardships that spawn despair, hopelessness, and personal anomie, which may independently engender drug use. Using cross-sectional data from a cohort of 8th grade, urban, black
youth, the authors tested several latent-variable structural equation models which posited
that general deviance would mediate the influence of cognitive efficacy (i.e., skills mastery
and personal competence) and, separately, personal anomie. Models were psychometrically
sound and accounted for large portions of variation. Results showed that the influence of
hopelessness, loneliness, and suicidal thinking was entirely mediated by physical aggression,
sensation-seeking, unsafe, and unconventional behavior. Personal competence had both
direct and indirect influences on drug use. Findings underscore the continued primacy of

deviance in predicting drug use for minority youth and the necessity of incorporating affective influences into current cognitive-behavioral intervention strategies.

Journal of Child & Adolescent Substance Abuse. 1996 Vol 5(1) 1-26

[512]
Schlesinger, Susanna; Susman, Marilyn; Koenigsberg, Judy

Self-esteem and purpose in life: A comparative study of women alcoholics.
Investigated the relationship between self-esteem (SE) and purpose in life (PIL) in 4 groups (alcoholic and nonalcoholic men and women) of 30 Ss each matched for age (20+ yrs), race, marital and employment status, and length of sobriety. Significant differences were found between SE and PIL scores for alcoholic and nonalcoholic women. No statistical difference was found between SE and PIL scores for alcoholic and non-alcoholic men. Women alcoholics may constitute an identifiable group with a unique configuration of symptoms, and treatment approaches need to establish therapeutic goals consistent with those symptoms and to design sex-specific methods of addressing them.

Journal of Alcohol & Drug Education. 1990 Fal Vol 36(1) 127-141

[513]
Steyn, M.; Greeff, M.; Poggenpoel, M.

Perception of life's meaning by drug-dependent patients
This study aims to determine how the drug dependent patient subjectively experiences his purpose in life, as well as establishing guide-lines for activating an experience of a life with a purpose during the rehabilitation programme of the drug dependent patient. A qualitative model of research using an explorative and descriptive contextual study was used. By using a non-probable convenience selection method, 15 voluntary drug dependent patients were defined as units of analysis in order to determine the extent of their subjective experience of their purpose in life, using a semi-structured interview with the help of the "Purpose in life Test". The units of analysis complied with the criteria for drug dependency and were studied within the given context, i.e. the short term unit inside the hospital environment. Data obtained, after completing the instrument of measurement, was processed using the point allocation system of the attitude scale in the first section, a coding and frequency analysis of important words in the second section, and the phenomenological method of Giorgi in the third section. The results indicated that 14 out of the 15 units of analysis experienced their purpose in life as weak. From these results a programme for the activating of purpose in life experience was proposed and implemented on a single drug dependent patient who was selected as a case study. The data obtained during the presentation of the programme consist of summaries made by the therapist during the course of each session, and independent evaluations of the therapist and the patient.

Curationis. 1991 Jul;14(1):30-6.

[514]
Testoni, I.; Zamperini, A.

Nihilism, drug addiction and representation of death.
Reports the results of a field study on drug-addiction which examined 100 Ss treated in both public and private centres in Italy. The results were compared with a group of 120 non-addict controls (aged 15-40 yrs). The investigation concerned the representation of

death between living and knowing that death leads to total "annihilation" and living and thinking that death is a "passage". The investigation was based on a questionnaire made up of 2 items concerning the representation of death, items from the Reasons for Living Inventory-48; and 2 semantic differentials to clarify the links between "death" and "annihilation". Results demonstrate that there are significant differences between the 2 groups of Ss with regard to the representation of death, that "reasons for living" may change depending on the representation of death, and that in their "reasons for living" addicts differ from non-addicts who like them maintain that death means "annihilation".

Giornale Italiano di Suicidologia. 1998 Apr Vol 8(1) 13-21

[515]
Tonigan, J. Scott

Benefits of Alcoholics Anonymous attendance: Replication of findings between clinical research sites in Project MATCH.
Compared findings on the benefits associated with Alcoholics Anonymous (AA) attendance across eleven clinical sites in Project MATCH. 1,726 clients were recruited for the study. Results found that the largest benefit associated with AA attendance was increased abstinence, followed by reductions in alcohol-related consequences. The magnitude of these benefits did not differ between sites. A positive association was also found between AA attendance and increased purpose in life, but the size of this relationship was very small and was statistically significant only after controlling for measurement error. Several explanations are offered to reconcile findings in this study with earlier work concluding that: (1) treatment setting moderated subsequent AA benefit, and (2) AA attendance was associated with psychosocial improvement.

Alcoholism Treatment Quarterly. 2001 Vol 19(1) 67-77

[516]
Waisberg, J. L.

Purpose in life and outcome of treatment for alcohol dependence.
Examined the relationship of purpose in life to treatment outcome assessed 3 mo after completion of treatment among 131 adult Ss in inpatient treatment programs or awaiting treatment for alcoholism (in some cases in addition to other drug addictions). The mean Purpose in Life Test (PIL) score before treatment was significantly below the normal range and the mean PIL score at the end of in-patient treatment was within the normal range. Furthermore, the PIL score at the end of treatment was predictive of changes in intimate relationships and health at follow-up. It was also predictive of follow-up drinking drug use status. However, the pattern of prediction differed in the two treatment groups. Post-treatment PIL score was a positive predictor of improvement in a skill-based treatment center, and a negative predictor in a more authoritarian, confrontation-based program.

British Journal of Clinical Psychology. 1994 Feb Vol 33(1) 49-63

Antisocial Behavior/Delinquency/Violence

[517]
Addad, Moshe

Neuroticism, extraversion and meaning of life: A comparative study of criminals and non-criminals.
Investigated possible connections between neuroticism, extraversion, and the meaning of life in a population of incarcerated criminals (89 males and 21 females) and 306 noncriminals. Ss were aged 17-51 yrs. Findings show a negative correlation between the meaning of life and neuroticism. No connection was found between extraversion and the meaning of life. It was found that only in specific cases can criminal solutions be a substitute for the meaning of life. Findings are discussed in terms of V. Frankl's (1970) theory of logotherapy.
Personality & Individual Differences. 1987 Vol 8(6) 879-883

[cf. 376]
Addad, Moshe

Psychogenic neuroticism and noogenic self-strengthening.
International Forum for Logotherapy. 1987 Spr-Sum Vol 10(1) 52-59

[518]
Addad, M.; Benezech, M.

Neuroticism, existential significance, and self-reinforcement of the ego: Comparative study of delinquents and nondelinquents.
(Nevrosisme, signification existentielle et auto-renforcement du moi: Enquete comparative entre delinquants et non-delinquants.)
Studied the possible link between neuroticism (anxiety level) and meaning of life. Human subjects: 140 male and female Israeli adolescents and adults (17-51 yrs) (incarcerated criminals). 306 normal male and female Israeli adolescents and adults (17-51 yrs). Tests used: The Maudsley Personality Inventory and Purpose in Life Test.
Annales Medico-Psychologiques. 1986 Sep-Oct Vol 144(8) 777-789

[519]
Addad, Moshe; Leslau, Avraham

Moral judgment and meaning in life.
Examined the relationship between V. E. Frankl's (published 1959-1978) concept of meaning in life and moral judgment (MJ) in 88 male criminals and 444 male and female noncriminals. It was hypothesized that (1) MJ was affected by the development, conditioning, and imitation of the individual and (2) the degree to which humans find meaning was related to the prevalence of the human dimension in their MJ. The relation between MJ levels and meaning in life held for males and females regardless of education or religiosity, and for criminals and noncriminals.
International Forum for Logotherapy. 1989 Fal Vol 12(2) 110-116

[520]
Bonner, Ronald L.; Rich, Alexander R.

Cognitive vulnerability and hopelessness among correctional inmates: A state of mind model.
Studied an interactional state-of-mind model of hopelessness among correctional inmates within a stress-cognitive vulnerability paradigm. 146 male inmates completed measures of problem-solving appraisal, perceived social alienation, rigid irrational beliefs, reasons for living, hopelessness, and depression. Jail stress was related to hopelessness through interaction with cognitive mediators. Depression, low appraised problem-solving effectiveness, and few reasons for living also had main effects in predicting hopelessness. Results provide preliminary support for the state-of-mind model of hopelessness.
Journal of Offender Rehabilitation. 1992 Vol 17(3-4) 113-122

[521]
Carter, Robert E.

The explosion in meaning.
Describes experiences gained in a lecture and seminar program offered by a university philosophy department to inmates serving life sentences at a nearby correctional institution. Ss were particularly interested in Zen Buddhist philosophy, an introspective approach to self-understanding. Many Ss developed full and rich introspective lives for themselves while continuing with the nearly constant routines of prison life. It is suggested that Ss were not denying the situation, but discovering a dimension in themselves that was not imprisoned. It is concluded that a small change in perspective or attitude may unleash an explosion that enlarges capacity for meaning. (
International Forum for Logotherapy. 1984 Fal-Win Vol 7(2) 100-102

[522]
Cole, David A.

Validation of the Reasons for Living Inventory in general and delinquent adolescent samples.
Administered a slightly modified version of the inventory of reasons for living in 2 separate studies to 285 10th, 11th, and 12th graders and to 79 juveniles (aged 12-18 yrs) living in a community-based state probation facility. As with adults, adolescents who reported more reasons for staying alive were less apt to report past or recent suicidal thoughts or behaviors. Evidence of convergent validity emerged via correlations of subscales with depression, hopelessness, and other suicide inventories. Evidence of discriminant validity emerged in low correlations with social desirability. Evidence of construct validity emerged in that the subscales related to suicidal thoughts and behaviors over and above depression and hopelessness.
Journal of Abnormal Child Psychology. 1989 Feb Vol 17(1) 13-27

[523]
DuRant, Robert H.; Cadenhead, Chris; Pendergrast, Robert A.; Slavens, Greg; et al.

Factors associated with the use of violence among urban Black adolescents.
Examined the social and psychological factors of violence among 225 Black adolescents,

aged 11-19 yrs and 44% male, in 9 high-crime, housing projects. Ss completed an anony-
mous questionnaire that was read to them to eliminate any bias based on reading ability.
The questionnaire contained selected items from the Denver Youth Study Self-Reported
Delinquency Questionnaire; the Centers for Disease Control and Prevention's Youth Risk
Behavior Survey; Richters and Martinez's Survey of Exposure to Community Violence;
Conflict Tactics Scale; Home Environment Interview, Version II; Children's Depression
Inventory; Hopelessness Scale for Children; and Purpose in Life test. Results show a corre-
lation between self-reported use of violence and exposure to violence, especially victimiza-
tion, family conflict, and severity of corporal punishment and discipline and between
depression and self-reported use of violence independent of exposure to violence
American Journal of Public Health. 1994 Apr Vol 84(4) 612-617

[cf. 578]
Greene, Kathryn; Krcmar, Marina; Walters, Lynda H.; Rubin, Donald L.; Hale, Jerold L.

Targeting adolescent risk-taking behaviors: The contribution of egocentrism and sensation-seeking.
Journal of Adolescence. 2000 Aug Vol 23(4) 439-461

[cf. 440]
Ivanoff, Andre; Jang, Sung Joon; Smyth, Nancy J.

Clinical risk factors associated with parasuicide in prison.
*International Journal of Offender Therapy & Comparative Criminology. 1996 Jun Vol 40(2)
135-146*

[cf. 441]
Ivanoff, Andre; Jang, Sung Joon; Smyth, Nancy J.; Linehan, Marsha M.

Fewer reasons for staying alive when you are thinking of killing yourself: The Brief
Reasons for Living Inventory.
Journal of Psychopathology & Behavioral Assessment. 1994 Mar Vol 16(1) 1-13

[524]
Jackson, Javel

Outcome research with high-risk inmates.
Presents pilot findings from a suicide prevention program employing a psychoeducational
approach in which treatment is administered in a group format. The goal of the program
was to train inmates in coping skills that can be used to deal with stressful situations. After
inmates completed the initial program they were assigned to a long-term therapeutic group
that was designed to provide inmates with a support system to help them cope with suicide-
related thoughts, feelings, and impulses. Coping skills learned in the first groups were then
reinforced and served as the basis for the support system. Participants were 18 high risk
inmates (aged 19-53 yrs) from 2 prison settings who completed the treatment in groups
ranging from 6-14 inmates. The Reasons for Living Inventory was used to measure changes
in attitude. Results for inmates participating at one of the prisons show significant pre- to

posttreatment differences. Difficulties of developing empirical support for treatments conducted within this setting as well as implications for future research are discussed

Behavior Therapist. 2003 Jan Vol 26(1) 215-216

[525]
McShane, Frank J.; Lawless, John; Noonan, Barrie A.

Personal meaning in the lives of a shoplifting population.
Evaluated the effectiveness of personal meaning as measured by the Purpose in Life Test (PILT) and Seeking of Noetic Goals (SONG) Test in discriminating shoplifters from non-shoplifters. Another objective was to provide a more systemic examination of the relationship between demographic, psychosocial stressor, and attitudinal variables and the act of shoplifting. Data were collected from 70 persons (aged 18-88 yrs) immediately after they had been apprehended for shoplifting and compared with data obtained from 70 undergraduate student nonshoplifters. PILT and SONG Test scores alone did predict group membership for almost 78% of Ss. Shoplifters were more likely to lack clear purpose in life, to live below the poverty level, to be socially isolated, and not to perceive psychological stressors than nonshoplifters

International Journal of Offender Therapy & Comparative Criminology. 1991 Fal Vol 35(3)
190-204

[526]
McShane, Frank J.; Noonan, Barrie A.

Classification of shoplifters by cluster analysis.
Developed an empirically derived multivariate taxonomy of shoplifters by cluster analysis. Previously collected data from 75 suspected shoplifters (aged 18-88 yrs), including demographic characteristics, past history, psychosocial stressors, and purpose in life measures as defined by the Purpose in Life and Seeking of Noetic Goals tests, were analyzed. Results indicate that shoplifters are a heterogeneous population consisting of at least 4 subgroups: rebels, reactionaries, enigmas, and infirms. Results suggest that psychosocial stressors provide a useful basis for classifying shoplifters, and identity and perception needs should be addressed in any treatment program oriented to reduce recidivism.

International Journal of Offender Therapy & Comparative Criminology. 1993 Spr Vol 37(1)
29-40

[527]
Newberry, Angela L.; Duncan, Renae D.

Roles of boredom and life goals in juvenile delinquency.
Examined the relationship between possible selves and boredom in juvenile delinquency in 418 high school students (aged 14-18 yrs). Participants completed questionnaires. The construct Possible Selves refers to the representation of the self that each person would like to become, could become, and is afraid of becoming. Participants who acknowledged high levels of delinquent behaviors reported more negative possible selves, a higher tendency to experience boredom, and fewer positive possible selves than did adolescents who engaged in lower levels of delinquent behaviors. Also, the number of negative possible selves, the number of positive possible selves, boredom proneness, and gender accounted for 32% of the variance in juvenile delinquency. Overall, the authors suggest that the results provide evi-

dence that boredom and a negative view of one's future play a significant role in adolescent delinquent behavior.

Journal of Applied Social Psychology. 2001 Mar Vol 31(3) 527-541

[528]
Qouta, Samir; Punamaeki, Raija-Leena; El Sarraj, Eyad

Prison experiences and coping styles among Palestinian men.
Investigated different types of prison experience and analyzed their relations with background and psychological variables. 79 male Palestinian ex-prisoners (mean age 25.4 yrs) were interviewed about their prison experiences, ways of coping, personality, and psychological well-being. The results of qualitative analysis revealed 7 different types of prison experience; only 1 of these reflected exclusively negative feelings, characterized by suffering and disillusionment. The others included relatively rewarding perceptions characterized as a struggle between strength and weakness, heroic fulfillment, developmental tasks, a normative stage in a man's life, growth in personal insight, and return to religion. Results showed that older men, town residents, and those exposed to a high level of torture perceived the imprisonment more as suffering and disillusionment than other men. Ex-prisoners who perceived their experience as suffering and disillusionment typically coped by using wishful thinking, avoidance, escape, and distraction. Torture and ill-treatment increased wishful thinking and self-controlling as coping styles.

Peace & Conflict: Journal of Peace Psychology. 1997 Vol 3(1) 19-36

[cf. 044]
Rahman, Tania; Khaleque, Abdul

The purpose in life and academic behaviour of problem students in Bangladesh.

Social Indicators Research. 1996 Sep Vol 39(1) 59-64

[529]
Reker, Gary T.

The Purpose-in-Life Test in an inmate population: An empirical investigation.
Administered the Purpose-in-Life (PIL) Test, the Life Areas Survey, Rotter's Internal-External Locus of Control Scale, and the Edwards Personality Inventory to 48 male inmates of a federal penitentiary to (a) assess the reliability and validity of the PIL in an inmate population; (b) investigate the relationship between the PIL and attitudes, locus of control, personality factors, and several demographic variables; and (c) compare PIL scores of the inmates with scores of normal samples reported by J. C. Crumbaugh and L. T. Maholick (1969) and W. A. Black and R. A. Gregson (1973). The PIL was shown to be a reliable and valid instrument and correlated significantly and positively with self-concept, self-esteem, internal locus of control and 2 EPI scales (Plans and Organizes Things and Carefree). Significant relationships were also found between PIL scores and age, IQ, and family relations. When compared to normal samples, inmates scored significantly lower on meaning and purpose in life. These data support the continued use of the PIL in research and applied settings.

Journal of Clinical Psychology. 1977 Jul Vol 33(3) 688-693

[530]
Rodrigues, Roberto

Noodynamisms of value deficiencies.
Examined the use of logotherapy to address patients' clinical symptoms, and presents the
noodynamisms of value deficiencies (NVD) classification. The clinical cases of approximately 100 individuals were examined. Results show that clinical issues were correlated with
deficiencies, difficulties, or lack of value actualization. Those who presented the maximum
searching for value actualization were also those in whom emerged the most value deficiencies. The NVD classification system comprises specific value deficiencies of major areas of
love, creativity, attitude, faith and creed, morality and ethics, and sensible life
International Forum for Logotherapy. 2001 Spr Vol 24(1) 30-34

[531]
Sappington, Andrew. A.; Goodwin, S.; Palmatier, A.

An experimental investigation of the relationship between anger and altruism.
24 college students who reported anger problems completed the Purpose-In-Life test and
the State-Trait Anger Inventory (C. Spielberger, 1988). Participants randomly assigned to
one group received self-administered booklets designed to increase the number of altruistic
acts (i.e., "giving to the world"). A 2nd group received self-administered booklets with
placebo exercises. A 3rd group received no treatment. The difference between pre- and
posttest scores indicate that the group who received the altruism exercises increased their life
purpose scores more than the other two groups, but not at a statistically significant level.
The altruism group decreased their trait anger scores with statistical significance.
International Forum for Logotherapy. 1996 Fal Vol 19(2) 80-84

[532]
Sappington, Andrew A.; Kelly, Patrick J.

Purpose in life and self-perceived anger problems among college students.
Three experiments investigated the relationship between anger problems and purpose in life
and its contributing variables of enjoyment of life, altruism, and cognitive reactions to evens.
Also investigated were the extent to which college students perceive themselves as having
anger problems and their interest in getting help. 253 college students (aged 17-43 yrs)
completed questionnaires on self-perceived anger problems, interest in participating in an
anger management study, completed a purpose in life (PIL) test, and other measures of
enjoyment of life, altruistic contributions to life, and cognitve reactions to umnpleasant
events. Anger problems correlated negatively with PIL scores, positive affect, and altruism
and correlated positively with negative affect and a tendency to respond to unpleasant
events by dwelling on problems or blaming others. 34-64% of Ss were interested in anger
and anxiety or depression management techniques. Implications from Frankl' s theory for
helping students deal with such problems are discussed.
International Forum for Logotherapy. 1995 Fal Vol 18(2) 74-82

[cf. 152]
Shek, Daniel T. L.; Ma, H. K.; Cheung, P. C.

Meaning in life and adolescent antisocial and prosocial behavior in a Chinese context
  Psychologia: An International Journal of Psychology in the Orient. 1994 Dec Vol 37(4) 211-218

[533]
Tashman, Nancy A.; Weist, Mark D.; Nabors, Laura A.; Shafer, Micheal E.

Involvement in meaningful activities and self-reported aggression and delinquency among inner-city teenagers.
163 9th-grade students from an inner-city high school completed self-report measures assessing their participation in meaningful activities, behavioral problems, and locus of control. In multivariate analyses, Gender * Activity Level interaction effects were shown: Males with higher levels of meaningful activity had significantly lower scores on aggression and delinquent behavior subscales than males with lower levels of meaningful activity. However, this relationship was not shown for females. Of youth who reported clinically significant levels of aggression and/or delinquency, females reported significantly higher levels of meaningful activities than males. Gender differences in findings and future research directions are discussed.
  Journal of Clinical Psychology in Medical Settings. 1998 Sep Vol 5(3) 239-248

[534]
Tehrani, S. Muhammad M. J.

Prison as a growth community: A prison reform project in Iran.
Reports on a project using religious integration therapy delivered through intensive psychological services to create a therapeutic prison environment in Iran. 42 male inmates were classified according to personality characteristics based on assessment by the Clinical Analysis Questionnaire. Efforts were made to provide growth opportunities in the physical, economic, social, cognitive, psychological, and spiritual aspects of the inmates. Humanistically oriented milieu therapy, individual, group, and family therapy were some of the service delivery modes. Higher levels of meaning in life and lower depression levels were among the measurable changes. Immeasurable changes include greater feelings of community, empathy, understanding, and patience in both inmates and staff.
  Journal of Humanistic Psychology. 1997 Win Vol 37(1) 92-109

[535]
Whiddon, Michael F.

Logotherapy in prison.
Treated 115 male prisoners with logotherapy over 18 mo. 20 Ss (most aged 27-33 yrs) participated in the 1st logotherapy group. Ss met 3 hrs night, 3 nights wk for 24 wks. The logotherapy program, designed to assist incarcerated adults in finding a purpose in their lives that might lead to rehabilitation, was based on exercises to help Ss become aware of their resources and values. Socratic dialog was used extensively to help Ss discover meaning for themselves. The program consisted of 5 phases: psychoeducational training in the principles of logotherapy, expansion of self-awareness, restructuring of self-esteem, de-reflection

toward values societal implications, and development of personal meaning and goals for the future. Results were based on reports of life meaning, behavior during the group, and a 2-yr follow-up on the presence or absence of criminal life-styles. All Ss' scores on a purpose-in-life test improved after the training. Group cohesion developed to the point that Ss spontaneously requested to be able to be housed together. Ss were moved to a unit where they developed a self-governing therapeutic community that functioned without guards for 18 mo. Of 9 Ss released from prison, 8 showed no indications of a criminal life-style. The case of a 28-yr-old serving time for robbery and kidnapping is presented.

International Forum for Logotherapy. 1983 Spr-Sum Vol 6(1) 34-39

Specific Logotherapeutic Approaches and Techniques

OCD and Anxiety Disorders: Paradoxical Intention

[536]
Ascher, L. Michael

Paradoxical intention in the treatment of urinary retention.
Although most cases of psychogenic urinary retention can be ameliorated by a program composed of various behavioral techniques, a small percentage of cases resist the behavioral treatment of choice. The present multiple case paper focused on the treatment of several resistant cases of functional urinary retention in 3 males and 2 females (19-47 yrs old). Following a 2-wk baseline period, each S was exposed to 8 weekly behavioral sessions. Whereas most cases of urinary retention have significantly improved by this time, the Ss chosen for the present study were dissatisfied with their progress. Thus, following the 8th week, paradoxical intention was employed. Within 6 wks treatment for the urinary problem was terminated as all Ss were comfortable with this aspect of their daily behavior. It was hypothesized that cases of psychogenic urinary retention that resist behavioral techniques are possibly exacerbated by performance anxiety. Such anxiety can be efficiently handled by paradoxical intention.
Behaviour Research & Therapy. 1979 Vol 17(3) 267-270

[537]
Ascher, L. Michael

Employing paradoxical intention in the treatment of agoraphobia.
Assessed the efficacy of paradoxical intention in ameliorating the travel restriction of 10 23-58 yr old agoraphobics. A combined score indicating proximity to 2 difficult target locations represented the dependent variable. A multiple baseline across Ss was used with each of 2 groups of 5 Ss. This was accomplished by sequentially staggering introduction of treatment. At the conclusion of baseline phase, Group A received 6 wks of gradual exposure followed by paradoxical intention to criterion. Group B received paradoxical intention to criterion immediately after baseline. Results indicate that paradoxical intention produced greater movement toward targets for Ss in Group B when compared both with their baseline and with the performance of Group A following an equal period of gradual exposure.
Behaviour Research & Therapy. 1981 Vol 19(6) 533-542

[538]
Ascher, L. Michael; Efran, Jay S.

Use of paradoxical intention in a behavioral program for sleep onset insomnia.
Sleep onset insomnia seems often to be based on performance anxiety associated with a client's fears of being able to fall asleep; in some cases, a therapeutic program might actually exacerbate this performance anxiety by focusing on the client's efforts to voluntarily control the sleep onset process. Five Ss aged 23-41 yrs and experiencing sleep onset difficulty

unusually resistant to a conventional behavioral program for this problem (i.e., deep muscle relaxation and systematic desensitization), were exposed to paradoxical intention suggestions requiring that they try to remain awake as long as possible, rather than attempt to fall asleep. A rapid reduction of sleep onset latency occurred following the shift from the conventional program to the paradoxical intention instructions.

Journal of Consulting & Clinical Psychology. 1978 Jun Vol 46(3) 547-550

[539]
Ascher, L. M.; Schotte, David E.

Paradoxical intention and recursive anxiety.
Investigated the relationship between "recursive anxiety" and paradoxical intention. Ss were 20 professional employees (aged 23-53 yrs) with public speaking concerns, and for whom fear of fear or recursive anxiety clearly represented an important element, or was completely absent from the clinical profile. These Ss were offered a standard in vivo treatment program for public speaking phobia with inclusion or exclusion of paradoxical intention. A 2 * 2 factorial design was employed. Those Ss whose public speaking anxiety was complicated by recursive anxiety experienced greater improvement when paradoxical intention was included in the treatment program than when it was not employed. In contrast, Ss reporting simple public speaking phobia demonstrated greater success with a treatment program in which paradoxical intention was absent. D. M. Wegner's (e.g., 1994) hypothesis of "ironic" cognitive processing was used to explain the proposed relationship between paradoxical intention and fear of fear.

Journal of Behavior Therapy & Experimental Psychiatry. 1999 Jun Vol 30(2) 71-79

[540]
Ascher, L. Michael; Schotte, David E.; Grayson, John B.

Enhancing effectiveness of paradoxical intention in treating travel restriction in agoraphobia.
Techniques ancillary to paradoxical intention (PI) were used to reduce anxiety and depression in 15 22-61 yr old agoraphobic clients. It was hypothesized that such enhancement would produce greater improvement in terms of increased travel capabilities during the initial portion of therapy than would be the case for individuals receiving component treatment. Ss were asked to indicate those situations that they would like to have entered but had avoided because of excessive anxiety. Two target locations were selected for every S. For all targets selected, a prescribed travel plan was developed and divided into 10 serial components; the final component of the series required that the S remain in the designated situation until he she was comfortable. Three groups of 5 Ss each were provided with the enhanced PI procedure, the PI alone, or the enhancement package alone. Following the 4th session, Ss in the enhanced PI group were performing significantly better than Ss in the 2 remaining groups. Results demonstrate the effectiveness of PI in ameliorating the travel restrictions of agoraphobics and indicate that PI can be enhanced by including ancillary cognitive and behavioral treatment components.

Behavior Therapy. 1986 Mar Vol 17(2) 124-130

[541]
Ascher, L. Michael; Turner, Ralph M.

Paradoxical intention and insomnia: An experimental investigation.
Partially replicated R. M. Turner and L. M. Ascher's (1978) study in which paradoxical intention was found to be equally as effective as progressive relaxation and stimulus control in ameliorating sleep onset insomnia. The present study with 25 adult complainants of sleep discomfort found that Ss exposed to the paradoxical intention procedure reported significant improvement compared to Ss in placebo and no-treatment groups.
Behaviour Research & Therapy. 1979 Vol 17(4) 408-411

[542]
Ascher, L. Michael; Turner, Ralph M.

A comparison of two methods for the administration of paradoxical intention.
Recent research in the treatment of insomnia by paradoxical intention has utilized 2 different methods of instruction. Studies utilizing the random assignment of Ss to treatment groups employ a procedure in which clients are provided with a straightforward explanation based on the present authors' understanding of the use of paradoxical intention with insomnia (Type A administration). In contrast, controlled case studies have employed reframing, a procedure that explains the need for the paradoxical intention in a manner that best suits the specific understanding of the individual client (Type B administration). The present study employed the Type B method in a design employing the random assignment of 40 clients (mean age 37 yrs) to groups. Three additional groups (Type A administration, placebo control, no-treatment control) completed the design. Results indicate that the Type A method was superior to the Type B procedure when the same method for administering paradoxical intention was applied to a randomized group of individuals.
Behaviour Research & Therapy. 1980 Vol 18(2) 121-126

[543]
Ataoglu A, Ozcetin A, Icmeli C, Ozbulut O.

Paradoxical therapy in conversion reaction.
Paradoxical therapy consists of suggesting that the patient intentionally engages in the unwanted behaviour such as performing compulsive ritual or wanting a conversion attack. In this study, the subjects were selected by the emergency unit psychiatrist from patients who were admitted to the emergency unit with pseudoseizure. The diagnoses was based on DSM-IV criteria. Paradoxical intention was applied to half of the 30 patients with conversion disorders; the other half were treated with diazepam in order to examine the efficiency of the paradoxical intention versus diazepam. In both groups the differences of the anxiety scores at the beginning of the study were found to be insignificant ($z=1.08$, $p=0.28$). Of the 15 patients who completed paradoxical intention treatment, 14 (93.3%) responded favorably to paradoxical intention. On the other hand of 15 patients who completed diazepam therapy, 9 (60%) responded well to therapy and 6 patients carried on their conversion symptoms at the end of 6 weeks. Paradoxical intention-treated patients appeared to have greater improvements in anxiety scores ($z=2.43$, $p<0.015$) and conversion symptoms ($t=2.27$, $p=0.034$) than the diazepam-treated patients. The results of the present study are

encouraging in that paradoxical intention can be effective in the treatment of conversion disorder.

Journal of Korean Medical Science. 2003 Aug;18(4):581-4. *

[544]
Broomfield, Niall M.; Espie, Colin A.

Initial insomnia and paradoxical intention: An experimental investigation of putative mechanisms using subjective and actigraphic measurement of sleep.
Paradoxical Intention (PI) is a cognitive treatment approach for sleep-onset insomnia. It is thought to operate by eliminating voluntary sleep effort, thereby ameliorating sleep performance anxiety, an aroused state incompatible with sleep. However, this remains untested. Moreover, few PI studies have employed objective sleep measures. The present study therefore examined the effect of PI on sleep effort, sleep anxiety and both objective and subjective sleep. Following a seven-night baseline, 34 sleep-onset insomniacs were randomly allocated to 14 nights of PI, or to a control (no PI) condition. Consistent with the performance anxiety model, participants allocated to PI, relative to controls, showed a significant reduction in sleep effort, and sleep performance anxiety. Sleep-onset latency (SOL) differences between PI participants and controls using an objective sleep measure were not observed, although an underlying trend for significantly lowered subjective SOL amongst PI participants was demonstrated. This may relate to actigraphic insensitivity, or more probably confirms recent suggestions that insomniacs readily overestimate sleep deficit, due to excessive anxiety about sleep.

Behavioural & Cognitive Psychotherapy. 2003 Jul Vol 31(3) 313-324

[545]
DeBord, Jeffrey B.

Paradoxical interventions: A review of the recent literature.
Compared 25 outcome studies (published 1980-1986) involving paradoxical psychotherapeutic techniques (paradoxical intention, symptom prescription, or reframing) in their methodology. Findings indicate that all the techniques may be effective therapeutic strategies for a variety of client concerns. However, the reframing studies were the best controlled and were all effective in alleviating client concerns. Reframing, with or without any type of directive, may be especially effective for treatment of depression.

Journal of Counseling & Development. 1989 Mar Vol 67(7) 394-398

[546]
Efran, Jay S.; Chorney, Robert L.; Ascher, L. Michael; Lukens, Michael D.

Coping styles, paradox, and the cold pressor task.
Investigated how coping style differences affected performance on the cold pressor task among 92 undergraduates. Reactions of monitors (individuals who prefer having information about stressors) and blunters (individuals who avoid cues connected with stressors) were compared, using different instructional sets. The effectiveness of paradoxical intention was also compared with S. M. Miller's Behavioral Style Scale. All instructional sets improved performance in comparison with a control condition, and Ss generally did better when an instructional set supported their preferred coping style. Paradoxical intention did not show

a decided advantage over other strategies. The desirability of designing stress management programs to fit individual coping style patterns is discussed.

Journal of Behavioral Medicine. 1989 Feb Vol 12(1) 91-103

[547]
Espie, Colin A.; Lindsay, William R.

Paradoxical intention in the treatment of chronic insomnia: Six case studies illustrating variability in therapeutic response.
Noting that the relatively limited behavioral literature contains encouraging reports evidencing the effectiveness of paradoxical intention therapy as a treatment for sleep-onset insomnia, the present authors contribute a further 6 case studies of chronic insomniacs, referred for treatment within the context of a major treatment comparison study, who were randomly allocated to receive paradoxical intention. Ss were aged 29-58 yrs. Therapy typically lasted for 8 wks, consisting of 2 4-wk phases, the first of which involved a counterdemand manipulation designed to control for demand and expectancy factors. Considerable variability in response to therapy was observed, with 3 Ss obtaining a rapid reduction in sleep-onset latency, while the sleep pattern of the other 3 Ss was significantly exacerbated. Although 1 S from this latter group did improve after several weeks of treatment, the other 2 Ss were ultimately successfully treated with progressive relaxation training, having been unable to persevere with paradoxical intention. Results are discussed with reference to the consideration of individual patient characteristics.

Behaviour Research & Therapy. 1985 Vol 23(6) 703-709

[548]
Espie, Colin A.; Lindsay, William R.; Brooks, D. Neil; Hood, Eileen M.; et al

A controlled comparative investigation of psychological treatments for chronic sleep-onset insomnia.
70 physician-referred chronic insomniacs (mean age 44.9 yrs) were randomly allocated to either progressive relaxation, stimulus control, paradoxical intention, placebo, or no treatment conditions. Treatment process and outcome were investigated in terms of mean and standard deviation (night to night variability) measures of sleep pattern and sleep quality. Only active treatments were associated with significant improvement, but the nature of treatment gains varied. Stimulus control improved sleep pattern, whereas relaxation affected perception of sleep quality. All improvements were maintained at 17 mo follow-up. Results are discussed with reference to previous research and guidelines are given for clinical practice.

Behaviour Research & Therapy. 1989 Vol 27(1) 79-88

[549]
Fava GA, Rafanelli C, Ottolini F, Ruini C, Cazzaro M, Grandi S.

Psychological well-being and residual symptoms in remitted patients with panic disorder and agoraphobia.
BACKGROUND: Little is known about psychological well-being in remitted patients with panic disorder and agoraphobia and its interactions with residual symptoms. METHODS: Thirty patients with panic disorder and agoraphobia who displayed a successful response to exposure therapy, and 30 control subject matched for sociodemographic variables, were

administered both observer-rated and self-rated scales for assessing residual symptoms and well-being. RESULTS: Patients had significantly more residual symptoms — as assessed by the Clinical Interview for Depression (CID) and the Symptom Questionnaire (SQ) — than controls. They also had significantly less environmental mastery, personal growth, purpose in life and self-acceptance — as measured by the Psychological Well-being Scales (PWB) — and less SQ physical well-being than controls. LIMITATION: The findings apply to patients with panic disorders who had been treated by behavioral methods and may be different in drug-treated subjects. CONCLUSIONS: The results indicate that successful reduction of symptomatology in panic disorder cannot be equated to a pervasive recovery (encompassing psychological well-being) and may pave the way for sequential therapeutic strategies of more enduring quality.

Journal of Affective Disorders. 2001 Jul;65(2):185-90.

[550]
Fogle, Dale O.; Dyal, James A.

Paradoxical giving up and the reduction of sleep performance anxiety in chronic insomniacs.

Paradoxical intention has been shown to improve sleep performance in chronic insomniacs, presumably by interrupting their overly anxious sleep efforts. It was hypothesized that instructions to simply give up such sleep intentions—without trying to stay awake—could have a similar effect. Giving-up instructions framed as a paradoxical sleep-improvement method ("try giving up") were compared with giving up presented as a way to improve nighttime comfort and morning restedness without any sleep improvement ("give up trying"), along with a placebo-attention (self-monitoring) treatment. The 3 treatments were embodied in a printed booklet delivered by mail and evenly distributed among 33 20-56 yr old chronic insomniacs recruited from the general community. All 3 treatment groups improved in daily sleep estimates ("sleep efficiency") after treatment, but only the giving-up groups improved on a self-report measure of sleep performance anxiety. It is suggested that such a reduction in performance anxiety may be an important therapeutic outcome, with or without sleep improvement.

Psychotherapy: Theory, Research & Practice. 1983 Spr Vol 20(1) 21-30

[551]
Hsu, L. George; Lieberman, Stuart

Paradoxical intention in the treatment of chronic anorexia nervosa.

Treated 8 patients with chronic anorexia nervosa with a paradoxical approach. This involved suggesting to the patient that he she might keep the illness and discussing the "benefits" it supplied. At follow-up 2-4 yrs later, 4 patients had maintained a normal weight (within 15% of average weight), and only 1 patient was at a very low weight. Despite the encouraging results of this technique, it does not address the individual's personality difficulties, for it did not appear to have improved the patients' social and sexual functioning. However, paradoxical intention seems worthy of further study in treating chronic anorexia nervosa.

American Journal of Psychiatry. 1982 May Vol 139(5) 650-653

[552]
Lacks, Patricia; Bertelson, Amy D.; Gans, Leslie; Kunkel, John

The effectiveness of three behavioral treatments for different degrees of sleep onset insomnia.
64 Ss (mean age 40.6 yrs) with mild, moderate, or severe insomnia participated in 4 1-hr weekly treatment sessions using 1 of 4 treatment procedures: progressive relaxation, stimulus control, paradoxical intention, and quasi-desensitization placebo control. Ss with the most severe sleep disturbance demonstrated the largest treatment gains, whereas those with mild or moderate insomnia accomplished proportionately less. No interaction was observed between severity of insomnia and type of treatment. Stimulus control resulted in the greatest reduction in sleep onset latency (SOL), while the other 3 treatments resulted in similar smaller reductions. In contrast to the successful outcome with stimulus control, paradoxical intention actually led to an increase in mean SOL, although SOL did decrease at a 16-wk follow-up. It is suggested that the positive effects of the placebo condition may have been due to expectation of therapeutic gain, support from group members, and development of a perceived control over sleep, which may also explain some of the effectiveness of other treatments.
Behavior Therapy. 1983 Nov Vol 14(5) 593-605

[553]
Ladouceur, Robert; Gros-Louis, Yves

Paradoxical invention vs stimulus control in the treatment of severe insomnia.
Assessed the effectiveness of 4 treatments for 27 Ss (mean age 41.8 yrs) with sleep onset insomnia—paradoxical intention, stimulus control, information on sleep habits, and self-monitoring of sleep onset latency (control group). Results show that paradoxical intention and stimulus control were equally effective, and they were significantly better than the information and control groups. It is suggested that treatment be adapted according to data collected from intensive behavioral analysis of each case.
Journal of Behavior Therapy & Experimental Psychiatry. 1986 Dec Vol 17(4) 267-269

[554]
Mavissakalian, Matig; et al

Cognitive-behavioral treatment of agoraphobia: Paradoxical intention vs self-statement training.
26 agoraphobics (mean age 41.5 yrs) were randomly assigned to either paradoxical intention (PI) or self-statement training (SST) that consisted of 12 weekly 90-min group sessions with 4-5 patients group. Major assessments were carried out at pretreatment, at the 6th and 12th wks of treatment, and at 1- and 6-mo follow-ups. Measures included clinical ratings of severity of condition, phobia, anxiety, and depression. A behavioral test was also administered during which changes in subjective units of discomfort and cognitions were assessed. Results indicate significant improvement over time with both treatments. ANCOVA revealed superior effects on several agoraphobia measures for the PI condition at posttreatment. However, by the 6-mo follow-up, the groups were equivalent due to marked improvement during the follow-up phase in the SST condition. Cognitive changes were marked by a decrease in self-defeating statements without concomitant increase in coping statements.
Behaviour Research & Therapy. 1983 Vol 21(1) 75-86

[555]
Michelson, Larry

Treatment consonance and response profiles in agoraphobia: The role of individual differences in cognitive, behavioral and physiological treatments.
39 severe and chronic agoraphobics received either paradoxical intention, graduated exposure, or progressive deep muscle relaxation training consisting of 12 2-hr weekly sessions. 31 Ss (mean age 40 yrs) completed the program and were administered a test battery that assessed severity, phobia, anxiety, depression, and avoidance with measures including the Fear Survey Schedule and the Beck Depression Inventory as well as measures of behavioral, cognitive and psychophysiological response systems before, during, and after treatment and at a 3-mo follow-up. Ss who were consonantly vs nonconsonantly treated were compared based on their initial response profiles. Findings confirm the hypothesis that Ss receiving consonant treatments would exhibit significantly greater treatment gains and concordance compared to nonconsonantly treated Ss. Consonantly treated Ss manifested enhanced levels of functioning and short-term maintenance. The most pronounced differences between groups were observed on measures of severity, fears, phobias, anxiety, depression, general symptomatology, and physiological functioning.
Behaviour Research & Therapy. 1986 Vol 24(3) 263-275

[556]
Michelson, Larry; Ascher, L. Michael

Paradoxical intention in the treatment of agoraphobia and other anxiety disorders.
Defines the paradoxical intention procedure, briefly reviews the literature relevant to this technique, and discusses the role of paradoxical treatment programs for agoraphobic clients. The cognitive and exposure components of paradoxical intention are described, and the procedure is compared with flooding and cognitive behavioral methods, such as self-statement training and anxiety management and rational-emotive therapy. Unlike cognitive behavioral strategies that consist of rational, graduated relabeling of self-defeating cognitions, paradoxical intention is an experiential, intuitive, and nonrational modality in which clients attempt to increase their symptoms by willing themselves to become as anxious and phobic as possible. A study conducted by the 1st author et al (1982) indicated that paradoxical intention, accompanying instructions to practice self-directed exposure, can be an effective treatment for agoraphobia.
Journal of Behavior Therapy & Experimental Psychiatry. 1984 Sep Vol 15(3) 215-220

[557]
Michelson, Larry; Bellanti, Christina J.; Testa, Sandra M.; Marchione, Norman

The relationship of attributional style to agoraphobia severity, depression, and treatment outcome.
Examined the relationship between attributional style, measured with a revised version of the Attributional Style Questionnaire (ASQ), and measures of agoraphobia severity, depression, and treatment outcome in 73 Ss who met Mental Disorders-III (DSM-III) criteria for agoraphobia with panic attacks and participated in 1 of 3 13-wk treatment conditions: paradoxical intention, graduated exposure, or progressive deep muscle relaxation training. Ss completed assessments at 4 periods: pretreatment, midtreatment, posttreatment, and at 3 mo follow-up. In addition to dimensions typically examined on the ASQ, this revised ver-

sion also measured Ss' estimates of the perceived importance, and future likelihood for both positive and negative events. Moderate but inconsistent associations were observed between attributional style and depression both within and across assessment periods. Predictions about associations between attributional style and agoraphobic severity were not supported; however, an interaction was observed between depression and attributional style with respect to severity of agoraphobia. There was no evidence of group differences across treatment types, although there were several significant changes in attributional style across time. Attributions for health related events were also examined.

Behaviour Research & Therapy. 1997 Dec Vol 35(12) 1061-1073

[558]
Michelson, Larry; Mavissakalian, Matig; Marchione, Karen

Cognitive, behavioral, and psychophysiological treatments of agoraphobia: A comparative outcome investigation.
88 severe and chronic adult agoraphobics with panic attacks, diagnosed using Diagnostic and Statistical Manual of Mental Disorders (DSM-III) criteria, were randomly assigned to 1 of 3 cognitive, behavioral or psychophysiological treatments: paradoxical intention, graduated in vivo exposure, or progressive deep muscle relaxation training. All Ss received extensive programmed practice instruction and feedback, in addition to their primary treatment. A comprehensive assessment battery was administered at pre-, mid- (6 wks), post- (12 wks), and at 3-mo follow-up. Analyses revealed significant improvement across all domains and treatments, with few between-group differences. Composite measures of endstate functioning and improvement at posttreatment and 3-mo follow-up revealed that the treatments were equally effective, yet incomplete. The role of pretreatment clinical and historical measures was examined with regard to therapeutic outcome and maintenance. The phenomenon of tripartite concordance was investigated with regard to both treatment outcome and short-term follow-up.

Behavior Therapy. 1988 Spr Vol 19(2) 97-120

[559]
Michelson, Larry; Mavissakalian, Matig; Marchione, Karen

Cognitive and behavioral treatments of agoraphobia: Clinical, behavioral, and psychophysiological outcomes.
39 severe and chronic agoraphobics with panic attacks, diagnosed using the Diagnostic and Statistical Manual of Mental Disorders (DSM-III) criteria, were randomly assigned to 1 of 3 cognitive-behavioral treatments: paradoxical intention (PI), graduated exposure (GE), or progressive deep muscle relaxation training (RT). Treatment consisted of 12 2-hr weekly sessions conducted by experienced therapists whose treatment integrity was objectively monitored. All 31 23-63 yr old Ss who completed the program received an extensive rationale emphasizing self-directed exposure and programmed practice in addition to their primary treatment. A comprehensive assessment battery consisting of clinical ratings of severity, phobia, anxiety, depression, and panic, as well as direct measures of behavioral, psychophysiological, and cognitive response systems was administered at pre-, mid- (6 wks), and posttreatment (12 wks) and at 3-mo follow-up. Analyses revealed significant improvement for all Ss. GE and RT tended to evoke more rapid effects. At follow-up, GE and RT evidenced the greatest potency and stability, as compared with PI. The GE condition expe-

rienced twice the drop-out rate of PI and RT. The phenomenon of synchrony appeared to be associated with overall improvement at 12 wks and follow-up.

Journal of Consulting & Clinical Psychology. 1985 Dec Vol 53(6) 913-925

[560]
Michelson, Larry; Mavissakalian, M.; Marchione, K.; Dancu, C.; Greenwald, M.

The role of self-directed in vivo exposure in cognitive, behavioral, and psychophysiological treatments of agoraphobia.
To examine the role of self-directed in vivo exposure practice in cognitive, behavioral, and psychophysiological treatments of agoraphobia, 31 severe and chronic agoraphobics (mean age 40 yrs) were randomly assigned to either paradoxical intention, graduated exposure, or progressive deep-muscle relaxation training. Treatment consisted of 12 2-hr sessions weekly, with all Ss receiving programmed-practice exposure instructions as a concomitant strategy to their primary treatment. Systematic behavioral diary recordings of all self-directed exposure practice, in vivo anxiety, duration, and accompaniment were analyzed across and within treatments. Differential temporal patterns of self-directed exposure were revealed across treatments. Multiple linear regressions of self-directed exposure practice and in vivo anxiety levels during treatment were significantly associated with endstate functioning at posttreatment. Results highlight the importance of developing, early in treatment, effective anxiety-management and cognitive-coping skills among agoraphobics and of subsequently encouraging them to use their skills in vivo. Conceptual and clinical dimensions of habituation processes and agoraphobia treatment are discussed.

Behavior Therapy. 1986 Mar Vol 17(2) 91-108

[561]
Michelson, Larry; Marchione, Karen; Marchione, Norman; Testa, Sandra; et al

Cognitive correlates and outcome of cognitive, behavioral and physiological treatments of agoraphobia.
39 Ss with agoraphobia with panic attacks were assigned to 1 of 3 cognitive-behavioral treatments: paradoxical intention, graduated exposure, or progressive deep muscle relaxation training. Results suggest that cognitive and behavioral strategies, accompanied by instructions to practice self-directed exposure, exerted significant therapeutic effects on salient (percent negative, percent positive) cognitive measures.

Psychological Reports. 1988 Dec Vol 63(3) 999-1004

[562]
Michelson, Larry; Mavissakalian, Matig R.; Marchione, Karen; Ulrich, Richard F.; et al

Psychophysiological outcome of cognitive, behavioral and psychophysiologically-based treatments of agoraphobia.
Analyzed psychophysiological process and outcome phenomena to determine differential temporal patterns within and across cognitive, behavioral, and physiologically based treatments of agoraphobia. Data were obtained from 73 severe and chronic agoraphobics with panic attacks (aged 22-63 yrs) who completed a clinical research protocol involving 1 of 3 treatments: paradoxical intention, graduated exposure, or progressive deep muscle relaxation. 21 nonphobic cohorts also participated. Analyses revealed numerous significant reductions on in vivo psychophysiological measures for the relaxation condition; there were

a few improvements in the exposure treatment. Patterns of synchrony-desynchrony (e.g., S. J. Rachman and R. Hodgson, 1974), or covariation of measures across assessment, are discussed.

Behaviour Research & Therapy. 1990 Vol 28(2) 127-139

[563]
Morin, Charles

Cognitive and behavioral perspectives in the treatment of chronic insomnia.
(Perspectives cognitivo-comportementales dans le traitement de l'insomnie chronique.)
Discusses the nature, incidence, etiology, and diagnosis of chronic insomnia; and presents a critical review of cognitive and behavioral approaches to treatment of this disorder. These approaches include relaxation training, biofeedback, paradoxical intention, stimulus control, sleep deprivation, cognitive therapy, and patient education. Based on a meta-analysis of 43 studies, data on the characteristics of patients with insomnia, the effectiveness of cognitive and behavioral interventions, and factors influencing treatment results are presented. Recommendations for research and practice are offered.

Science et Comportement. 1991 Vol 21(4) 273-290

[564]
Morin, Charles; Hauri, P.J.; Espie C.A.; Spielman, A.J.; Buysse, D.J.; Bootzin, R.R.

Nonpharmacologic treatment of chronic insomnia. An American Academy of Sleep Medicine review.
This paper reviews the evidence regarding the efficacy of nonpharmacological treatments for primary chronic insomnia. It is based on a review of 48 clinical trials and two meta-analyses conducted by a task force appointed by the American Academy of Sleep Medicine to develop practice parameters on non-drug therapies for the clinical management of insomnia. The findings indicate that nonpharmacological therapies produce reliable and durable changes in several sleep parameters of chronic insomnia sufferers. The data indicate that between 70% and 80% of patients treated with nonpharmacological interventions benefit from treatment. For the typical patient with persistent primary insomnia, treatment is likely to reduce the main target symptoms of sleep onset latency and/or wake time after sleep onset below or near the 30-min criterion initially used to define insomnia severity. Sleep duration is also increased by a modest 30 minutes and sleep quality and patient's satisfaction with sleep patterns are significantly enhanced. Sleep improvements achieved with these behavioral interventions are sustained for at least 6 months after treatment completion. However, there is no clear evidence that improved sleep leads to meaningful changes in daytime well-being or performance. Three treatments meet the American Psychological Association (APA) criteria for empirically-supported psychological treatments for insomnia: Stimulus control, progressive muscle relaxation, and paradoxical intention; and three additional treatments meet APA criteria for probably efficacious treatments: Sleep restriction, biofeedback, and multifaceted cognitive-behavior therapy. Additional outcome research is needed to examine the effectiveness of treatment when it is implemented in clinical settings (primary care, family practice), by non-sleep specialists, and with insomnia patients presenting medical or psychiatric comorbidity.

Sleep. 1999 Dec 15;22(8):1134-56.

[565]
Neeleman, J.

The therapeutic potential of positive reframing in panic.
Describes the use of interventions reminiscent of paradoxical intention (PI) with 4 patients suffering from panic attacks associated with atypical chest pain and avoidance. PI was originally described by V. E. Frankl (1955, 1975) for the treatment of anticipatory fear, which he regarded as the core element of phobias. The reported cases suggest that a consistently positive connotation of symptoms may be a useful therapeutic tool against anxiety symptoms. The cognitive restructuring inherent in positive connotation may be sufficient to achieve therapeutic change in panic.
European Psychiatry. 1992 Vol 7(3) 135-139

[566]
Ogawa, Takayuki; Ikezuki, Makoto

Treatment of obsession by use of paradoxical intention.
Describes the treatment of obsession through achievement of paradoxical intention in 9 cases: 8 male and female adults (aged 21-55 yrs), and an 11-yr-old boy in 5th grade. The importance of urging clients to turn to a consequentially paradoxical intention once acceptive counseling has made them more aware of their symptoms, and warning clients' supporters vs interfering with the clients' achievement of this intention is discussed.
Japanese Journal of Counseling Science. 1991 Mar Vol 24(1) 37-44

[567]
Ott, Brian D.; Levine, Bruce A.; Ascher, L. Michael

Manipulating the explicit demand of paradoxical intention instructions.
Determined the effect of using a procedural component to emphasize the explicit demands of paradoxical intention instructions. 56 18-55 yr olds who reported an average weekly sleep onset latency (SOL) of at least 60 min were assigned to 4 groups. Two groups received identical paradoxical intention instructions. One was required to present "objective" data along with their subjective sleep report, while the other had only to present the subjective data. Two control groups were included in the design that used SOL as a dependent variable. As hypothesized, results indicate that the paradoxical intention group submitting objective data reported latencies that were significantly longer than those of the no-treatment control, while the paradoxical intention group that was not required to submit objective data reported SOLs that were significantly shorter than those of the no-treatment control group.
Behavioural Psychotherapy. 1983 Jan Vol 11(1) 25-35

[568]
Petit L, Azad N, Byszewski A, Sarazan FF, Power B.

Non-pharmacological management of primary and secondary insomnia among older people: review of assessment tools and treatments.
BACKGROUND:primary and secondary insomnia, especially among older adults, is frequently encountered by family physicians. Pharmacological interventions, although effective in some circumstances, can be detrimental in others. Non-pharmacological management of insomnia may allow the patients to self-administer the treatment. OBJEC-

TIVES:review of published literature of assessment tools and treatments for primary and secondary insomnia. RESULTS:two frequently used self-reporting methods for obtaining sleep data are sleep diaries and Pittsburg Sleep Quality Index. A large amount of research supports the use of non-pharmacological treatments such as stimulus control, sleep restriction, sleep hygiene education, cognitive therapy, multi-component therapy and paradoxical intention. CONCLUSION: assessing the nature of insomnia by using an effective assessment tool and providing patients with a non-pharmacological treatment should be the first intervention for insomnia. It is shown that non-pharmacological treatments for primary and secondary insomnia are feasible and effective alternatives to the use of benzodiazepines, and that family physicians should consider these when managing older patients with insomnia.

Age & Ageing. 2003 Jan;32(1):19-25

[569]
Reesal, Robin T.; Bajramovic, Hifzija; Mai, Francois M.

Anticipatory nausea and vomiting: A form of chemotherapy phobia?
Presents the cases of 2 male cancer patients (aged 22 and 52 yrs), which support the proposal that the phenomenon of anticipatory nausea and or vomiting is a component of a phobic response to chemotherapy. Ss described symptoms consistent with a "fight or flight" response, and were able to accept treatments after systematic desensitization or in vivo paradoxical intention.

Canadian Journal of Psychiatry. 1990 Feb Vol 35(1) 80-82

[cf. 467]
Roehrig, Helmut R.; Range, Lillian M.

Recklessness, depression, and reasons for living in predicting suicidality in college students.

Journal of Youth & Adolescence. 1995 Dec Vol 24(6) 723-729

[570]
Saldana, Carmina; Diest, Alicia; Talarn, Antonio

Behavior therapy in sleep-onset insomnia: A pilot-study of three procedures through an intrasubject analysis.
(Tratamiento conductual del insomnio de iniciacion: Estudio piloto de tres procedimientos mediante un analisis intrasujeto.)
Conducted a within-S analysis of different therapeutic procedures (stimulus control, paradoxical intention, and placebo treatment) applied to sleep-onset insomnia. Six individuals, aged 19-59 yrs, who had had problems with insomnia for periods longer than 2 yrs participated. Results indicate that while paradoxical intention and stimulus control were effective, the placebo treatment showed contradictory results. Methodological alternatives are proposed to conclusively determine the specific weight of each component of the reviewed procedures.

Revista del Departamento de Psiquiatria de la Facultad de Medicina de Barcelona. 1984 Mar-Apr Vol 11(2) 109-122*

[571]
Ralph M.; Ascher, L. Michael

Controlled comparison of progressive relaxation, stimulus control, and paradoxical intention therapies for insomnia.
Assessed the effectiveness of treatment programs based on progressive relaxation, stimulus control, and paradoxical intention in the context of sleep difficulties for 50 volunteer Ss. The results indicate that each of the therapeutic procedures significantly reduced sleep complaints in contrast to placebo and waiting list control groups. No differences were observed among the 3 active techniques.

Journal of Consulting & Clinical Psychology. 1979 Jun Vol 47(3) 500-508

[572]
Turner, Ralph M.; Ascher, L. Michael

Therapist factor in the treatment of insomnia.
Attempted to replicate the author's study contrasting progressive relaxation, stimulus control, and paradoxical intention therapies for the treatment of insomnia using clinicians-in-training as therapists. 30 Ss, aged 18-79 yrs, participated. Progressive relaxation and stimulus control were again shown to be effective; paradoxical intention instructions were not. A significant therapist effect was found, which is discrepant with previous findings by researchers including P. Nicassio and R. R. Bootzin (1974) and S. W. Steinmark and T. D. Borkovec (1974).

Behaviour Research & Therapy. 1982 Vol 20(1) 33-40

Hyper- and Dereflection

[573]
Baron, Pierre; Hanna, Jayne

Egocentrism and depressive symptomatology in young adults.
Administered the Adolescent Egocentrism-Sociocentrism scale and the Beck Depression Inventory to 152 undergraduates. As predicted, Ss with high egocentrism showed significantly more depressive symptoms than those with low egocentrism. Results replicate those obtained by P. Baron with adolescents and suggest an association between egocentrism and depressive symptomatology across ages.
Social Behavior & Personality. 1990 Vol 18(2) 279-285

[574]
Beck, J. Gayle; Barlow, David H.; Sakheim, David K.

The effects of attentional focus and partner arousal on sexual responding in functional and dysfunctional men.
The effects of attentional-focus instructions (self vs partner focus) and level of partner arousal (high, low, and ambiguous) on sexual responding, both objectively and subjectively measured, were examined with 8 sexually functional and sexually dysfunctional heterosexual males (aged 21-60 yrs). These instructional sets were delivered just before Ss viewed an erotic film depicting a heterosexual couple, in which they identified with the male. When both groups were focusing on themselves rather than their partner, higher tumescence was observed when their partner was displaying low arousal. When the partner's level of arousal was ambiguous, highest tumescence was achieved during partner attentional focus. When the partner was displaying high sexual arousal, functional Ss reached highest levels of tumescence during partner focus, while dysfunctional Ss reached highest levels of tumescence during self-focus. High partner arousal seemed to inhibit dysfunctional Ss' tumescence under partner focus. Examination of self-report of arousal data, as measured by a subjective lever, revealed interesting group differences. Results are discussed in light of possible maintaining factors in sexual dysfunction and their treatment implications.
Behaviour Research and Therapy. 1993. 21, 1-8

[575]
Brockner, Joel; Hjelle, Larry; Plant, Robert W.

Self-focused attention, self-esteem, and the experience of state depression.
Examined the effect of self-focused attention and self-esteem on self-reported state depression, using 162 undergraduates. Ss completed a self-esteem scale before taking part in an exercise designed to induce either strong (strong condition) or mild (weak condition) feelings of temporary depression. Before rating their mood, Ss waited for a short period either in the presence or absence of a mirror. A significant depression manipulation by mirror no mirror interaction effect emerged: Ss who waited in the presence of the mirror reported feeling more depressed in the strong condition and less depressed in the weak condition, relative to those who waited in the absence of the mirror. Moreover, this interaction effect was attributable mainly to the low self-esteem Ss, rather than to the medium or high self-esteem

Ss. Findings support the awareness hypothesis (i.e., self-focus affects individual's self-reports of their emotionality by making them more aware of their true level of emotionality).
Journal of Personality. 1985 Sep Vol 53(3) 425-434

[576]
Dove, Natalie L.; Wiederman, Michael W.

Cognitive distraction and women's sexual functioning.
Past research on the role of cognitive distraction in sexual dysfunction typically has focused on males and has been conducted in the laboratory using artificial stimuli. In the current study, 74 18-21 yr old women with coital experience completed questionnaires regarding cognitive distraction and their sexuality. Those women who reported greater cognitive distraction during sexual activity with a partner also reported relatively lower sexual esteem, less sexual satisfaction, less consistent orgasms, and higher incidence of pretending orgasm even after the women's general conflict, sexual desire, general self-focus, general sexual attitudes, and body dissatisfaction were statistically controlled. Results are discussed with regard to directions for future research and implications for sex therapy.
Journal of Sex & Marital Therapy. 2000 Jan-Mar Vol 26(1) 67-78

[577]
Greenberg, Jeff; Pyszczynski, Tom

Persistent high self-focus after failure and low self-focus after success: The depressive self-focusing style.
Assessed the spontaneous self-focusing tendencies of depressed and non-depressed individuals after success and failure. Based on a self-regulatory perseveration theory of depression, it was expected that depressed individuals would be especially high in self-focus after failure and low in self-focus after success. Ss (41 and 42 undergraduates in Exps I and II, respectively) were administered the Beck Depression Inventory and a measure of spontaneous self-focusing tendencies. Results of Exp I suggest that immediately after an outcome, both depressed and nondepressed Ss were more self-focused after failure than after success. This finding led the authors to hypothesize that differences between depressed and nondepressed individuals in self-focus following success and failure emerge over time. Specifically, immediately following an outcome, both types of individuals self-focus more after failure because of self-regulatory concerns. However, over time, depressed individuals persist in higher levels of self-focus after failure than after success, whereas nondepressed individuals shift to the opposite, more hedonically beneficial pattern. Results of Exp II provide clear support for these hypotheses.
Journal of Personality & Social Psychology. 1986 May Vol 50(5) 1039-1044

[578]
Greene, Kathryn; Krcmar, Marina; Walters, Lynda H.; Rubin, Donald L.; Hale, Jerold L.

Targeting adolescent risk-taking behaviors: The contribution of egocentrism and sensation-seeking.
One widely used individual difference variable, sensation-seeking, has been incorporated in health message design to some extent, but it fails to take development into account. Research on adolescent egocentrism suggests adolescents experience personal fable which can lead to an exaggerated sense of invulnerability. The present study sampled 381 11-18 yr

old junior and high school students and 343 18-25 yr old college students to examine relative contributions of egocentrism and sensation-seeking to risk-taking behavior. Results indicate a latent factor labeled risk-seeking (primarily indicated by disinhibition and risk-taking personality, and to a lesser degree by invulnerability, experience-seeking, boredom susceptibility, and thrill and adventure-seeking) indeed predicted a latent factor labeled delinquent behavior (primarily indicated by alcohol consumption and delinquency, and to a lesser degree by drug use, drinking and driving, and risky driving). Other results indicate consistently high personal fable combined with high sensation-seeking explained most risk-taking behavior. Implications and directions for future research are discussed.

Journal of Adolescence. 2000 Aug Vol 23(4) 439-461

[cf. 021]
Halama, Peter

Dimensions of Life Meaning as Factors of Coping

Studia Psychologica. 2000. 42:4. 339-350

[579]
Heilbrun, Alfred B.; Frank, Michelle E.

Self-preoccupation and general stress level as sensitizing factors in premenstrual and menstrual distress.
Examined the role of general stress level and self-preoccupation (SPO) in sensitizing 55 female undergraduates to symptoms of menstrual (MD) and premenstrual (PD) distress. Ss were categorized according to reports of distress: 19 had greater MD, 17 had greater PD, and 17 had equal distress (ED) in both periods. PD Ss demonstrated significantly greater SPO and reported higher general stress than either MD or ED Ss. When both sensitizing factors were introduced into the same analysis, high SPO and a high level of general stress were found only in PD Ss. Data suggest that stress and personality sensitize premenstrual symptoms in women with premenstrual syndrome (PMS) and are prominent features in normal women who report more serious symptoms during the premenstrual period.

Journal of Psychosomatic Research. 1989 Vol 33(5) 571-577

[580]
Ingram, Rick E.; Lumry, Ann E.; Cruet, Debra; Sieber, William

Attentional processes in depressive disorders.
Investigated self-focused attentional processes in clinical depression by administering the Self-Focus Sentence Completion Scale to 12 depressed psychiatric outpatients (mean age 29.6 yrs). Results indicate that depressed Ss evidenced significantly more self-focused attention than did an age- and sex-matched nondepressed control group (mean age 31.3 yrs). The proportion of attention that was personally unfavorable was also substantially greater in the depressed group. Results are discussed in terms of the manner in which increased self-focused attention might potentially be related to the onset and course of depression.

Cognitive Therapy & Research. 1987 Jun Vol 11(3) 351-360

[581]
Ingram, Rick E.; Smith, Timothy W.

Depression and internal versus external focus of attention.
653 college students participated in 2 studies to examine a hypothetical relationship between self-attentional processes and several depressive phenomena. In Study 1, a replication of earlier research by T. W. Smith and J. Greenberg demonstrating a relationship between depression and the dispositional tendency to self-focus attention was obtained using 3 samples (584 Ss); each S completed the Beck Depression Inventory and a private self-consciousness scale. In Study 2, 37 depressed and 32 nondepressed Ss were compared on a measure of current level of self-focusing. Results indicate that depressed Ss evidenced a greater self-focused responding and less externally focused respondng. The possible role of self-focused attention in contributing to the negative affect, negative internal attributions, and lowered self-esteem in depression is discussed.
Cognitive Therapy & Research. 1984 Apr Vol 8(2) 139-151

[582]
Ingram, Rick E.; Wisnicki, Kathleen

Situational specificity of self-focused attention in dysphoric states.
Although research has shown that heightened self-focused attention characterizes dysphoria, few studies have examined what factors are linked to increases in this process. The current study examined whether mood states affect the elevation of self-focused attention among dysphoric individuals. A sample of 70 college students with elevated dysphoria was compared with a control sample after either a negative or a positive mood induction. Results show that dysphoric and nondysphoric Ss self-focus in different ways in response to mood-eliciting events. Dysphoric Ss showed higher self-focus than control Ss after both mood conditions. These data suggest a generalized self-focusing responsivity among dysphoric Ss that may contribute to the intensity and duration of the dysphoria.
Cognitive Therapy & Research. 1999 Dec Vol 23(6) 625-636

[583]
Lantz, Jim; Harper, Karen V.

Logotherapy and the hypersomatic family.
Describes the use of family logotherapy to treat 16 hypersomatic families, whose members consistently hyperreflect about physical health because of a need to fill their existential vacuum. Socratic dialog, dereflection, and paradoxical intention were used to facilitate existential reflection. As measured in scores on the Purpose in Life Test and mean number physician visits, logotherapy was helpful to 13 families, with benefits maintained during a 1-yr follow-up.
International Forum for Logotherapy. 1988 Fal-Win Vol 11(2) 107-110

[584]
McCann, Joseph T.; Biaggio, Mary K.

Egocentricity and two conceptual approaches to meaning in life.
Tested the hypothesis that if self-actualization raises the level of egocentricity, then individuals high in self-transcendent striving will exhibit less egocentricity. 48 staff members of a

university and their spouses completed the Purpose in Life Test, the Personal Orientation Inventory, the Selfism Scale (W. J. Phares and N. Erskine, 1964), and the Crowne-Marlow Social Desirability Scale. Findings suggest that purpose in life and self-actualization were similar constructs for Ss. Results do not support the contention that self-actualization raises the level of egocentricity.

International Forum for Logotherapy. 1988 Spr-Sum Vol 11(1) 31-37

[585]
Melchior, Lisa A.; Cheek, Jonathan M.

Shyness and anxious self-preoccupation during a social interaction.
58 female 1st-yr college students completed a shyness (SH) scale developed by J. M. Cheek and A. H. Buss, conversed with another S for 5 min, and rated themselves and their partner immediately after the conversation ended. Shy Ss reported more time spent self-focusing and more anxious thoughts and other SH symptoms than Ss who were not shy. Shy Ss who conversed with a socially self-confident partner experienced the greatest difficulties during the interaction and rated themselves more negatively than their partners rated them. Results are interpreted as supporting the distribution-of-attention model of SH as a propensity for engaging in anxious self-preoccupation.

Journal of Social Behavior & Personality. 1990 Vol 5(2) 117-130

[586]
Mor, Nilly; Winquist, Jennifer Affili

Self-focused attention and negative affect: A meta-analysis.
This meta-analysis synthesized 226 effect sizes reflecting the relation between self-focused attention and negative affect (depression, anxiety, negative mood). The results demonstrate the multifaceted nature of self-focused attention and elucidate major controversies in the field. Overall, self-focus was associated with negative affect. Several moderators qualified this relationship. Self-focus and negative affect were more strongly related in clinical and female-dominated samples. Rumination yielded stronger effect sizes than nonruminative self-focus. Self-focus on positive self-aspects and following a positive event were related to lower negative affect. Most important, an interaction between foci of self-attention and form of negative affect was found: Private self-focus was more strongly associated with depression and generalized anxiety, whereas public self-focus was more strongly associated with social anxiety.

Psychological Bulletin. 2002 Jul Vol 128(4) 638-662

[587]
Nix, Glen; Watson, Cheryl; Pyszczynski, Tom; Greenberg, Jeff

Reducing depressive affect through external focus of attention.
Investigated the effect of manipulating focus of attention on the experience of depressive affect among depressed and nondepressed Ss. In Study 1, 21 depressed and 23 nondepressed Ss, randomly assigned to either self or external focus conditions, were administered a story-writing task (A. Fenigstein and M. P. Levine 1984) for manipulating attentional focus, and their depressed and anxious moods were assessed on the Profile of Mood States. The procedure was replicated in Study 2 (25 depressed and 35 non depressed Ss), using premeasures of depression and anxiety before attention manipulation. Results show that externally

focused depressed Ss reported less depressive affect compared to internally focused Ss. External focus reduced anxiety, regardless of Ss initial levels of depression. In depressed Ss, reduced self-focus lowered depressive affect, while its increase did not produce a corresponding increase in depressive affect.

Journal of Social and Clinical Psychology, 14 (Spring), 36-52

[588]
Pyszczynski, Tom; Greenberg, Jeff

Evidence for a depressive self-focusing style.
Assessed the possibility that depressed persons have a unique self-focusing style in which they increase their level of self-focus (SF) after failures and decrease their level of SF after successes. 32 nondepressed and 33 mildly depressed (Beck Depression Inventory) college students were randomly assigned to succeed or fail on a supposed test of verbal abilities or to a no-outcome control group that did not take the test. Ss were then taken to another room and given 10 min to work on 2 sets of puzzles, one of which was positioned in front of a large mirror. As in previous research on SF, the amount of time spent in front of the mirror was taken as a measure of aversion to SF. As predicted, depressed success Ss spent significantly less time in front of the mirror than did depressed control, depressed failure, or nondepressed success Ss. The time spent in front of the mirror by nondepressed Ss, however, was apparently unaffected by their performance outcomes. Implications of this depressive self-focusing style for the esteem, attributions, affect, motivation, and performance of depressed persons are discussed.

Journal of Research in Personality. 1986 Mar Vol 20(1) 95-106

[589]
Pyszczynski, Tom; Hamilton, James C.; Herring, Fred H.; Greenberg, Jeff

Depression, self-focused attention, and the negative memory bias.
On the basis of self-regulatory perseveration theory, we hypothesized that the negative memory bias commonly found among depressed people is mediated by excess levels of self-focused attention and thus can be reduced by preventing depressed people from focusing on themselves. In Experiment 1, nondepressed and subclinically depressed college students were induced to either focus on themselves or externally and then to recall 10 events that had happened to themselves during the previous 2 weeks. Consistent with our hypotheses, events recalled by depressed Ss were more negative than events recalled by nondepressed Ss under conditions of self-focus but not under conditions of external focus. We conducted Experiment 2 to determine whether this effect was specific to self-referent events or generalizable to events that happened to other people. Experiment 2's findings replicated the previous findings for self-referent events but showed a different pattern for recall of events that happened to others, suggesting that self-focus reduces the negative memory bias among depressed individuals by deactivating their self-schemas. Theoretical and practical implications of these findings are discussed.

Journal of Personality & Social Psychology. 1989 Aug Vol 57(2) 351-357

[590]
Sakamoto, Shinji

A longitudinal study of the relationship of self-preoccupation with depression.
Self-preoccupation, the tendency to focus more on the self and to maintain self-focused attention, is believed to be a vulnerability factor to depression. The present study investigated this hypothesis in a longitudinal design, using Japanese undergraduates. At Time 1, both self-preoccupation and depressive symptoms at that time, measured by the Zung Self-rating Depression Scale (SDS), were assessed. At Time 2, 3 months later, life events experienced from Time 1 to Time 2 and depressive symptoms at that time were assessed. Data from 169 undergraduates who scored less than 50 on the SDS in Time 1 were analyzed and the above hypothesis was suggested. When experiencing a greater number of negative events, those high in self-preoccupation became more depressed than those who were low in that tendency, though when there were a smaller number of negative events, this difference disappeared.

Journal of Clinical Psychology. 1999 Jan Vol 55(1) 109-116

[591]
Sakamoto, Shinji; Tomoda, Atsuko; Iwata, Noboru; Aihara, Waka; Kitamura, Toshinori

The relationship among major depression, depressive symptoms, and self-preoccupation.
Investigates whether highly self-preoccupied people (exhibiting a tendency to focus primarily on the self and to maintain self-focused attention) were more likely to experience major depressive episodes (MDEs) than those without such tendencies. 119 young community residents (aged 18-21 yrs) took part in semistructured interviews, during which the authors investigated their past and present history of mental illness, including MDEs, as delineated by the Diagnostic and Statistical Manual of Mental Disorders-III-Revised (DSM-III-R). Self-preoccupation was measured by the Self-Preoccupation Scale (SPS). Of the 119 participants interviewed, the lowest and highest quarters in the SPS scores formed the low- and high-self-preoccupation (SP) groups. The lifetime prevalence of the DSM-III-R MDE was significantly greater among those high in SP than in the low SP group. Moreover, the high-SP group had significantly more depressive symptoms than the low-SP group. The contributory role of self-preoccupation to suicide ideation and the interpersonal aspects of self-preoccupation were discussed.

Journal of Psychopathology & Behavioral Assessment. 1999 Mar Vol 21(1) 37-49

[592]
Smith, Timothy W.; Ingram, Rick E.; Brehm, Sharon S.

Social anxiety, anxious self-preoccupation, and recall of self-relevant information.
Theoretical and empirical efforts concerning cognitive processes associated with anxiety have typically emphasized either cognitive deficits (i.e., reduced learning, memory, and task performance) or cognitive excesses (i.e., increased self-focused, ruminative thought). Evidence of these 2 types of cognitive processes has primarily been based on different types of sources (performance measures and self-reports), which precludes direct comparisons of the extent to which cognitive deficits and or excesses characterize anxiety states. The present study attempted to directly compare the cognitive excesses and deficits associated with social anxiety by operationalizing both types of cognitive phenomena with similar performance measures. 97 undergraduates, selected on the basis of high or low scores on the

Social Avoidance and Distress Scale, performed a modified self-referent depth-of-processing paradigm under stress or no-stress conditions. Socially anxious Ss in a socially evaluative situation evidenced a specific type of cognitive excess (i.e., concern over evaluations by others) but not cognitive deficits. Results are discussed in terms of person-by-situation models of anxiety and the nature and treatment of social anxiety.

Journal of Personality & Social Psychology. 1983 Jun Vol 44(6) 1276-1283

[593]
Wink, Paul; Donahue, Karen

The relation between two types of narcissism and boredom.
Investigated the relation between 2 types of narcissism and boredom, as measured by the Boredom Proneness Scale (BPS), in 106 female undergraduates. Confirming the findings of P. Wink and K. Donahue (1996), the MMPI based measures of overt and covert narcissism both correlated positively with the BPS and its subscale measuring a need for challenge and excitement. Only overt narcissism, characterized by extroversion and rebelliousness, correlated with the BPS subscale measuring feelings of restlessness and impatience in response to external constraints on behavior. Only covert narcissism, characterized by a sense of inner depletion, correlated with BPS subscales measuring difficulties in keeping oneself entertained (lack of internal stimulation), feelings of meaninglessness, and the perception that time is passing slowly. Findings support the view that both types of narcissism and boredom are related

Journal of Research in Personality. 1997 Mar Vol 31(1) 136-140

[594]
Wood, Joanne V.; Saltzberg, Judith A.; Neale, John M.; Stone, Arthur A.; et al

Self-focused attention, coping responses, and distressed mood in everyday life.
Several questions concerning the relation between self-focused attention and depressed mood were examined: (a) Does the association involve global negative affect, rather than sadness per se? (b) is self-focus associated with specific negative affects other than sadness? and (c) does the association occur at the between-subjects or within-subject level? Also hypothesized was that self-focus is associated with coping responses that may perpetuate negative mood. In an idiographic nomothetic design, 40 male community residents completed daily reports for 30 days. Results suggest that self-focus is linked with global negative mood as well as specific negative affects other than sadness and that the association occurs on a between-persons, rather than a day-to-day within-person, basis. In addition, highly self-focused men reported using passive and ruminative coping styles, which in turn were associated with distressed affect.

Journal of Personality & Social Psychology. 1990 Jun Vol 58(6) 1027-1036

PART III

TESTS AND RESEARCH
INSTRUMENTS

Research on Logotherapeutic Tests

[cf. 003]
Balcar, K.

Standardization of the "Logo-Test" questionnaire in a sample of the Czech university students.
(Standardizace dotazniku "Logo-test" na vzorku studujicich ceskych vysokych skol.)
Ceskoslovenska Psychologie, 1995, 39, 400 – 405

[cf. 004]
Balcar, Karel

Meaningfulness of life and personality.
(Zivotni smysluplnost a osobnost.)
Ceskoslovenska Psychologie. 1995 Vol 39(6) 496-502

[cf. 088]
Chamberlain, Kerry; Zika, Sheryl

Measuring meaning in life: An examination of three scales.
Personality & Individual Differences. 1988 Vol 9(3) 589-596

[cf. 007]
Chang, Rosanna H.; Dodder, Richard A.

The modified Purpose in Life Scale: A cross-national validity study.
International Journal of Aging & Human Development. 1983-1984 Vol 18(3) 207-217

[595]
Coward, Doris D.

Self-transcendence and emotional well-being in women with advanced breast cancer.
Self-transcendence has been associated, in previous studies, with stressful life events and emotional well-being. This study examined the relationships among self-transcendence, emotional well-being, and illness-related distress in women with advanced breast cancer. The study employed a cross-sectional correlational design in a convenience sample (n = 107) of women with Stage IIIb and Stage IV breast cancer. Subjects completed a questionnaire that included Reed's Self-Transcendence Scale; Bradburn's Affect Balance Scale (ABS); a Cognitive Well-Being (CWB) Scale based on work by Campbell, Converse, and Rogers; McCorkle and Young's Symptom Distress Scale (SDS); and the Karnofsky Performance Scale (KPS). Data were analyzed using factor analytic structural equations modeling. Self-transcendence decreased illness distress (assessed by the SDS and the KPS) through the

mediating effect of emotional well-being (assessed by the ABS and the CWB Scale). Self-transcendence directly affected emotional well-being (beta = 0.69), and emotional well-being had a strong negative effect on illness distress (beta = -0.84). A direct path from self-transcendence to illness distress (beta = -0.31) became nonsignificant (beta = -0.08) when controlling for emotional well-being. Further research using longitudinal data will seek to validate these relationships and to explain how nurses can promote self-transcendence in women with advanced breast cancer, as well as in others with life-threatening illnesses.

Oncological Nursing Forum. 1991 Jul;18(5):857-63*

[596]
Coward, Doris D.

Meaning and purpose in the lives of persons with AIDS.
Little research has been reported that explores meaning-discovery and meaning-making in persons with AIDS. Self-transcendence experiences, as proposed by Reed (1991), may lead to maintenance or restoration of mental health in persons facing end-of-life issues. Nurses who work with persons with life-threatening illness, such as men and women with AIDS, have opportunities to facilitate choices that lead to experiences from which meaning and emotional well-being may be obtained. This study used a phenomenological approach to describe experiences of 10 men and 10 women with AIDS that led to feelings of increased self-worth, purpose, and meaning in their lives. Participants provided oral or written descriptions of experiences associated with feelings of increased connectedness with others, sense of well-being, and hope for longer life. Data were analyzed using Colaizzi's phenomenological technique (1978). Although men and women with AIDS faced some of the same issues, their responses were different. By incorporating gender and individual differences, nurses may be better able to create therapeutic exchanges in which self-transcendence views and behaviors are fostered in both men and women with AIDS.

Public Health Nursing. 1994 Oct;11(5):331-6*

[597]
Coward, Doris D.

Self-transcendence and correlates in a healthy population.
The purpose of this study was to document the presence of self-transcendence perspectives in a healthy population and to compare self-transcendence and related concepts with previous findings in elderly well persons and in those with life-threatening illness. Levels of self-transcendence, as assessed by the Self-Transcendence Scale and the Purpose-in-Life Test in a sample of 152 persons (mean age = 46 years), were similar to those found in other populations. Moderate correlations with self-transcendence and female gender; older age, and higher self-report of health status were found. Self-transcendence was strongly correlated with sense of coherence, self-esteem, hope, and variables assessing emotional well-being.

Nursing Research. 1996 Mar-Apr;45(2):116-21*

[cf. 484]
Crumbaugh, James C.

The Seeking of Noetic Goals Test (SONG): A complementary scale to the Purpose in Life Test (PIL).

Journal of Clinical Psychology. 1977 Jul Vol 33(3) 900-907

[cf. 011]
Crumbaugh, James C.; Henrion, Rosemary

The PIL Test: Administration, interpretation, uses theory and critique.
International Forum for Logotherapy. 1988 Fal-Win Vol 11(2) 76-88

[cf. 012]
Debats, Dominique L.

The Life Regard Index: Reliability and validity.
Psychological Reports. 1990 Aug Vol 67(1) 27-34

[cf. 014]
Debats, Dominique L.; Van der Lubbe, Petra M.; Wezeman, Fimmy R.

On the psychometric properties of the Life Regard Index (LRI): A measure of meaningful life: An evaluation in three independent samples based on the Dutch version.
Personality & Individual Differences. 1993 Feb Vol 14(2) 337-345

[cf. 096]
DeVogler-Ebersole, Karen; Ebersole, Peter

Depth of meaning in life: Explicit rating criteria.
Psychological Reports. 1985 Feb Vol 56(1) 303-310

[598]
Dittmann-Kohli, Freya; Westerhof, Gerben J.

The SELE-Sentence Completion Questionnaire: A new instrument for the assessment of personal meanings in aging research.
Presents the SELE-instrument (a sentence completion test) and an accompanying coding scheme which is designed to study cognitions about self and life. The related theoretical construct is the personal meaning system, which encompasses different meaning domains, like "self," "activities," and "social relations," as well as evaluations and time perspectives. It is argued that especially in aging research, it is necessary to use more open instruments in studying self- and life-cognitions. A short history of sentence completion instruments in psychology is presented in order to better understand the specific contents of the SELE-instrument. The SELE provides sentence stems in the 1st form singular (I) in combination with verbal functors, which express different combinations of evaluation and time perspective, to which the respondents have to react in their own words. The sentence completions are coded with an extensive coding scheme, which is hierarchically and dimensionally organized. Some figures on the coding reliability as well as on the validity and stability of the instrument are presented. The different uses to which the SELE-instrument has been put are briefly described.
Anuario de Psicologia. 1997 Vol 73(2) 7-18

[cf. 428]
Durak, A; Yasak-Gultekin, Y.; Sahin, N. H.

Validity and reliability of the Reasons for Living Inventory.
(Insanlari yasama baglayan nedenler? Yasami surdurme nedenleri envanterinin (YSNE)
guvenirligi ve gecerligi.)
                                        Teurk Psikoloji Dergisi. 1993 Vol 8(30) 7-19

[599]
Dyck, Murray J.

Assessing logotherapeutic constructs: Conceptual and psychometric status of the Purpose
in Life and Seeking of Noetic Goals tests.
Reviews logotherapy research to evaluate the conceptual and psychometric validity of 2
principal measures used to assess logotherapeutic constructs—the Purpose in Life (PIL) test
and the Seeking of Noetic Goals (SONG) test. These tests are designed to reflect V. Frankl's
(1955) concepts of existential vacuum and will to meaning, respectively. The PIL was
judged to be mainly an indirect measure of depression, but may also be related to an existential vacuumlike construct. The SONG was found to be an invalid measure of will to
meaning; will to meaning appears to be an unmeasurable construct. It is concluded that a
new measure of existential vacuum is required if the empirical evaluation of logotherapy is
to progress.
                                        Clinical Psychology Review. 1987 Vol 7(4) 439-447

[600]
Ebersole, Peter; Levinson, Rhoda; Svensson, Cheryl

Purpose in Life Test: Parts B and C.
17 members of a creative writing class anonymously completed Part B (sentence completion items) of the Purpose in Life Test; the 2nd author, who knew the Ss well, felt certain
that she was able to identify 16 of the participants from the results.
                                        Psychological Reports. 1987 Oct Vol 61(2) 452

[601]
Ebersole, Peter; Quiring, Gogi

Social desirability in the Purpose-in-Life Test.
Administered the Marlowe-Crowne Social Desirability Scale (SDS) and the Purpose-in-Life
(PIL) test to 132 undergraduates in 1984 and 105 undergraduates in 1987 to investigate
the degree of social desirability (SD) in the PIL. The relationship between the SDS and the
PIL was modest. While findings were consistent with those of H. R. Snavely (1962) and
supported the PIL's critics' contention that there is SD confounding in the PIL, these correlations accounted for a small proportion of the total variance. It is concluded that SD is
only a minor factor on the PIL.
                                        Journal of Psychology. 1989 May Vol 123(3) 305-307

[602]
Ebersole, Peter; Quiring, Gogi

Meaning in life depth: The MILD.
Describes a rating system for measuring meaning in life depth (MILD), after clarifying some of the ambiguity surrounding the phrase "meaning in life." A number of examples are given of how essays by respondents about their life meanings are scored using the criteria of the MILD instrument. Some problems and complexities of scoring are also identified.
Journal of Humanistic Psychology. 1991 Sum Vol 31(3) 113-124

[603]
Ebersole, Peter; Sacco, John

Depth of meaning in life: A preliminary study.
Two independent raters of meaning depth were used to check interrater agreement on essays on meaning obtained from 124 undergraduates. A correlation of .51 indicated moderate interrater agreement on depth of meaning.
Psychological Reports. 1983 Dec Vol 53(3, Pt 1) 890

[cf. 432]
Ellis, Jon B.; Smith, Peggy C.

Spiritual well-being, social desirability and reasons for living: Is there a connection?
International Journal of Social Psychiatry. 1991 Spr Vol 37(1) 57-63

[cf. 230]
Giorgi, Bruno

The Belfast Test: A new psychometric approach to logotherapy
International Forum for Logotherapy. 1982 Spr-Sum Vol 5(1) 31-37

[cf. 433]
Gutierrez, Peter M.; Osman, Augustine; Kopper, Beverly A.; Barrios, Francisco X.

Why young people do not kill themselves: The Reasons for Living Inventory for Adolescents.
Journal of Clinical Child Psychology. 2000 Jun Vol 29(2) 177-187

[cf. 435]
Gutierrez, Peter M.; Osman, Augustine; Barrios, Francisco X.; Kopper, Beverly A.; Baker, Monty T.; Haraburda, Cheryl M.

Development of the Reasons for Living Inventory for Young Adults
Journal of Clinical Psychology. 2002 Apr Vol 58(4) 339-357

[604]
Halama, Peter

Noodynamic Test and some of its psychometric qualities.
(Test noodynamiky a niektoré jeho psychometrické kvality.)
Popielski's Test Noodynamic focuses on qualitative and quantitative analysis of processes
and activity of the noetic dimension. The conception of the noetic dimension follows
Frankl's theory of spiritual existence of man. The noetic dimension is understood as a theoretical construct used for a qualitative description of existential matters, which are considerably important in man's life. The author of this paper concentrated on preliminary
verification of some psychometric qualities (internal conistence, discrimination of individual dimensions) of the Slovak translation of the Test Noodynamic. Also the preliminary
sten norm for college students was created and differences between men and women and
between believers and nonbelievers was described.
*Êeskoslovenská Psychologie. 1999. Vol 43 (2), 133-142**

[cf. 021]
Halama, Peter

Dimensions of life meaning as factors of coping.
Studia Psychologica. 2000 Vol 42(4) 339-350

[605]
Halama, Peter

Development and construction of life meaningfulness scale.
(Vyvin a konstrukcia skaly zivotnej zmysluplnosti.)
The paper presents the first experience with the newly developed scale concerning life
meaningfulness. The scale is based on the three component model of personal meaning
(Reker, Wong, 1988), which considers three basic aspects of life meaningfulness: the cognitive (beliefs, cognitive schemas, interpretations), the motivational (commitment to goals
and values), and the affective (happiness, fulfilment, satisfaction). The scale contains three
dimensions corresponding to these three components. It has 18 items (six for every
dimension). The process of development of the scale using the sample of university students is described. The basic psychometric features of the scale presented in the paper
show adequate factor structure of the scale, satisfactory internal consistency, and good
validity with regard to several other meaningfulness scales.
*Ceskoslovenska Psychologie. 2002 Vol 46(3) 265-276**

[cf. 023]
Harlow, Lisa L.; Newcomb, Michael D.; Bentler, P. M.

Purpose in Life Test assessment using latent variable methods.
British Journal of Clinical Psychology. 1987 Sep Vol 26(3) 235-236

[cf. 024]
Harris, Alex H. S.; Standard, Samuel

Psychometric properties of the Life Regard Index-Revised: A validation study of a measure of personal meaning.
Psychological Reports. 2001 Dec Vol 89(3) 759-773

[606]
Hutzell, Robert, R., Peterson, T.J.

An MMPI Existential Vacuum Scale.
The International Forum for Logotherapy. (1985) 8:97-100.

[607]
Hutzell, Robert R.

A review of the Purpose in Life Test.
Reviews the literature concerning the Purpose in Life Test (PILT), which is used to measure the degree to which individuals experience life as meaningful. Data support the validity of the PILT as a measure of this variable. Part A, which has been used with adults and adolescents in a wide variety of settings, is well-suited for this purpose in noncompetitive situations. However, for groups that depart from middle-class American values, the generalization of the PILT is questioned.
International Forum for Logotherapy. 1988 Fal-Win Vol 11(2) 89-101

[cf. 489]
Hutzell, Robert R.; Finck, Willis C.

Adapting the Life Purpose Questionnaire for use with adolescent populations.
International Forum for Logotherapy. 1994 Spr Vol 17(1) 42-46

[cf. 385]
Juros, Andrzej

Personality correlates of the feeling of the meaning of life.
(Korelaty osobowosciowe poczucia sensu zycia.)
Roczniki Filozoficzne: Psychologia. 1984 Vol 32(4) 97-112

[cf. 238]
Kass, Jared D.; Friedman, Richard; Leserman, Jane; Caudill, Margaret; et al

An inventory of positive psychological attitudes with potential relevance to health outcomes: Validation and preliminary testing.
Behavioral Medicine. 1991 Fal Vol 17(3) 121-129

[cf. 387]
Kishida, Y. ; Kitamura, T.; Gatayama, R.; Matsuoka, T.; Miura, S.; Yamabe, K.

Ryff's psychological well-being inventory: factorial structure and life history correlates among Japanese university students.
Psychological Reports 2004 Feb;94(1):83-103

[cf. 446]
Labelle, Real; Lachance, Lise; Morval, Monique

Validation of a French-Canadian version of the Reasons for Living Inventory.
(Validation d'une version canadienne-francaise du Reasons for Living Inventory.)
Science et Comportement. 1996 Vol 24(3) 237-248

[cf. 031]
Leontyev, Dmitry A.; Kalashnikov, Mikhail O.; Kalashnikova, Olga E.

The factor structure of the Purpose in Life Test
Psikhologicheskiy Zhurnal. 1993 Jan-Feb Vol 14(1) 150-155

[cf. 441]
Linehan, Marsha M.; Goodstein, Judith L.; Nielsen, Stevan L.; Chiles, John A.

Reasons for staying alive when you are thinking of killing yourself: The Reasons for Living Inventory.
Journal of Consulting & Clinical Psychology. 1983 Apr Vol 51(2) 276-286

[cf. 242]
Liu SJ.

The construction and evaluation of the reliability and validity of a life attitude scale for elderly with chronic disease.
Journal of Nursing Research 2001 Jun;9(3):33-42

[608]
Lukas, Elisabeth Lukas

ICD-10 diagnoses and logotherapeutical terminology.
(Zuordnung der klinisch-diagnostischen Leitlinien der ICD-10 zur logotherapeutischen Terminologie.)
This is an attempt to correlate the principal diagnostic concepts of logotherapy with the categories introduced by the "International Classification of Psychic Disorders" (ICD-10) published by the World Health Organisation. The authors of ICD-10 are not shy in admitting that disorder is a somewhat inexact concept. The expression is used to denote "a clinically discernible complex of symptoms and disordered behavior in combination with stress and with an impairment of certain functions. Social deviations or conflicts as such shall not be considered as psychic disorders." The concept of "disease" was eliminated, and so was almost any kind of differentiation between psychic disorders on the basis of their origin. ICD-10 is based on a purely descriptive-phenomenological analysis, as opposed to an etio-

logical-pathogenetic one. The reason for this is purely pragmatic: only in this manner the representatives of various psychotherapeutic schools were able to arrive at a compromise in defining a set of common diagnostic criteria. As an example, the classification group F0 is defined as comprising all disorders "that may be related to a distinctively organic cause". However, the doubtlessly endogenous factor in schizophrenia, in certain affective disorders, in cognitive impairment and in some developmental disorders is completely disregarded here. Thus the specific sensitivity of logotherapy for that dimension of human existence which is affected in a given crisis is quite lost. The important discrimination between depressions that are of endogenous, exogenous/reactive, or noogenic origin - each requiring a completely different therapeutic approach - is missing. In this context the following defects of the IDC-10 categorisation must be mentioned: (a) The description and definition of noogenic neuroses and depressions is missing, (b) The description and definition of somatogenic pseudoneuroses is missing, (c) The description and definition of iatrogenic neuroses and traumata is missing, (d) ICD-10 does not distinguish between psychogenic diseases with somatic effects (e.g. cardial neurosis) and psychosomatic diseases (e.g. gastric ulcer). Both are categorised under the new concept of "somatoform disorders and non-organic functional disorders". In this way the existence or non-existence of a previous organic defect prior to the appearance of psychic triggers is not registered. ICD-10 lists pathological reactions to serious stress; however, the equally important group of pathological reactions to sudden stress relief is disregarded. Also, the concept of "adaptational disorder" for "states of subjective suffering and emotional impairment following decisive changes in life" is questionable. Explicitly mentioned is the case of mourning, which leads to the consequence that the grief of a wife mourning for her husband would have to be categorised as an "adaptational disorder" with regard to her new status as widow.

The International Journal of Logotherapy and Existential Analysis / The Journal of the Viktor Frankl Institute. 1997: Volume 5, Number 2 (Fall/Winter 1997)*

[cf. 036]
Martin, John D.; Martin, Elinor M.

The relationship of the Purpose in Life (PIL) Test to the Personal Orientation Inventory (POI), the Otis-Lennon Mental Ability Test scores, and grade point averages of high school students.

Educational & Psychological Measurement. 1977 Win Vol 37(4) 1103-1105

[cf. 246]
Mayers, Aviva M.; Khoo, Siek-Toon; Svartberg, Martin

The Existential Loneliness Questionnaire: Background, development, and preliminary findings.

Journal of Clinical Psychology. 2002 Sep Vol 58(9) 1183-1193

[cf. 039]
Meier, Augustine; Edwards, Henry

Purpose-in-Life Test: Age and sex differences.

Journal of Clinical Psychology. 1974 Jul Vol 30(3) 384-386

[cf. 158]
Okamoto, Kaori

On existential tendency for life and family satisfaction in modern college students.
Japanese Journal of Family Psychology. 1990 Sep Vol 4(2) 83-95

[cf. 454]
Oquendo, Maria A.; Baca-Garcia, Enrique; Graver, Ruth; Morales, Miguel; Montalvan, Viviana; Mann, J. John

Spanish adaptation of the Reasons for Living Inventory
Hispanic Journal of Behavioral Sciences. 2000 Aug Vol 22(3) 369-380

[cf. 456]
Osman, Augustine; Gifford, Jody; Jones, Teresa; Lickiss, Laura; et al.

Psychometric evaluation of the Reasons for Living Inventory.
Psychological Assessment. 1993 Jun Vol 5(2) 154-158

[609]
Osman, Augustine; Jones, Keith; Osman, Joylene R.

The Reasons for Living Inventory: Psychometric properties.
Examined the test-retest reliability, internal consistency, reliability, and the normative and item analysis data of the Reasons for Living Inventory (M. M. Linehan et al. [1983]) for 110 college students. The inventory has 6 subscales, each of which assesses a category of adaptive beliefs and expectations considered reasons for not committing suicide. The inventory was administered twice, with a 3-wk interval between testings. Test-retest coefficients were moderate to high. The alpha coefficients and item-total correlations for the subscales and the total inventory provide strong support for internal consistency. 26 items were consistently endorsed by 30% or more of the total sample as extremely important, while only 4 were suggested as not important reasons for not committing suicide.
Psychological Reports. 1991 Aug Vol 69(1) 271-278

[cf. 457]
Osman, Augustine; Kopper, Beverly A.; Linehan, Marsha M.; Barrios, Francisco X.; Gutierrez, Peter M.; Bagge, Courtney L.

Validation of the Adult Suicidal Ideation Questionnaire and the Reasons for Living Inventory in an adult psychiatric inpatient sample.
Psychological Assessment. 1999 Jun Vol 11(2) 115-123

[cf. 043]
Peacock, Edward J.; Reker, Gary T.

The Life Attitude Profile (LAP): Further evidence of reliability and empirical validity.
Canadian Journal of Behavioural Science. 1982 Jan Vol 14(1) 92-95

[610]
Picardi, Angelo; Mannino, Gherardo

Personal meaning organizations: Toward an empirical validation.
(Le organizzazioni di significato personale: Verso una validazione empirica.)
Studied the construction of an instrument designed to evaluate the clinical validity of the personal meaning construct. Ss included 98 male and female psychology and psychotherapy students in (mean age 20-35 yrs) in Italy. Data on sociodemographic variables and general way of feeling, thinking, and acting were obtained by questionnaire. Factor structure and convergent, content, and discriminant validity were determined. The results show that the instrument does not measure personal meaning but does measure personality trait variables that may correspond to the construct of personal meaning organization. Models of personal meaning are discussed.
Rivista di Psichiatria. 2001 Jul-Aug Vol 36(4) 224-233

[cf. 046]
Reker, Gary T.

Logotheory and logotherapy: Challenges, opportunities, and some empirical findings.
International Forum for Logotherapy. 1994 Spr Vol 17(1) 47-55

[611]
Reker, Gary T.; Cousins, J. B.

Factor structure, construct validity and reliability of the Seeking of Noetic Goals (SONG) and Purpose in Life (PIL) tests.
Examined the factor structure, construct validity, and reliability of the Seeking of Noetic Goals test (SONG) and the Purpose in Life test (PIL) in 248 undergraduates. 10 interpretable independent dimensions of satisfaction with life were extracted, with 6 factors that loaded on the PIL and 4 that loaded on the SONG. These data support J. C. Crombaugh's (see record 1978-24352-001) assertion that the SONG is a complementary scale to the PIL contributing factors that deal with the strength of motivation to find meaning and purpose in life. In addition, the SONG and the PIL are shown to be highly reliable (Spearman-Brown coefficients for both tests .87) and valid instruments. Further research that uses SONG-PIL factor scores and profile analysis is recommended.
Journal of Clinical Psychology. 1979 Jan Vol 35(1) 85-91

[cf. 046]
Reker, Gary T.; Fry, Prem S.

Factor structure and invariance of personal meaning measures in cohorts of younger and older adults.
Personality & Individual Differences. 2003 Oct Vol 35(5) 977-993

[cf. 049]
Ruini, Chiara; Ottolini, Fedra; Rafanelli, Chiara; Ryff, Carol; Fava, Giovanni Andrea

Italian validation of Psychological Well-being Scales (PWB)
(La validazione italiana delle Psychological Well-being Scales [PWB].)
Rivista di Psichiatria. 2003 May-Jun Vol 38(3) 117-130

[612]
Salmon P, Manzi F, Valori RM.

Measuring the meaning of life for patients with incurable cancer: the life evaluation questionnaire (LEQ).
Clinical observation, systematic research and popular anecdote indicate that, when confronted by death, people change the criteria by which they evaluate their lives. Questionnaires used routinely to assess quality of life in people with poor-prognosis cancer tend to be symptom-based and do not assess factors which become important when confronted by fatal illness, such as the meaning of life and the degree to which life has been enriched by the illness. To develop a questionnaire which would be sensitive to these areas, patients with incurable cancer and carers of such patients were interviewed in depth. Responses were reviewed by a panel of patients, clinicians and carers and formed into an inventory which was completed by 200 similar patients. Principal components analysis identified five dimensions: clearer perception of the meaning of life; freedom versus restriction of life; resentment of the illness; contentment with past and present life; past and present social integration. Only the most symptom-oriented scales (freedom, resentment) correlated with the Rotterdam Symptom Checklist. Scale scores showed that younger patients were more resentful of their illness, but also gained a clearer perception of the meaning of life. This questionnaire can evaluate psychological needs of people with incurable cancer which are neglected by existing instruments.
European Journal of Cancer. 1996 May;32A(5):755-60*

[613]
Shapiro, Stewart B.

Development of a life-meaning survey.
The Life-meanings Survey is a semistructured, depth interview which assesses the outcomes of various humanistically oriented, confluent educational projects. It attempts to reach a deeper, more personal level of response than the usual paper-and-pencil personality, attitude, or achievement measures by probing into relatively enduring effects which make a difference in the lives of the participants. It investigates some of the major philosophical psychological domains of what is substantially worth believing in, doing, and living for, and what is a coherent, useful philosophy of life. Divided into 5 areas of meaning, the interview technique includes intentionality, significance, symbols, sense, and the meaningful impact of a given project. Research results are reported from 3 studies: the effects of confluent education on 40 middle-class high school students, the outcomes of a humanistically oriented medical program with 14 participants, and the results of a 1-yr program in confluent education for 18 school administrators. These studies indicate that quantitative assessments can be made using this instrument. Rough reliability and validity measures of the interview have indicated its usefulness and stability.
Psychological Reports. 1976 Oct Vol 39(2) 467-480

[cf. 054]
Shek, Daniel T.

Reliability and factorial structure of the Chinese version of the Purpose in Life
Questionnaire.
Journal of Clinical Psychology. 1988 May Vol 44(3) 384-392

[cf. 055]
Shek, Daniel T.

Measurement of pessimism in Chinese adolescents: The Chinese Hopelessness Scale.
Social Behavior & Personality. 1993 Vol 21(2) 107-119

[cf. 057]
Shek, Daniel T.; Hong, Eric W.; Cheung, Mary Y.

The Purpose In Life Questionnaire in a Chinese context.
Journal of Psychology. 1987 Jan Vol 121(1) 77-83

[cf. 060]
Sink, Christopher A.; van Keppel, John; Purcell, Mark

Reliability estimates of the Purpose in Life and Seeking Noetic Goals tests with rural and
metropolitan-area adolescents.
Perceptual & Motor Skills. 1998 Apr Vol 86(2) 362

[cf. 407]
Stanich, John; Oertengren, Ilona

The Logotest in Sweden.
International Forum for Logotherapy. 1990 Spr Vol 13(1) 54-60

[cf. 063]
Van Ranst, Nancy; Marcoen, Alfons

Meaning in life of young and elderly adults: An examination of the factorial validity and
invariance of the Life Regard Index.
Personality & Individual Differences. 1997 Jun Vol 22(6) 877-884

[cf. 066]
Walters, Lynda H.; Klein, Alice E.

A cross-validated investigation of the Crumbaugh Purpose-in-Life test.
Educational & Psychological Measurement. 1980 Win Vol 40(4) 1065-1071

[cf. 470]
Westefeld, John S.; Badura, Amy; Kiel, Jeffrey T.; Scheel, Karen

The College Student Reasons for Living Inventory: Additional psychometric data.
Journal of College Student Development. 1996 May-Jun Vol 37(3) 348-350

[cf. 471]
Westefeld, John S.; Cardin, Denise; Deaton, William L.

Development of the College Student Reasons for Living Inventory.
Suicide & Life-Threatening Behavior. 1992 Win Vol 22(4) 442-452

[cf. 472]
Westefeld, John S.; Scheel, Karen; Maples, Michael R.

Psychometric analyses of the College Student Reasons for Living Inventory using a clinical population.
Measurement & Evaluation in Counseling & Development. 1998 Jul Vol 31(2) 86-94

EPILOGUE

Concluding Remarks
We offer this bibliography to the members of the helping professions and to researchers in the empirical behavioral sciences in the hope that they might find it helpful. To us, collecting the studies included in this book – and seeing the number of studies growing almost daily over the months – reassured us that logotherapy and existential analysis have a living empirical branch, albeit one that is relatively rarely acknowledged, even by logotherapists themselves. Certainly, for most psychiatrists, psychotherapists, and counsellors working as logotherapists or who make use of logotherapeutic concepts, individual patients' and clients' paths to healing, recovery, and a renewed sense of purpose and meaning serve as daily evidence of the usefulness, validity, and efficiency of Frankl's life work.

All the more do we, as should the logotherapeutic community in general, thank those researchers who, aware of the inherent limits of empirical research, nonetheless strive to maintain logotherapy as a scientific discipline. Our work would not have been possible were it not for those researchers who conduct research in a field where numbers and statistics often give only a glimpse of the true scope, depth and breadth of the phenomena investigated.

Viktor E. Frankl repeatedly expressed his wish that logotherapy and existential analysis would be seen as a therapy, as well as a discipline, with the latter being concerned with both theoretical and empirical research. Frankl first anticipated, and later saw, that the basic concepts of logotherapy would stand the empirical test, and, in his lectures, articles, and books, repeatedly quoted the growing number of studies that were conducted by his students and colleagues. Now, on the occasion of his 100th birthday, we believe that he would have been proud of the state of empirical research in logotherapy today.

Nevertheless, after reviewing and closely examining the more than 600 entries in this bibliography, we became astutely aware of the need for more research, and, for more networking among researchers in logotherapy. For example, many of the studies summarized in this bibliography have not yet made it into the standard logotherapeutic canon of empirical research findings, although they are highly relevant, and often explore new concepts and methods in measuring the basic ideas and applications of logotherapy. We hope that the bibliography will change this situation; and that it will inspire researchers from different disciplines and nations to connect and build interdisciplinary and international networks and research groups dedicated to the scientific advancement of research in logotherapy and existential analysis.

In this context, we also would like to mention the fact that logotherapy and existential analysis are, in a number of countries (e.g., in Eastern Europe, especially the new members of the European Union), still in need of official recognition as a school and method of applied psychotherapy and clinical psychology. We believe that only more research (and more dedicated and, above all, concerted international and interdisciplinary action) will change this situation and bring forth the official recognition logotherapy and existential analysis deserve, in both academic and health-care circles. And as the more than 600 studies presented in this bibliography testify, logotherapists have no reason to shy away from putting their theory to the test, but rather should welcome even more research.

Thus, we want to close this book with both a note of gratitude and a call to action: gratitude to those logotherapists who keep the empirical and applied branch of our discipline alive and striving, and a call to action to researchers working in any of the many disciplines to which Frankl contributed: a petition for more research, especially in those areas where only a few empirical studies have been published.

If this bibliography helps in getting the empirical branch of logotherapy a better hearing, in, as well as outside, the logotherapeutic community, it has served its first purpose. But only if it helps to strengthen an important branch within logotherapy – namely, the advancement of its empirical validation – has it fulfilled the second, and main, intention of the authors — and, we believe, Viktor E. Frankl's intention, too.

Appendix I. English-Language Books by Viktor E. Frankl

The Doctor and the Soul. From Psychotherapy to Logotherapy.
Random House, London, 1986.
Souvenir, London, 2004.

Man's Search for Meaning. An Introduction to Logotherapy.
Beacon Press, Boston, 2000.

On the Theory and Therapy of Mental Disorders:
An Introduction to Logotherapy and Existential Analysis (with an Introduction by James M. DuBois)
Routledge, New York and London, 2004.

Psychotherapy and Existentialism. Selected Papers on Logotherapy.
Simon & Schuster, New York, 1985.
Souvenir, London, 1985.

The Will to Meaning: Foundations and Applications of Logotherapy.
New American Library, New York, 1988.

The Unheard Cry for Meaning. Psychotherapy and Humanism.
Simon & Schuster, New York, 1988.
Hodder and Stoughton, London, 1988.

Viktor Frankl - Recollections. An Autobiography.
Insight Books, New York, 1997.
Perseus Book Group, New York, 2000.

The Unconscious God. Psychotherapy and Theology.
Simon & Schuster, New York, 1985.
Hodder and Stoughton, London, 1985.

Man's Search for Ultimate Meaning. (A revised and extended edition of *The Unconscious God*;
with a Foreword by Swanee Hunt).
Perseus Book Group, New York, 2000.

Appendix II. Logotherapy Journals and Periodicals

The International Journal of Logotherapy and Existential Analysis
(formerly Journal des Viktor-Frankl-Instituts) appeared from 1993 to 1998
Published by the Viktor Frankl Institute, Vienna, Austria at Vienna University Press

Journal des Instituto Viktor Frankl
(Spanish edition of Journal des Viktor-Frankl-Instituts)
Published by the Catedra Abierta Viktor E. Frankl (CAVEF), Buenos Aires, Argentina

The International Forum for Logotherapy
Published by the Amercian Viktor Frankl Institute of Logotherapy, Abilene, TX, USA

Existenz und Logos
Zeitschrift für sinnzentrierte Therapie / Beratung / Bildung
Published by the Deutsche Gesellschaft für Logotherapie und Existenzanalyse (DGLE),
Pfaffenweiler, Germany

Ricerca di Senso (formerly: Attualita in Logoterapia)
Analisi esistenziale e logoterapia frankliana
Published by the Associazione di Logoterapia e Analisi Esistenziale Frankliana (ALAEF),
Rome, Italy

Comprehensive Medicine
Published by the Japanese Society for the Study of Logotherapy, Hamamatsu City, Japan

Viktor Frankl Foundation Journal
Published by the Viktor Frankl Foundation of South Africa, Benmore, South Africa

Revista Mexicana de Logoterapia
Published by the Sociedad Mexicana de Analisis Existencial y Logoterapia S. C., Mexico
DF, Mexico

Revista Logo-Teoria/Terapia/Actitud
Published by the Sociedad Argentina de Logoterapia 'Viktor E. Frankl', Capital Federal,
Argentina

Journal del Instituto Viktor Frankl
Published by the Catedra Abierta Viktor E. Frankl (CAVEF), Buenos Aires, Argentina

Revista Brasileira de Logoterapia
Published by the Sociedade Brasileira de Logoterapia (SOBRAL), Sao Paulo, Brasil

Bulletin Logotherapie en Existentiele Analyse
Published by the Netherlands Institute for Logotherapy and Existential Analysis,
Amsterdam, Netherlands

Nous - Boletin de Logoterapia y Analisis Existencial
Published by the Asociacion Espanola de Logoterapia (AESLO), Madrid, Spain

Chratta
Published by the Schweizerische Gesellschaft für Logotherapie und Existenzanalyse (SGLE), Chur, Switzerland

Appendix III. Logotherapy Societies and Institutes

There are more than 70 logotherapy institutes and societies worldwide. The Viktor Frankl Institute in Vienna hosts an international list of addresses of these institutes.

The Viktor Frankl Institute, Vienna
Director: Dr. Gabriele Vesely-Frankl

The Viktor Frankl Institute in Vienna, Austria, is a scientific not-for-profit organization whose primary mission is to promote logotherapy and existential analysis as a comprehensive psychiatric, psychological and philosophical research discipline and as an applied clinical therapy. The Institute was founded by an international and interdisciplinary group of colleagues, friends, and family members of Viktor Frankl (on his behalf) in 1992. It is the world's primary accrediting and regulatory body for logotherapy and existential analysis.

Its task is to foster the lifetime work of Viktor Frankl and to provide access to accurate information about logotherapy and existential analysis to the interested general public and the scientific and medical communities. The Institute also hosts the private archives of Viktor E. Frankl and the largest collection of books, articles, audio- and videotapes, and historical documents on the life and work of Viktor Frankl and the international history of logotherapy and existential analysis.

Together with the City Council of Vienna, the Viktor Frankl Institute cofounded the Viktor Frankl Foundation, which was established in December 1999 and formally constituted in April 2000. It supports the work of both young and senior researchers by regular endowments (bestowed yearly). It also supports and stimulates relevant scientific and practical projects by the yearly announcement of the Viktor Frankl Award. Additionally, the yearly Honorary Viktor Frankl Award honors the lifework of exemplary scientists and humanists, who, although not necessarily logotherapists, live up to its basic ideas and values (previous laureates are: Heinz von Foerster, Paul Watzlawick, Cardinal Franz König, and Dame Cicely Saunders).

An international list of about 70 affiliated or befriended institutes and societies dedicated to the advancement of the life work of Viktor Frankl is available on the Web site of the Institute. The site also hosts a comprehensive bibliography of logotherapeutic literature. A regularly updated news section informs readers about current developments and news items of interest to the worldwide logotherapy community.

Viktor Frankl-Institut
Langwiesgasse 6
A-1140 Vienna
Austria

Internet: www.viktorfrankl.org

The North American Viktor Frankl Institute of Logotherapy
Director: Robert C. Barnes, Ph.D.

The American Viktor Frankl Institute of Logotherapy was founded by Joseph Fabry. What started as a private and pioneering initiative in Fabry's home in El Cerrito, California, soon turned into an active Institute, which was officially incorporated on February 14, 1978, as the Viktor Frankl Institute of Logotherapy.

In 1993, at the Ninth World Congress on Logotherapy held in Toronto, Robert C. Barnes, PhD, was elected president of the International Board of Directors of the Viktor Frankl Institute of Logotherapy. The A.B. Shelton Professor and Chairman of the Department of Counseling and Human Development at Hardin-Simmons University in Abilene, Texas, Barnes had previously served as Chairman of the Institute's Education and Credentialing Committee, and, since 1990, as Vice-President of the board.

In addition to on-site Continuing Education workshops and seminars, the Institute began, in 1994, to develop a Distance Learning opportunity for presenting its educational curriculum worldwide.

Aside from offering courses in logotherapy, the American Viktor Frankl Institute of Logotherapy publishes the International Forum of Logotherapy (starting in Winter 1978), which is the oldest scientific periodical in the world of logotherapy. The American Viktor Frankl Institute of Logotherapy also hosts the Annual World Congresses of Logotherapy.

Viktor Frankl Institute of Logotherapy
Box 15211
Abilene, TX 79698-5211
USA

Internet: www.logotherapyinstitute.org